TREASURE NEVERLAND

'Captain Teach commonly call'd Black Beard', from *A General History of the Lives and Adventures of the Most famous Highwaymen, Murderers, Street-Robbers, &c.* (London, 1734).

TREASURE
NEVERLAND

REAL AND IMAGINARY PIRATES

NEIL RENNIE

OXFORD
UNIVERSITY PRESS

OXFORD
UNIVERSITY PRESS

Great Clarendon Street, Oxford, OX2 6DP,
United Kingdom

Oxford University Press is a department of the University of Oxford.
It furthers the University's objective of excellence in research, scholarship,
and education by publishing worldwide. Oxford is a registered trade mark of
Oxford University Press in the UK and in certain other countries

First Edition published in 2013

Impression: 1

British Library Cataloguing in Publication Data

Data available

Library of Congress Cataloging in Publication Data

Data available

ISBN 978–0–19–967933–1

Printed by the MPG Printgroup, UK

Preface

This book is about factual and fictional pirates and is therefore a deliberate combination of history and literary history. Swashbuckling eighteenth-century pirates were the ideal pirates of all time and are still popular today. Most people have heard of Blackbeard and Captain Kidd, for example, although they lived about three hundred years ago. But most people have also heard of other pirates, such as Long John Silver and Captain Hook, although those pirates never lived at all, except in literature. So there have been two kinds of pirates—real and imaginary—but the real, historical pirates are themselves somewhat legendary, somewhat fictional, belonging on the page and stage rather than on the high seas. The solid basis for the research is in primary material, much of it in manuscripts, inky scribbles in the National Archives and in the British Library—testimonials, narratives, legal statements, colonial and mercantile reports—which are the best firsthand evidence of actual piracy. Of course the pirates who appeared in such reports, written or spoken by themselves or their victims, can never be simply and transparently factual, but those pirates are nevertheless distinguishable from the literary characters in plausibly 'realistic' or amusingly 'fantastic' fictions about pirates who never existed, except in the collaborating imaginations of writers and readers. The aims of the book are to discriminate and describe the ascertainable facts of the real eighteenth-century pirate lives and then to investigate how such facts were subsequently transformed artistically, by writers like Defoe and Stevenson, into fictions of various kinds: historical novels, popular melodramas, boyish adventures, Hollywood films. The aim is to watch, in other words, the long dissolve from Captain Kidd to Johnny Depp.

There are surprisingly few scholarly studies of the factual pirates—properly analysing the basic manuscript sources and separating those documents from popular legends—and there are even fewer literary-historical studies of the fictional pirates, although those imaginary pirates form a distinct and coherent literary tradition—instalments of a single, continuing story, written by Scott, Washington Irving, Fenimore Cooper, Poe, Stevenson, and Barrie. *Treasure Neverland* is a study of this Scots-American literary tradition and also of the inter-relations between the factual and fictional pirates—pirates who are intimately related, as the nineteenth-century writings about fictional pirates began with the eighteenth-century writings about supposedly real pirates. 'What I want is the *best* book about the Buccaneers', wrote Stevenson when he began *Treasure Island* in 1881. What he received, rightly, was indeed the best book: the sensational and unreliable *History of the Pyrates* (1724).

I should add that all translations and mistranslations are my own, unless otherwise indicated, and I must thank the following friends who did their best to make this a better book than it is: Claire, Hugo, John, Kevin, Louis, Marilyn, Philip.

Contents

List of illustrations

I

Every and all the Averys

Come all you brave Boyes whose Courage is Bold
Will you venture with me and I'le glut you with Gold –
Make haste into Coruna a Ship you will finde
Now called the *Fancy* which will pleasure your minde

('A Copy of Verses Composed by Capt. Henry Every', 1694)[1]

Piracy has been called by many names, but—by any name—it is basically and simply robbery at sea. Although, as such, it is probably as old as seafaring, its so-called 'golden age', the period of its flourishing—distantly, invisibly, at sea in ships, and also legibly, saleably, on land in print—is the late seventeenth and early eighteenth centuries. This is the age of the historical pirate who is still, who doubles as, the imaginary pirate of today. The leader of those who inhabit both the 'golden age' and our imagination, the first of those pirates who are historical as well as fictional, is arguably a man called Henry Every, who invaded and opened up the era of the golden age. Because Every has thus a double life, as the authentic original and almost immediately, almost inseparably, as a legendary hero, because he is ambiguous in his authenticity as well as his morality, inspiring not only emulation by pirates but fiction by writers, we should therefore attempt to observe him in the clearest transparency possible—in the words of those closest to his actions at sea, before he is rewritten as fiction. We need to read the words of witnesses at first hand, or even second or third hand, before we rewrite them—and him. Some of his deeds will seem surprisingly undramatic, then, and some of their words unprofessionally crude.

Intended as part of an expedition to the West Indies but delayed and unpaid for several months, the men of the English ship *Charles II*

mutinied at Coruña in May 1694. Some of the evidence about their
mutiny was given as testimony in a trial, so some of our first witnesses
of piracy are witnesses in a court of law—by no means a neutral
medium, of course. At the trial of some of the alleged mutineers at the
Old Bailey in 1696, a witness, David Creagh, recalled that on the eve
of the mutiny he had joined the captain of the *Charles*, a Captain Gibson, in drinking a bowl of punch with an officer named Every and
some others aboard the ship. That night Creagh heard 'a great Noise
above Deck' and was confined to his cabin.[2] When he was allowed on
deck he saw 'Every was cunning the Ship' (by which he explained that
he meant directing 'the Steering of her').[3] 'Every took me by the hand',
Creagh testified, 'and ask'd me if I would go with him?'[4] To this question Creagh answered that 'I did not know his Design'.[5] There was
some prevarication and discussion of this 'Design', which seemed clear
enough to two of Every's companions whom he described as 'true
Cocks of the game, and old Sports-men'.[6] Creagh went below, threatened by one of these 'Sports-men' that otherwise 'I will knock you on
the Head'.[7] In his testimony Creagh then described an exchange he
had heard between Every and Captain Gibson, to whom Every
announced that 'I am a Man of Fortune, and must seek my Fortune'.[8]
Offered a choice, Gibson chose not to follow Every's fortune but to go
ashore. He was joined in a boat by the witness, David Creagh, and 13
or 14 others. The precise nature of Every's 'Design' remains unknown
but, in response to a petition of protest about unpaid wages from some
of the sailors' wives, two to three months after the mutiny, the principal
owner of the *Charles* enclosed a copy of a ballad which he said the
mutineers had left behind at Coruña, 'A Copy of Verses Composed by
Capt. Henry Every now gone to Sea to Seek his Fortune', which
plainly declared, as the owner pointed out, the sailors' 'intentions of
Pyrating'.[9]

Whatever his 'intentions' might have been, Every's actions after the
mutiny are clear enough. The *Charles* (renamed the *Fancy*) sailed to the
Cape Verde Islands off the west coast of Africa, then to the coast of
Guinea where they captured 'several Negroes', and to Fernando Po
and the Portuguese colonial island of Principe, where they encountered and captured two Danish ships, thereby acquiring 'a great quantity of Brandy', 'about 640 Ounces of Gold Dust', 'a quantity of
Elephants Teeth', and 14 Danish men who joined them.[10] Thereafter
they sailed to the nearby Portuguese island of Annobon, where they

took on provisions before rounding the Cape of Good Hope and sailing to Madagascar in the Indian Ocean, where they 'watered their Ship, and got Provisions, and Cows to salt up', before sailing to the nearby Comoro Islands.[11] There they reprovisioned and took aboard 13 French sailors who had lost their ship and a further 40 Frenchman from 'a French Pyrating Junk' which they fought and defeated.[12]

The men of the *Fancy* then decided to make for the Red Sea, and on the way encountered and were joined by two American ships, the *Dolphin* and the *Portsmouth Adventure*, 'two Saile which came up with us & prov'd to be upon the same Account'.[13] At the entrance to the Red Sea, the strait of Bab-el-Mandeb, the three ships with a common purpose were joined by three more American vessels, the *Susanna*, the *Pearl*, and the *Amity*, a sloop commanded by Thomas Tew, a sailor commended by the Governor of New York despite Tew's 'rude habit of swearing' and prior experience of Red Sea piracy.[14] These ships also agreed to work in partnership with the *Fancy* and under the command of Every.

After some time spent waiting at the entrance to the Red Sea, the pirates began to fear that the Muslim pilgrim ships (and their valuable cargo of trade) would not emerge on their way back to Surat from Mocha, so they captured some local men in boats, who confirmed the imminence of 'the Moors Shipps'.[15] When the Mughal fleet did come, as promised, it passed the pirates unseen at night, so the pirates set off in pursuit of the returning pilgrims on their course to Surat. The *Dolphin* was slow in the pursuit and was abandoned, therefore, and her crew added to the *Fancy*, which also took the *Pearl* in tow. The *Amity* also fell behind, as did the *Susanna*, while only the *Portsmouth Adventure* was able to keep up with the *Fancy*.[16] Somewhat in disarray, the pirates nevertheless overtook and awaited one of their intended prey, 'a slight ship' that unwarily came 'within about a Pistoll shott' of the *Fancy*, which captured 'about 50 or 60,000 l. [pounds] in that ship in Silver and gold', and then came upon another Mughal vessel, better armed, with about 40 cannon and 800 men.[17]

This 'great Ship' was 'called the *Gunsway*', properly the *Ganj-i-Sawai*, a substantial vessel owned by the Grand Mughal Aurangzeb, emperor of Mughal India.[18] There was a fight for two to three hours before the *Gunsway* yielded. The men of the *Gunsway* fired at the *Fancy* and threw fireworks at her sails to try to set them on fire, but one of the *Gunsway*'s own guns exploded and a pirate gun damaged her mainmast, which emboldened the pirates to board.[19] 'When we were on board', one of the pirate invaders remembered, 'they being all run into the Hold we called them up & gave them good Quarter' (mercy on condition of surrender).[20] The *Fancy* 'lost not a single man, and had only one man wounded on boarding' the *Gunsway*, but, according to a later source, Captain Tew finally stopped swearing, being 'killed by a great Shott from [the] Moors ship'.[21] An even later account provided even more details: 'a Shot carried away the Rim of Tew's Belly, who held his Bowels with his Hands some small Space [until] he dropp'd'.[22] A contemporary Indian historian gives a Mughal version of events, featuring the cowardice of the captain of the *Ganj-i-Sawai*, who ran down into the hold of his ship where there were some concubines he had bought himself in Mocha: 'He put turbans on their heads and swords into their hands, and incited them to fight', but they 'fell into the hands of the enemy, who soon became perfect masters of the ship', transferring 'the treasure and many prisoners to their own ship'.[23] The pirates then

busied themselves for a week searching for plunder, stripping the men, and dishonouring the women, both old and young...Several honourable women, when they found an opportunity, threw themselves into the sea, to preserve their chastity, and some others killed themselves with knives and daggers.[24]

A crewman on the *Fancy* reported that they kept the two captured Mughal ships for two days (not a week) taking

Treasure which was very great tho little in comparison to what was on board, for tho they putt Sevll. to the Torture they would not confess where the rest of their Treasure lay. They took great quantities of Jewells & a Saddle & Bridle set with Rubies designed for a present for the great Mogull. The Men lay with the Indian Women aboard those Ships &...sevll. of them by their Habitts & riches in Jewells appeared of better quality than the rest.[25]

By this account, then, piracy involved torture and rape as well as robbery. Another member of the *Fancy*'s crew subsequently denied (or dodged) such stories: 'there were no women of any quality on board nor any ravished as is reported, therefore if any thing of that kind was done it was done by some of the Ships that are still out'.[26] The crewman's denial is perhaps subject to some suspicion, but in any case the agents of the East India Company at Bombay heard something like the Mughal account, felt the consequent wrath of the Muslims, and wrote to the government in London to protest:

It is certain the Pyrates, which these People affirm were all English, did so very barbarously by the People of the *Gunsway* and Abdul Gofors Ship [the ship of a merchant, Abdul Gofor, the first taken by the pirates], to make them confess where their Money was, and there happened to be a great Umbraws Wife [the wife of a grandee of the Grand Mughal's court] (as Wee hear) related to the King, returning from her Pilgrimage to Mecha, in her old age. She they abused very much, and forced severall other Women, which Caused one person of Quality, his Wife and Nurse, to kill themselves to prevent the Husbands seing them (and their being) ravished. All this will raise a black Cloud att Court, which We wish may not produce a severe storme.[27]

Unmindful of this storm, the pirates who had engaged in the fight were rewarded with the proceeds: gold and silver in coins and plate which, added to their previous takings, made up a share of about £1,000 a man for 180 men, with a double share for Every.[28] The distribution of the loot was mutually agreed and principled, with some exceptions in need of correction. When the men of the *Fancy* found that the men of the *Pearl* had been clipping the takings of gold coins, they confiscated the *Pearl*'s share of the treasure, providing them with 'only 2000 peices of Eight to buy provisions'.[29]

The enriched pirates went their several ways, two ships to Saint Mary's Island off the north-east coast of Madagascar, a regular pirate resort, and Every himself and the *Fancy* eventually to Providence (or New Providence) in the Bahamas. Some of his men mutinied on the way, wishing the *Fancy* would sail instead to Cayenne, French Guiana, but Every defeated them and, after leaving as many as wanted ashore on the French Indian Ocean island now called Réunion, he sailed back round the Cape of Good Hope. An English captain, collecting slaves from West Africa, recorded in his journal in December 1693 that, at the Portuguese-controlled island of St. Thomas, off the African coast, Every had paid the Governor for provisions with 'a bill of exchange payable at London, but drawn upon John a-Nokes [colloquially, a simpleton], or the pump at Algate' (a well-known landmark in central London).[30] This may be a legend already taking shape, an apocryphal tale in the making, but certainly Every sailed across the Atlantic to the Caribbean.

At the Danish-controlled island of St. Thomas in the Virgin Islands (sharing its name with the African island), a place that provided a free and uncontrolled port, a visiting French priest described the abundant booty emanating from an English pirate ship that had 'pellé les

Vaisseaux du Grand Mogol, qui portoient à la Mecque quelques-une de ses femmes, avec des merchandises & des richesses très grandes' (that had pillaged the ships of the Grand Mughal, which were carrying to Mecca some of his wives with great wealth and merchandise).[31] This may be Every's ship or another to which his legend was attached, but the loot in the West Indies was real—real, not fictional, pirate treasure. Jewellery, gold coins, and rupees with Arabic lettering, according to Père Labat, were permeating the islands from this pirate ship. Cotton prints and fine muslins were flooding the market. Père Labat borrowed money to invest in the bargain booty, listing his purchases: feathered quilts sewn with layers of precious materials, at 15 crowns each, although worth a hundred each in France; blue and white striped cloths, three-and-a-half metres long by one-and-a-quarter wide, at one crown each, providing magnificent table cloths and hangings; fine spices, including nutmeg and cinnamon, for two crowns a pound weight. From the same dealer, and perhaps the same source, he also bought several less exotic items, books—to prevent other people reading them, he explained—'cloaques d'ordures' (filth, pornography), which he read as he sailed on among the islands, throwing them into the sea as he read them, because 'ils ne méritoient pas autres chose' (they merited no better).[32]

From St. Thomas—perhaps—Every sailed on more definitely to the island of Providence in the Bahamas, where a large bribe of pieces-of-eight (those Spanish but international coins) and other less portable items, including the *Fancy* itself, its guns and 'Elephants Teeth', was successfully offered to the British Governor, Nicholas Trott, for permission to come ashore and go safely wherever they wished.[33] The hospitable but punctilious Governor entertained the pirates 'at his House, at which, one of the Men breaking a Drinking Glass, he made him pay for it 8 Chequeens' (sequins, gold coins).[34] Another pirate, Joseph Morris, was 'left Mad at Providence looseing all his Jewells upon a Wager'.[35] Yet another, Edward Short, was 'killed by a Shirk'.[36] Some men bought their own ship to sail for Carolina and Every and about 20 others bought a sloop to sail for England, Every taking on the alias of Bridgman. Every-alias-Bridgman landed at Dunfanaghy, County Donegal, in Ireland. He was said to have gone to Scotland but was expected to head for Exeter, England, 'being a Plymouth man', according to the court witness, mariner John Dann, who was himself seized at his home town of Rochester, 'by meanes of a Maid, who found his Gold Quilted up in his Jackett hanging with his coate'.[37] The contents of mariner Dann's jacket and pockets, confiscated by the Mayor of Rochester, were calculated as £1,045 in gold sequins, plus ten guineas.[38]

The judge, Sir Charles Hedges, correctly and invitingly informed the jury at the Old Bailey that 'Piracy is only a Sea term for Robbery', but the jury returned an unexpected verdict of 'Not Guilty' on the six prisoners from the *Fancy*, whereupon the trial was adjourned and the case retried, so that five of them were satisfactorily condemned to be 'Hanged by the Necks, until you, and every one of you be Dead', a sentence carried out in November 1696 at Execution Dock, Wapping, London.[39] *An Account of the Behaviour, Dying Speeches, and Execution* described their crimes generally as 'plundering and rifling all the Vessels they met with, Ravishing and Deflowering the Virgins and Women, and then turning them out naked, to starve upon shore, amongst Rocks and Desarts'.[40] Even these 'unheard-of Barbarities' were surpassed, however, by

their Suprizing a Ship of the King of the Indies, where they first took away an infinite Treasure, most inhumanely Ravisht a Young Princess, and the rest of her Female Train, and afterwards left the Ship disarm'd and disabled, floating as a wreck upon the Sea.[41]

The published information was sensational, therefore, feeding a public appetite for pirate barbarity.

In their 'dying speeches' the condemned men were suitably 'inclined to penitence', but their captain, Every, or Avery, or Bridgman, had escaped their fate, and was instead condemned to everlasting speculation and legend.[42] The last recorded trace of him was left by the witness John Dann, who reported that Every had been consorting in Ireland with another pirate's wife, Mrs Adams, acquired at Providence, whom Dann subsequently saw at St. Albans, near London, catching a stagecoach. She told him 'that shee was goeing to Captaine Bridgmans but would not tell him where he was'.[43] A few days later another crewman of the *Fancy*, William Phillips, reported that Every's wife (Mrs Adams or another?) 'lives in Ratcliffe Highway' by the Thames, London, where she 'Sells Periwiggs'.[44] Perhaps inspired by hope of a reward for information leading to Every's capture, Phillips provided the only description we have of our elusive hero: 'A tall well sett man aged about 40 wears a light coloured Wigg most commonly, pretty swarthy, Grey Eyes, a flattish Nose'.[45]

Meanwhile the *Susanna* had reached the refuge of Saint Mary's in December 1695, where the ship was careened (the essential protective cleaning of the hull) and the men were sold some goods, and 'stayed at St. Maries till the middle of April, where the Captain and Master and most of his men dyed' of some 'Sickness'.[46] The *Amity* arrived a few days after the *Susanna*, and sailed only five days later, in successful pursuit of another ship, the *Charming Mary*, which the *Amity* captured and took over for pirating with.[47] Most of this information about Saint Mary's comes from its main proprietor at the time, Adam Baldridge, who gave a detailed statement in New York in 1699. According to this informative (if not impartial) piece of pirate history, Baldridge (who had 'turned Pirate' after reportedly killing a man in Jamaica), established himself on Saint Mary's, a few miles off the north-east coast of Madagascar, about May 1691, introducing '70 head Cattel and some slaves', and had built a house and 'a Fort with 22 Guns' to guard an excellent harbour (see Figure 1.1).[48] An account by Henry Watson, captured by pirates in 1696, reports that Baldridge was in partnership with one Lawrence Johnston, and that both men 'are factors for one Frederick Phillips'.[49] According to Watson:

These two are both of them married to country women, and many of the others are married at Madagascar. They have a kind of fortification of seven or eight guns upon St. Mary's. Their design in marrying the country women is to ingratiate themselves with the inhabitants, with whom they go into war against other petty kings.[50]

The number of guns varied according to reports and probably also according to circumstances, but Watson was correct in stating that Baldridge was kept supplied by an ostensibly respectable New York trader, Frederick Philipse, whose cargo for Saint Mary's in 1693 consisted of shoes, stockings, speckled shirts, breeches, hats, carpenter's tools, rum, wine and spirits, grindstones, saws, jars of oil, cannon powder, some books and Bibles, some garden seeds and tools, implying a variety of requirements. In return Baldridge despatched '1100 pieces 8/8 [pieces-of-eight] and Dollers, 34 Slaves, 15 head of Cattel, 57 barrs of Iron'.[51]

In his statement to colonial officialdom in New York, Baldridge recorded a previous visit to Saint Mary's, on 19 October 1693, by Thomas Tew, who was later to die in the fight with the *Gunsway*. According to Baldridge, Tew and his men in 1693, 'haveing taken a

Figure 1.1. Harbour of Saint Mary's Island, an imaginary view, crudely adapted from an illustration of a water spout.

Ship in the Red Seas that did belong to the Moors,...took as much money in her as made the whole share run 1200l. [pounds] a man'.[52] Tew had preceded Every, then, in pillaging the Moors. Having careened the *Amity* at Saint Mary's and restocked her supplies, Tew sailed on 23 December 1693, 'bound for America'.[53] An American customs official grumbled at Tew's untroubled arrival at Rhode Island: 'Thomas Tew a pyrate, came thither from the Read Sea in the year 1694 and brought with him 100,000 lbs [pounds] in Gold and Silver'.[54] Despite or because of this success, Tew and the *Amity* were eager for more Red Sea wealth in 1695, when he joined Every's pirate fleet. Baldridge recorded the fatal effect when the *Amity* returned to Saint Mary's on 11 December 1695: 'Arrived the Sloop *Amity*, haveing no Captain, her former Captain Thomas Tew being killed by a great Shott from a Moors ship'.[55] Another informant, an ex-pirate, remembered that he had heard on Madagascar of a dispute between 14 pirates, some of them Tew's men, who

had by consent divided themselves into two sevens, to fight for what they had
(thinking that they had not made a voyage sufficient for so many) and that one
of the said Sevens were all killed, and five of the other, so that the two which
survived enjoyed the whole Booty.[56]

The precise date of this dispute is vague and it may be a legend reflect-
ing notions of pirate justice rather than historic truth, but Baldridge's
reports were more reliable.

Saint Mary's was thus a natural port of call for the captainless *Amity*
and the *Susanna* after Every's spectacular success of 1695. Indeed Baldridge's business proceeded happily until in 1697 Baldridge left his personal colony to undertake some trading by ship, and in his absence
some Malagasy rebelled against his white settlement, killed many, and
destroyed and pillaged Saint Mary's.[57] Baldridge explained in his statement that the Malagasy rebelled in protest at the abuse and theft practised by the white pirates, but Baldridge himself had been involved in
inter-tribal warfare and, as we know, slaving.[58] Although Baldridge's
career at Saint Mary's was over, his pirate resort continued prosper-
ously under new management, while across the waters the reputation
of the Madagascar pirates grew and spread.

An argument for pardoning these pirates, who were 'most of them
English', was put to the House of Commons in 1707, and published as
Reasons for Reducing the Pyrates at Madagascar.[59] The proposer argued
that the pirates would be more effectively suppressed by negotiation
and pardon than by force. The case was carefully reasoned. The pirates'
'Treasure' could not be returned to its original owners because it was

taken (mostly, if not wholly) from the Subjects of the Great Mogull, and other
Indians and Mahometans, in the most remote Parts of the World, and now lies
Buried or Useless in or near the said Island of Madagascar; it's much better
they should be permitted to bring it to England with safety, where it may do
Good, than to let it remain where it is (as Useless and Unprofitable as the
Earth that covers it).[60]

So the wastefully buried pirate treasure should be relocated to England,
'where it may do Good'.

In *The Review* of 18 October 1707, Daniel Defoe took up and played
with some of these suggestions (though adding some sarcastic com-
ments of his own). He acknowledged the growing fame of the pirates:
'That Madagascar has for a few Years past been a Receptacle of Pyrates,
of all Nations, most People have heard, and long Tales we have had told

us of their Wealth.'[61] These pirates were often Englishmen, he noted, and were supposed to have offered large sums in return for pardons and a return to England. Defoe considered a pardon a reasonable and practical solution to the pirate problem, remarking also that piracy was not so distinctly different from some supposedly acceptable and legal business practices.

Sir Charles Hedges's explanation to the jury at the Old Bailey trial of the *Fancy*'s men was simple: 'Piracy is only a Sea term for Robbery'. As such—robbery at sea—piracy must have been almost as old as going to sea. A celebration of the deeds of the fierce and powerful Pharoah Thutmosis III, inscribed proudly on the walls of a temple at Karnak, boasts of 'a seizing of two ships' that were 'loaded with everything, with male and female slaves, copper, lead, emery, and every good thing'.[62] This very bad thing, this robbery at sea, *c.* 1475 BC, has been called 'the first act of piracy on record', but of course piracy is older than writing.[63]

The word 'pirate' is derived, via the Latin 'pirata', from the Greek πειρᾶν (peiran), to attempt, attack, assault, but the Greek word for pirate from that derivation, πειρατής (peirates), is not in use until the third century BC.[64] In Homer's usage the word for 'pirate' is λῃστής (leistes) which occurs, for example, in what is a formal, formulaic question, asked by Nestor in the *Odyssey* of the visiting Telemachus, and also by the Cyclops when visited—or invaded—in his cave by Odysseus and his men. 'Strangers, who are you?' asks the Cyclops:

Whence do you sail over the watery ways? Is it on some business [κατὰ πρῆξιν, for trade], or do you wander at random over the sea, as pirates [λῃϊστῆρες, leisteres] do, who wander hazarding their lives and bringing evil to men of other lands?[65]

The question implies a distinction, between sailing peacefully to trade and aggressively to bring 'evil', but also an ambiguity, which the question is meant to resolve. If peaceful trade and aggressive piracy are hard to distinguish, except when it is too late, the difference between war and piracy is even harder to tell, a matter of opinion, of definition and verbal distinction. All evidence of piracy in the classical world is necessarily textual in any case, as piracy cannot be deduced across time from material remains, from bits of ships' tackle or even far-fetched artefacts which may have been traded or plundered or both.[66]

Homer's hero is perhaps another man's pirate. On Ithaca the loyal swineherd Eumaeus tells how he was abducted as a child and brought to Ithaca by Phoenician seafarers, but Odysseus himself was not so different from those fierce seafarers, telling Eumaeus that 'oared ships were ever dear to me, and wars, and polished spears, and arrows'.[67] Even before the Trojan war, he says, 'I had nine times led warriors and swift-faring ships against foreign folk, and great spoil had ever fallen into my hands'.[68] Wily Odysseus was hiding his royal identity on Ithaca, speaking to Eumaeus in disguise as a Cretan, and 'Cretans are always liars', as Saint Paul remarked, quoting the sixth-century BC Cretan poet Epimenides, and noting with amusement that 'he told the truth!'[69] Epimenides spoke in conundrum but Odysseus was a liar as well as an impostor, and Homer himself composed fiction.

Pirates were stock characters in those subsequent, more novelistic stories of love and travel, the Greek romances, serving the authors' purpose by capturing the hero or heroine to delay the happy ending. In *Daphnis and Chloe* of the third century AD, Tyrian pirates briefly capture the young goatherd Daphnis until he is rescued by swimming cows who upturn the pirate ship, drowning the pirates in their heavy armour, while Daphnis swims to safety ashore with the cows, only to see the shepherdess Chloe naked for the first time, washing herself:

That wash seemed to him more terrible than the sea. He felt as though his life was still at the mercy of the pirates [ληστais]; for he was young and lived in the country and as yet knew nothing of the piracy of Love ['Ερωτος ληστήριον].[70]

Love and piracy go together, then, like cows and swimming.

There are pirates by deed if not by name in Boccaccio's mid-fourteenth-century *The Decameron*, specifically a lover too poor to marry his sweetheart, who 'cominciò a costeggiare la Barberia' ('began to coast, to pirate, along the Barbary coast').[71] Piracy and a woman are connected again by the plot of another brief tale in *The Decameron*. A sexually abstemious husband takes his wife sailing for pleasure, whereupon she is abducted by 'a notorious corsair', a 'molto famoso corsale', who provides her with so much sexual attention that she refuses to return to her husband.[72] In his fifteenth-century *Testament* the poet François Villon recognized the pirate's role as a poor man's hero by recounting an anecdote about a pirate taken for judgement before Alexander the Great, who asks the shackled prisoner why he is a 'larron de mer', a pirate? 'Why do you call me a robber?' the pirate asks Alexander. 'Is it simply because you see me skimming the seas in my little boat?'

'Se comme toy me peusse armer,
Comme toy empereur je feusse.'[73]

('If I could arm myself like you, I would make myself like you, an emperor.')

Villon's anecdote derives from Augustine in the fifth century, who was not justifying piracy but justice, which made the difference, he said, between kingdoms and criminals. 'Remove justice', said Augustine, 'and what are kingdoms but gangs of criminals'?[74] Augustine plainly preferred kingdoms to sea criminals, but there were legal difficulties in establishing their respective rights. Kingdoms had laws and powers to enforce justice, but did those laws and powers stretch over the ocean, the no-man's land of the high seas, beyond any nation's jurisdiction? Augustine's anecdote derived in turn from Cicero in the first century BC, who argued that pirates were not beyond the law.[75] Nations could control the freedom of the lawless ocean because 'a pirate' was legitimately the enemy—not of one nation or another— 'sed communis hostis omnium', 'but the common enemy of all'.[76] Cicero's way of controlling the anomalous pirate, by bringing him within the legal reach of nations, as the 'enemy of all mankind', was echoed and endorsed in the seventeenth century, when seafaring European nations stretched out their laws to reach him, the universal enemy, skimming freely on the high seas.[77]

Mediterranean pirates, the corsairs, appear in *Don Quixote* (1605 and 1615), specifically 'cosarios Franceses' who took a captive lady's jewels but not her most precious jewel, 'la joya que mas valia, y ella mas estimaba'.[78] On 27 September 1575, Cervantes himself was captured by a corsair galley and lost 'one of the most precious gifts the gods gave to man', his freedom.[79] Another corsair, 'un Corsaire de Salé' (on the Moroccan coast), attacked a luxurious galley in Voltaire's *Candide* (1759), a corsair ship with a corsair crew who took female captives— more frequent in fiction, perhaps, than on ships—and inserted fingers speculatively into their captives' most precious parts, 'pour voir si nous n'avions pas caché là quelques diamants' ('to see if we hadn't hidden some diamonds there').[80]

Meanwhile there had been English pirates as well as Mediterranean corsairs. Thomas Walton and Clinton Atkinson, for instance, overstepped the poorly-defined boundary between legal privateering and illegal piracy and were defeated at sea and taken in 1583 for execution at Wapping, London, the location described in John Stow's *Survay of*

London (1598) as 'the usuall place of Execution for the hanging of Pyrates and sea Rovers, at the lowe water marke, and there to remaine, till three Tydes had overflowed them'.[81] Before these executions and tidal punishments, however, 'Walton as he went toward the gallowes rent his venetian breeches of crimosin taffata, and distributed the same to such his old acquaintance as stood about him'.[82] Stow also notices that Atkinson had already given to his friends 'his murrey [purple-red] velvet doublet with great gold buttons, & his like coloured velvet venetians laid with great gold lace, apparell too sumptuous for sea rovers, which he had worne at the seas'.[83] These flamboyant characters, too sumptuously attired for sea rovers, stepped posthumously from the scaffold to the stage, in Heywood and Rowley's *Fortune by Land and Sea* (*c.*1607), in which the dramatists' imaginary piratical hero is on the side of the nation and in receipt of a knighthood because he defeats at sea and thereby acquires the fortune of the real Walton and Atkinson, who are led to execution at Wapping again, distributing their piratical costumes in the final Act: 'The work man [that] made them took never measure on a Hangmans back', says Walton.[84] Our clothes were not made to be worn by a hangman, so 'Wear them for our sakes, and remember us.'[85] Their friends will wear their clothes and remember the 'two valiant Pirats', as they call themselves, and the play's hero will be rewarded by their fortune acquired by piracy at sea.[86] The hero is nearly a pirate and the pirates are nearly heroes. A pamphlet published in 1639, *A True Relation, of the Lives and Deaths of the two most famous English Pyrats, Purser and Clinton*, condemned their piratical lives but admired their brave deaths. When Clinton Atkinson and Thomas Walton (alias Purser) were 'turned off from the Ladder, it appeared to all the multitude that were then present, that they could not live more irregularly, than they dyed resolutely: and so there they [remained] hanging till from that ebbe two Tydes had overwhelmed their bodies' (see Figure 1.2).[87]

Some English pirates joined the North African corsairs, such as John Ward, for instance, who featured in a play by Robert Daborn, *A Christian turn'd Turke* (1612), in which Ward turns from Christian to Muslim, turns 'renegade' in the contemporary term, tempted by a Muslim lady, Voada. 'Turne Turke I am yours', she tells him, and he obediently undergoes circumcision, but she herself falls for one of Ward's crew, a young girl who disguised herself by 'putting on the weed of a Sailers boy'.[88] 'I have not seene so much of beauty in a man', says Voada,

Figure 1.2. 'The two Pirats Purser and Clinton', from *A True Relation, of the Lives and Deaths of the two most famous English Pyrats, Purser and Clinton* (1639).

unsuspecting, but it all ends badly, as of course it should, Ward vengefully stabbing faithless Voada and then Ward and his cross-dressed sailor stabbing themselves.[89] Ward was celebrated and deprecated in a pamphlet and ballads sold in London in 1609, before the play. One ballad, 'The Seaman's Song of Captain Ward, the Famous Pirate', admired his social mobility, rising from 'a simple fisherman' in England to a Muslim prince in Tunis, but hoped that his exotic 'honors' would 'prove like letters written in the sand'.[90]

The authentic Ward, unlike the dramatic Ward, was not circumcised for love, nor circumcised at all—so far as we can tell—nor crewed by cross-dressed sailors, but lived to a good age in Tunis, according to a Scots traveller, William Lithgow, who 'dyned and supped' with Ward in his 'faire Palace, beautified with rich Marble and Alabaster stones', a palace he hospitably shared with 'some fifteene circumcised English Runagates'.[91] 'He hath built a very stately house, farre more fit for a Prince, then a pirate', according to the London pamphlet, *Two notorious*

Pyrates (1609).[92] Like the ballad and using some of the same words, the pamphlet conceded Ward's survival and princely status in Tunis, but pointed out ominously that 'these honors are like letters written in the sand, which are blown away with every gust of winde, and in the end shall prove sorrows to his heart, being paind with a thousand passions, and stung with a continuall gnawing of conscience, for committing so many impieties'.[93] In this pamphlet, as well as in the ballad and the play, the immorality of piracy, a redistribution of wealth making a prince of a pirate, is confused with treachery to the nation and with apostasy, as circumcision is with sexual temptation.

A pirate by yet another name, a prototypical pirate, the buccaneer, emerges from the seventeenth-century colonization of the Caribbean islands by the French, English, and others, acting nationally but also irregularly and independently, invading territory that was papally decreed to be Spanish. (François I of France asked sarcastically to see the relevant clause in Adam's will.[94]) On Saint-Domingue (alias Hispaniola) and neighbouring Tortuga, transnational Europeans either planted or hunted or pirated, pillaging Spanish shipping and the Spanish colonies on the Spanish Main. For these adventures, ships on the sea were mostly a means for the delivery of fierce fighting men to the American mainland. The fierce, wild buccaneers (see Figure 1.3) hunted wild cattle and hogs and preserved the meat as the indigenous Indians did, placing it over a fire on a rack called a 'barbacoa' (hence 'barbecue') in a smoking process called 'boucaner' (hence 'buccaneer').[95] Mostly French and English, they were rascals and refugees from many places, rendered skilful and brave by hunting and being hunted themselves by the Spanish who gave no quarter.[96] In fear of these merciless enemies, the buccaneers ate back to back, guns cocked, surrounded by their packs of dogs.[97] One careful and anthropological observer called them Europeans who had become American savages—civilized savages, in other words, a new world of vagrant, invading Europeans who rediscovered themselves as colonists in reverse, colonized by savagery, tribalized and culturally reinvented.[98] The buccaneer anticipated the white wild man of the nascent Anglo-American colonies, the frontiersman, the future cowboy, but the buccaneer was more free of national constraints, free to go native and to reinvent himself. The new world that turned the old one upside down was the stimulus, the basis, for the revolution on the ocean.

Figure 1.3. 'Buccaneers and scenes from the life of buccaneers', from A.O. Exquemelin, *Histoire des Avanturiers* (Paris, 1686).

For clothing the buccaneers wore a shirt smeared and imbued with grease and animal blood, trousers even filthier, and a belt of hairy cowskin which held up on one side a sheath containing several knives and on the other a cartridge case.[99] Their shoes were made of pigskins tied on with a thong and their hats had brims cut to a point at the front. Also around the waist they wore a bag into which they crawled at night for protection from the bites of mosquitoes and other insects that sucked their blood.[100] Besides their Flemish knives and a Spanish machete they had guns called 'boucaniers' like themselves, with barrels four-and-a-half feet long, with which they could hit a coin at 120 paces.[101] Without wives or children, they formed themselves into couples by an arrangement they called 's'amateloter', 'becoming shipmates', one could say, their term deriving from the original sense of 'matelot', 'sailor', meaning 'companion de couche', or hammock-sharer, sleeping partner, bedfellow.[102] They called themselves 'Frères de la côte', 'Brothers of the coast', obeying no national laws but following what they called 'la coutume de la côte', customs of their own, explaining that all former obligations were 'noyé', drowned, when they had crossed the tropical line.[103] They were brothers of each other, then, a tribal reformulation of their sexual as well as national alignments, their kinship systems. Observers distinguished the buccaneers from flibustiers (their name derived from the English 'freebooter') but both types inhabited the same regions, the coasts of Saint-Domingue and nearby Tortuga. Flibustiers were amphibious buccaneers, it could be said, buccaneers who had taken to the sea. They hated the whole of humanity but especially Spaniards.[104] Instead of hunting they would make or steal a boat and set out on the sea to die or make their fortunes, crowded, cramped, exposed to sun and rain, hoping to steal a better boat and some loot, which they would instantly spend in debauchery.[105] They were forever in extremities, said one reporter, either of excessive joy or unbearable misery.[106] 'Mourir ou faire fortune; en attendant, se divertir, c'etoit là toutes leur maximes.'[107] ('To die or make a fortune; meanwhile to amuse oneself: that was their entire philosophy.') The reports of these prototypical pirates indicate the significance of the prospective pirate type for cosmopolitan readers. These seafaring Europeans, like the savages, were discoverers of new rights for mankind: to take what they wanted of colonial spoil by violence not toil, by colonizing the ocean not the land. On the ocean a man could rise above his station, or die trying, could profit, could win.

Hardy, sharp-shooting, avaricious, and unstable, these buccaneers gradually turned their hunting and survival skills to raiding the Spanish colonies. The English buccaneer Basil Ringrose described a fight in 1680 off Panama between 68 raiding buccaneers in canoes and piraguas (large canoes) and 228 defending Spanish, blacks, and mulattos in three barks. A lucky shot from a buccaneer gun hit the man at the wheel of the largest Spanish bark, so that the unsteered ship turned into the wind and its flapping sails filled the wrong way, sending the ship backwards. A buccaneer canoe came under the stern of this stricken bark and fired at any man who attempted to take the wheel. While a buccaneer piragua grappled at close quarters with a second Spanish bark, two buccaneer canoes made for the third bark, which sailed off and escaped. At the stern of the largest bark the buccaneers jammed its rudder and killed two thirds of its men, including the captain and the pilot, whereupon those on board finally surrendered. The buccaneers boarded this defeated bark and sent two canoes to support the piragua grappling with the remaining undefeated bark. Again the buccaneers were fortunate, as powder containers exploded on the Spanish ship, burning and blowing up many men aboard. In the resulting carnage and chaos, the buccaneers boarded and took the Spanish bark. Ringrose went aboard to find the Spanish forces killed, wounded, and 'horribly burnt with Powder'.[108] On the largest Spanish bark, which he then visited, he found only 25 men had survived of the original force of 86 and only 8 of those survivors were in a condition to fight, 'all the rest being desperately wounded'.[109] 'Their blood ran down the decks in whole streams', he wrote.[110] Ringrose survived to describe what he saw but a Spanish ambush nearly six years later, in 1686 in Mexico (New Spain), left a party of buccaneers 'so cut and mangl'd' as to be unrecognisable, as William Dampier reported.[111] 'We had about 50 Men killed, among the rest my ingenious Friend Mr. Ringrose was one'.[112]

The buccaneers were the subject of a brief history by a man of appropriately uncertain nationality—perhaps French, probably Dutch— the variously-spelled Esquemeling, who wrote in Dutch *De Americaensche Zee-Roovers* (1678), rapidly translated into German, Spanish, French, and English (from the Spanish), as *Bucaniers of America* (1684). He claimed to write as 'an Eye-witness', a status which has been disputed, though his accounts tally generally—if not completely—with information from other sources and colonial records.[113]

The work begins as a travel book, delivering information—from a distance and thus at a premium—about the islands of the Caribbean, where civilized European rivalries were exported and given room for more blatant savagery. Esquemeling describes the competitive struggles of the white invaders against the indigenous Indians, against the packs of wild dogs imported to extirpate the Indians, and against each other.

He carefully describes the local flora and fauna, pestilent crocodiles and mosquitoes, beneficial glow-worms, 'shining so brightly' that 'I could easily read in any Book, although of never so small a print'.[114] He describes especially what is edible or profitable—how to grow tobacco, for example—how the islands are frequented by turtles with such reliable senses of direction that lost ships can follow their navigations. The options for the buccaneers who adapted to these circumstances were, he explained, planting, hunting, or pirating. As itinerants the buccaneers preferred hunting to planting, whether game or gold. Wild and desperate, they were willing to risk themselves, even puncturing their own small and overcrowded vessels—often one-masted barks or even canoes—to ensure they would capture another and better vessel rather than drown in their own.[115] They were characterized by ferocity and sometimes cruelty. One buccaneering leader, Francis Lolonois, was said to have torn out the tongue of a Spanish captive, 'to bite and gnaw it with his teeth, like a ravenous Wolf', as a warning to his other captives that he was to be feared and obeyed.[116] Tortures were devised to extract the whereabouts of hidden loot. Prisoners had 'burning Matches placed betwixt their fingers', cords 'twisted about their heads, till their eyes bursted out of the skull'.[117] 'Some were hang'd up by the Testicles ... till they fell unto the ground, those private parts being torn from their bodies ... Others had their feet put into the fire, and thus were left to be roasted alive'.[118] Propelled by greed for gold, the buccaneers spent it quickly in 'Taverns and Stews', experiencing rapidly rising and falling fortunes.[119] Some 'will spend two or three thousand pieces of eight, in one night, not leaving themselves peradventure a good shirt to wear, on their backs, in the morning'.[120] Esquemeling 'saw one of them give unto a common Strumpet, five hundred pieces of eight, only that he might see her naked'.[121] Another buccaneer spent 3,000 pieces-of-eight in three months, only to be sold himself to pay his debt to a tavern.[122] Brutal Lolonois deservedly perished, as 'God Almighty' had 'appointed the Indians of Darien' to pull him apart, burn his pieces in a fire and throw his ashes into the air so as to disperse his wicked person for ever.[123]

Free of the laws of their own nations of origin, inhabiting the ungoverned spaces before formal colonization, the buccaneers made laws of their own, some later incorporated into the rules of conduct for the pirates. The buccaneer principles were communal, transnational. Leaders could be changed by popular demand. Loot should be divided and was the only remuneration. 'No prey, no pay', was a slogan.[124] Compensation schemes were collectively agreed and tabulated: 'for the loss of a right Arm six hundred pieces of eight, or six slaves...For an eye, one hundred pieces of eight, or one slave'.[125]

Esquemeling described the rise and fall of Lolonois, a Frenchman from Les Sables d'Olonne on the Atlantic coast, Bartholomew Portugues, presumably Portuguese, and Roche or Rock Brasiliano, supposedly a Dutchman, before establishing his major character, the man who scrambled to the greatest success and even respectability, a Welshman, Henry Morgan, whose profitable exploits were robberies on land, not sea, and who organized and coordinated hundreds of otherwise unruly and separately greedy buccaneers into collectively raiding and pillaging Spanish colonial centres: Portobello in 1668, Maracaibo in 1669, and famously, in 1671, Panama, after crossing the Isthmus, to confront the Spanish on their safer Pacific coast. Esquemeling considered the reward of only 200 pieces-of-eight for an ordinary buccaneer at Panama was mean and the result of cheating by Morgan, but the proceeds were nevertheless considerable and spread naturally to the incipient British Caribbean colonies, especially their taverns and brothels, no doubt, and to England inevitably.[126] Panama was, as Morgan boasted in his triumphant report, a pivotal point in the traffic from the New World to the Old of the products of colonial mines, and thus 'the greatest Mart for Silver and gold in the whole World'.[127] Although considered 'an honest brave fellow' by the Governor of Jamaica, Morgan was arrested and shipped back to England in 1672, principally to satisfy the Spaniards, as the Governor wrote: 'I shall send him home so as he shall not be much disgusted, yet the order obeyed, and the Spaniards satisfied'.[128]

In England Morgan was celebrated, described after dinner in John Evelyn's diary as the man 'who undertooke that gallant exploit from Nombre de Dios to Panamà'.[129] In effect an unofficial agent of British colonial interests, Morgan was rewarded in 1675 by a knighthood and appointment as Deputy Governor of Jamaica. A respectable as well as wealthy figure, increasingly inhabiting a hammock in his dotage in Jamaica, and alarming Dr Hans Sloane by his appearance, 'lean, sallow coloured, his Eyes a little yellowish, and Belly a little jetting out', and by his behaviour, 'drinking and sitting up late', Morgan died and was publicly and officially mourned in 1688.[130] His buccaneering successes were military rather than nautical or piratical and were manifestations

of the long-standing British colonial rivalry with the prevailing European power on the mainland of America, the Spanish. Indeed, as the
buccaneers became susceptible to organization and to British and
French colonial policy, so they tended to settle legitimately and become
absorbed in the consolidating colonial arrangements.

Piracy is almost as old as seafaring and as old as fiction, or travelling
and lying, those two old companions, but the great phase of piracy, in
fact and in fiction, the so-called 'golden age', came in the late seventeenth and early eighteenth centuries, with the opening of the world's
oceans to mobile, exploring Europeans. There are many names for
such maritime highwaymen—buccaneers in the West Indies, for example, who preyed on the Spanish colonial empire, or the corsairs of the
Mediterranean, for another example, plunderers from the Barbary
coast of North Africa, like those who stole the freedom of
Cervantes—but the pirates of the golden age are defined by their own
historical circumstances: the opening of the world's oceans before they
were closed by colonial grasp, oceans that made room for precolonial
rivalry, peacetime hostility and especially the interception of the transit
of the colonial spoils—silk, jewels, slaves, gold—that measured—as
piracy did—the prosperity of the European seafaring nations. These
particular pirates, who are the ideal pirates for all time, our own time
as well as theirs, have a literary context as well as a maritime one,
emerging in print from cities with writers and readers, pirates of the
imagination as well as the high seas, the open oceans and colonial
prospects. The pirates of the so-called golden age were born of a coincidence between the circumstances at sea, the opening oceans, opening opportunities for theft, and the circumstances on shore, readers
horrified and delighted by lawbreaking, robbery, and social mobility,
readers opening opportunities for profit. Pirates were made in London
as well as Madagascar, by hacks in the back streets as well as by sailors
changing sides on the high seas.

The Homeric sea was wine-dark and dangerous, an obstacle course
between Odysseus and Ithaca. There was no ocean in Eden. The Flood
was God's punishment of mankind. The Presbyterian divine John Flavel was enthusiastically metaphorical but not blatantly unChristian
when he informed seventeenth-century sailors, 'you who float upon
the great Deeps' which are not only 'the Bottom of the Sea, but of Hell
also', that 'you...have the roaring Waves and Billows...gaping for
you'.[131] Until the Romantic age oceans were voids, wastelands, or

worse, confining not liberating. 'Why, Sir,' Johnson told Boswell in 1773, 'no man will be a sailor who has contrivance to get himself into a jail, for being in a ship is being in a jail with the chance of being drowned'.[132] As well as better 'safety' than a man at sea, Johnson explained, a man in jail 'has more room, better food, and commonly better company', but for many men the sea was nevertheless a means of escape.[133] In the eighteenth century the repulsive and terrifying emptiness of the oceans was becoming traversable and was filling with attainable treasures.[134]

Of course seamen led hazardous lives, nearer to death, at times, than life. 'Seamen', according to John Flavel's meditative *Navigation Spiritualized*, 'are, as it were, a third Sort of Persons, to be numbered neither with the Living nor the Dead; their Lives hanging continually in Suspense before them'.[135] Edward Barlow's journal describes the hazards more nearly:

> in stormy weather, when the ship rolled and tumbled as though some great millstone were rolling up one hill and down another, we had much ado to hold ourselves fast by the small ropes from falling by the board; and being gotten up into the tops, there we must haul and pull to make fast the sail, seeing nothing but air above us and water beneath us, and that so raging as though every wave would make a grave for us.[136]

A slip in the rigging could send a man to that watery grave, to take his 'habitation among the haddocks', to quote one grim sailor, or to make 'meat for the fishes', to quote another.[137] The seaman, according to witty Richard Brathwait, 'goes not the way of all flesh, but the way of all fish'.[138] Despite such macabre humour, however, for many sailors, such as John Morris, 'tired of hanging around' in a dockside tavern, paying three shillings and sixpence a week for bed and food, a precarious life at sea with some added violence, some fierce fighting against men as well as the elements, had its potential rewards as well as dangers.[139] 'Either a golden chain or a wooden leg', as he wrote from that tavern to his brother.[140] Fortune decided that John Morris lost his life, not his leg, but many sailors were prepared to venture themselves on the ocean.[141]

The sailors of the *Charles* (named in honour of Carlos II of Spain) were hired to salvage the sunken treasure of Spanish galleons in the West Indies but instead became the pirates of the *Fancy*, 'which will pleasure your minde', became men of 'Fortune', like their Captain

Every, and sought their own treasure in adventure. Edward Short was killed by a shark; James Morris lost his jewels and his mind in a wager; five others from the *Fancy* were hanged at Execution Dock; but by far the majority of its crew escaped such premature fates and found fortunes. The oceans were navigable, traversable, but uncontrollable, opening new worlds to discoverers, new opportunities not yet closed by national and colonial rule. The taking of the Danish ships by the *Fancy* was excused by a supposed Anglo-Danish war, but some Danish sailors chose to join the notional enemy aboard the *Fancy*.[142] The 12 or so Frenchmen who 'had lost their ship' in the Comoros and were taken into the *Fancy* 'had been privateering in those Seas under English Colours'.[143] The next recruits were 40 men from a defeated 'French Pyrating Junk'.[144] One of the *Fancy*'s Englishmen took a tally of her crew at this point in the voyage, 'being now in all about 170 Men vizt. 14 Danes, 52 French & 104 English'.[145] They would soon be swelled by two more ships from America and then '3 Englishmen more [three ships more] from America'.[146] Piracy transcended national boundaries as well as legal bounds and flourished profitably in far-flung islands beyond the reach of European powers, like the pirate haven in uncolonized Madagascar.

The popular idea of the pirate formed in the late seventeenth and early eighteenth century was an ambivalent expression of the power of the individual to transcend his or her circumstances and achieve sexual freedom, immense wealth, and political revolution, a reworking, therefore, of the conventions of romance, economics, and politics, to achieve complete personal self-gratification by means of an aggression that recast the ideals of heroism into an ideology of self-assertion. The pirate was a figure who could move credibly between the fantasy of romance and the plausibility of the novel. Indeed, pirates are perfect Defoe characters, like the narrators of his novels from Colonel Jack to Moll Flanders: deviant and anomic, marginal and therefore socially mobile, their pseudo-autobiographical medium offering an intimate moral consciousness to absorb and absolve the thrilling criminality of the narrative.[147]

Some of these ideological rearrangements are implicit in the title of an anonymous pamphlet published in London in 1709: *The Life and Adventures of Capt. John Avery, the Famous English Pirate, (rais'd from a Cabbin-Boy, to a King) now in Possession of Madagascar*. The title page stated that *The Life* was 'Written by a Person who made his Escape'

from Madagascar, and a Preface supplied the further information that
this author was 'one Adrian Van Broeck', a Dutch merchant captured
by Avery's men and brought to Madagascar, where Avery had trusted
and befriended him.[148]

Born at Plymouth in 1653—according to Van Broeck's supposed
journal—Avery was resourceful and successful in various maritime
exploits but inadequately rewarded for his services and also shamefully
defrauded of his rightful inheritance from his father of modest wealth
and property. After some account of this early career, Avery is described
in preparation for a new turn in his story:

He was, as to his Proportion, middle-siz'd, inclinable to be fat, and of a gay
jolly Complexion... His Temper was of a Piece with his Person, daring and
good-humour'd, if not provok'd, but insolent, uneasy, and unforgiving to the
last Degree, if at any Time impos'd upon.[149]

He is thus likeable but frightening, and his prowess at sea and the theft
of his inheritance incline us to admiration and sympathy, but he is now
presented and assessed because 'he was just upon the Point of seeing
himself a Great Man by honest Practices, when an unlucky Accident
shipwreck'd his good Fortune, and occasion'd his being enroll'd in the
List of Robbers himself', along with those who had 'plunder'd... his
Patrimony'.[150] The 'unlucky Accident' was Avery's attraction to a farm-
er's daughter whose father never paid a promised dowry and who
herself delivered a son the spitting image of a local inn-keeper.

Enraged by these deceits, Avery turned to fraud himself, obtaining
command of a ship and crew to whom he offered the prospect of personal wealth by contrast with the misery they would experience, as he
had, from the injustices of the world. Instead of such misery 'he
promis'd one Day's resolute Fight should make the Residue of their
Lives an uninterrupted Scene of Pleasure'.[151] After some cruising in
the Indian Ocean,

Fortune... threw in his Way a Vessel of a great Burthen,... freighted with the
richest Merchandizes of all the East, and had got a Prize of greater Value about
her, I mean a Grand-Daughter of Aurenzebe, who was then Great Mogul.[152]

The 'Indians' were easily and quickly defeated by the English, who
acquired a cargo amply satisfying their piratical appetites:

The Cargo of this Ship was so very rich, that it even satiated the Appetites of
the most covetous of the Mariners; for above the Value of a Million of Money

in Silver, and rich Stuffs, was found therein, and a very agreeable Lady into the Bargain.[153]

When Avery saw the lady in tears, he became 'of an amorous Disposition' and, 'instead of ravishing the Princess, which some Accounts have made Mention of', respectfully took her aboard his own ship.[154] The fabulous wealth of the cargo was, it seemed, originally intended as a dowry for the Princess, to be married to 'a Persian Potentate', and so it was appropriate that Avery (previously deprived of his own dowry) acquired this new dowry and married the Princess, which he did with her consent, and according to the rites of 'those Foreigners'.[155] His crew less romantically drew lots for her female attendants but politely 'stay'd their Stomachs 'till the same Priest had said Grace for them'.[156] Thus supplied by Fortune with wealth and wives, the pirates 'came in Sight of the Island of Madagascar'.[157]

At Madagascar Avery made an alliance with an indigenous king and set about securing a harbour which, by design or coincidence, does seem to resemble the pirate resort established by Baldridge in about 1691.[158] Here Avery made sure that the loot recently acquired was equitably distributed, 'according to the Law of Pirates, who, though they make it their Business to prey on Persons of a different Life and Conversation, yet among themselves observe the strictest Rules of Justice'.[159] Using this base on Madagascar, Avery resumed piracy, taking two more 'Moorish Vessels, and an English East India Ship' and 'another Prize, which was full of French-Men'.[160] The Crews of these ships were offered a ship to escape with, or the opportunity to join Avery's Madagascar 'Republic Of Pirates'.[161] One of the Frenchmen, ominously named 'Mons. de Sale', became Avery's deputy, and led a voyage 'in Quest of Women' which 'soon return'd with a Cargo of Ladies' who were attractive even though 'their Complexion was none of the fairest'.[162] So Avery's 'new-structur'd Commonwealth' propagated itself and multiplied by attracting 'Pirates of all Nations'.[163]

Unfortunately, however, Mons. de Sale covets Avery's wife and status and incites a French revolution, but fortunately his plot is betrayed to Avery and the rebels are tried and executed. Avery's power and authority are consequently enhanced but he begins to think of returning to his own country and of what he may expect 'at a Heavenly Tribunal'.[164] Inspired by these considerations, Avery writes a patriotic letter to the East India Company requesting a pardon and offering a

Figure 1.4. Captain Avery in Madagascar, from *The History and Lives of all the most notorious Pirates, and their Crews* (London, 1729).

payment of 'some Millions of Money'.[165] There is no response to this offer, so Avery continues on Madagascar (see Figure 1.4), consolidating his power there, expelling the French colonial presence and even conquering the Malagasy king, his former ally. He now commands 15,000 soldiers and more than 40 warships.[166] The pamphlet concludes with a description of Madagascar and a suggestion that the British government should either 'suppress these Pyrates by Force' and thus 'get possession of this wealthy Island' or else achieve the same result by negotiating a pardon for Avery.[167]

This fictional account of Avery, designed to satisfy popular requirements of a pirate type rather than record or reveal facts about Every, contains no distressing details of violence, although invoking the secular mechanisms of Fortune and bodily appetite. Avery deserves a successful legitimate career at sea, deserves his due inheritance from his father, and deserves also to love and marry a faithful wife. When his social circumstances deprive him of these deserts, he obtains better rewards by piracy, travelling 'from a Cabbin-Boy, to a King'. Although a king, he rules over an egalitarian republic. The pirates are utopians who break laws but make their own and 'among themselves observe the strictest Rules of Justice'.[168] He rules justly over his kingdom-republic and even comes to repent his deviations from piety, home country, and patriotic duty. *The Life and Adventures of Capt. John Avery, the Famous English Pirate* thus turns him into the hero of a political legend of piracy, a story with some precedents in the reality of the buccaneers in the Caribbean, but now shaped into a saleable fiction—a fiction masquerading as fact and still believed by some modern historians.[169]

As the quasi-legal manuscripts that are the basic records of piracy turn into commercial print, the oral testimonies and statements of sailors take the retrospectively recognizable shape of those innovatory fictions that are now better known as the novel. The pirates acquire biographical contexts that are explanatory, even exculpatory, supplying reasons for the pirate hero, an individual now, a hero whose adventures, whose fortunes, turn the plot, correcting the errors of an unjust society on shore that defrauded him of love and money, rewarding him at sea with an exotic princess and unimaginable, intangible treasure, exotic as well as mysterious in its incalculability. This hero is an ordinary man who becomes an exotic colonial king because of his irrepressible natural ability in a happy coincidence with fortune, not by means of his brutal violence, which is invisible in the factitious but pleasing tale, a fantastical romance of his love and courage, not lust and violence, a romance made credible now in a new literary genre, utilizing the crude but vivid language of ordinary speakers who have now become—in a revolution that anticipated the hero's own—readers and purchasers, a genre not suspending disbelief, but eliminating it.

Some reports of the Madagascar pirates were not so flattering. Returning from the voyage that found and rescued Selkirk, 'a Man cloth'd in Goat-Skins, who look'd wilder than the first Owners of them', Captain Woodes Rogers reported from the Cape of Good Hope in 1711 that

I spoke with an English and an Irish-man, who had been several Years with the Madagascar Pirates, but were now pardoned, and allowed to settle here:

They told me, that those miserable Wretches, who had made such a Noise in the World, were now dwindled to between 60 or 70, most of them very poor and despicable, even to the Natives, among whom they had married. They added, that they had no Embarkations, but one Ship, and a Sloop that lay sunk; so that those Pirates are so inconsiderable, that they scarce deserve to be mentioned.[170]

Nevertheless those pirates continued to be mentioned. In 1712, the year of publication of Rogers's *Voyage*, the members of the audience of Charles Johnson's *The Successful Pyrate* at the Theatre Royal in Drury Lane, London, were requested by the Prologue to 'Believe your selves in Madagascar's Isle'.[171] A character called Arviragus is presently King but has been a pirate, after some events resembling those in *The Life and Adventures of Capt. John Avery*. His gallant naval service has been unrewarded because he fought a superior officer, as he did in *The Life*, and this officer has cheated him of his estate and married his mistress. On an Indian expedition Arviragus has married instead 'an Omrah's Daughter' and had a son by her whom he laments leaving behind and hopes one day to find and install as his heir on Madagascar.[172] We are thus introduced to Arviragus's personal history, but the first event of the play is the capture of a new prize which 'Fortune has convey'd': 'The Grand-daughter of the Great Mogul is taken, with her whole Dow'r and Train'.[173]

Arviragus loves Zaida, this grand-daughter of Aurangzeb, the Grand Mughal, but she loves another, her fellow-passenger and fellow-captive, Aranes. Meanwhile some of King Arviragus's subjects plan a rebellion, led by one in particular, named De Sale, who jealously aims to ensure that 'Zaida and his throne shall both be mine'.[174] Although a benevolent monarch, Arviragus orders the death of his rival, Aranes, and the incipient rebellion is betrayed and suppressed, but the lovely Zaida still mourns Aranes and Arviragus feels ashamed of himself. Success inevitably beckons, however, as Aranes has survived and owns a bracelet confirming that his long-lost father is Arviragus, who offers Zaida and his throne to his newly-discovered son and heir. Arviragus has been yearning for his home in Britain and regrets that his bribe of gold has been rejected. An Epilogue explains that Arviragus is really Avery, the historical pirate whom he resembles not at all, though clearly a theatrical heir to the hero of the pamphlet *Life and Adventures*. The fictional Avery is clearly taking shape as a rising man who achieves success in love and war, starting an exotic royal family and ruling justly as King of an exotic kingdom, but yearning, even so, for home and country.

The Successful Pyrate was not itself particularly successful, but the critic (and dramatist) John Dennis protested at a play which could celebrate a mere sailor and real pirate:

> was any thing wanting to the Extravagance of this degenerate Age, but the making a Tarpawlin and a Swabber, and a living Tarpawlin and a Swabber, the Hero of a Tragedy? who, at the same time that he is strutting in Buskins here, is lolling at Madagascar with some drunken sun-burnt Whore over a Can of Flip.[175]

Making a hero of such a man (drinking a sailor's cocktail of beer and brandy) was 'introducing upon the Stage a Hero of Execution-Dock'.[176]

This mixture of aesthetic and ethical protest did not deter other writers from turning Avery into art—and potential profit. The 'golden age' of the pirate at sea was also an age of the pirate on stage and the page. The real pirate was immediately fictional. He became a go-between, a medium of exchange, between authors and a market: the pirate as product, in short. The commercial opportunities for the pirate on the ocean thus coincided with commercial opportunities for his fictional double, the popular hero. The original at sea was nearly invisible but his representative on shore was on public display, by popular demand, and was masquerading as the real pirate, was purporting to be the real Every. The Avery on stage or in print was replacing the real Every, who had vanished. In disguise, perhaps, under a pseudonym, probably, Every—in his 'light coloured Wigg most commonly, pretty swarthy', with 'Grey Eyes, a flattish Nose'—real Every . . . had escaped.

In 1720, not long after *Robinson Crusoe*, a work was published in London which has been (speculatively but not implausibly) attributed to Defoe.[177] Its full and rambling title was *The King of Pirates: Being an Account of the Famous Enterprises of Captain Avery, the Mock King of Madagascar. With his Rambles and Piracies; wherein all the Sham Accounts formerly publish'd of him, are detected. In Two Letters from himself; one during his Stay at Madagascar, and one since his Escape from thence.* The titular reference to the *Mock King of Madagascar* and the claims to detect *all the Sham Accounts formerly publish'd* immediately announce the theme of correcting fiction with fact. The fictions are now in competition, one Avery with another, supposedly more authentic. The 'Preface' repeats this emphasis, signalling that the account will show 'the readers how much they have been impos'd upon in the former ridiculous and extravagant Accounts'.[178] By comparing these letters written by Avery himself with 'the extravagant Stories already told', the readers will be able to judge 'which is most likely to be genuine'.[179] In particular: 'The Account given of Captain Avery's taking the Great Mogul's Daughter, ravishing and murdering her, and all the Ladies of her Retinue, is . . . differently related here'.[180] Previous accounts were untrue and crudely inconsistent, for 'it was but ill laid together of those who publish'd, that he first ravish'd her, then murder'd her, and then marry'd her'.[181] This new version of events, on the contrary, 'stripp'd of all the romantick, improbable, and impossible Parts of it, looks more like the History of Captain Avery, than any Thing yet publish'd ever has done'.[182] Exposing the fiction, then, has become an essential part of the Avery fiction, and plausible realism the medium for doing so.

The opening of the First Letter touches immediately on this theme again, expressing Avery's 'Resentment' at 'a most ridiculous Book, entitled *My Life and Adventures*'.[183] The earlier part of the 'First Letter' has no relation, however, to what is known of the historical career of the real Every.[184] This new Avery carries out various buccaneering deeds—predations on the Spanish colonies in South America, in company with real buccaneers such as Sharp and Sawkins (whose stories had been published in a second edition in 1684 of the English translation of Esquemeling's *Bucaniers of America*). He rises in the ranks of various fluctuating buccaneering alliances and accumulates loot as well as status until eventually a decision is reached to retreat to Madagascar, 'where we might all settle ourselves undisturb'd'.[185] The description of Madagascar is rudimentary, and the settlement is at an unspecific location on the west coast, or north-west coast, not at the actual pirate rendezvous of St. Mary's Island, off the north-east coast. After a period back in London, Avery's life perhaps coincides with the real Every's, as this Avery, who is perhaps Defoe's, leads a mutiny off the coast of Spain before returning to Madagascar. The geographical circumstances of his most famous action are a little different, however, as he is at a port in Sumatra when he hears of two ships of the Grand Mughal, carrying the Mughal's grand-daughter to wed the King of Pegu (in South Burma). Avery is insistent that he did no ravishing of 'the Queen (for such she was to have been)'.[186] He was the first to enter her cabin, and found her all in Gold and Silver, but frighted; and crying, and at the Sight of me she appear'd trembling, and just as if she was going to die...she was, in a Manner, cover'd with Diamonds, and I, like a true Pirate, soon let her see that I had more Mind to the Jewels than to the Lady...I have heard that it has been reported in England that I ravish'd this Lady, and then used her most barbarously; but they wrong me, for I never offer'd any Thing of that Kind to her, I assure you.[187]

As proof he informs us that 'I did not like her; and there was one of her Ladies who I found much more agreeable to me'.[188] Avery 'had more Mind to the Jewels than to the Lady', then, preferred robbery to rape, and also—by way of variation from alternative accounts—preferred a lady-in-waiting to the Queen herself. The legend of Every and a Muslim lady persisted in the East as well as in London. The sailor Edward Barlow recorded in his journal in 1697 what he had heard at Bombay, that 'one Everrey, a pirate...had ravished a great lady of the Court of the Great Mogul, who had been at Mocha to pay her devotions to their prophet Mahomet's tomb'.[189] A Captain Alexander Hamilton reported, in *A New Account of the East Indies* (1727), that Every had 'carried a young Mogul Lady with him, and some of her female Servants, who had been at Mecca to perform a Vow, laid upon her by her Mother on her Death-bed'.[190] *The King of the Pirates* is not genuinely concerned with correcting legends with facts, however. The point here is to give the illusion of fact by contradicting the previous published fiction, not to establish Avery as a chivalrous man of principle, which he certainly is not. His relations with his subordinate pirates are matters of mere convenience, uncomplicated by friendship or even loyalty.

Back at the pirates' lair on Madagascar, another legend is now rearranged, for Avery contradicts the exaggerated accounts of his strength and wealth on Madagascar:

for, as I have understood, they were told at London, that we were no less than 5000 Men; that we had built a regular Fortress for our Defence by Land, and that we had 20 Sail of Ships...But nothing of all this was ever true, any more than it was true, that we offer'd ten Millions to the Government of England for our Pardon.[191]

Avery even finds that these stories have come to find him in Madagascar, where (without 'letting them know that I was Avery himself') he hears from visiting sailors about his huge army and fleet of ships, as well as that 'he ravish'd the Great Mogul's Daughter' while his men 'ravish'd and forc'd all the Ladies attending her Train, and then threw them into the Sea, or cut their Throats'.[192] In return he spreads his own legend, anonymously telling the visitors of a prospective force of 'twenty thousand Men' and of Avery's probable offer of 'five or six Millions of Ducats' for a pardon.[193] He is thus the author—and denier—of his own legend. 'This Discourse', he informs his reader, 'was the Ground of the Rumour you have had in England, that Avery has offer'd to come in and submit, and would give six Millions for his Pardon'.[194]

In his letters in his own *King of Pirates* he reveals that he feels no solidarity for the people of Madagascar and little for his pirate companions, not wishing to be 'burying myself alive, as I call'd it, among Savages and Barbarians' (piratical, perhaps, as well as indigenous).[195] His main concern is how to escape and take his wealth somewhere he can spend it. He embarks with a select band of his men in a sloop to Bassora (Basra, in Iraq), from where he travels upriver to Baghdad, where he and his men disguise themelves as Armenian merchants before he and a companion travel, for no apparent reason, to Isfahan in Persia, from where he travelled overland to Constantinople. From there he writes his second letter, which he promises to send from 'Marseilles in France; from whence I intend to go and live in some inland Town, where, as they have, perhaps, no Notion of the Sea, so they will not be inquisitive after us'.[196]

These prose works about Avery are all anonymous or pseudonymous, a condition characteristic of the kind of writings that they are, situated on the borderline between fact and fiction, a location characteristic of a new genre, the novel, a businesslike writing emerging from growing London, a thriving kind of writing by and for citizens who were not writers or readers of literature hitherto deemed respectable. The fictional pirates are an invasion of the high seas by the venturesome hacks of London, redeploying the pirates to meet the aspirations, political and commercial, of new, emerging readers with pennies to spend on pirates of the mind, of the imagination, of happily—and profitably—suspended disbelief.

The writer whose name is most connected, correctly and incorrectly, with these anonymously written pirates is Daniel Defoe, though none of the writings about Avery carried his name. Few of Defoe's works did carry his name—*Robinson Crusoe*, for example, was 'Written by Himself', by Robinson Crusoe. Defoe, the anonymous author, was

born and died in the near neighbourhood of a London street described
in his lifetime as 'but indifferent, as to its Houses and Inhabitants; and
sufficiently pestered with Courts and Alleys', the street called Grub
Street, its name derived from 'grube', a drain or ditch.[197] Although
Defoe has risen posthumously from his death in Ropemaker's Alley,
round the corner from Grub Street, from where he has risen with the
acquired respectability of the novel, he was nevertheless in his day a
citizen of metaphorical Grub Street, as defined knowingly in Johnson's
Dictionary, 'a street in Moorfields in London, much inhabited by writers of small histories, dictionaries, and temporary poems'.[198]

From such a street of London, then, emerged the pirate from the
pen of the money-grubbing, anonymous hack, for sale—pen and
pirate—to the rising readers who had pennies enough to pay for reading that combined the thrilling, rising pirates with the documentary,
matter-of-fact realism of plausible fiction. From Grub Street the pirate
sailed the high seas, credible but out of reach of verification, provoca-
tively thrilling but properly evil. His undistinguished origins are in the
catch-penny pamphlets about the bad deeds and consequent last days
of popular convicted rogues, publications that were usually labelled
'True' but were more adapted to the fantasies of writers and readers
than to the facts of rogues—or pirates, for that matter.[199] These writings about sensational crimes and their humble but notorious perpe-
trators interacted with the increasingly realistic direction of fiction, a
tendency with particular scope in the literature of travel, which could
celebrate the adventure of individualism achieved by departure from
home and country in comfortable conjunction with the freedom and
impunity from observation and contradiction afforded by distance
over the seas. From the factual fictions there naturally emerged unmit-
igated fictions to realize the commercial potential of the imagination.
From the novelization came the novel, as we can see from the accounts
of Avery, fictions that were credible still and realistic, indistinguishable
from the truth, but coming, not from the confessions of criminals or
the records of their trials (sources that were dubious in their own
ways), but from the imaginations of hacks in indifferent streets pestered
with alleys—streets like metaphorical Grub Street, from whose over-
flowing drain or ditch emerged Defoe's piratical Captain Singleton as
well as respectable Robinson Crusoe.

Pirates coincide with the novel and are quickly fictitious by way of
rumour, legend, fake reports of facts, and the novel's own deliberately

plausible narrative, a medium congenial to pirates, a medium passively following the fortunate self-creation of the adventurer hero who plots his way through the illegal, subcultural, and unverifiable margins of society and history, escaping detection by way of the empty but enriching oceans, most himself and most at home in fiction. Defoe's *The Life, Adventures, and Pyracies, of the Famous Captain Singleton* (1720), published soon after *The King of Pirates*, falls quite distinctly into two halves. The first tells the pseudo-autobiographical story of young Singleton, stolen aged about two from a pub garden near Islington, acquired by a beggar-woman, then by a gypsy for 12 shillings, transferred from town to town, taken to sea, captured by Turkish pirates and from them by Portuguese sailors. He is a lost and displaced child, at sea with the Portuguese and put ashore with others on Madagascar, which is just another such displacement. Singleton was not his real name, but he is certainly single by nature. On Madagascar he begins to fill a leadership role, finally sailing with his fellow-castaways to the east coast of Africa and then, with much help from Africans they capture, extraordinarily (and rather tediously) crossing the entire continent from east to west. Eventually they near the west coast and begin accumulating gold and tusks, especially with the help of a naked Londoner, a Crusoe turned Kurtz (who seems to have had a real original, named Freeman).[200]

Enriched Singleton returns to England, where he has no known relatives or friends and foolishly spends his African wealth on 'Folly and Wickedness'.[201] The second part of *Captain Singleton* is more like an expansion of *The King of Pirates* and begins—as Every's historical piracy did—with Singleton's joining in a mutiny on an English ship at 'the Groyn' (Coruña).[202] He embarks on a career as a pirate, accompanied by a Quaker, William, who has principles (supposedly, though willing to sell captured blacks as slaves) and by Wilmot, the pirate leader. Because of his previous experience, Singleton suggests they use Madagascar as a centre of activity. Various adventures follow and he encounters the supposedly real Avery, who has captured a ship 'with the great Mogul's Daughter, and an immense Treasure in Money and Jewels'.[203] Failing to fulfil the promise of the title page of *Captain Singleton*, that the work would contain *an Account of his many Adventures and Pyracies with Captain Avery*, Singleton and William separate from Avery and Wilmot and proceed with various repetitive piratical successes which serve the principal plot, an account of the accumulation of wealth. Some fights with the local peoples of a potentially Tasmanian, or vaguely Austral land, and of Ceylon, help to relieve the impending tedium of repetitive piracies and lists of loot. An account of the genuine narrative of Robert Knox, *An Historical Relation of the Island Ceylon* (1681), is given for comparison with the account of Singleton's own experiences, which 'agreed so well' with Knox's.[204]

William and Singleton consider returning to their usual port at Madagascar but William begins a conversation with Singleton about repentance, thus returning to a religious concern touched on earlier with some 'Reflection on my former Life' that followed a frightening storm (as had happened also to real William Dampier, who 'made very sad reflections on my former Life', as did fictional Robinson Crusoe).[205] Singleton's serious reflections with William (which resemble an internal debate between a single character's conflicting ideas) lead to consideration of whether men have a natural yearning to return home, 'especially when they are grown rich'.[206] But Singleton replies that he feels nothing for the country of his birth, not so much even as 'for the Island of Madagascar', which 'has been a fortunate Island to me'.[207] They speak of the necessity of 'Repentance', but seem to think it would be potentially consistent with keeping their stolen wealth (a hypocrisy which the reader can notice, as with Moll Flanders's 'repentance').[208] Following the escape route taken by Avery and his companion in *The King of Pirates*, Singleton and William travel in disguise as 'Persian Merchants', for example, and as 'Armenian Merchants', from Basra to Baghdad and then via Aleppo eventually to Venice.[209] From there William writes to a sister in England sending money and requesting secrecy. Singleton also sends her money and after some years in Venice the two former pirates travel to England, with immense wealth, and Singleton finally informs us that he has married William's sister and will 'say no more for the present, lest some should be willing to inquire too nicely after Your Old Friend, Captain Bob'.[210] *Captain Singleton* was never as popular as *Robinson Crusoe* but is evidence that the pirate has arrived and is at home in the new genre. The pirate is now, for all time, a character in a novel.

Defoe paid another fictional visit to Madagascar in his *A New Voyage Round the World* (1724), in which the first person narrative (of circumnavigation from west to east) contains an episode with the pirates at Madagascar. Some of the officers of the ship hold the supposedly typical received opinions:

they had received such Ideas of the Figure those people made in Madagascar, from the common Report in England, that they had no Notion of them, but as of a little Common Wealth of Robbers; that they were immensely rich, that Captain Avery was King of the Island, that they were near 8000 Men, that they had a good Squadron of stout Ships.[211]

The narrating captain knows better, however, and the events of his story show the majority of the pirates to be disaffected, and keen to turn from pirates to legitimate sailors, and sail with Defoe's *New Voyage*. There are no signs of Captain Avery.

Avery was at Madagascar in the preconceptions of Defoe's visitors in *A New Voyage*, but absent from their imaginary experience of the island. His story, however, was still to be told again. Earlier in 1724, some months before *A New Voyage*, there appeared (with corrections and additions that same year and in 1725 and 1726) *A General History of the Robberies and Murders of the most notorious Pyrates*. The author on the title page was an unidentifiable and probably pseudonymous 'Captain Charles Johnson', but the work was ascribed to Defoe in 1932, without good reason. The ascription was, however—and still is— widely accepted, perhaps because pirates are characters who seem to belong in novels—and are therefore Defoe's authorial property—and because factual fictions were his kind of writing. Such confusions arise, therefore, from the prevailing popular conception of pirates, as characters indigenously inhabiting a verisimilitudinous but fictional world, a literary world, and although the *General History* was credibly expelled from the canon of Defoe by convincing arguments advanced in 1988, the work is still ascribed to him in the catalogues of many libraries.[212] Whoever the author, the *General History* is a work of fundamental importance for the history of piracy and also for its perception, those almost indistinguishable things, but for present purposes we should notice in particular that the title page in 1724 announced 'An Account of the famous Captain Avery and his Companions; with the Manner of his Death in England'. Indeed the opening chapter of the *General History* told this story of 'Captain Avery, and Others of his Crew'. Once again we were informed of the popular but erroneous portrayal of Avery, who

was represented in Europe, as one that had raised himself to the Dignity of a King, and was likely to be the Founder of a new Monarchy; having, as it was said, taken immense Riches, and married the Great Moguls Daughter, who was taken in an Indian Ship . . . ; that he had built Forts, erected Magazines, and was Master of a stout Squadron of Ships.[213]

In England a 'Play was writ upon him, call'd, the *Successful Pyrate*; and, these Accounts obtain'd such Belief,' that schemes were planned for subjecting his men by force, or seducing them 'to England, with all their Treasure'.[214] All such ideas were, however, 'no more than false Rumours':

for, while it was said, he was aspiring at a Crown, he wanted a Shilling; and at the same Time it was given out he was in Possession of such prodigious Wealth in Madagascar, he was starving in England.[215]

This new account, then, like many previous ones, purported to replace legend with fact, and indeed the circumstances of the mutiny at Coruña are given in some detail, with some dialogue from the published *Tryals* (1696) and some apparently imagined. The account of Every's encounter with other ships in his pirate company is inaccurate, however, despite the consistent and credible evidence in the trial and other witness statements, and a story also inconsistent with more credible accounts is given of Every's swindling of the crews of the other ships of their shares of the looted proceeds. One of the Grand Mughal's daughters 'was said' to have been aboard the prize he took, travelling incorrectly to Mecca, not from Mecca, but nothing is made of her supposed presence.[216] There is some sense in the statement that the fierce reaction by the Grand Mughal and the consequent alarm of the East India Company were the real reasons for 'the great Noise this Thing made', which was itself the reason for 'all those Romantick Stories which were form'd of Avery's Greatness'.[217]

The new account was the best connected to the historical events of any yet, but by no means tied to them. Its innovation, as announced, was its attention to Every's return, which was more or less accurately described, from Providence Island via Ireland to England, and then supplemented, probably unreliably, by way of hearsay or, more likely, invention. He was (plausibly) in some difficulty with cashing in his stolen diamonds and therefore contracted with some merchants to sell them for him. Meanwhile he 'changed his Name, and lived at Biddiford' (Bedeford, in Devonshire).[218] When he received no payment for his diamonds he confronted these merchants, who 'silenced him by threatning to discover him, so that our Merchants, were as good Pyrates at Land as he was at Sea'.[219] After this poetic justice he 'fell sick and died' at Bedeford, 'not being worth as much as would buy him a Coffin'.[220] This is of course a possible ending to the real Every's story, but it seems more likely to have been dictated by a narrative concern for a moral outcome than by conscientious historical accuracy. We may never know what actually happened to Henry Every but we can be sure that—certainly—he became a fiction.

II

Yo-Ho-Ho and a Cup of Bumbo

Many long leagues from shore
I murdered William More,
And laid him in his gore, when I sail'd,...
Because a word he spoke,
I with a bucket broke
His scull at one sad stroke, while I sail'd.

('Captain Kid's Farewel to the Seas', 1701)[1]

Every was famous in his day but he vanished—not just from detection and arrest, but from enduring fame. We should now follow the known facts about some of the more persistently popular pirates who followed Every into the 'golden age', the final decade of the seventeenth century and the first two decades of the eighteenth. These pirates—unlike Every—are still known today, household names, some of them, others less widely remembered, but still appearing and reappearing in print, their stories, or legends, still retold and resold. These are the pirates who have generated the most retellings since their own 'golden age'—the pirates who represent the typical and ideal pirates of all time, including our own.

The anthropologist Claude Lévi-Strauss wondered why a Kwakiutl Indian who frequently used to visit and inform another anthropologist, Franz Boas, in New York, would, after satisfying Boas's curiosity about Kwakiutl culture, 'reserve all his [own] intellectual curiosity for the dwarfs, the giants and the bearded ladies who were at that time exhibited in Times Square'.[2] The explanation, Lévi-Strauss decided, was that, of all the aspects of exotic 'civilization' that the Kwakiutl was confronted by in New York, it was only a freak show which 'mettait en

cause sa propre culture', only freaks who brought into question the
Kwakiutl Indian's own culture, which was what exclusively concerned
him and what he sought to recognize in New York.[3] For Lévi-Strauss
the Kwakiutl Indian was a potential analogue for the professional
anthropologist who—for all his scientific objectivity—was perhaps
only interested in the aspects of an 'other' culture that seemed to speak
directly, if mysteriously, to the anthropologist's own. The anthropological observation has an obvious historical parallel. In a documentary film
about the making of the Disney *Pirates of the Caribbean* films, we cut to
a stand-in for Boas's Kwakiutl Indian, a talking head, Stuart Beattie,
screenwriter for those films, who reports from behind the scenes:

> When I came across Blackbeard, it was just…[he pauses for thought and
> words] like a lightbulb going off, you know what I mean. This guy was straight
> out of central casting as far as Hollywood's concerned. I mean you wouldn't
> believe it if it wasn't in a book—that this guy did what he did. It's just fantastic
> stuff and you couldn't make it up.[4]

The Hollywood screenwriter sees in eighteenth-century Blackbeard
someone from twenty-first-century Hollywood, 'straight out of central casting', but also 'in a book', and therefore true. Like the Kwakiutl
Indian, the Hollywood man sees in the eighteenth-century pirate only
what speaks to him of his own—and our own, successfully marketed—
Disney culture.

The aim in this chapter, then, is to ascertain the plain facts about
Every's successors as best we can before assessing the fictions that have
made these particular pirates famous—not just in their own historical
moments, the brief spans of their own short lives, but subsequently for
centuries. The pirates' real lives have not merited their enduring fame but
have provided the points of departure, the prefatorial beginnings, for
their fictional lives, and have significance in themselves as well as in relation to their legends, because facts as well as fictions have tales to tell.
Facts as well as fictions speak for a time and a place, truths as well as
myths provide anthropological evidence. The fascination of the Kwakiutl
Indian with the freak shows in New York is an anthropological fact
which has something to say about him just as his Kwakiutl myths have
something to say—perhaps, for example, that in New York he recognized
that he was…a freak. The pirate myths have fascinated non-piratical audiences for all time because—somehow—those myths put ourselves into
question, because those myths are really and recognizably ours. Before

the myths, however, and in order to know the myths, we must first try
to follow the facts.

Pirates are famous for their obscure beginnings and William Kidd's
are no exception. Certainly he was Scottish and possibly born at
Greenock as the son of a Presbyterian minister, about 1645.[5] He
emerges from his obscurity in 1689, when he is in the Caribbean privateering (another word, like 'buccaneering', to describe supposedly
legitimate, or authorized pirating which coincided with the national
interest). As captain of a stolen ship renamed the *Blessed William*, Kidd
was successfully (and patriotically) fighting the French, until his crew
abandoned him ashore and sailed away.[6] Caught between patriotic privateering and criminal piracy, Kidd figures in a changing phase of
piracy. While European powers contended for colonies, slaves, and
other plunder, privateering steered a fine line between national rivalry
and simple 'Robbery', as Sir Charles Hedges had defined piracy to a
jury at the Old Bailey. As British colonial power became established,
however, its interests, except in times of war, came into contradiction
with piracy, and even privateering, as colonial and non-piratical power
gradually took control on land, at sea, and in law.

Kidd married in 1691 and settled respectably in the community of
New York, observing the local politics and the local commerce in the
products of distant trade and distant piracy (on Madagascar, for example).[7] Then in 1695 he made a voyage to London and managed to trade
in his checkered maritime experience for a more legitimate role in a
consortium of aristocratic investors planning to turn pirate on the
pirates and legally profit from their spoils. To this purpose Kidd was
provided with a ship, the *Adventure Galley*, and a crew prepared to
forgo wages for shares of the loot expected to be relooted. After revis-
iting his wife and daughters in New York (and recruiting more crew),
Kidd set off in 1696 with the *Adventure Galley* for the Indian Ocean,
where piracy had travelled in flight from British and French colonization in the Caribbean and in emulation of the success of Henry
Every.

After a few encounters with naval ships and colonial officials which
served to raise suspicions that he was more pirate than pirate-catcher,
Kidd reached Tulear, on the south-west coast of Madagascar, in January
1697.[8] Then, instead of proceeding round Madagascar to Saint Mary's
Island and pirating the pirates there, Kidd sailed for the nearby Comoro
Islands, where he careened the *Adventure Galley* and lost many of his

crew to some indigenous or imported disease.[9] From there he sailed
north up the African coast and headed for the Red Sea, a foray omitted
from his subsequent 'Narrative', as indicative, no doubt, of his real aim,
to seek—not pirates, but what pirates sought, the Muslim pilgrim fleet.
When the awaited fleet finally appeared from Jeddah, however, it was
convoyed by European ships, supplied in response to the Grand
Mughal's fury at the depredations of Every. One of these protective
ships was commanded by Edward Barlow, who recorded in his journal
the approach of Kidd's *Adventure Galley*, which 'showed no colours but
had only a red broad pennant out without any cross on it'.[10] Barlow's
ship pursued and attacked the *Adventure Galley* 'but he sailed far better
than we did', according to Barlow, 'and away he went' and sailed for
India.[11] Off the west coast Kidd and his men took and looted a small
English trading ship, hoisting some of the Arab or Indian crew up by
their arms and slapping them with the flats of cutlasses in an attempt
to extract any information about hidden money.[12] Kidd thus moved
from ambiguity to outright piracy, but brazenly proceeded south down
the Indian coast, visiting the ports of Karwar and Calicut and explaining his pirate seeking mission to increasing official disbelief.[13] His own
men were also increasingly sceptical, about his failure to provide them
with satisfying booty, piratical or antipiratical. On 30 October 1697,
Kidd confronted the ship's gunner, William Moore, who was speaking
to others on deck about taking a nearby Dutch ship. Furious, Kidd
called him a 'Lousie Dog', to which Moore retorted, 'If I am a Lousie
Dog, you have made me so'.[14] Kidd picked up a bucket and swung it
down on Moore's head. He died of his injury, a fractured skull, the
next day.

In November Kidd seized a local trading ship, Dutch-owned, by
displaying French colours and tricking the Dutch captain into presenting him with a French pass. Because Britain and France were at war at
the time of Kidd's pirating-privateering contract, it allowed him to
take French ships. On receiving the French pass Kidd reportedly cried
out gleefully: 'By God, Have I catch'd you? You are a Free Prize to
England'.[15] The Dutch ship had enough cargo to warrant its sale ashore
and a distribution of some remuneration to Kidd's crew. Other minor
prizes were taken over the next few weeks, but yielded merely some
supplies rather than wealth for Kidd and his crew. In January 1698
the *Adventure Galley* had a better success, taking a large trading ship,
the *Quedah Merchant*, with a more valuable cargo, which was once

again partly sold and some proceeds distributed. Again Kidd had displayed French colours and received a French pass from the *Quedah*, at the time on lease to Muslims in the Grand Mughal's court entourage.[16] With the captured *Quedah* in tow, and accompanied by the captured Dutch ship, Kidd set off across the Ocean for the pirate haven of Madagascar, the island of Saint Mary.

As the *Adventure Galley* approached the narrow entrance to the pirate harbour on Saint Mary, a canoe came out to her with a crew of European men. They knew Kidd was out to catch pirates, but they also knew Kidd. According to his ship's doctor, Kidd assured them that he had not 'come to take them, and hang them'.[17] 'He told them, it was no such thing for he was as bad as they.'[18] He accompanied them to their ship, in Saint Mary's harbour, where he reassured their captain, Robert Culliford, who was one of the crew of the *Blessed William* who had abandoned their captain—Kidd—on Antigua in 1690. Kidd and Culliford celebrated their reunion with a rum cocktail. According to the doctor, an eye-witness, Kidd 'took a cup of Bomboe, and swore to be true to them'.[19] Aboard the *Adventure Galley*, piloted into the harbour by Culliford himself, and welcomed to Saint Mary, Kidd's crew celebrated with another distribution of some of their disposable spoils, in cash and cloth, which could be exchanged for drink or other goods by Edward Welsh, who reportedly 'came from New England thither when he was a Boy', and had taken over as manager of the pirate island after the departure of Baldridge.[20] Some of Kidd's men reported that he had 'proposed to his men to take' Culliford's ship, the *Mocha*, but that most of them told him that in that case 'they would fire two guns into him rather than one into the other [the *Mocha*] and immediately departed the sd Gally [the *Adventure*] and went on board the Mocco'.[21] Nearly one hundred men, the vast majority of Kidd's crew, decided to exercise their pirate rights to transfer themselves to Culliford's command, in hopes of more remunerative piracy, and sailed off aboard his ship.[22] As one of them later complained, 'Capt. Kidd had made no good voyage'.[23]

Kidd's own subsequent 'Narrative' presents events at Saint Mary's rather differently. When he arrived at the 'Port of St. Maries', there was 'a Pyrate Ship' at anchor there, commanded by Robert Culliford, 'who with his men left the same at his [Kidd's] coming in, and ran into the Woods'.[24] Kidd very properly proposed chasing after Culliford but

Kidd's 'mutinous Crew' refused 'and thereupon 97 deserted' and joined Culliford.[25] These 'Deserters' subsequently looted the *Adventure Galley* and its prize, the *Quedah Merchant*, and 'threatned several times to murder the Narrator' (Kidd) 'which they designed in the Night to effect but was prevented by his locking himself in his cabin at night, and securing himself with barrocading the same with bales of Goods, and having about 40 small Armes, besides Pistols, ready charged'.[26] Indeed their 'wickedness was so great, after they had plundered and ransacked sufficiently', that they provided an excuse for Kidd's not producing his ship's journal in evidence.[27] In the excess of their wickedness, they

went four miles off to one Edward Welche's house, where his the Narrator's Chest was lodged, and broke it open, and took out 10 Ounces of Gold, forty Pounds of Plate, 370 pieces of Eight, the Narrator's Journal, and a great many papers that belonged to him.[28]

In additional wickedness, the 'Deserters' deprived Kidd of the 'Moors' (captured Arab or Muslim Indian sailors) he was using constantly to pump the leaking *Adventure Galley*, 'so that the Moors he had to pump and keep the *Adventure Galley* above Water being carried away, she sunk in the harbour'.[29] Kidd says he and his depleted crew had to transfer to the *Quedah*, and 'he was forced to stay five months for a fair Wind', before setting off—for New York, presumably, to explain himself to his consortium and any curious authorities in Mughal India, England, and America.[30]

His minimal crew supplemented by some recruits from Saint Mary's and some slaves, Kidd's prize, the *Quedah*, eventually reached Anguilla in the West Indies in April 1699, where he acquired food and water and heard that the British government (encouraged by the East India Company) had declared him a pirate.[31] He sailed to the safer Danish island of St. Thomas and then to a small island between Puerto Rico and Hispaniola, and then to a river in or near Hispaniola.[32] There (wherever it was) he unloaded and sold bales of cloth from the *Quedah* to interested ships who could dispose of the goods profitably and discreetly.[33] He bought one of these ships, the *Saint Antonio*, abandoned the *Quedah* and whatever remained of her cargo, and set sail to meet his fate in colonial North America.[34]

In Delaware Bay the *Saint Antonio* transferred, by chance or arrangement, goods to a ship from New York City.[35] Then on Long Island Kidd met his wife and daughters. He began cautious negotiations with the Governor of New York and Massachusetts Bay, Lord Bellomont, a member of Kidd's original consortium but now fearful and distrustful. Through an intermediary Kidd offered various presents to Bellomont's wife, the Countess, including 'three or four small Jewells', a 'green silk bag of about 5lb. weight of bar gold' and two children Kidd had bought at Saint Mary's, a black girl and a boy named Dundee, bribes which were not accepted.[36] Meanwhile Kidd sailed at the eastern end of Long Island, in the vicinity of Gardiner's Island, and goods were dispersed in multifarious ways.[37] Some slaves were put ashore in the custody of John Gardiner, the proprietor of Gardiner's Island, who supplied Kidd with 'Six Sheep' and 'a barrel of Cyder', and received in return some muslin and Bengal cloth.[38] A few days later Kidd put into Gardiner's safekeeping several bundles of goods, including more muslin cloth, 'Romals [handkerchiefs] and flowered Silke', and a box containing gold 'being Fifty Pound Weight or upwards in Quantity'.[39]

In July 1699, Bellomont, suffering from greed, fear, and a bad attack of gout, and calculating that the cargo of the abandoned *Quedah* should be 'worth Seventy Thousand pounds', required that Kidd make his case to the Massachusetts council, who insisted he provide a written narrative of his voyage, while Bellomont finally decided to arrest him.[40] Kidd was also required to itemize some of the loot unloaded at Gardiner's Island, for instance the contents of a chest. Here, then, in a statement signed by Kidd himself, are the exact contents of a real pirate treasure chest, subsequently a topic of endless speculation and fiction:

Captn. William Kidd declareth and saith That in his chest wch he left at Gardiners Island there was three small baggs or more of Jasper Antonio or Stone of Goa [a medicine for fever invented in India by one Gaspar Antonio] severall pieces of Silk stript [striped] with silver and gold Cloth of Silver about a Bushell of Cloves and Nutmegs—mixed together and strawed [strewed] up and down, severall books of fine white Callico's, severall pieces of fine Muzlins severall pieces more of flowred Silk, he does not well remember what further was in it . . . there was neither gold or silver in the Chest. It was fastned with a Padlock and nailed and corded about.[41] (See Figure 2.1.)

Meanwhile Bellomont assembled evidence to secure Kidd's conviction, in particular a statement by one Joseph Palmer, 'of New York in America', aged about 30, a sailor who had abandoned Kidd at Saint Mary's and joined Culliford for pirating aboard the *Mocha*.[42] Under examination at Newport, Rhode Island, on 29 July 1699, Palmer

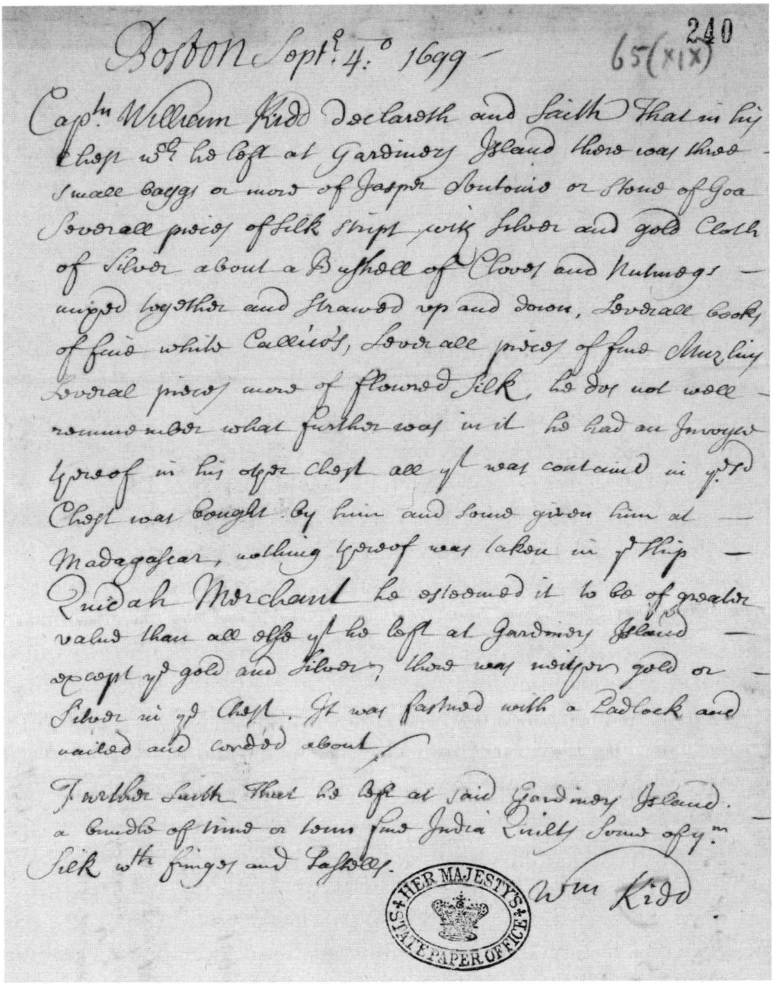

Figure 2.1. Captain William Kidd, Declaration.

saith that Capt. Kidd in a passion struck his Gunner, as it was said, with an Iron bound Bucket, wch. blow he lived not above twenty four hours after; but he [Palmer] was not upon the Deck wn. the blow was struck.[43]

We may notice that Palmer did not witness the murder of Moore, the Gunner, but Bellomont enclosed this statement to the Council of Trade and Plantations in London, remarking that 'your Lordships may

please to observe that he accuses Kidd of murdering his Gunner, wch.
I never heard before'.[44]

Robert Bradinham, the ship's doctor on the *Adventure Galley*, was
another of Kidd's crew who had joined the *Mocha* at Saint Mary's and
had then shipped back to America, where he was taken prisoner, and
his loot confiscated, a large collection of coins of various currencies,
some silver and gold, silk cloths and handkerchiefs, loot which he
claimed that 'he got by practice' of his medical profession.[45] Bellomont
considered Bradinham 'the obstinatest and most hardned of 'em all',
but William Penn, Governor of Pennsylvania, where Bradinham was
captured, informed London that 'I have several times discoursed with
him and urged an ingenuous confession'.[46] Meanwhile Kidd was
imprisoned in Boston jail, awaiting shipment, with his former crewman, Joseph Palmer, and his black boy, Dundee, and black girl of
unknown name, to London, which he reached in April 1700.

From the ship, the *Advice*, he wrote to Lord Orford, one of the consortium, protesting his innocence and mentioning that the cargo of the
Quedah was, he estimated, of 'the value of ninety thousand pounds',
which he was confident he could bring 'without any diminution' to
England 'when I am clear of this trouble'.[47] In mid-April he was called
to testify to a collection of dignitaries at the Admiralty. He was then
committed to Newgate, from which he was released to be interviewed
again by the House of Commons, twice in late March 1701. Kidd's black
boy and girl were examined by judges on behalf of the High Court of
Admiralty, but 'nothing more could be learned of them, in regard that he
[Dundee] did not understand English'.[48] Joseph Palmer and Robert
Bradinham were more usefully examined on 25 April.[49] On the 8th and
9th of May that year, Kidd was put on trial at the Old Bailey, with a few
of his crew and some others of them who would speak out as witnesses
in return for a pardon. Kidd himself was tried first for the murder of his
gunner, William Moore, and then, with others, for piratically taking the
Quedah. He began by asking for his trial to be postponed because he had
not yet had returned to him the two French passes he had taken from
two ships he had pirated, and was in any case unprepared to defend
himself. He was told the trial must proceed. Joseph Palmer and Robert
Bradinham were called, and Palmer described the 'Lousie Dog' dialogue
and the bucket blow to Moore's head, while Bradinham, the ship's doctor, verified the cause of death. Palmer's description of the stricken
Moore's words when carried to the Gunroom—'Farewel, farewel,

Captain Kidd has given me my last'—was extremely similar to Bradinham's, a coincidence which could be seen as collusion or corroboration,
or a combination, and Palmer, who had stated previously at Newport
that he 'was not upon the Deck wn. the blow was struck', when asked
in the Old Bailey 'Did you see the Prisoner give the Blow with the
Bucket?' replied 'Yes, my Lord'.[50] When Bradinham was asked in court
'Was you there when the Blow was given?' he replied 'No'.[51] Palmer
probably perjured himself but Kidd did not deny the murder. He
defended himself by claiming that the death of Moore was in the course
of 'a Mutiny on board'.[52] When this supposed mutiny could not be
credibly connected to the context of Moore's death, Kidd argued against
a murder charge, saying 'It was not designedly done, but in my Passion,
for which I am heartily sorry'.[53]

   While the jury considered its verdict, the second trial was started,
'for Piracy and Robbery on a Ship called the *Quedah Merchant*'.[54] An
account of Kidd's voyage was being delivered to the court and to a
new jury when the first jury returned with their verdict on the murder
charge: 'Guilty'.[55] Palmer and Bradinham were called as witnesses
again, of piracy this time, and Bradinham described Kidd's attempt to
prey on 'the Moorish Fleet' at the Red Sea and the taking of the *Quedah* by trickery with French colours.[56] Both Palmer and Bradinham
described Kidd's use of torture—a routine practice of pirates—on the
crew of a ship captured off the Indian coast. Palmer testified that Kidd
'ordered some of the Men to be hoisted up by their Arms, and drubb'd
with a naked Cutlass' ('drub'd with a naked Cutlace', echoed Bradinham).[57] Asked 'for what reason', Palmer replied, 'They were beat with
a naked Cutlass to make them discover what Money was aboard'.[58]
The legal issue here was not Kidd's cruelty but his piratical pursuit of
money. Bradinham also gave his eyewitness account of Kidd's 'cup of
Bomboe' with the pirates at Saint Mary's.[59] Palmer testified to Kidd's
relish at the prospect of the 'Moco [Mecca] Fleet'—'I heard him say,
Come Boys, I will make money enough out of that Fleet'—and vividly described the meeting of Kidd and Culliford at Saint Mary's,
quoting Kidd's warm words on Culliford's ship:

And on the Quarter-deck they made some Bomboo, and drank together, and
Captain Kid said, Before I would do you any harm, I would have my Soul fry
in Hell-fire; and wished Damnation to himself several times, if he did. And he
took the Cup, and wished that might be his last, if he did not do them all the
good he could.[60]

Did Palmer really see and hear this scene on Culliford's ship—or is it a dramatization with dialogue, perhaps a pirate fiction? When asked in court 'Was you there then?' Palmer implied he was not.[61] 'This was on the Quarter-Deck of the *Moco* Frigate' (Culliford's ship) was his answer.[62] Bradinham, however, when asked in court about the Faustian bumbo pact 'How came you to know all this? Was you aboard then?' (on Culliford's ship), replied 'I was aboard then, and I heard the words'.[63]

In his defence, Kidd maintained that the *Quedah* was somehow French and he 'had a Commission to take the French'.[64] When asked why he had told Culliford 'I will fry in Hell before I will do you any harm', he replied 'That is only what these witnesses say'.[65] The jury returned after about half an hour with their verdicts: Kidd was guilty of piracy and so were the other prisoners, except three who were servants and could therefore be considered of diminished responsibility. The court was adjourned and proceedings resumed the next day with further charges of piracy concerning Kidd's other captured ships. Rather hopelesssly he accused Bradinham of stealing the surgeon's chest when he had absconded to Culliford's command at Saint Mary's and, more poignantly, asked 'Mr Bradinham, are you not promised your Life, to take away mine?'[66] Bradinham was officially told he need not answer that question, but in truth both Bradinham and Palmer were pardoned because they 'have been made use off as Witnesses agst Capt William Kidd'.[67] Sentence was pronounced: the guilty prisoners would be 'severally hanged by your Necks until you be dead'.[68] Kidd spoke the last words: 'My Lord, It is a very hard Sentence. For my part, I am the innocentest Person of them all, only I have been sworn against by perjured Persons.'[69] The historical rather than legal point, however, is not whether Kidd in particular was guilty of piracy but simply that a pirate is hard to tell from a violent plunderer.

Back—all too briefly—at Newgate, Kidd wrote, dangling his 'treasure' once again, to Robert Harley, the Speaker of the House of Commons, requesting him to inform the House

that in my late proceedings in the Indies I have Lodged goods and Tresure to the value of one hundred thousand pounds which I desiere the Goverment may have the benefitt of, in order thereto I shall desiere no manner of liberty but to be kept prisoner on board such shipp as may be appointed for that purpose.[70]

We have further news of Kidd's few remaining days in a published notice by Paul Lorrain, the pastor (or 'ordinary') of Newgate, who attended the prisoner assiduously, recommending him to faith and repentance, but on the day of execution, 23 May 1701, the pastor 'was afraid the Hardness of Capt. Kidd's Heart, was still unmelted'.[71] Lorrain 'therefore apply'd my self with particular Exhortations to him' but found that, when Kidd arrived for execution at Wapping, 'he was inflamed with Drink; which had so discomposed his Mind, that it was now in a very ill frame, and very unfit for the great Work, now or never, to be perform'd by him'.[72] Lorrain passes over Kidd's 'Dying-Words' (advertised in his title), suspicious of 'his Sincerity' and noting his tendency 'to excuse and justify himself'.[73] But executions, like trials, can be seen from different points of view, and the anonymous author of a rival publication supplies more details: that Kidd accused his accusers at his trial of lying, excused his blow to William Moore as given 'in a Passion', and expressed sorrow at leaving his wife and children without being able to see them.[74] The last words of Darby Mullins, Kidd's former crewman, now his convicted pirate companion at Execution Dock, were more to Lorrain's taste, who quoted Mullins's confession that he

had of late very much given up himself to Swearing, Cursing, profaning the Sabbath-day, &c. which he now acknowledged had deservedly brought this Calamity upon him.[75]

At about six in the evening Kidd was pushed off the scaffold at Wapping but not into eternity. The rope broke, not his neck, and he fell to the ground, 'and by this means', reported Lorrain, 'had opportunity to consider more of that Eternity, he was launching into'.[76] Lorrain now 'found him in much better temper than before', and persuasively followed him half way up the ladder from which he fell again, repentantly and successfully.[77] Posthumously, nevertheless, he was encased in chains (see Figure 2.2) and hung as an admonitory spectacle further down the Thames at Tilbury Point, a job for which a carpenter was paid ten pounds and a smith four pounds, plus expenses of 19 shillings and threepence at two taverns.[78]

Ballads immediately celebrated him, such as 'Captain Kid's Farewel to the Seas', and of course his legendary treasure survived him, glittering in the imaginations of generations of relentless diggers with maps, and authors with readers and audiences to thrill with stories of Kidd and the Mughal's daughter, murdered as well as robbed for her treasure, glittering still.[79] As the popular *Pirates Own Book, or Authentic*

Figure 2.2. 'Capt. Kidd hanging in chains', from *The Pirates Own Book* (1837).

Narratives of the Lives, Exploits and Executions of the Most Celebrated Sea Robbers informed its eager American readers in 1837: 'The report of his [Kidd's] having buried great treasures of gold and silver which he actually did before his arrest, set the brains of all the good people along the coast in a ferment.'[80] Any rotting hulk beneath a deep covering of rich mud must be the vanished *Quedah Merchant*, soon (in 1844) 'to be successfully operated upon by the present improved and philosophical methods of submarine operations', and to disclose, no doubt, solid gold and 'coins with Moorish inscriptions'.[81] These tales roamed the shores of America and various scattered islands during the nineteenth century, 'with more freedom than the pirates ever did', as a sceptical commentator remarked in 1871.[82] Then the thrill of Kidd's unspent treasure spread into the twentieth century and across the Atlantic. In 1935 we were told of the discovery in 'a pretty seaside town' in England of a wooden chest, inscribed 'Capn Kidd his chest', with a 'false bottom' which contained 'a treasure chart of an island in a certain remote Far Eastern sea' (unnamed, like the pretty seaside town).[83] Such is Kidd's eternity—so far, at least.

The story of Kidd's lifetime rise as pirate-fighter and then fall as pirate from the scaffold—to be haunted by posthumous fame—illustrates the increasing attempts of the national state to fight a war against piracy, particularly in times of peace between national states.[84] In peacetimes the nation states were more determined to assert a monopoly of maritime violence and commerce, treating pirates as enemies not allies of capitalism and colonialism. Attempts were made to control governors who supported or condoned piracy (such as Governor Trott of the Bahamas, who was bribed into opening a door for Every back into the civilized western world, or Fletcher of New York, who was succeeded by Kidd's partner and captor, Bellomont).[85] Legal arrangements were made to enable trial and execution to be delivered colonially and locally, and there were decisions, in principle, at least, to maintain a naval presence in colonial waters in peacetime, with ships on permanent station in North America and the West Indies, to protect commercial trade and colonial power from piratical eruption and intrusion. Another, weaker measure was to offer, from time to time, pardons.

Despite such measures, the tide of piracy rose and fell periodically, often surging in peacetimes, or in response to particular local conditions. A pamphlet by 'an Officer of an East-India Ship', published in 1701, the year of Kidd's execution, explained the development of Indian Ocean piracy as a response to news of the rich booty seized in the East, which

stirred up the Old Bucaneer Gang, (who found it more difficult now to rob the Spaniards than formerly and finding their Prizes in the West Indies grow scarce) to direct their Course to the East. And their success answering their Expectation, their Numbers daily increased by the News of the rich Booties they had taken and reposed at Madagascar.[86]

Nevertheless the mobile, world-straddling pirates persisted in the West Indies, shifting their bases among the many islands and preying upon the North American coast in the summers, particularly in areas, such as the Carolinas, where colonial control was still relatively weak. Indeed the decade from about 1715 to 1725 can be seen as a peak of piracy, partly, no doubt, because of its actual prevalence and partly because it was coming to wider notice, with the *General History of the Pyrates* (1724) and the contemporary proliferation of newspapers in England and even the colonies.

As well as directly and indirectly spreading this public knowledge, the pirates themselves were more aware of themselves as a coherent maritime community, provoking public fear as well as attention, and making common use of cultural equipment, such as the symbols of impending death on their flags: cutlasses, hourglasses, skeletons, skulls, crossbones. By 1720 the piratical signs were well enough known for Defoe's Singleton to relate that 'we let them soon see what we were, for we hoisted a black Flag with two cross Daggers in it'.[87] Red flags as well as black sent the same signals: Singleton later states that 'we spread our Black Flag or Ancient on the Poop, and the bloody Flag at the Top-mast Head'.[88] The symbols were sometimes more elaborate, such as those on the pirate flag displayed at the execution of twenty-six pirates at Newport, Rhode Island, in 1723, who were hanged

under their own deep Blew Flagg which was hoisted up on their Gallows, and had pourtraid on the middle of it, an Anatomy [i.e. a skeleton] with an Hour-glass in one hand and a dart in the Heart with 3 drops of blood proceeeding from it, in the other.[89]

This flag 'they called, "Old Roger", and often us'd to say they would live and die under it'.[90] The pirates' term 'Old Roger' was a current cant term for the Devil but the more usual 'Jolly Roger' has been explained—conjecturally and dubiously—as an English pronunciation of the French 'jolie rouge'.[91]

There was particular trouble in the Bahamas, where the tide of piracy rose, with pirates infesting Providence Island, as a local colonist complained in 1716, causing 'great disorders in that Island, plundering

the inhabitants, burning their houses, and ravishing their wives'.[92]
Pirates freely and repeatedly used the port of Nassau on Providence
as a base, particularly a Captain Hornigold, and one sailor had taken
control ashore, a Thomas Barrow, who boasted 'that he is the Governor of Providence and will make it a second Madagascar'.[93] A ship's
captain encountered fugitives on another Bahamian island who 'had
left Providence by reason of the rudeness of the pirates'.[94] These fugi-
tive colonists named several pirate captains who 'made the harbour of
Providence their place of rendevous': Benjamin Hornigold, who
commanded 'a sloop with 10 guns and 100 men', and another whose
name now emerges from obscurity, 'Thatch, a sloop 6 gunns and
about 70 men'.[95]

One of those who made a public impression in this 'golden' period
and was magnified in the published rendering of that vivid impression,
was this Edward Thatch, or Teach, known then and now as 'Blackbeard', who 'hoisted his Black Flag' in the second decade of the eighteenth century.[96] Virtually nothing is known about his early life and
career, and little until his last years. He was not brought to trial, so
there is no official, legal rehearsal of his particular crimes and the
alleged evidence of them. He is said to have been born in Bristol, England, but there is no proof of this.[97] The Governor of the Leeward
Islands, sailing through his gubernatorial waters in 1717, had a ship and
sloop pointed out to him, as he reported back to London.

The ship is commanded by one Captain Teatch, the sloop by one Major Bonnett, an inhabitant of Barbadoes, some say Bonnett commands both the ship
and sloop. This Teatch it's said has a wife and children in London, they have
comitted a great many barbarities'.[98]

Blackbeard (whose London family is unknown—as well as innocent
of 'barbarities', of course) was thus sighted in company with Stede
Bonnet, an unusually gentlemanly pirate, who was not in command of
Blackbeard but under his thumb.[99] The *Boston News-Letter* reported the
activities in October 1717 of 'a Pirate Sloop called the Revenge, of 12
Guns 150 Men, Commanded by one Teach'.[100] Blackbeard was preying
on the maritime traffic of trade to and from British America, pillaging
the ships' cargoes but also jettisoning goods that were undesired by the
pirates. His men threw overboard most of the cargo of a ship sailing
from Liverpool and Dublin, 'excepting some small matters they fan-
cied'.[101] 'One Merchant had a thousand Pounds Cargo on board, of

which the greatest part went over board, he begg'd for Cloth to make him but one Suit of Cloth's, which they refus'd to grant him.'[102] Likewise Blackbeard and his men captured a Bristol ship, a snow, the *Sea Nymph*, 'loaden with wheat for Oporto, which they threw over board, and made a Pirate of the said Snow', disposing of its crew aboard another captured ship.[103] From a sloop sailing from Madeira, however, 'they took 27 Pipes of Wine'.[104] The *Boston News-Letter* also reported the presence aboard Blackbeard's ship of Bonnet:

On board the Pirate Sloop is Major Bennet, but has no Command, he walks about in his Morning Gown, and then to his Books, of which he has a good Library on Board.[105]

This portrait of Bonnet—more Hamlet than pirate—may be fanciful or true (he was said to be recuperating, 'not well of his wounds that he received by attacking of a Spanish Man of War') but French colonial records provide a more empirical report of Blackbeard's activities the following month, November 1717, when he took the *Concorde*, an inappropriately-named French slaving ship transporting 516 slaves from the Guinea Coast to Martinique.[106] Not far from this West Indian destination the *Concorde* 'fut attaqué par deux forbans anglais, l'un de douze, l'autre de huit canons, montés par deux cent cinquante hommes, commandant Edward Titche' (was attacked by two English pirate ships, one of twelve, and the other of eight guns, carrying 250 men, commanded by Edward Titche).[107] Blackbeard deposited the French crew and most of the slaves on a nearby island but took 14 slaves (ten by force and four who volunteered) and he took the *Concorde*, which he renamed—in a Jacobite vein—the *Queen Anne's Revenge*. This was the 'large ship', with '36 guns mounted and 300 men', which, in company with a pirate sloop, took another sloop, the *Margaret*, on the 5th of the next month, December.[108] As the *Margaret*'s master, Henry Bostock, reported, 'He was ordered on board' the *Queen Anne's Revenge* 'and Capt. Tach took his cargo of cattle and hogs, his arms books and instruments'.[109] The pirates 'did not abuse him or his men, but forced 2 to stay and one Robert Bibby voluntarily took on with them'.[110]

Some months later, in May 1718, Blackbeard in alliance with Bonnet blockaded the harbour of Charleston, South Carolina, taking hostages and threatening their death unless he was given, for some reason, 'a chest of medecines', which he eventually received.[111] Shortly after this episode, Blackbeard accidentally or deliberately ran the *Queen*

Anne's Revenge aground and consequently or coincidentally decided to abandon Bonnet and to maroon some of his own (Blackbeard's) men on an islet off the coast of North Carolina, 'a small Sandy Hill or Bank, a League distant from the Main; on which Place there was no Inhabitant, nor Provisions'.[112]

Late September that year, Bonnet and his crew, supplemented by some of Blackbeard's marooned but rescued men, were pursued by an expedition from Charleston commanded by a daring Colonel Rhett. Bonnet's men made fun of the Colonel at first: 'The Pirates made a Wiff [a whiff, a hoisted signal] in their bloody Flag, and beckon'd with their Hats in derision to our People to come on board them'.[113] But they were defeated and taken prisoner by the daring Colonel and put on trial in Charlestown in October and November 1718, in particular for taking two sloops, the *Francis* and the *Fortune*. A list of thefts was read in evidence, for example 'twenty five Hogsheads of Molosses . . . one Pair of Silver Buckles, Value ten Shillings', and witnesses called, including the mate of the *Francis*, who described the pirates piratically coming aboard.[114] When they entered the cabin,

the first thing they begun with was the Pine-Apples, which they cut down with their Cutlasses . . . They asked me what Liquor I had on board? I told them some Rum and Sugar. So they made Bowls of Punch, and went to Drinking the Pretender's Health . . . Then sung a Song or two.[115]

Some of Bonnet's men claimed they had been coerced by Blackbeard, who then 'marooned us on an Island', and meanwhile Bonnet, awaiting trial, escaped on 24 October to hide in the wildness of Sullivan's Island, where he was recaptured on 6 November by the indefatigable Colonel Rhett.[116] On trial he argued that 'I never took a Vessel but with Capt. Thatch'.[117] The Judge protested that he had taken the *Fortune* without Blackbeard, to which Bonnet replied feebly that 'It was contrary to my Inclinations', that he had been coerced by his men, and that at the time 'I was asleep'.[118] He was found guilty, given a lecture about his abominable mixture of gentility and piracy, and hanged on 10 December 1718 'at White Point near Charles-Town' (see Figure 2.3).[119]

Meanwhile Providence Island, that 'second Madagascar', had a Governor, the former privateer, Woodes Rogers. As he reported to London, he arrived on 26 July 1718 at the port of the capital, Nassau, a straggling set of wooden houses, church, jail, and shaky fort, to find a captured French ship, a piratical prize, set ablaze as a threatening fireship

Figure 2.3. 'Major Stede Bonnet hanged', from *Historie der Engelsche Zee-Rovers* (Amsterdam, 1725).

by the pirate Charles Vane, who 'fled away in a sloop wearing the black flag, and fir'd guns of defiance'.[120] The pirate Benjamin Hornigold, however, had already accepted King George's latest pirate pardon and Rogers sent him in pursuit of Charles Vane, although, 'not hearing from Capt. Hornigold', Rogers 'was afraid he was either taken by Vaine or begun his old practice of pirating again'.[121] From a distance Vane continued his impudence, sending the new Governor a message, as Rogers reported, that 'He expects soon to joyne Majr. Bonnet or some other pirate, and then I am to be attack'd by them'.[122]

Hornigold's old shipmate Blackbeard had also received an official pardon (one of those periodically on offer) from Governor Eden of North Carolina and apparently took up respectable residence in the local capital at Bath Town, but briefly, resuming some piracy (with the capture of a French ship) and spending time happily anchored in Ocracoke Inlet, on the south side of Ocracoke Island, between the Atlantic and the more sheltered waters of Pamlico Sound.[123] Governor Spotswood of Virginia considered himself a better protector of the colonies than his more indulgent neighbouring Governor Eden, and feared a local Madagascar:

a design of the most pernicious consequence to the trade of these Plantations, wch. was that of the pyrats fortifying an Island at Ocracock Inlett and making that a general rendevouze of such robbers.[124]

He formed a plan with the help of the two naval ships currently stationed at Jamestown, Virginia, 'to extirpate this nest of pyrates'.[125] As a result two sloops, manned by sailors from the ships *Pearl* and *Lyme*, and commanded by a Lieutenant Maynard, set sail for Teach's Ocracoke Inlet in November 1718.

Maynard gave an account himself, in a letter published in *The Weekly Journal or British Gazetteer*, which can be supplemented by a fuller but second-hand account given in the *Boston News-Letter*, and another by Governor Spotswood. According to Maynard, Teach began proceedings when 'he drank Damnation to me and my Men, whom he stil'd Cowardly Puppies, saying, He would neither give nor take Quarter'.[126] Maynard then described the fighting, mentioning that the officer commanding his companion sloop was killed and that several of his own men were wounded when he rowed his own sloop nearer to Teach's ship. According to the *Boston News-Letter*, 'Teach fired some small Guns, loaded with Swan shot, spick Nails and pieces of old Iron in upon

Maynard, which killed six of his Men and wounded ten'.[127] The *Boston News-Letter* also added a tactic adopted by Maynard, who then concealed some of his men 'in the Hould', which lured Teach and his men into boarding Maynard's sloop and engaging in fierce hand-to-hand fighting.[128] The *Boston News-Letter* gave more details of this fighting than Maynard's letter. Maynard and Teach fought each other with swords, Teach breaking the handguard of Maynard's sword and wounding his fingers, whereupon Maynard 'Jumpt back, threw away his Sword and fired his Pistol, which wounded Teach'.[129] At this juncture Teach was attacked by 'a Highlander', according to the Boston paper,

who gave Teach a cut on the Neck, Teach saying well done Lad, the Highlander reply'd, if it be not well done, I'll do it better, with that he gave him a second stroke, which cut off his Head, laying it flat on his Shoulder.[130]

Maynard's version is less graphic and lacks this decapitation and dialogue, though he does note precisely that Blackbeard 'fell with five Shot in him, and 20 dismal Cuts in several Parts of his Body'.[131] This brief statement would seem perhaps to call into question the Highlander's newspaper decapitation, which would be somewhat more remarkable than '20 dismal Cuts', and in some contradiction with Maynard's further statement that 'I have cut Blackbeard's Head off, which I have put on my Bow-spright, in order to carry it to Virginia'.[132] The Boston newspaper helpfully explained that 'Teach's [headless] body was thrown overboard', presumably into Ocracoke Inlet.[133] Spotswood's account mentioned a dastardly plan by Teach to blow up his own ship which was prevented by a prisoner opportunely in the hold at the time.[134]

Dastardly, dangerous, but decapitated, his head a trophy on a bowsprit, Blackbeard survived not only in Hollywood and in print, but his pirate ship, the *Queen Anne's Revenge* (formerly the *Concorde*) has perhaps been found, unlike Kidd's *Quedah Merchant*. Twentieth and twenty-first-century marine archaeology is more sophisticated than in the nineteenth century. Various discoveries by divers at the bottom of the sea off the North Carolina coast—some French and British cannons, oak planking of an appropriate date, some flakes of gold dust—are none of them conclusive but collectively suggestive that the wreck is—perhaps—Blackbeard's ship.[135]

Blackbeard was killed in North Carolina on 22 November 1718, and Bonnet executed at Charlestown, South Carolina, on 10 December, but Rogers's pirate-catching pirate, Benjamin Hornigold, had failed to eliminate Charles Vane. Instead Hornigold captured a smaller fry, John Augur and his piratical crew, so Rogers was able to put on a local pirate trial in Nassau which produced verdicts of guilty and an opportunity for a public show of strength. On 13 December 1718 the condemned men were escorted to the top of the ramparts of Nassau's dilapidated fort where the Governor and an audience of about one hundred officials, soldiers and others awaited them. Several prayers and psalms were read in concert by the spectators and the prisoners, who were then escorted down a ladder to the foot of the fort's wall, 'where was a Gallows erected, & a black Flagg hoisted thereon & under it a Stage, supported by three Butts, on which they assended by another Ladder'.[136] They then 'had 3/4 of an houre Allow'd under the Gallows which was spent by them in Singing of Psalms' and some other performances which an official observer described with care.[137] The captain John Augur 'all along appeared very penitent'.[138] When he was offered a glass of wine, he 'drank it with Wishes for the Good Success of the Bahama Islands, & the Governour'.[139] Dennis McKarthy, aged 28, had been an ensign in the local militia and had hoped to escape execution,

but when he thought he was to dye, & the morning came without his Expected Reprieve, he put on a clean shift of Cloaths, adorn'd at Neck, Wrists, knees, & Capp with long blew Ribbons when on the Rampart lookt Cheerfully arround him, Saying he knew the time when there was many brave fellows on the Island that would not suffer him to dye like a dog, at the same time pull'd of his Shoes kicking them over the Parapet...saying he had promised not to dye with his shoes on.[140]

Thomas Morris, 'aged about 22 had been a very incorragable youth & Pirate...and a little before he was turn'd off, said aloud that he might have been a greater Plague to these Islands, & now wisht he had been so'.[141] After these various speeches, 'the Butts having Ropes about them, were hauld away, upon which the stage fell & the Eight Swang off'.[142]

Charles Vane had escaped Hornigold and Rogers and took ship after ship for month after month in 1718 until about 23 November, when his pirate brigantine attacked a French man-of-war which fought them off. Hosea Tisdell, a Kingston tavern-keeper and captive aboard Vane's ship, reported that after this defeat 'the Pirates quarrelled among themselves', with the result that 'the Quarter-Master, being made Captain of their Brigantine, they turn'd out Charles Vane' and 16 of his supporters, and sent them off separately in a small sloop the pirates had in their possession.[143] Vane was thus deposed and ousted by his quartermaster, John Rackam, but continued to pirate to the end of the year 1718. In 1719, however, he was wrecked by a tornado on an uninhabited island, from where he was rescued but recognized and taken prisoner to Jamaica. There he was tried on 22 March 1721, and executed at Gallows-Point at Port-Royal on 29 March and 'afterwards hung on a Gibbet in Chains at Gun-Key'.[144]

One of those who had been Blackbeard's guests at Ocracoke with Vane on a previous occasion was Vane's quartermaster at the time, John (or Jack) Rackam, 'alias Callico Jack, (so called, because his Jackets and Drawers were always made of Callico)'.[145] On 22 August 1720 Rackam sailed from the harbour at Nassau with a stolen sloop of about 12 tons named *William*, armed with four mounted guns and two swivel guns. A 'Proclamation' by the Governor, Woodes Rogers, named those who were responsible: Rackam, five other men 'and two Women, by Name, Ann Fulford, alias Bonny, & Mary Read'.[146] With this purloined sloop they had robbed a boat to the south of Providence and a sloop in the Berry Islands, north of Providence.[147] Rogers officially declared 'that the said John Rackum and his said Company are hereby proclaimed Pirates and Enemies to the Crown of Great-Brittain'.[148] Rogers had sent a sloop with 45 men in pursuit of Rackam and then on 2 September another sloop with 54 men and 12 guns.[149] The following day, 3 September, Rackam and his pirate crew stole 'the Fish, and Fishing Tackle' from seven fishing boats on Harbour Island, to the north of the long, thin Bahamian island of Eleuthera.[150] They then sailed the *William* some distance south-east to Hispaniola, where they pillaged two merchant sloops on 1 October.[151] Around this time also, they abducted John Besneck and Peter Cornelian, two Frenchmen who had been 'hunting wild Hog' on the western, French-controlled part of Hispaniola.[152] With these two Frenchmen aboard Rackam headed for Jamaica and on 19 October, somewhere near Jamaica, he fired at and boarded a schooner, the *Neptune*, under the command of a Thomas Spenlow.[153] From Spenlow and his schooner the pirates stole 50 rolls of tobacco, nine bags of pimiento (allspice) and ten black slaves, valued at 300 pounds.[154] We hear no more of these slaves but Rackam kept Spenlow and his schooner for another 48 hours, so Spenlow witnessed the pirates' next assault, on 20 October, on a merchant sloop, the *Mary and Sarah*, at anchor in Dry Harbour in the north of Jamaica. On entering the bay the *William* fired a gun and the *Mary and Sarah*'s master, Thomas Dillon, and his crew rapidly abandoned ship and went ashore, where more shots were fired at them.[155] Dillon hailed the *William* from the shore and one of the pirates, George Fetherston, who had aided Rackam in stealing the *William*, answered 'That they were English pirates, and that they [Dillon and his crew] need not be afraid, and desired [him, Dillon] to come on Board', which he did, to find Rackam in command.[156]

The next encounter of the *William* was with a solitary woman, Dorothy Thomas, in a canoe with 'some Stock and Provisions' somewhere at sea off the north coast of Jamaica.[157] The pirates 'took out of the Canoa, most of the Things that were in her', Dorothy reported, and let her paddle away.[158] A day or so later, on 22 October, the *William*, ominously flying 'a white Pendant', came across nine men turtling with a canoe at Negril Point, the westernmost tip of Jamaica, who were persuaded to come aboard for 'a Bowl of Punch' and obediently came onto the *William*, armed with their guns and cutlasses.[159]

Meanwhile the Governor of Jamaica, Sir Nicholas Lawes, had sent a vessel in pursuit of the *William*, under the command of a Jonathan Barnet, who sighted the *William* off Negril Point, with her nine turtling guests. Rackam forced these turtlers to help raise his anchor and then attempted to escape by rowing the *William* away.[160] Barnet hailed her for identification and was answered 'John Rackam from Cuba' and by a shot from one of the *William*'s swivel guns and another from a pistol or musket.[161] Barnet's response was immediate and the result conclusive, according to the fullest account of the encounter, by James Spatchears, aboard Barnet's vessel. In reply to the shots from the *William*,

Barnet order'd his Men to fire a Broad-side and Volley of Small-shot at the said Sloop, which they did, and carried away the Enemy's Sloops Boom, and then they called to Barnet for Quarter, which he gave them, and afterwards took the said Sloop.[162]

After this surrender, without hand-to-hand resistance, without fighting at close quarters, those aboard the crippled *William*—a single-masted ship with its boom destroyed—were all, including the nine turtlers, taken ashore on Jamaica and put under guard by a Major Richard James, a militia officer, for escort to jail in Spanish Town.[163]

On the 16th of the next month, November, Rackam and eight of his men were put on trial at the Jamaican town of St. Jago de la Vega, by a court presided over by the Governor, Sir Nicholas Lawes. *The Tryals of Captain John Rackam, and other Pirates*, a rare pamphlet published in Jamaica in 1721, gives a record of the proceedings. Charges were read out of the piratical acts committed on fishing boats, 'two Merchant Sloops' (un-named) and Spenlow's *Neptune* and Dillon's *Mary and Sarah*.[164] The prisoners pled 'Not Guilty'.[165] Witnesses were produced against them: Thomas Spenlow, the two Frenchmen, with an interpreter, and James Spatchears, Barnet's man. The court decided that the prisoners were 'all of them Guilty', whereupon Sir Nicholas 'pronounced Sentence of Death upon them'.[166]

On the following day, 17 November, two more of Rackam's men, Thomas Brown and James Fenwick, were charged specifically with piracy on the *Neptune*. The master, Thomas Spenlow, testified against them. They had 'nothing to say for themselves', were removed from court and then returned to be declared guilty and sentenced to death.[167] On the next day, the 18th, Rackam and four of his crew were hanged at Gallow's Point, at the town of Port Royal, and Rackam and two of them were subsequently 'hung on Gibbets in Chains, for a publick Example, and to terrify others from such-like evil Practices'.[168] On Saturday the 19th four more of Rackam's men were executed—at Kingston, for some reason—and on Monday the 21st Brown and Fenwick were executed at Gallow's Point, Port Royal.

A week later, on Monday 28 November, Sir Nicholas and his court convened again, to try 'Mary Read, Ann Bonny, alias Bonn'.[169] They were charged as the dead men were, with pirating fishing boats, two merchant sloops, Spenlow's schooner and Dillon's sloop. The two prisoners pled 'Not Guilty' and witnesses were called.[170] Thomas Spenlow testified that both women were aboard Rackam's sloop when the schooner *Neptune* was taken by Rackam. Thomas Dillon testified more particularly

That the two Women, prisoners at the Bar, were then on Board Rackam's Sloop; and that Ann Bonny, one of the Prisoners at the Bar, had a Gun in her Hand, That they were both very profligate, cursing and swearing much, and very willing to do any Thing on Board.[171]

One of them was armed, then, and both used bad language. Dorothy Thomas, robbed in her canoe, gave a description of the women's clothing as well as their behaviour. She reported

That the Two Women, Prisoners at the Bar, were then on Board the said Sloop, and wore Mens Jackets, and long Trouzers, and Handkerchiefs tied about their Heads; and that each of them had a Machet [a machete, or cutlass] and Pistol in their Hands.[172]

She also testified that these two armed women 'cursed and swore at the Men, to murther the Deponent [Dorothy Thomas]; and that they should kill her, to prevent her coming against them'.[173] We may notice that the piratical women were heavily armed but had to ask the men to kill Dorothy, another woman, and that the men did not do so. As it happened, of course, Dorothy did indeed come 'against them'. In conclusion, Dorothy 'further said, That the Reason of her knowing and believing them to be Women then was, by the largeness of their Breasts'.[174]

A court at that time and place would see in Dorothy's words evidence that the two prisoners were armed participants in piracy, but we may interpret her testimony to address our modern questions about the role played by these two women subsequently famous for mixing their gender with piracy. The clothing they wore was not a disguise but the usual attire of sailors. An eighteenth-century dictionary of nautical usage gave the following definition: 'Trowsers, a sort of loose breeches of canvas worn by common sailors'.[175] With their trousers, sailors typically wore a short jacket that would not tangle with ropes, spars or rigging, and a handkerchief loosely tied around the neck or the head.[176] Two other witnesses, the Frenchmen John Besneck and Peter Cornelian, who had been captive aboard the *William* and had witnessed the two women for several days sustainedly, had observed their complicity in piracy, but also their dress. They reported, through their interpreter, that the two women

were very active on Board, and willing to do any Thing; that Ann Bonny, one of the Prisoners at the Bar, handed Gun-powder to the Men, That when they saw any Vessel, gave Chase, or Attacked, they wore Men's Cloaths; and, at other Times, they wore Women's Cloaths; That they did not seem to be kept, or detain'd by Force, but of their own Free-Will and Consent.[177]

The two Frenchmen had been aboard the *William* at the taking of the *Neptune* and of the *Mary and Sarah* and their testimony, no doubt at the court's direction, is aimed at establishing the women's free participation in piracy, in particular Ann Bonny's acting as a powder monkey, supplying powder to the men. They also provide us, however, with a clear description of the women's shipboard dress: as women, except in

times of action, when they wore the sailors' clothes described by
Dorothy Thomas. There is no question of Ann Bonny and Mary
Read being disguised as men. They were described as 'Two Women' by
Rogers in his 'Proclamation' of 5 September, reporting the theft of the
William from the harbour at Nassau, and nobody who saw them was
in any doubt of their gender.

In the court in St. Jago de la Vega, Jamaica, on 28 November 1720,
Ann Bonny and Mary Read, confronted by the testimony, said 'That
they had no witnesses, nor any Questions to ask'.[178] They were removed
while the court unanimously decided that they 'were both of them
Guilty'.[179] Brought back and told of this judgement they said that they
had nothing 'to say, or offer, Why Sentence of Death should not pass
on them', so they were sentenced accordingly, to death, whereupon
'both the Prisoners inform'd the Court, that they were both quick
with Child, and prayed that Execution of the Sentence might be
stayed'.[180] The court then 'ordered, that Execution of the said Sentence
should be respited, and that an Inspection should be made'.[181] Nothing is known of the results of that inspection and nothing more of
Bonny and Read, except for a report in a Jamaican parish register of
the burial on 18 April 1721 of Mary Read.[182] We may note that their
sentences were 'respited', not annulled, but that there is no record of
their executions, and also that, in the margins of their story, the nine
turtlers who came aboard the *William* for a bowl of punch at Point
Negril were tried for piracy on 24 January. Their spokesman protested
'That Rackam had used violent Means to oblige them…to help
weigh the Sloops Anchor', and the two French witnesses testified that,
when Barnet had opened fire, all the turtlers 'went down under Deck',
but the Frenchmen also testified, damningly, that 'some' (they couldn't
say which) of the turtlers had 'helped to row the Sloop, in order to
escape from Barnet', and that 'they all seemed to be consorted together'—that the turtlers were complicit with the pirates, in other words.[183]
All nine turtlers were found guilty of 'Piracy and Felony' and condemned to death, but only six were executed.[184]

These petty and pathetic facts—stolen fishing tackle and six hanged
turtlers—seem far from the romance we associate with the 'golden age'
of piracy. They do not explain, for example, why there have been published in the twentieth century two plays and seven novels—and four
more novels in the twenty-first century, so far—novels and plays purporting to be firmly, truthfully based on the historical facts about

Bonny and Read.[185] The persistently famous pirates of the 'golden age' are hardly the swashbuckling treasure-seekers of the high seas, of subsequent legend and literature. From whence, then, came the pirate of our imagination, the pirate still in our mind today, the pirate for all time? From what eighteenth-century facts did he—or she—emerge? As we shall see, he was more a man of words than facts.

III

Some Rambling Lives

'The odd Incidents of their rambling Lives, are such, that some may be tempted to think the whole Story no better than a Novel or Romance...'

(*A General History of the Robberies and Murders of the most notorious Pyrates*)[1]

A few years after the events related in the previous chapter, some of those pirates—Kidd, Blackbeard, Rackam, Bonny, Read—and their piracies were brought before a wider audience in the work entitled *A General History of the Robberies and Murders of the most notorious Pyrates* (London, 1724), which was announced as written by an unidentified Captain Charles Johnson, and was supplemented by a second volume in 1728. Kidd, so well-known 'that his Actions have been chanted about in Ballads', appeared in the second volume, and the principal source for its account of him was the published account of his trial, *The Arraignment, Tryal, and Condemnation of Captain William Kidd* (London, 1701), from which he is quoted—sometimes not exactly—saying, for example, of 'the Moca Fleet': 'We have been unsuccessful hitherto, but Courage, my Boys, we'll make our Fortunes out of this Fleet'.[2] A more or less accurate account follows of his predations on other ships off the Indian coast, with his trickery about French flags and passes, and his killing of Moore, and the taking of the *Quedah Merchant*. At Madagascar he meets former shipmates, assures them he is 'just as bad as they; and calling for a Cup of Bomboo, drank their Captain's Health'.[3] Nevertheless his crew absconds for Culliford's command. Kidd is arrested on return to New York, shipped to England and tried at the Old Bailey for piracy and the murder of Moore. The trial is rehearsed from the source, and its conclusion stated. The whole account is a fair, if not precisely accurate, summary of Kidd's voyage and its consequences, drawn from the published *Tryal*.

Blackbeard preceded Kidd before the public, in the first volume of the *General History*. He begins his career under Hornigold, renames his prize *Queen Anne's Revenge*, allies himself with Bonnet, whose 'Humour of going a pyrating, proceeded from a Disorder in his Mind...which is said to have been occasioned by some Discomforts he found in a married State'.[4] Bonnet's gentlemanly piracy psycho-sexually explained, he is—as indeed he was—dominated by Blackbeard, who takes over Bonnet's command by 'committing a sort of Pyracy upon him'.[5] Blackbeard subsequently blockades Charleston, as he did. Some of this period of Blackbeard's career would have been known by way of the published *The Tryals of Major Stede Bonnet, and other pirates* (London, 1719), such as his splitting up of his forces and marooning of men (who were rescued by Bonnet). He proceeds to receive a pardon from Governor Eden, as he did, but his sexual activities in Carolina are something new, and perhaps to be suspected. He marries a 16-year-old, his 'fourteenth Wife', to whom he customarily invites 'five or six of his brutal Companions', forcing her 'to prostitute her self to them all, one after another, before his Face'.[6] There is no independent record of this marital or extramarital behaviour, unless, of course, the *General History* can be considered such a record.[7] The *General History* also interrupts Blackbeard's various piratical acts to mention the 'Liberties, (which 'tis said,) he and his Companions often took with the Wives and Daughters of the Planters'.[8] Governor Spotswood plans his expedition and Maynard and his two sloops set out in November 1718 and confront Teach in the 'Okerecock Inlet'.[9]

The opening dialogue quite closely follows what had been reported in the newspapers, with Blackbeard and Maynard sparring with the words 'come aboard' in friendly and aggressive senses, and Blackbeard's drinking a toast to Maynard: 'Damnation seize my Soul if I give you Quarters, or take any from you'.[10] Maynard's tactic, described in the *Boston News-Letter*, of tricking Blackbeard by hiding men in the hold, is described, and an additional detail, that 'Thatch's Men threw in several new fashion'd Sort of Grenadoes', in effect hand-grenades of exploding bottles.[11] The details of the hand-to-hand fighting are much like those in the *Boston News-Letter*, Blackbeard breaking Maynard's sword but receiving a wound from his pistol and cuts from one of

Maynard's men. Blackbeard's death is a little different, however. The *Boston News-Letter* allocated the final, killing blow to the Highlander, with his quip, 'I'll do it better', but Maynard's own letter did not mention this, and neither does the *General History*, numbering Blackbeard's wounds at 'sixteen' (revised in the second edition to 'five and twenty', matching Maynard's figure) and saying merely that he 'fell down dead', but remarking: 'Here was an End of that couragious Brute, who might have pass'd in the World for a Heroe, had he been employ'd in a good Cause'.[12] Another extra piece of information is introduced, also, which had been mentioned by Governor Spotswood in his official account: that Blackbeard had installed a man in the powder room of his ship, ready to blow it up, but this man had been dissuaded by two prisoners (one, according to Spotswood) who happened to be aboard.[13] In summary, then, the report of the battle in the *General History* quite closely (though not precisely) follows the newspaper accounts (which in any case differ from each other), but in some details contain new information, accurate or inaccurate, derived either from alternative sources, true or false, or from imagination. What follows the battle in the *General History* is, however, of considerable significance for the characterization of Blackbeard, 'that couragious Brute, who might have pass'd in the World for a Heroe'.

He is given a full and vivid description, much more particular than Maynard's brief remark that 'he went by the name of Blackbeard, because he let his Beard grow, and tied it up in black Ribbons'.[14] Blackbeard is presented in the *General History* as the terrible flamboyant pirate we know to this day, a strange hero:

our Heroe, Captain Thatch, assumed the Cognomen of Black-beard, from that large Quantity of Hair, which like a frightful Meteor, covered his whole Face, and frightened America, more than any Comet that has appear'd there a long Time.

This Beard was black, which he suffered to grow of an extravagant Length; as to Breadth, it came up to his Eyes; he was accustomed to twist it with Ribbons, in small Tails, after the Manner of our Ramellies Wigs [which had a single plait at the back of the head], and turn them about his Ears: In Time of Action, he wore a Sling over his Shoulders, with three brace of Pistols, hanging in Holsters like Bandaliers; he wore a Fur-Cap, and stuck a lighted Match on each Side, under it, which appearing on each Side his Face, his Eyes naturally looking Fierce and Wild, made him altogether such a Figure, that Imagination cannot form an Idea of a Fury, from Hell, to look more frightful.[15]

Mysteriously, in the second edition later in 1724, Blackbeard has lost his 'Fur-Cap', which was properly depicted in the illustration to the first edition, and replaced in the illustration to the second edition with a conventional three-cornered hat. The alteration is mysterious but matches the description in the second edition which removes the words 'he wore a Fur-Cap'[16] (see Figures 3.1 and 3.2). The illustrations—frequently reproduced ever since, as if they were portraits from life—quite carefully correspond to the textual details and indeed emphasize the extraordinary and the strikingly characteristic, the two different illustrations of 'Blackbeard the Pirate' in the first and second editions both showing the lighted matches protruding 'on each Side his Face'.[17]

In keeping with this portrait of 'a Fury, from Hell', some anecdotes are told. One that he gratuitously shot and lamed one of his men, still 'alive at this Time in London, begging his Bread', by firing his pistols under the table at which they sat drinking in his cabin.[18] Blackbeard's explanation of this arbitrary violence was 'that if he did not now and then kill one of them, they would forget who he was'.[19] What is signalled by this story is Blackbeard's concern to dramatize his self-presentation, or the author's concern to dramatize him, or both. Another significant story is told to exemplify this role-playing by Blackbeard, some of whose 'Frolicks of Wickedness, were so extravagant, as if he aim'd at making his Men believe he was a Devil incarnate'.[20] Thus, 'being one Day at Sea, and a little flushed with Drink:– Come, says he, let us make a Hell of our own, and try how long we can bear it'.[21] In order thus to enact a Hell, Blackbeard and some of his men sealed themselves in the hold and set alight several pots of brimstone, enduring near suffocation, with Blackbeard triumphantly enduring the longest. Whatever the truth of these stories, their selection and presentation in the *General History* are clear indications of an aim to demonize Blackbeard into a piratical incarnation of Satan, an attractively horrible creation (or self-creation) as an enduring type of fiendish evil. The showman in a pantomime act of real evil, mixing cruelty with play in his 'Frolicks of Wickedness', he is indeed 'such a Figure, that Imagination cannot form an Idea of a Fury, from Hell, to look more frightful'.

The first volume of the *General History* also gave an account of John Rackam, outlining the West Indian piracies he was charged with at his

Figure 3.1. 'Blackbeard the Pirate', from *A General History of the Robberies and Murders of the most notorious Pyrates* (first edition, London, 1724).

trial, and then turning to the two lives of the women on his ship, who were featured on the title-page of the *General History*, which advertised *The remarkable Actions and Adventures of the two Female Pyrates, Mary Read and Anne Bonny.* Their stories were entitled as full biographies, 'The Life of Mary Read' and 'The Life of Anne Bonny', and jointly introduced as 'a History, full of surprizing Turns and Adventures'.[22] Indeed, we are warned by the author that

the odd Incidents of their rambling Lives, are such, that some may be tempted to think the whole Story no better than a Novel or Romance; but since it is supported by many thousand Witnesses, I mean the People of Jamaica, who were present at their Tryals, and heard the Story of their Lives, upon the first

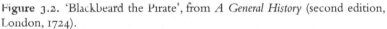

Figure 3.2. 'Blackbeard the Pirate', from *A General History* (second edition, London, 1724).

discovery of their Sex; the Truth of it can be no more contested, than that there were such Men in the World, as Roberts and Black-beard, who were Pyrates.[23]

So, to doubt the *General History*'s account of Bonny and Read would be to doubt the very existence of Bartholomew Roberts, famous for his dandified death in 'rich crimson Damask', and of Blackbeard.[24] Such doubt would be absurd, especially when the two women's biographies were witnessed by many thousand Jamaican colonists who attended their trial, when their genders were first discovered. So says the author of the *General History*.

The life of Mary Read (about whom no history emerged in the printed Jamaican account of her trial) is given first, from its very beginning. She is born in England, illegitimate and fatherless, brought up as a boy in order to receive money under false pretences from the grandmother of a previous, deceased, legitimate son. Independent-minded—'growing bold and strong, and having also a roving Mind'— Mary becomes in male disguise a sailor and then a soldier.[25] She falls in love with a fellow soldier, a comrade-in-arms, reveals her gender to him, resumes 'Womens Apparel', and marries him.[26] On his death, she 'again assumes her Man's Apparel' and becomes a soldier and a sailor again, taking a passage to the West Indies on a ship captured by pirates, who take her into their company.[27] She continues her pirate career in male disguise and eventually ships with Rackam and Ann Bonny, also in male disguise (her Christian name spelled with and without an 'e').[28] The *General History* remarks that, although Mary 'often declared, that the Life of a Pyrate was what she always abhor'd', nevertheless some of the witnesses at her trial, conscripted men who

had sail'd with her, deposed upon Oath, that in Times of Action, no Person amongst them was more resolute, or ready to Board, or undertake any Thing that was hazardous, as she and Ann Bonny; and particularly at the Time they were attack'd and taken, when they came to close Quarters, none kept the Deck except Mary Read and Ann Bonny, and one more; upon which, she, Mary Read, called to those under Deck, to come up and fight like Men, and finding they did not stir, fired her Arms down the Hold amongst them, killing one, and wounding others.[29]

This was not evidence given in the published record of her trial. If it had been stated by a witness it would probably have been recorded in the account of her trial, which would have had no reason to omit such evidence of her participation in piratical action, not to mention murder. Nor is it consistent with Spatchears's account of Barnet's capture of the *William*, which had its boom destroyed by a broadside and small-shot from a distance, and then called out in surrender, 'called to Barnet for quarter, which he gave them', with no fighting at close quarters. Nevertheless it obviously pleases the author of the *General History* to describe his two female characters as fiercer and more violent than their male pirate companions, whom Mary Read called upon to 'fight like Men'.

Contrary to the evidence in the published account of her trial, that Mary Read and Ann Bonny were obviously women 'by the largeness of their Breasts', and only 'wore Men's cloaths' in times of action, the *General History* reports of Mary Read that

Her Sex was not so much as suspected by any Person on Board, till Ann Bonny...took a particular liking to her; in short, Ann Bonny took her for a handsome young Fellow, and for some Reasons best known to herself, first discovered her Sex to Mary Read; Mary Read knowing what she would be at, and being very sensible of her own Incapacity that Way, was forced to come to a right Understanding with her, and so to the great Disappointment of Ann Bonny, she let her know she was a Woman also.[30]

Having invented this amusing misunderstanding (contrary to the published witness statements), the author of the *General History* introduces a love triangle, informing us that Rackam 'was the Lover and Gallant of Ann Bonny'.[31] As such, Rackam 'grew furiously jealous' of the man he believed Mary Read to be, and 'told Ann Bonny, he would cut her new Lover's Throat, therefore, to quiet him, she let him into the Secret also'.[32] Nevertheless, despite this disclosure, we are told that 'Captain Rackam, (as he was enjoin'd,) kept the Thing a Secret from all the Ships Company'.[33] Another 'Scene of Love' ensued, however, when Mary fell in love with a conscript pirate and let him into the secret, 'by carelessly shewing her Breasts, which were very White'.[34] To save the life of this lover, she fought a duel in place of him with a real pirate, whom she killed with a sword. To this lover 'was owing her great Belly, which she pleaded to save her Life'.[35]

In introducing 'The Life of Ann Bonny', the author of the *General History* says that, as he has 'been more particular in the Lives of these two Women, than those of other Pyrates', it was therefore necessary 'to begin with their Birth'.[36] He does not explain why female pirates require fuller biographies than male ones, but he begins Ann Bonny's story well before her birth. Her father was a lawyer in Ireland and Ann was born there illegitimately. This requires a long explanation by way of a convoluted story, irrelevant to piracy and generically like a fabliau or a picaresque romance, with little characterization but much complication of plot, featuring tricks and misunderstandings. This prebirth story occupies almost as much space as Ann's own life.

An attractive servant girl in Ann's father's household was wooed by a young man, a tanner, who stole three silver spoons from the house. The servant girl, a maid, missed the spoons and challenged the young man with their theft, whereupon he hid them between the sheets of her bed, guessing that she would find them there and he would explain that the theft had only been a joke. When he immediately departed the house, however, the maid concluded that he had made off with the spoons. She informed the policeman, who pursued the young man, who went into hiding, thinking that she must have found the spoons and decided to keep them for herself, while blaming him.

The lawyer's wife, who had been away from home for some time, now returned, with her mother-in-law, to be informed by the maid of the young man's theft of the spoons, which he independently confessed to the wife, pretending it was a jest not a theft. The wife found the three spoons where the tanner said he had hidden them, in the maid's bed. The wife therefore suspected the maid—not of stealing the spoons, but of not sleeping in her bed, and perhaps sleeping in the lawyer's instead, in the wife's absence. The wife then decided to sleep in the maid's bed (which sets the scene for the theatrical plot device known as 'the bed trick'). The maid's bed was therefore remade in preparation for the wife by the maid, who thus found the hidden spoons, still there, which she hid in her trunk. That night the wife in the maid's bed was visited by her husband, who 'play'd the vigorous Lover; but one Thing spoil'd the Diversion on the Wife's Side, which was, the Reflection that it was not design'd for her'.[37]

Jealous of the maid and vengeful, the wife accused her the next day to the policeman, who found the spoons in the maid's trunk and sent her to prison, where 'it was discovered she was with Child'.[38] She was in due course released 'for want of Evidence' and 'was delivered of a Girl'.[39] This is piratical Ann's arrival at last in her biography. Is she supposed to have known all this that happened before her birth? If so, did she believe it? Are we supposed to believe it?

Now another twist in the plot of Ann's supposed story: 'it was discovered the Wife was with Child also', although the lawyer 'had had no Intimacy with her' (no intimacy that he knew of, presumably), and 'she was delivered of Twins'.[40] The mother-in-law nevertheless made a will in favour of the wife and twins, disinheriting her son the lawyer, who was however given an allowance by his separated wife when the mother-in-law died. At this point Ann Bonny's cross-dressing is explained. The lawyer father, wishing to live with his illegitimate daughter, had her 'put into Breeches, as a Boy', pretending that she was a relative's son, not his own daughter.[41] The wife suspected this supposed boy and employed a snooper who, 'by talking with the Child, found it to be a Girl'.[42] The wife therefore stopped the allowance to her husband, who then cohabited publicly with the girl's mother, the maid, until, the scandal damaging his legal practice, he travelled with maid and daughter to Carolina. There he acquired 'a considerable Plantation' but the maid, 'who passed for his Wife, happened to dye, after which his Daughter, our Anne Bonny, now grown up, kept his House'.[43]

Ann was 'of a fierce and couragious Temper', however, and without her father's consent married a penniless sailor named Bonny, with whom she shipped to the island of New Providence in the Bahamas, where she met John Rackam, who was smitten with love for her. An 'Appendix' to the second volume of the *General History* (1728) supplied more details of her affair with Rackam, who spent his looted treasures to impress her, having 'nothing but Anne Bonny in his Head'.[44] She suggested to her husband, James Bonny, that he should formally sell her to Rackam, a scheme which the Governor (who would have been Woodes Rogers) prevented, threatening Ann with prison and a whipping, which Rackam would be compelled to give her. In response, she and Rackam planned the theft of a sloop, which Ann boarded, 'having a drawn Sword in one Hand and a Pistol in the other', threatening the sailors on guard that if they resisted 'she would blow out their Brains, (that was the Term she used)'.[45]

In this stolen sloop, the *William*, which the *General History* enlarges from about 12 tons to 'betwixt thirty and forty Tun', Ann sailed with Rackam into her career of piracy.[46] According to the 'Appendix', the first piratical episode after the theft of the *William* was an attempt to take revenge on the man who had informed the Governor of Ann and Rackam's proposal to buy her from James Bonny. This informer was turtling with his sloop at an island, known to Rackam, who sailed there directly in the *William* but failed to find him, hiding in the woods. To punish him they pillaged his sloop and abducted three of his crew, Richard Connor, John Davis, and John Howel, before sinking his sloop in deep water. This episode, which integrates the piratical actions of Ann and Rackam with their romance, may or may not have happened, but does not fit the documented details, that John Davis and John Howell were two of the men named in Rogers's 'Proclamation' as responsible for the theft of the *William* from Nassau on 22 August 1720. The subsequent piratical career of Ann Bonny with Rackam, which would have lasted about two months in total, from the theft of the *William* to arrest by Barnet, is briefly described in the *General History*:

In all these Expeditions, Anne Bonny bore him Company, and when any Business was to be done in their Way, no Body was more forward or couragious than she, and particularly when they were taken; she and Mary Read, with one more, were all the Persons that durst keep the Deck.[47]

There was no such evidence presented, according to the published account of her trial, which would have had every reason to notice such piratical behaviour. Ann's story in the *General History* is concluded with an anecdote demonstrating her admiration for manliness:

The Day that Rackam was executed, by special Favour, he was admitted to see her; but all the Comfort she gave him, was, that she was sorry to see him there, but if he had fought like a Man, he need not have been hang'd like a Dog.[48]

The biographies of Bonny and Read in the *General History* have little basis in the only known records about them, those in Rogers's 'Proclamation' and those of the evidence at their trial, securing their conviction as pirates. As the author of the *General History* said himself, to disarm us, 'the odd Incidents of their rambling Lives, are such, that some may be tempted to think the whole Story no better than a Novel or Romance', and indeed the 'suprizing Turns and Adventures' of their biographies are much more like the plots of fiction than the lives of real people.[49] The *General History* belongs to the dawning age of the novel and its author is aware that his stories of Bonny and Read are generically related to the new literary form, as he shows when he reverts again to 'the Lives of our two female Pyrates' in his Preface to the *General History*:

If there are some Incidents and Turns in their Stories, which may give them a little the Air of a Novel, they are not invented or contrived for that Purpose, it is a Kind of Reading this Author is but little acquainted with, but as he himself was exceedingly diverted with them, when they were related to him, he thought they might have the same Effect upon the Reader.[50]

Is this as good as a nudge and a wink from the author, the supposed but unidentified Captain Charles Johnson?

What we can reliably know about Mary Read and Ann Bonny— apart from Mary Read's burial in April 1721—is that they sailed with Rackam aboard the *William* for about two months and participated in his piracies during that time. They were sometimes dressed in men's clothes (sailors' clothes) but never disguised as men. The story in the *General History* of Ann disguised as a man falling in love with Mary disguised as a man is not consistent with the known historical details and is much more consistent with the theatrical disguises and plot

devices of fiction. We do not even know that Ann and Rackam had a
romance in ramshackle Nassau or at sea in the cramped spaces of the
William. The author of the *General History* claimed that the truth of his
fictions of Bonny and Read was 'supported by many thousand Witnesses, I mean the People of Jamaica', who attended the trial (surely
not in thousands) and 'heard the Story of their Lives, upon the first
discovery of their Sex'.[51] As some parts of the *General History*'s account
of Bonny and Read are directly derived, word for word, from the
account in *The Tryals of Captain John Rackam*, we can be sure that the
author of the *General History* knew the *Tryals* and knew when he was
deviating into fiction.[52] He knew what we do, that the story of the
lives of Bonny and Read, as told in the *General History*, was not told in
the course of their trial, which did not suddenly reveal that they were
women.[53] The myth in the *General History* is nevertheless persistent,
repeated again and again, even today, by *The Oxford Dictionary of
National Biography*, for example, which repeats the principal fictions of
the *General History*: that the two women were disguised as men and
were fiercer than men.[54]

With his 'surprizing Turns and Adventures' the author of the *General
History* is introducing Bonny and Read into the repetitively male plot
of piracy. They are not simply demonic types of barbarity, like Blackbeard, but, as supposed cross-dressers, also crossing generic boundaries.

Figure 3.3. 'Ann Bonny and Mary Read', from *A General History* (first edition, London, 1724).

Their legend is literary and a romance, with its background in fictions of gender and fables of disguise and substitution, tricks and missing spoons, literary devices that belong in London, where the novel is being created, along with a popular book, the *General History*, which has been attributed—though mistakenly—to the novelist Defoe.

Female pirates are a distinctive pirate variant, a kind of paradox, a combination of femininity and ferocity, as can be seen in the illustration in the first edition of the *General History*, in which Bonny and Read are dressed as sailors in trousers (see Figure 3.3). They are not disguised as men, however, but advertised as women, with long flowing hair beneath their shoulders, as they are in the illustrations to the Dutch translation of the *General History*, the *Historie der Engelsche Zee-Roovers* (Amsterdam, 1725), in which they display breasts as well as aggression in threatening poses (see Figures 3.4 and 3.5). What is essential in their depiction is the simultaneous combination of femininity and piracy, with the two women heavily armed in the English illustration, brandishing and wearing cutlasses and axes. In the Dutch illustrations they are wearing pistols and axes and Mary has a cutlass in hand and Ann a pointing pistol, while both women expose their naked breasts—obviously not in disguise but in manifestation of their explicit femininity. They are icons of the paradox of the female pirate, a kind of oxymoron, simultaneously displaying breasts and weapons. The illustrations are in some apparent contradiction with the story of the *General History*, which insists on the women's being disguised as male pirates as well as being more manly, more fierce and aggressive, more piratical than male pirates. The two essential features of Bonny and Read to be inferred from the textual inventions are, then, their disguise as men and their superiority in maleness. These are the two principal fictions of the *General History* when compared with the evidence of the witnesses published in the *Tryals*. The witnesses testified that Bonny and Read were sometimes dressed like the men but were not disguised as men. The witnesses did not testify that the two women were fiercer—more manly—than the men.

The illustrations and the text both indicate the basic requirements of the woman pirate, who can bring love and the generic effects of romance into the male adventure of piracy. In fact, we know nothing about Bonny's and Read's loves, not even that Bonny was Rackam's lover. What we know is simple and starkly so: they were two women who participated in male piracy and were saved from execution by

Figure 3.4. 'Anne Bonny captured in Jamaica', from *Historie der Engelsche Zee-Rovers* (1725).

their distinctive female manifestations, the largeness—not of their breasts, which Dorothy Thomas noticed—but of their bellies. As women pirates they are paradoxical and double deviants. Like male pirates they are transgressing the conventions of ownership but as female pirates they are also transgressing the conventions of their genders, or at least mixing the male and female plots—bringing romance into the piratical adventure.

Of course there were some women who went to sea disguised as men. Doubtless there were many more who were not discovered and

Figure 3.5. 'Mary Read has died in jail in Jamaica', from *Historie der Engelsche Zee-Rovers* (1725).

are therefore unknown to us. Captain Thomas Phillips recorded in his journal on 18 November 1693 that the wind was 'shuffling between the W.S.W and S.S.W.' and also that John Brown, one of the Royal African Company's soldiers aboard his ship, had suffered an ailment which led the surgeon's assistant to administer an enema, only 'to find more sally-ports [openings] than he expected'.[55] The black soldier, an attractive African woman of about 20, confessed her gender, was assigned by Captain Phillips to more suitable work, and 'prov'd very useful in washing my linnen'.[56] Another who was discovered was an eighteenth-century marine called William Prothero, who sailed aboard the aptly named *Amazon*, and was actually an 18-year-old Welsh woman, according to the journal of the surgeon's mate, who recorded— romantically or accurately—that the supposed William Prothero 'had followed her lover' to sea.[57] A little later in the century a Frenchman named Jean Baré turned out to be a Frenchwoman named Jeanne Baré, as the Tahitians discovered when the explorer Bougainville's ships visited their island in 1768.[58] She too had a possible amatory motive, as the companion of a scientist accompanying the naval voyage. These stories are true and some have charming and romantic explanations which resemble the plots of fictions. But the cross-dressing in the *General History*, which takes the form of disguises which keep the two women's genders unknown to their fellow-pirates, is a well-rehearsed theatrical convention, far more commonplace than the historical reality aboard ships at sea. Indeed it has been assiduously calculated that about a quarter of the plays staged in London between 1660 and 1700—eighty-nine out of three hundred and seventy-five—contained roles in which actresses wore men's clothes.[59]

Even before there were actresses on the London stage there were actors playing piratesses. In Thomas Heywood's *The Fair Maid of the West* (c.1600), the 'fair maid' is a pirate leader who appears on deck dressed 'like a Sea-captain', so convincingly disguised that her lover thinks her a 'young Gentleman'.[60] In Robert Daborn's *A Christian turn'd Turke* (1612), a play we have already noticed, a young girl on a pirate ship disguises her gender by 'putting on the weed of a Sailers boy', successfully deceiving the men as well as a young woman who falls in love with her, thus affording a kind of dramatic irony, amusing the audience which knows more than the characters, as well as extending the scope of female roles.[61] In Fletcher and Massinger's *The Double Marriage* (c.1621), Martia, the pirate Duke's daughter, is not disguised as a man, but is a 'brave wench', according to the pirate boatswain.[62] A 'Martiall maid' by nature as well as name, she is sensually 'soft for sweet embraces' but simultaneously fierce and 'manly'.[63] Later still, when female roles were played by actresses, the hero of William Wycherley's *The Plain-Dealer* (1677), Captain Manly, is protected by a lady who is 'in Love with Manly, and follow'd him to Sea in Man's Cloaths'.[64] This devoted lady, under the significant name of Fidelio, deceives masculine Manly into believing that she is a man, and she deceives also the faithless lady whom Manly foolishly pursues, who passionately falls for the apparently male Fidelio, who is subsequently discovered very palpably to be a lady, an heiress no less, a suitable as well as faithful bride for Manly. It need hardly be said: Bonny and Read have fictional precedents.

One example of an actress cross-dressing occurs in an operetta half a century later, by John Gay, *Polly* (1729), the sequel to Gay's popular *The Beggar's Opera*. (We should notice—in parenthesis—that robbers like Gay's imaginary Macheath, and like pirates, were thrilling popular heroes at the time, when Defoe (probably) wrote the *Life* (1725) of the real Jonathan Wild, the London thief, thief-taker, and underworld gang-leader.) Gay's heroine, Polly, one of Macheath's wives, follows him to the West Indies, where he has disguised himself as a black man and become a pirate. The moral ambiguity of *The Beggar's Opera*, in which the criminal fraternity of thieves satirically echoes the respectable political authorities, is replaced by a simpler contrast between the immoral colonial authorities and pirates, on the one hand, and on the other the principled noble savages who are the local indigenous Indians. Polly, disguised as a man 'To protect me from the violences and insults to which my sex might have expos'd me', is captured by the pirates and escapes with a fellow-prisoner, the principled Indian Prince Cawwawkee.[65] The happy ending leaves her preferring the principled Indians and in particular the Prince (who is pleased to discover her real gender) to the double-dealing and bigamous Macheath. Contrary to the belief of one modern pirate historian that Gay's Polly cross-dressed and went 'to sea as a pirate', she was never a pirate but, more to the theatrical point, her cross-dressing in the wild West Indies gives rise to titillating ironies when, for example, she is kissed and wooed by Macheath's latest wife, the Londoner Jenny Diver (a 'diver' is thieves' cant, or slang, for 'pickpocket').[66] The scene has resemblances, of course, to the scene of Bonny's attraction to Read in the *General History*, but Polly is not a pirate and Gay's West Indian pirates are more of a transposition of his London thieves to a new setting than authentically piratical characters. It is not a case of Gay's theatrical fiction copying from piratical fact so much as a coincidence of theatrical conventions in both *Polly* and the *General History*. The female pirate had a long career ahead of her—where she belonged, in fiction.

In 1728 the second volume of the *General History* appeared, opening with the life 'Of Captain Misson'. Unusually, Misson was French and unusually, too, the supposed source for his story was the accidental possession by the author of 'a French manuscript, in which he himself

[Misson] gives a Detail of his Actions'.[67] His life was therefore followed from his birth 'in Provence, of an ancient Family'.[68] Inspired by reading 'Books of Travels', he went to sea on board the *Victoire*, commanded by a relation.[69] This captain allows him to visit Rome, where the sight of ecclesiastical luxury and licentiousness suggested to him that 'Religion' was a conspiracy of disbelievers to control 'the Minds of the Weaker', an opinion confirmed by his confessor, a Signor Caraccioli, firmly of the view that the church was 'govern'd with the same Policy as were secular Principalities and Kingdoms'.[70] Impressed, Misson suggests that Caraccioli take up a career at sea instead, and they sail together on the *Victoire*.

In the course of their voyaging, Caraccioli 'made a perfect Deist of Misson, and thereby convinc'd him, that all Religion was no other than human Policy'.[71] He reasoned likewise with other crewmen and moved from religion to politics, arguing that 'every Man was born free'.[72] When the *Victoire* engaged off Martinique with the English warship the *Winchelsea* and the captain and senior officers of the *Victoire* were killed, Misson and Caraccioli took command and defeated the *Winchelsea*, which 'blew up' and sank, with the loss of all aboard, who died as free as they were born, presumably.[73] The author of the *General History* claims that 'None ever knew before this Manuscript fell into my Hands how the *Winchelsea* was lost', but in historical reality she was lost in a hurricane in 1707.[74] After this fictitious victory (and authorial attempt to infiltrate historical authenticity), Caraccioli encourages Misson to declare himself captain of the *Victoire*. Caraccioli's reasoning is inconsistent with his previously stated principles, of freedom and equality, and is blatantly hypocritical therefore. He tells Misson that, with the ship and its crew under his command, Misson could 'bid Defiance to the Power of Europe, enjoy every Thing he wish'd, reign Sovereign of the Southern Seas, and lawfully make War on all the World'.[75] Misson is successfully convinced by this appeal to gratify himself and, offering the crew the option to follow him or be set ashore, he is welcomed with a unanimous cry of 'Vive le Capitain Misson et son Lieutenant le Scavant Caraccioli'.[76] The boatswain proposes they sail under black colours but Caraccioli objects, with much political rhetoric, that, as they 'do not proceed upon the same Ground with Pyrates, who are Men of dissolute Lives and no Principles, let us scorn to take their Colours'.[77] Instead, as 'Ours is a brave, a just, an innocent, and a noble Cause', he proposes 'a white Ensign, with Liberty printed in the Fly' (on the free-flying end of the flag).[78]

Their first victim was an English ship from which they took some rum and sugar but with no harm to its crew. An English privateer from Jamaica was similarly captured and released. They next encountered two Dutch trading ships, one of which Misson decided to sink: 'he pour'd in a Broad-Side, which open'd such a Gap in the Dutch Ship, that she went directly to the Bottom, and every Man perish'd'.[79] Misson's reiterated principles are thus in obvious contradiction with his piratical practice. The other Dutch ship, suitably impressed, is captured, plundered, and sold on as a prize.

A decision is made by Misson—and democratically agreed to—that the *Victoire* and its crew should make for the west-African coast, where they take a Dutch ship which they man as a consort. The slaves aboard were freed and joined the pirate ranks, informed by Misson, persuasively, that religious men who 'sold Men like Beasts...prov'd that their Religion was no more than a Grimace'.[80] The *Victoire* and its consort, captained by Caraccioli, make for Madagascar but on the way, at the adjacent Comoro Islands, Caraccioli advises Misson to heighten the local hostility between Johanna and another Comoro island, Mohilla, as he could then 'hold the Ballance of Power between them'.[81] Misson followed this advice and married the Queen of Johanna's sister, while Caraccioli married the daughter of the Queen's brother and several subordinate pirates also 'took Wives'.[82] Whether by coincidence or design, this echoes the reports that Baldridge and others at Saint Mary's married local women 'to ingratiate themselves with the inhabitants, with whom they go into war against other petty kings'.[83] When the King of Mohilla attacked Johanna, Misson and his men successfully defended it and then invaded Mohilla and carried out reprisals. Misson was still keen to foster the rivalry of the islands and refrained, therefore, from completely defeating the Mohillans. (We may note, incidentally, that Misson's relationship with Caraccioli is rather like Singleton's with his hypocritically principled friend William.)

The chapter 'Of Captain Misson' closes with the establishment and settlement on Madagascar of Misson's colony 'which he called Libertalia' but also with a promise that the story will be continued, which it is in a subsequent chapter, 'Of Captain Tew, And his Crew'.[84] Misson's fictional life is a dateless one but events of 1707–8 provide a vague historical background when his life occasionally connects with real things and events (the loss of the *Winchelsea*, for example). Despite this historical context, however, the fiction of Misson is also blended with facts and historical pirates of a much earlier period, such as Tew himself, who died in 1695.[85] Thus, in the chapter 'Of Captain Tew', Misson encounters Tew's ship, which joins the *Victoire* and its latest prize, a Portuguese ship, and sails to visit Libertalia. An account of Tew's career is interspersed at this point, to some extent repeating the account already given in the first volume of the *General History* during the chapter 'Of Captain Avery', and to a greater extent expanding it, to provide real Tew with a fictional role in the continuing story of Misson.

Tew is thus sent by Misson on a mission to strengthen his growing colony by the capture of a slaving ship and he consequently takes a Dutch galley and a larger English ship with 240 Angolan slaves aboard, who are immediately freed on Misson's orders and taken to join the Madagascar colony (rather than repatriated to Angola). Caraccioli then takes a Dutch prize at Mascarenhas (modern Réunion) and Misson and Tew easily capture a Mughal pilgrim ship bound for Jeddah. They release the passengers and crew ashore but keep the ship, its cargo, and '100 Girls, from 12 to 18 Years old', whom they transport for stock to Libertalia, much as captured women were used to populate and propagate Avery's fictional 'Republic of Pirates' in *The Life and Adventures of Capt. John Avery*.[86] Misson's colony is flourishing but threatened by five well-armed Portuguese ships, which are duly resisted, pursued, and defeated. This engagement with Misson was ignorantly mistaken for one with Avery, remarks the author of the *General History*, as Avery had supposedly 'taken upon him the State and Title of King, a Mistake we have already spoken to in the first Volume'.[87] The author thus shows his hand: having debunked the myth of Avery's Madagascar utopia, he has substituted an alternative fictional version of it, Misson's Madagascar utopia.

The utopia in the *General History* comes to grief quite quickly. The *Victoire* and her crew are lost in a storm and Misson has to escape the island and abandon his colony when it is attacked by the indigenous people of Madagascar, who 'made a great Slaughter', including Caraccioli, 'for what Reason he could not imagine'.[88] This repeats or coincidentally parallels the Malagasy attack on Baldridge's colony on Saint Mary's. Tew proposes 'their going to America' but Misson is considering returning to Europe, though he can make no decision, only that 'his Misfortunes had erased all Thoughts of future Settlements'.[89] They set sail in separate ships but a storm sinks Misson and his crew and Tew proceeds to America, with some Frenchmen by whom the manuscript of Misson's life came to La Rochelle and thence into the hands of the author of the *General History*. Tew himself lives tranquilly and comfortably until pressed by some of his men to make another voyage, which takes him to his actual historical fate, to be shot and killed by 'a Ship belonging to the Great Mogul'.[90]

Some modern scholars have swallowed Misson whole and regurgitated him undigested into their own histories: Hubert Deschamps, for instance, in *Les Pirates à Madagascar* (1949).[91] J.R. Moore was more concerned with the authorship of Misson and of the whole of the *General History*, gullibly and implausibly building up a case in *Defoe in the Pillory and Other Studies* (1939) for the attribution of the work to Defoe, a case dismantled by P.N. Furbank and W.R. Owens in *The Canonisation of Daniel Defoe* (1988).[92] Some, believing Misson to be Defoe's work, indeed 'one of Defoe's most remarkable and neglected works of fiction', have attempted to explain why he should apparently have made his hero a Deist, but have not noticed the hypocrisy of Misson's Machiavellian principles.[93] Yet others, more recently, have reluctantly acknowledged the fictitiousness of Misson but argued that his utopia is a real and historical reflection of the political ideals of genuine piracy.[94] Again his hypocrisy has not been noticed (nor the close resemblance of his utopia to the principled humbug and actual practice of colonization). Clearly the fictional Libertalia of Misson is a continuation of the political theme of piracy, beginning in historical actuality with the buccaneer 'frères de la côte' in the Caribbean and then echoed in fictional accounts of historical Every's Madagascar 'Republic of Pirates' and now in the pure fiction of Misson.

In a review of the *General History* that has been (plausibly) attributed to Defoe, he is most intrigued by the political schemes of the pirates, which he finds 'as excellent for Policy as any Thing in Plato's Commonwealth'.[95] 'Some may be diverted with the Boldness of their Enterprizes, or Stratagems to catch their Prey, or the Strangeness of two Women's engaging in Life of Blood and Rapine', but what most engages the reviewer is the utopian and dystopian prospect of 'the Settlement of the Pyrates upon the Island of Madagascar, and their making themselves Princes there', for good and ill.[96] The alternative ethics and politics of the pirates are remarkable, for 'tho' they are Rogues to all the World besides, they are Men of Honour to one another'.[97] Whether Defoe wrote the *General History* or not (and there is no evidence that he did and no reason to assume so) his authorship haunts the work, and his review of it—if it is indeed his review—suggests the alternative politics of piracy as a recognized theme in the work. What Defoe wrote and in what character need not concern us here, nor the identity of the real author who played the role of the pseudonymous, fictitious Captain Charles Johnson at a time when booksellers' hacks 'lay three in a bed, at the Pewter-Platter Inn in Holborn'.[98] We may notice instead that the fiction of Misson has been constructed from something resembling the fictional story of the historical Every and the rise and fall of his supposed Madagascar empire.

Indeed the second volume of the *General History*, opening with the entirely fictional but credible Misson, follows events on Madagascar as a kind of plot, a thread of continuity to connect the otherwise episodic and sporadic lives of its sometimes real and historical pirates. The real, historical pirates themselves—in so far as we can follow their traces in more reliable sources—do seem to have led lives that were interconnected on Madagascar itself, as well as in Grub Street, by their shifting alliances, by their ships and shore bases, social institutions that inevitably intertwined and entangled the individual pirates. If we follow as best we can the historical traces of one or two actual pirates, we can observe the subculture of these pirates, who were colonists by another name, as Swift satirically and correctly noticed in *Gulliver's Travels* (1726):

A Crew of Pyrates are driven by a Storm they know not whither, at length a Boy discovers land from the Top-mast, they go on Shore to Rob and Plunder;...And this execrable Crew of Butchers employed in so pious an Expedition, is a *modern Colony*....[99]

It is in the mundane, sequential facts of the real pirate-colonists' lives—their itineraries, their alliances, their punctilious lists of crazy cargoes of trade and loot, their imprisonments—that we can glimpse the real, non-fictional history of piracy. In his *Cruising Voyage* of 1712 Woodes Rogers had reported, at second hand, that the Madagascar pirates, 'those miserable Wretches, who had made such a Noise in the World', and who were celebrated on stage that year at Drury Lane in *The Succesful Pyrate*, were meanwhile in Madagascar 'poor and despicable, even to the Natives'.[100] They possessed 'but one Ship, and a Sloop that lay sunk'.[101] Truly, 'those Pirates are so inconsiderable, that they scarce deserve to be mentioned'.[102] So the real lives of the pirates in Madagascar did not match their reputations in London, according to Rogers's informants, but it is in first-hand evidence, not second-hand, in ordinary, not imaginary glimpses of these Madagascar pirates that we can observe both them and their relation to their ghostly counterparts, written in inconsiderable Grub Street.

When Kidd was left ashore at Antigua in February 1690, his ship which sailed away from him was captained by a William Mason and crewed by at least two sailors who would meet again at Saint Mary's, Samuel Burgess and Robert Culliford.[103] After some petty piracies in the Caribbean, '400 peices of eight, severall boxes of sweet meats worth about 30 li. [£30], and eight black men', Kidd's men 'sold their blacks for 20 li. [£20] a peece' and sold Kidd's ship, the *Blessed William*, in New York, then transferred to another captured vessel they named the *Jacob*, and sailed for the Indian Ocean, where Burgess was unloaded at Madagascar 'upon a discovery of cheating', according to Culliford, and where Culliford himself defected at Mangalore, India.[104] In 1696 he was aboard the East India Company ship *Josiah* when the men mutinied and he emerged as captain. He then mysteriously reappears in a canoe with two other sailors from the *Josiah* at the Nicobar Islands, and is taken prisoner by the suspicious captain of a passing ship, who was then compelled by the pirates aboard another ship, the *Mocha*, to release him, whereupon he joined his fortunes with the *Mocha*.[105] Aboard that ship were the pirate captain, Ralph Stout, and the quartermaster, James Kelly, who had both been captured by an Indian Nawab who had supposedly converted them to Islam, a process that involved circumcision.[106] They were subsequently aboard the *Mocha*, another East India Company ship which had mutinied in 1696, its captain killed 'while [he] was asleep', allegedly by James Kelly, who 'had turned Moor, and was circumcised', according to the regular word, spoken here by William Cuthbert, ship's gunner.[107]

Meanwhile a Richard Shivers or Chivers, a Dutch New Yorker, had been chosen by a pirate crew to captain another ship called the *Resolution* (and other names) and was reported at Calicut seizing and ransoming ships there in November 1696, declaring in his blustering negotiations that he and his men 'acknowledged no countrymen, that they had sold their country and were sure to be hanged if taken, and that they would take no quarter, but do all the mischief they could'.[108] Somewhat thwarted, for all his bluster, Chivers sailed for the Dutch-controlled island of Mauritius and then to Saint Mary's.

In the Nicobar Islands the *Mocha*, commanded by Ralph Stout, joined forces with the *Charming Mary*, which had been pirating with some of Tew's men and others, and together the two pirate ships sunk an English ship of 500 tons, the *Satisfaction*, 'with a rich Cargoe of Sugar', in January 1696, and plundered a Dutch ship, whose master reported that the *Mocha* 'has now 125 English, Dutch and French'.[109] William Willock, the captain of the sunken *Satisfaction*, was kept a prisoner aboard the *Mocha* for 11 months, until 22 December 1697. He reported later that the *Mocha* and the *Charming Mary* took in February 1697 a Portuguese ship, 'richly laden, with at least 100lb. weight of gold and 2,300 pieces of silk'.[110] Later that month 'they captured a large Moor's ship' and sailed to the Maldives, where they ransacked and 'burned several villages' and quarrelled amongst themselves, according to Willock, with the result that the *Mocha* separated from the *Charming Mary* at the end of April.[111] Then on 5 June the *Mocha* took another Portuguese ship with 'a cargo worth 40,000 dollars' but, 'while that ship was robbing [being robbed] Capt. Ralph Stout going ashoare...to fetch water wth. 12 men, hee with 7 men were Cutt off by the Malays, upon which Colivei...was chosen Commander'.[112]

Later that June 1697, the *Mocha*, under Culliford's command, sighted an English ship, the *Dorrill*, in the Malacca Straits. Willock reports events from the *Mocha*:

Hell was never in greater confusion than was then aboard the Pyrate, some being for fighting under French Collours, some for shewing no Collours and some for not fighting at all. The Captain [Culliford] laid down his charge, because of such confusion. Then 'bout ship they go to choose another Captain...At length they concluded to fight, and the Captain [Culliford] resumed his place again.[113]

William Reynolds, supercargo aboard the *Dorrill* (in charge of its cargo and commercial transactions), described this erratic behaviour from his point of view. The *Mocha* came within range of the *Dorrill* and hoisted 'the Union Jack & lett fly a broad red Pendent at their maintopmast head'.[114] They then sailed parallel with the *Dorrill*, then veered off and three hours later approached the *Dorrill* again. There were some probing but not explicitly hostile questions between the two ships, about names and destinations, and the *Mocha* gave 'their Capts name Collyford'.[115]

The next day the *Mocha* continued to menace the *Dorrill*, and Reynolds recorded some more exchanges between the ships. A 'Hellish Imp'

who was 'wearing a Sword' on the Quarter Deck of the *Mocha* 'cryed
Strike [i.e. surrender] you Doggs, which [we] perceived was not by a
generall consent, for he was called away'.[116] In response the *Dorrill's* Boatswain 'in a fury run upon the Poop unknown to the Capt. & answered,
that wee wo'd strike to noe such Doggs as hee, telling him the Rogue
Every & his Accomplices were all hanged'.[117] The *Dorrill's* Captain now
reasserted his authority, asking the hellish imp 'what was his reason to
Dogg us'?[118] Another man on the *Mocha* now stepped forward, 'becken-
ing with his hand and said, Gentlemen, Wee want not your Ship nor men,
but money'.[119] 'That's well', replied the *Dorrill*.[120] 'Come and take it.'[121] At
this 'a percell of bloud hound rogues' on the *Mocha* 'clasht their Cutlassess,
& said they would have it or our hearts bloud'.[122] 'Do you not know us
to be the Moca?' they asked.[123] 'Yes, Yes', was the answer from the *Dorrill*.[124] The pirates gave three cheers at this, both ships opened fire, and the
Dorrill, as Reynolds says, 'gave them better than [they] did like', particularly several broadsides, with the result that Willock

could see the Pyrates become disheartened. Said they 'Here we shall get nothing but broken bones, and if we lose a mast, where shall we get another!' they
having received a great shott right in the heart of the foremast going clean
through. Says the Pyrate Captain [Culliford], 'We have wind enough, let us go
about ship and take him, for he lies by for us'. Says one, 'You may put her
about yourself an you will, for I'll fight no more.' 'Nor I', says another, which
then became the general cry.[125]

   The *Dorrill* defied the *Mocha*, then, but at some cost: the *Dorrill's*
mizzen mast was shot away, much of her rigging, her main yard was 'by
a Shott cutt 8 Inches deep', and another shot had penetrated the bread
room, opening a leak which ruined most of the store of bread.[126] The
human cost should not be forgotten: the Gunner's boy, Thomas Math-
ews, and the Quartermaster each lost a leg, and the Boatswain's boy,
George Mopp, aged 13, 'was shott into the Thigh which went through
& splindered his bone'.[127] In the following days the Gunner's and the
Boatswain's boys both died, as did two other sailors of their wounds.
Aboard the *Mocha* two were killed and Culliford sailed in search of
more susceptible prey, releasing Willock to tell his tale, and sailing the
Mocha back to Saint Mary's in March, 1698, to greet Kidd and share a
cup of bumbo. Most of Kidd's men transferred to the *Mocha* at Saint
Mary's, but at least one crewman of the *Mocha*, James Kelly, alias Gillam,
transferred to Kidd's command.

In May or June 1698, a Theophilus Turner, aboard a French ship at the island of Johanna, plundered by the *Mocha* for 'about Two Thousand pounds in money, besides wine Cloath and Hatts', was taken aboard Culliford's ship, now reinforced with defectors from Kidd's crew, and so Turner was sailing as a captive when the *Mocha* met with another pirate ship off the coast of India, commanded by Richard Chivers.[128] The two ships 'consorted' and took 'a Turkey Ship' from Surat, the *Great Mahomet*, on 23 September 1698, from which they stole, according to Culliford himself:

40,000 Thousand [*sic*] peices of Arabian Gould, about 60,000li [pounds], one thousand ounces of Gould, value 30,000 li, about 250,000 peices of 8, value 10,000 li., 3 Chests of Corall, vallue, 300 li., 2 Bales containing Beades and Dragons Blood [red plant resins], value 200 li.[129]

Two of the defectors from Kidd's crew who would later be witnesses against him, Brandinham and Palmer, were also participants in the taking of the *Great Mahomet*, Palmer reporting, under Examination in London, that there were horses aboard the captured ship. The pirates, he said,

turned the horses over board to swim on shore and also turned ashore allmost all the rest of the People except some few Lascars [Indian sailors] which they kept onbd. that ... came from India way & Turks and Moors [probably Arabs] and a pretty many weomen .[130]

Palmer's flowing sentence does not go on to describe the fate of these captured men and women, but Samuel Annesley, of the East India Company at Surat, passed on to his company the complaints of the *Great Mahomet*'s owner, that the pilgrims aboard his ship were 'turned adrift in the ships boats, without Oars, sail or Provisions', and that 'about sixty' women passengers 'were kept aboard, and inhumanely abused to avoid wch indignity five stabbed themselves'.[131] 'The Treasure Goods and Horses in the ship were computed to be worth 18,50000 Rups [rupees]', he added.[132] To what extent these reports by the pillaged ship's owner and the East India Company were made as demands for protection and compensation is a matter for speculation, but it is certain, as Palmer stated, that the pirates took the *Great Mahomet* to replace Chivers's ship, which they sunk, and they are reported to have shared the proceeds of the looting, which amounted to 'about Seven or eight hundred pounds a man'.[133] In consort with Chivers's new command, the ship 'he had taken from the Turks, having 22 Guns and being a bigger Ship than the Moco', the reluctant Turner sailed aboard the *Mocha* to Saint Mary's, where they arrived about Christmas 1698.[134]

Culliford's old shipmate on the *Jacob*, Samuel Burgess, had meanwhile rejoined at Madagascar the *Jacob* which had dismissed him there for cheating, and had returned in her to New York where the crew gave her to the Governor, Fletcher, Bellomont's more flexible predecessor, as a placatory present.[135] Burgess then went into the employ of Frederick Philipse, the wealthy New York trader and slaver, for whom he captained the *Margaret* to Madagascar for slaves to be supplied by Philipse's Saint Mary's agent, Adam Baldridge. A letter he carried to Baldridge conveyed Philipse's grumbles and protests at Baldridge's previous consignment of 1693 (particularly of humans: 'Itt is by negroes that I finde my chievest Profitt. All other Trade I onely look upon as by the by').[136] Instead of sending 'two hundered negroes or more', Baldridge had failed miserably:

of the 34. negroes that you putt aboard, there were 15 of them Childeren. 3. yet Sucking. And the Iron you sent was almoste Eat up with Rust; and the Alloways [alloys?] of little or no vallew here. For no body wil give any thing for itt.[137]

Presumably Philipse's 'cheif designe...for Negores' was better satisfied by Burgess's 1695–97 voyage, as Burgess was required to sail for Saint Mary's once more in June 1698.[138] To this purpose, 'to dispose thereof for negores &c.', Burgess was provided at New York with a meticulously listed cargo which included '1 Brass blunderbluss...24 Black hatts...100 paire of Pumps...11 hogsheads of Rum...2 Barrils Lime Juice'.[139]

Philipse did not have a monopoly on trade with Saint Mary's. Before Burgess reached the island in January 1699, it had been visited by another pirate, Giles Shelley, captain of the *Nassau*, who reported to his owner or agent in New York, Stephen Delaney, that at

St. Marie's on Madagasacar...I sold your goods for 17 bales of muslin, fine and coarse, and 24 bales of white calicoes, one ton of elephants' teeth, about 2 or 3 cwt. of opium, one bale of painted calicoes, &c., which goods I have on board.[140]

Back in New York, Governor Bellomont was informed, correctly or not, that at Saint Mary's this Shelley sold rum, which cost but 2s. per gallon at N.York, for 50s. and £3 per gallon at Madagascar, and a pipe of Madeira wine, which cost him £19 at N.York he sold there for £300. Strong liquors and gunpowder and ball are the commodities that go off there to best advantage.[141]

With this Madagascar trade, he complained, 'N.York will abound with gold. 'Tis the most beneficial trade, that to Madgascar with the pirates, that ever was heard of, and I believe there's more got that way than by turning pirates and robbing'.[142]

Shelley, trader not robber, had also taken on some passengers at Saint Mary's, from whom he received payment 'for their passage, &c., about 12,000 picces of eight and about 3,000 Lyon dollars'.[143] About 29 of these passengers were bound for America, including the reluctant pirate, Theophilus Turner, and one Darby Mullins, who had come to Saint Mary's with Kidd and would hang with him at Wapping, and Bradinham and Palmer, who would testify against Kidd at the Old Bailey. Some of Shelley's passengers were arrested on arrival at Cape May, New Jersey, by Jeremiah Basse, the Deputy Governor, who reported that they 'confess that [they] have been on the coast of India and have taken several prizes there'.[144] Two of them had loot, which Basse thoughtfully inspected: 'In their chests are about 7,800 Rix dollars and Venetians [silver and gold coins], about thirty pound of melted silver, a parcel of Arabian and Christian gold, some necklaces of amber and coral, sundry pieces of India silks'.[145]

Bellomont suspected Jeremiah Basse of hoping to acquire this loot for himself—and perhaps Bellomont was right—but later that year the punctilious Governor was able to capture the reported murderer of the East India Company captain of the *Mocha*. James Kelly, alias Gillam, who had quitted the *Mocha* at Saint Mary's, where he 'left the Ship, and Dwelt on Shore', had sailed to America with Kidd, only to be traced to Boston, Massachusetts, in November 1699, by way of his mare, which was identified 'tied up in the yard' of a Boston inn, and then by way of information about his whereabouts, revealed by the wife of a former Madagascar pirate.[146] By these means and some luck, as Bellomont acknowledged—such that 'one would believe there was a strange fatality in that m[an's] Starrs'—the supposed murderer of the captain of the *Mocha* was caught 'in the dark', returning after 'treating [entertaining] young women', and was conclusively identified when Bellomont 'had him search'd by a [Su]rgeon and also by a Jew in this Town, to know if he were Circumcised, and they have both declar'd on oath that he is'.[147] He was taken to London on the same ship as Kidd, tried for piracy, denied killing the *Mocha*'s captain, was found guilty, wrote his brief story at Newgate, which he signed 'the unfortunate, James Kelly', and was hanged for piracy on 12 July 1700.[148]

Back at Madagascar in 1699, as Shelley informed his New York agent—no doubt with some satisfaction, 'Captain Burges arrived at St. Marie's that day I sailed from thence'.[149] When Burgess in the *Margaret* did reach Saint Mary's that day, 9 January 1699, he found that Baldridge was no longer there, having sailed in a brigantine that eventually reached New York, but Burgess found another old acquaintance in a new ship, the frigate *Mocha*, 'the one called the moco frigot Commanded by Robard Colloford', who later testified that he had purchased 'the greatest part' of the *Margaret*'s trade goods, including 'small armes powder shott', and paid with 'about 6800 peices of eight'.[150] According to Theophilus Turner, the reluctant passenger aboard the *Mocha*, another pirate ship was present, Chiver's prize, the *Great Mahomet*. Turner gives a firsthand account of Saint Mary's, where there was

a Ship on Ground said to be brought in there by Capt. Kidd & reputed to be taken from the Moors or Turks and at the time of the Capture was Commanded by a Dutch man. There was likewise the bottom [the hull] of the Adventure Galley in which Capt. Kidd sailed from New York and the Ribbs of one other Turkish Ship taken either by Capt. Hoare or Capt. Glover [known pirates who used Saint Mary's]. There is no fortifications at St. Marys but Edwd Welch [Baldridge's successor] has 6 Guns at his House which have no Command of the place where the Shipping lye. At this place of St. Marys Fort live Capt Culliford and Capt Sivers [Chivers] who pretends to be a Dutchman. There, is one John Swann, a great Consort of Culliford [reputedly homosexual] & who lives with him; Also there are near an hundred English French and Dutch which use that island.[151]

When Burgess sailed from Madagascar again, the *Margaret* carried several paying white passengers from Saint Mary's, including Richard Chivers, and more than a hundred profitable black slaves.[152] On this return voyage, however, the *Margaret* was boarded at the Cape of Good Hope on 18 December 1699, by order of Matthew Lowth, commander of an East India Company ship, the *Loyal Merchant*, who possessed a licence, a 'Commission', to hunt pirates. Burgess protested that he was a legal and legitimate slaver, but the *Margaret*, Lowth noticed, 'was full of White men' as well as black.[153] So Lowth arrested Burgess and all the whites aboard the *Margaret*, put them in irons aboard the *Loyal Merchant*, and impounded a treasure for future historians, piles of documentary evidence of the bureaucracy of piracy, to which Lowth made his own gleeful contribution, a list of 'goods found on board the *Margaret* Prize December the 19 1699', including:

all Coynes in the Universe...
an English shipps bell
a very large English copper
One hundred Negroes
3 casks Cochineil.[154]

Two days later at the Cape, on 20 December, according to Lowth's poorly punctuated Journal,

appeared another small Vessell wch came in I sent for the Master whose name was Thomas Warren in the Vine pink [a small sailing vessel with a narrow stern] come from St Maries &c & has aboard 14 Pyrates or as he calls them Passengers whose of [of whom] Capt Culliford that was Commander of the Mocoa was one.[155]

Warren 'threw down one of his Majesties Proclamations' of pirate pardons in front of Lowth, who in return showed 'him my Commission' to hunt pirates and 'ordered him into Irons'.[156] The next day, however, Lowth was more impressed by Warren's credentials, releasing him from his irons and releasing also his ship, the *Vine*, and its passengers, so that Lowth and Warren 'parted good friends', according to Lowth.[157] A separate series of events had led to this clash of naval and commercial authorities at the Cape.

The Council of Trade and Plantations wrote to King William on 13 January 1698, reporting that it had spoken to a Captain Warren (the father of the commander of the *Vine*) and to the East India Company, but had not found out much about Saint Mary's (perhaps because that Captain Warren had never been there): 'we have been unable to obtain any information as to the fort or settlement at St. Mary's beyond that given by Captain Warren'.[158] They concluded that, 'if your Majesty be satisfied as to the existence of this settlement', they proposed sending a small naval squadron 'to offer your pardon to all pirates who will surrender' and to attack any who 'refuse to submit'.[159] The Council renewed its resolution the following month, as they had heard that 'the pirates in the East Indies do resort to St. Mary near Madagascar, where they are supplied by one Baldridge (who has made himself the head of a disorderly rabble of Europeans and natives)'.[160] While the King and Council deliberated, some garbled news of the indigenous attack on

Saint Mary's in July 1697 (as reported by Baldridge) was received in England in September 1698, 'there being but 40 men in the fort, which the islanders cut to peices, and seized their vast treasure', and Warren's mission was considered unnecessary.[161] A squadron did nevertheless set out, early the following year, 1699, with Warren in command, and a distracting duty, to convey an ambassador to India. Thus distracted, Warren sent his son in the *Vine* to communicate the pardon to whatever pirate remnants were still left at Saint Mary's. His son, also named Thomas, reported that he reached Saint Mary's in August 1699 'and the next Day one Robert Cullover attended with Severall Negro Servants came on Board the said Ship Vine' and inquired about the pardon.[162] On 8 September 1699, Robert Culliford and 16 others signed or placed their mark (as did his consort, John Swanes, and eight illiterate others) on Culliford's petition to Captain Warren, requesting that he 'Carry us as pasingers to any parte of his Majisties Dominions' so that 'wee may as soon as posible testifye ower Selves obedient Subjects to his Most gracious Majistye'.[163]

Culliford was free of Lowth's clutches at the Cape, therefore, when Lowth recognized Warren's naval authority, but Burgess's cargo of black slaves for Philipse in New York, a commodity which Lowth called 'my Slaves out of the Prize', was sold by Lowth at the Cape (with some slaves as bribes to the Dutch authorities, who also had a profitable role in this squabble) and Burgess himself and his white passengers had to travel with Lowth's *Loyal Merchant* to Bombay, where they were 'confined in the Castle Prison' and where Chivers died, before Burgess was returned to England, reaching Marshalsea prison on 29 August 1701.[164] Unfortunately for Culliford, whose voyage to England was not interrupted by a voyage to Bombay, his pardon was considered flawed (signed after its expiry date) and he was placed in Newgate and questioned for testimony about piracy.[165] In particular it was noted by the authorities that 'there is no other Evidence agst Burgess' but that 'Captn Collover cannot be brought as a Witness against him upon his Tryal unless he is first Pardoned'.[166] This legal process must have been understood by Culliford himself, whose 'Examination' at Newgate on 2 October 1701 specifies that 'he was formerly very well acquainted with the said Burges,...from whom he lately received a letter since he [Burgess] has been a prisoner in the Marshalsea, desireing the Examinant [Culliford] not to owne that he knew him'.[167] Judicial circles turned and a legal advisor to the Lord High Admiral wrote on 2 April 1702 that

> it being…certified by her majesties Advocates and Councill that the Said Culliford was a necessary witness against other Pirates in custody and that such Pirates cannot well be brought to tryall without his evidence, I am [of the] opinion that it may be for his Majesties Service to pardon the Said Culliford, if her Majesty in her Royal Wisdom shall think meet.[168]

With Queen Anne's approval, presumably, Culliford was duly pardoned but, a few months later, Burgess was pardoned also, with some help from the Philipse family.[169] Culliford vanishes from sight into the streets of London and Burgess took a post as first lieutenant aboard one of two ships led by William Dampier, bound for the Pacific, but was put in command of a French ship taken near Tenerife in the Canaries, turning up in November 1703 with this—not very plausible—explanation in Delaware Bay, from where he slips temporarily from view.[170]

Meanwhile another British punitive expedition achieved little. Two ships sent in 1703 to deal with the Madagascar pirates captured a couple of men, David Williams and John Pro, a Dutchman, who then escaped together by canoe in the Comoro Islands.[171] A better source of information is provided by way of the wreck in 1703 of a leaking ship returning from Bengal, run ashore on the southern tip of Madagascar. Most of its crew were massacred but a few survived, including a young boy, Robert Drury, who assimilated into and moved between various Malagasy tribes, walking vast distances 'singing Madagascar Songs; for I had forgot to sing in English', and living as a Madagascar man until rescued by a slaving ship, the *Drake*, in 1716.[172]

Reclothed, barbered, and reconstituted as an Englishman, Drury accompanied his new captain, William Mackett, to Masselage on the north-west coast of Madagascar, where they hoped to buy slaves from the local king, Deaan Toakoffu, known to the English as 'Long Dick' or 'King Dick'.[173] Drury travelled upriver to the king's town where he learned that the king was away at war, but that 'There were four white Men liv'd there, who came from the Island of St. Mary's'.[174] He is further informed that 'they have liv'd here some Years; Their Names are Capt. Burgess, Zachary, John Pro, and Nick'.[175] He meets two of them, one of whom affords us a portrait of a retired pirate, actually the man who was captured in the punitive expedition of 1703 and escaped by canoe in February 1704:

One was a Dutchman, named John Pro, who spoke good English; he was dress'd in a short Coat with some broad Plate-buttons, and other Things agreeable, but without Shoes or Stockings: In his Sash stuck a Brace of Pistols, and one in his Hand . . . [He] liv'd in a very handsome Manner, his House was furnish'd with Pewter Dishes, &c., a standing Bed with Curtains, and other Things of that Nature except Chairs; but a Chest or two serv'd for that Use well enough: He had one House on Purpose for his Cook-room and Cook-slave's Lodging, Store-house and Summer-house; all these enclos'd in a Palli-sade, as the great Mens Houses are in this Country; For he was rich, had many Cattle and Slaves.[176]

When Drury meets the other man, also armed with three pistols, 'Nick look'd me earnestly in the Face, and at length took hold of my Hand, saying, "Robert Drury, how have you done these many Years?"'[177] He is Nicholas Dove, one of the four other boys saved with Drury from the massacre of most of the ship's company, more than 13 years previously. He tells Drury of the pirate life he had lived since they last met, cruising mostly in pursuit of 'the Moors' (Muslim ships), with much profitable loot, which they used to carry to Saint Mary's: 'This Place they made their Settlement and general Rendez-vous, there being a good Harbour.'[178] Enriched, and their ship 'growing old and crazy [decrepit]', they moved to the mainland of Madagascar, where they made a carpenter, Thomas Collins, their Governor, built a small fort and 'liv'd most dissolute and wicked Lives, stealing away, and ravishing the Wives and Daughters of the Natives'.[179] Under the regime of this Thomas Collins (who may or may not have been a member of Every's crew) 'they had liv'd without going out a Pyrating for nine Years', before moving to the territory of Deaan Toakoffu.[180]

Drury also meets Zachary and Samuel Burgess, who has found his way back to Madagascar from Marshalsea (via Delaware Bay and other points unknown), but Drury does not say much about them, except that Burgess has possession of a sloop, which he uses for slaving.[181] Deaan Toakoffu returns home in a month from his battles, instigating many ceremonies and presenting Drury with 'a Girl of twelve Years old, which I sold immediately to John Pro'.[182] Despite the delay, Dru-ry's Captain Mackett achieved his full 'Cargo of Slaves' and Robert Drury returned to London in 1717, later to write and publish his *Journal* (1729), recently rescued from the expanding and now contracting canon of works attributed to Defoe.[183]

Drury's recollections are now generally credited (and not considered fiction by Defoe) and can provide a glimpse by chance of pirate life on Madagascar in 1716–17. The *General History*, although similarly expelled from the canon of Defoe, is less consistently reliable but does corroborate, or match, some of the detail accidentally encountered by Drury. The confusion of pirates' lives in the second volume of the *General History*—naturally endemic because of changing alliances, locations, ships' companies—is given some narrative coherence by the continuing story of Madagascar (the persistent presence), and this story does locate Burgess on the island at the right time for Drury's chance encounter. According to the *General History*, Burgess found his way back to Madagascar and for a few months inhabited a house on Saint Mary's, but tended to be based thereafter at Masselage, frequently slaving.[184] Drury mentions Burgess's being engaged in some business by Captain Mackett, on behalf of another ship, the *Henry*, and something very similar is described in the *General History*, in which Burgess was sent by the captain of the *Henry* to complain to the king, Deaan Toakoffu, about the delay in supplying slaves.[185] This disrespectful behaviour was resented by Deaan Toakoffu, according to the *General History*, with the result, perhaps, that Burgess was

carried to Dinner with some of the principal Blacks, and drank very plentifully with them of Honey Toke [an indigenous alcohol], in which it is supposed he was poison'd, for he fell ill and died soon after....[186]

This conjectured ('supposed') ending to the story 'Of Captain Samuel Burgess' is unconfirmed and hangs in a state of uncertainty, therefore, a state perfectly characteristic of pirate history.[187]

In April 1719, on the other side of Africa, at Sierra Leone, Captain William Snelgrave's ship, the *Bird*, was captured by a small consortium of pirates, and he himself aboard her. Three pirate ships were involved in this loose alliance, threatened by sudden quarrels, ships captained by Thomas Cocklyn, Howell Davis, and 'one Le Bousse a Frenchman'.[188] *The Weekly Journal or British Gazetteer* reported this gang and their 'unheard of Cruelties', hanging Captain Plumb of the *Princess* and, 'just as if they set themselves apart to study Cruelty', hanging 'Negroes by the Legs' before shooting them.[189] Plumb was not hanged, however, and the pirates' other reported cruelties to Africans, for example, were perhaps just as falsely reported, but Snelgrave's experience was at first hand. His account of his captors is attentive to their behaviour, which manifested the disorderly culture of piracy, and shows his curiosity as well as astonishment at finding himself in a topsy-turvy world which he describes deliberately in detail. 'I would not mention such trifling Circumstances', he says, 'but that I judge they serve to shew the Humours and Temper of these sort of People'.[190] He observed, for example, the piratical practice with the captured alcohol aboard the captured *Bird*:

They hoisted upon Deck a great many half Hogsheads of Claret, and French Brandy; knock'd their Heads out, and dipp'd Canns and Bowls into them to drink out of: And in their Wantonness threw full Buckets of each sort upon one another. As soon as they had emptied what was on Deck, they hoisted up more: And in the evening washed the Decks with what remained in the Casks.[191]

The bottled alcohol was disposed of with the same customary alacrity. They did not trouble to remove the corks, 'but nick'd the Bottles, as they called it, that is struck their necks off with a Cutlace'.[192]

When Snelgrave's own personal timepiece, a 'very good going Gold Watch', was delivered to the pirate quartermaster, 'he held it up by the Chain, and presently laid it down on the Deck, giving it a kick with his Foot; saying, "It was a pretty Foot-ball"'.[193] Snelgrave's two large chests of books were emptied and the contents

thrown overboard; for one of the Pirates, upon opening them [the chests], swore, 'There was Jaw-work enough (as he called it) to serve a Nation, and proposed they might be cast into the Sea; for he feared, there might be some Books amongst them, that might breed Mischief enough; and prevent some of their Comrades from going on in their Voyage to Hell, whither they were all bound.' Upon which the Books were all flung out of the Cabin-windows.[194]

Most of his bundles of possessions were likewise thrown overboard, except for one, containing 'a black Suit of Cloaths' and 'a good Hat and Wig'.[195] One of the pirates opened up this remaining bundle, whacking the mildly protesting Snelgave on the shoulder with the flat of a broadsword, warning him 'never to dispute the Will of a Pirate'.[196] Snelgrave thanked him for this advice and the pirate 'put on the Clothes, which in less than half an hour after, I saw him take off and throw overboard', because 'some of the Pirates seeing him dress'd in that manner, had thrown several Buckets of Claret upon him'.[197] That evening Snelgave retained only his hat and wig from the pirates' grasp, but unpredictably 'several brought me Liquor, and Slices of Ham broiled, a Biscuit being my Plate; saying "They pitied my Condition" '.[198] A little later, however, another pirate entered the cabin. 'The Hat and Wig I had left, being hung on Pins in the Cabin, a person half-drunk came in about eight a clock at night, and put them on; telling me "He was a great Merchant on Shore, and that his name was Hogbin" '.[199] This Hogbin, in Snelgave's hat and wig, was then beaten 'very severely' by the pirate quartermaster, 'for taking things he had no Right to'.[200]

The pirate quartermaster (a petty officer) was a baffling figure of authority but the captain who was Snelgrave's captor, Thomas Cocklyn, was civil to him, and Snelgrave approved of another pirate captain, Howell Davis, 'a most generous humane person' (who was soon to die) and of Davis's second in command (and rival), John Taylor, whom Snelgrave considered 'brisk and couragious', but he did not describe the other pirate captain, the Frenchman Olivier Le Vasseur, called La Buse (the Buzzard).[201] Davis proposed offering Snelgrave, in exchange for the *Bird*, a surplus pirate ship that La Buse had moved out of, an offer Snelgrave accepted, and sailed away to tell his tale, but some of these pirates would be heard of again, especially in the Indian Ocean. Davis did not survive long enough to round the Cape. He was joined by a sailor from Plumb's *Princess*, a pirate with a fierce future, Bartholomew Roberts, who succeeded Davis when he himself was killed by order of the Portuguese Governor of the island of Principe in the Gulf of Guinea.[202] Another pirate captain, Edward England, joined the loose alliance and John Taylor became captain of another prize, named the *Victory*, while La Buse sailed into the piratical opportunities of the Indian Ocean where he wrecked his ship at Mayotte, one of the Comoro Islands near Madagascar.[203]

At nearby Johanna (or Anjouan), while La Buse was rebuilding himself a ship, two other pirate ships appeared out of the blue in August 1720, the *Fancy*, captained by Edward England, who had named his ship after Every's, and the *Victory*, John Taylor's ship. A Captain Macrae, watching these arrivals at Johanna from his own ship, the *Cassandra*, decided to fight, unsupported by the other ships at Johanna, but with some success. The *Victory*, badly hit 'betwixt Wind and Water', according to Macrae's account, retreated for some repairs but the *Fancy* fiercely resisted and Macrae, in extremis, decided to run the *Cassandra* ashore, to be followed in remorseless pursuit by the *Fancy*, which beached on higher ground than the *Cassandra*, providing more of a target, to Macrae's delight, and with its bow exposed to the guns of the *Cassandra*'s broadside.[204] The *Victory* then reinforced the *Fancy*, however, 'with three Boats full of fresh Men', and rejoined the battle herself, so that Macrae ordered his men to abandon ship in 'the Long Boat under Cover of the Smoak of our Guns'.[205] Macrae himself, although 'wounded in the Head by a Musket Ball', reached the shore as others did by boats or by swimming.[206] The pirates helped themselves to the booty on the *Cassandra*, outward bound for Bombay, with a cargo of £10,000 worth of woollens for trade and—more usefully—£25,000 of silver coin for purchasing Indian goods.[207] After a few days lurking ashore meanwhile, Macrae began negotiations with the victorious and richly-rewarded pirates, who agreed to let him have the badly-damaged *Fancy* in return for the *Cassandra*, to which England and his men transferred.

Macrae was thus able to set off in the *Fancy* on a perilous voyage to Bombay, but one of his men, Richard Lasinby, was retained as a captive aboard England's new pirate ship, witnessing various routine acts of piracy, including the torture of some Moorish (Indian or Arab) sailors 'by Squeezing their Joynts in the vice', in the hope of learning of any hidden money.[208] Under Lasinby's unfavourable gaze the pirates also sailed to one of the Laccadive Islands, where the local men fled the village that the pirates invaded, the men leaving behind

only Abundance of Women & Children, which they [the pirates] found a day or two afterwards, hid in the Bushes; and forct them in Barbarous Manner, to their lascivious Inclinations; Destroying their Cocoa-trees and every thing they mett wth., setting fire to severall of their Houses & Churches.[209]

England and Taylor then proceeded to Cochin, where they took a small English ship with a captain who was 'very drunk' and reported a false rumour that Macrae was preparing a fleet to chase the pirates, who took out their rage at the perfidious Macrae on convenient Lasinby, who reported later that Captain Taylor 'fetcht his Cane and began to Labour me unmercifully', until dissuaded by other, more merciful pirates.[210]

The pirates knew no boundaries but sailed in waters shared by various colonial and commercial prevailing powers. The European nations competing for the eighteenth-century Eastern trade operated via national mercantile companies—the British East India Company and its Portuguese, Dutch, and French equivalents—with some local political and military powers to aid and abet their exchanges of a few national manufactures (such as British woollens) and a lot more hard cash in silver coins for the 'India goods', chiefly calico, muslin, and silks, and also, potentially, Arabian coffee, Malabar pepper (for food preservation in lieu of refrigeration), and China tea. (As Voltaire observed, 'Le superflu, chose très nécessaire, a réuni l'un et l'autre hémisphère': 'The superfluous, that very necessary thing, has joined our world's two halves in one'.[211])

Back at Cochin, where the Dutch were established, the pirates were supplied by a Dutchman, 'bringing with him a large Boat with Arrack which they Receiv'd with Abundance of Joy'.[212] They supplied the cooperative local Governor with 'a fine Table Clock' that had come with the *Cassandra* and supplied the helpful Dutchman with a generous fee, with three cheers and with handfuls of ducatoons (the silver coins taken with the *Cassandra*) tossed into his boat.[213] The pirates then debated whether to make for Madagascar or to cruise in search of a lucrative Moorish ship. Deciding on the latter course, they celebrated Christmas in pirate style, carousing for 'near 3 days', after which they proposed to go to the island of Mauritius to repair one of their ships which was leaking.[214] They reached Mauritius in February 1721 and— unreported by Lasinby—were joined by La Buse, with whom they sailed for 'the island Mascarine', the nearby French-controlled island now called Réunion.[215]

Taylor and Edward England in the *Cassandra* and La Buse in the *Victory* appeared at the harbour of Saint-Denis on Réunion on 8 April, only to find, as Lasinby later recorded:

a large 70 Gun Portugueze, whom they Immediately took with very little Resistance, She haveing lost all her Masts & likewise Guns save 21 in a Storm they had mett with . . . She had on Board when they took her the Vice Roy of Goa & severall other Gentlemen that were Passengers.[216]

A Frenchman, François Duval, gives a more detailed account of this event, written, Duval claims, with the help of the Vice Roy himself, the Count d'Ericeira, who mounted in his and Duval's account a gallant defence of his ship, *Nostra Senhora de Cabo*, cyclone-damaged, under-manned, and under repair, to which the two pirate ships were heading in a stiff breeze, flying black flags emblazoned with sculls.[217] Supported on the bridge of the *Nostra Senhora* by a handful of surviving and unflinching men, the valiant Vice Roy, dangerously distinctive in his scarlet clothing, his swordblade heroically broken, was sur-rounded by pirates who knocked him over, still fighting with his cane, and would have killed him if John Taylor had not shouted an order to save him. The Vice Roy was taken aboard the *Cassandra* and treated civilly, while La Buse and England negotiated a ransom with him over dinner, England demanding 2,000 piastres (Spanish-American dol-lars). The Vice Roy suggested he write to the French Governor of Réunion asking if the necessary funds could be supplied, a letter which La Buse delivered. The ransom duly arrived and the pirates sent the Vice Roy ashore to his expensive freedom in a specially capari-soned boat, with a 21 gun salute.

The pirates' other prisoner, Richard Lasinby, who was released with the Vice Roy, gives a below-decks version of the negotiations, which were preceded by 'a Great Caball among the Pyrates on the Vice Roys Acct.', some wishing to sail away with him and thereby perhaps increase the potential ransom, others arguing for a smaller but immediate ran-som, which was finally agreed at '2000 Dollars'.[218] Lasinby says, how-ever, that the Vice Roy told him of the value of something that exceeded that of the Vice Roy himself: the diamonds, proceeds of the Vice Roy's private trading, that the pirates found aboard the *Nostra Senhora*, which 'were to the Value of Between three & four Millions of Dollars'.[219] Whatever these figures in financial reality, in the first quar-ter of the eighteenth century and in the middle of the Indian Ocean, in piastres or in dollars, the *Senhora* was legendarily and perhaps truly the greatest pirate prize of the golden age.

The taking of the Vice Roy, told in different ways by sources at first hand, soon generated legends, such as the anecdote repeated as true by the future author of *Paul et Virginie*, Bernardin de Saint-Pierre, an anec-dote which features La Buse, although he is not named. According to Bernardin de Saint-Pierre's *Voyage* (1773), the Vice Roy was dining with the French Governor of Réunion when the pirate captain (by implication La Buse) joined them at the table, declaring politely, affa-bly, that the Vice Roy was now his prisoner and demanding a ransom of 'mille piastres' ('a thousand piastres').[220] 'C'est trop peu' ('that's too little') responded the Governor, suggesting that the Vice Roy should be ransomed for more than that, or for nothing.[221] 'For nothing, then', the pirate gallantly replied.[222]

There was no such gallantry in Réunion in 1721 but a lot of money, which was made by the pirates who sailed away, aboard the *Victory*, the

Cassandra, and the *Nostra Senhora*, with 200 slaves taken from their Portuguese owners on the *Nostra Senhora*, 200 Africans from Mozambique, destined for the Portuguese colony of Brazil, but whose new destinations and destinies are unknown.[223] Unlike piracy, slavery was legal as well as profitable, for colonists and pirates alike. At the island of Saint Mary, the pirates burned the *Victory*, careened the *Cassandra* and refitted the *Nostra Senhora*. According to one witness, the second mate of another pirate prize, 'they buried at St. Mary's abt. 80 men' at this time, but no reason is given.[224] Captains, ships and ships' names are in flux at this point and hard to tell. The *General History* told the tale 'Of Captain England' via the published letters of Macrae and the unpublished report of Lasinby, with a few embellishments, such as a probably imaginary anecdote about a pirate who received one large diamond as the equivalent of the 42 smaller ones allocated per pirate and consequently split his large one into 43 pieces, to outdo his fellow-pirates. Exactly what happened to Edward England is not reliably written and is therefore hard to know, but Taylor and La Buse, in the *Nostra Senhora* and the *Cassandra*, sailed together out of the harbour at Saint Mary's and in May 1721 at the south of Madagascar they captured a French ship, *La Duchesse de Noailles*, anchored awaiting slaves to be delivered by the local king.[225] The *Duchesse* was pillaged and also burned, for which La Buse would not be forgiven by the French colony at Réunion.[226]

Disputes were reported between Taylor and La Buse by a resentful French captive from the *Duchesse*, but in April 1722—perhaps steering clear of a British naval mission to seek out the Madagascar pirates—they jointly captured a Dutch fort at Mozambique, abducting a Dutch official, Jacob de Bucquoy, who reported that he shared Taylor's cabin, in which he witnessed that the pirate captain

would frequently awake with a start as if seized with terror, utter some horrible blasphemies, reach out for his pistols hanging close at hand, sit up, look all around him and, seeing that no danger threatened him, lie down again.[227]

Jacob de Bucquoy was released and Taylor and the *Cassandra* are next heard of a year later in May 1723 in the Caribbean, seeking a pardon, apparently. They were claiming 'that they can divide in Silver and Gold £1200 a Man & ... have a great Value aboard in Diamonds'.[228] A month later, the news from Portobello, Panama, via a British captain, was that the pirates of the *Cassandra* had received a Spanish not a British pardon

and 'were selling their Diamonds and India Goods'.[229] Taylor's former
captive, Jacob de Bucquoy, reported later news from an informant,
which may or may not be true, that Taylor (no doubt with some help
from his diamonds) had acquired a wife and four children, a plantation
in Cuba, a trading vessel, and in 1744 'was still living the miserable life
which is the typical fate of famous pirates'.[230] Taylor's fate does not
seem so miserable as morality would have it, but Edward England—
according to the unreliable account of a sailor called Downing—died
in Madagascar from the 'severe Stings of his Conscience', and La Buse
we know for certain had another piratical fate.[231] Reported with some
official distaste by the French colonial authorities as one of a few miserable surviving pirates, 'unhappy, boatless degenerates', still surviving
on Saint Mary's with 'some diamonds which were useless for procur-
ing the necessities of life', diamonds which follow the plot of their
lives, La Buse was taken prisoner by a French ship, the *Méduse*, reportedly with some trickery, then tried and hanged on 17 July 1730 on the
beach at Réunion, where he had captured the *Nostra Senhora* and the
Vice Roy, an execution that closed an era, a golden age, of piracy.[232]

What tentative conclusions can we draw, then, from our observations of some real pirates in the 'golden age', pirates who are no longer
famous, like Blackbeard and Captain Kidd, but who carried out two of
the richest raids, on the *Great Mahomet* and the *Nostra Senhora*, as well
as being fought off and repelled, as the *Mocha* was by the *Dorrill*? They
certainly looted and opportunistically raped, were certainly violent but
not particularly gallant or valiant. They tortured captives for information about hidden valuables, but were otherwise not much different
from other sailors or colonists who routinely grabbed land and traded
slaves. Contrary to the arguments of some modern historians, pirates
were not political revolutionaries (unlike fictional Misson) although
they sometimes chose or changed their captains.[233] They seemed
childishly and dangerously unruly in their 'Humours and Temper', as
William Snelgrave reported, throwing buckets of claret and brandy at
each other, throwing Snelgrave's books out of the cabin windows into
the sea, dressing up in his good suit and then throwing more 'Buckets
of Claret' over it. But the pirate who stole Snelgrave's 'good Hat and
Wig' was 'very severely' beaten by another pirate, 'for taking things he
had no Right to'.

The pirates were not confederated homosexuals (although Culliford had that reputation). Nor were they cross-dressing Feminists (like

the fictionalized Bonny and Read), nor melodramatic Satanists (like the Grub Street Blackbeard). They did not make their victims walk the plank, so far as we know, nor did they bury their treasure. The plots of their lives were fluid, and they themselves more like flotsam and jetsam than most sailors and colonial traders, but we can tell something about their plots from their endings. Some of our sample of Madagascar-related pirates were executed, like 'the unfortunate, James Kelly', as he called himself, or La Buse, whose diamonds did not save him from a hanging on the beach at Réunion. Some were imprisoned and pardoned, like Culliford and Burgess, but Culliford disappeared into the streets of London and Burgess died (perhaps poisoned) in Madagascar. Chivers died in prison in Bombay but Taylor reportedly recovered from his terrifying nightmares, sold his diamonds to the Spanish and prospered as a planter in Cuba. Some of them survived to become colonists on Madagascar, rather pathetically, like those encountered in mundane reality by Robert Drury, who saw John Pro living much like a Malagasy chief, with cattle, slaves, some pistols stuck in a sash, but no shoes or stockings.

Our sample suggests that pirates were not much different from other sailors and colonists, more unruly and unscrupulous, yes, but not principled revolutionaries in their masculinity, nor their occasional femininity, nor their occasional homosexuality.[234] Golden age pirates were not the characters some modern historians are looking for: were not typically Sodomites, nor Sadists, nor Marxists, but more like enterprising opportunists, heroic in taking their chances to sail away from their social and economic circumstances and then in taking more chances to loot the owners of the legitimate colonial plunder (the slaves and diamonds of the Vice Roy of Goa, for example). Eighteenth-century piracy does not seem very distinct as a subculture. The pirates were not as savagely separate as the buccaneers, the 'frères de la côte'. Unsurprisingly, the pirates were—although mixed in their nationalities—much like other seafaring and colonizing Europeans. What is more surprising, perhaps, is that some modern historians have declared them to be different. Modern historians—like the eighteenth-century author of the *General History*—have mythologized the pirates of the golden age, have made them what they would like them to be, sexual and political liberals, but those historical pirates were not dreamers and plotters of sexual and political utopias. The historians who see them as such are like the Kwakiutl Indian in New York, looking for himself. We may draw the curtain on the Madagascar men with some reports of two sorts of conclusions that commonly came to them—primitive colonialism or pure fiction.

In 1721 the British squadron—the trouble that Taylor and La Buse avoided—left England, four naval ships under Commodore Thomas Matthews. After touching at Madagascar before continuing to India, Matthews's ships returned to the island in 1722 and visited Saint Mary's. Clement Downing, a sailor aboard the *Salisbury*, published an account some years later which described his arrival in April 1722 at the pirate island, 'where we found the Wrecks of several Ships which the Pyrates had demolished, with their Cargo's of China Ware, rich Drugs, and all sorts of Spices, lying in great heaps on the Beach.'[235] A day or two later, ashore on the mainland of Madagascar, Downing was greeted by 'a white Man'

who said his Name was James Plantain; that he was born on the Island of Jamaica, at Chocolate-Hole, and that he had been a pyrating, but had now left off, and had settled at a Place about six or seven Miles higher up, called Ranter-Bay [presumably Rantabé, a village further north, in the bay of Antongil], where he fortified himself, and was called by the Natives, King of Ranter-Bay.[236]

Plantain's settlement was visited by the naval squadron and found to consist of 'a large Number of Slaves' and some other whites who joined him in 'a very profane and debauch'd Life, indulging themselves in all manner of Wickedness'.[237] To assist this wickedness, Plantain possessed

a great many Wives and Servants, whom he kept in great Subjection; and after the English manner, called them Moll, Kate, Sue or Pegg. These Women were dressed in the richest Silks, and some of them had Diamond Necklaces. He frequently came over from his own Territories to St. Mary's Island, and there began to repair several Parts of Capt. Avery's Fortifications.[238]

Downing's historical knowledge pertains to legend rather than reality; Every probably did not visit Saint Mary's and certainly did not fortify it. The profanity and debauchery of Plantain's people notwithstanding, the naval squadron

sold them several Hogsheads and Puncheons of Arrack, and Hampers of Wine, for which they paid a very large Price, in Diamonds, and Gold Pieces of about 10s. each. We had several Cattle sent down for the Benefit of the Squadron; and Plantain himself came down and delivered his Goods and Money . . . Our People likewise sold them Hats, Shoes, Stockings, and such other Necessaries as they wanted. His House, or rather Castle, was fortified with Guns, and strongly guarded.[239]

Downing was pleased to report that the squadron successfully cheated Plantain by forcibly removing all the alcohol he had expensively purchased, 'and also several of the Blacks, who were left to guard the said Arrack'.[240] He regretted, though, that 'We were not able to suppress those Pyrates, who after they had done all the vile Actions possible, were now settled on shore amongst a parcel of Heathens, to indulge themselves in all sorts of Vice.'[241]

Downing's tale of the pirate pirated was confirmed in statements made by other seamen, inhabiting those maritime parts of London where, as an observer remarked at the time: 'a man would be apt to suspect himself in another country. Their manner of living, speaking, acting, dressing, and behaving, are so very peculiar to themselves'.[242] One Samuel Nobber, 'living next Door to the Rising Sun near Canon Street in Ratcliff high Way Mariner', testified on 21 October 1724 that, at Charnock Point near Saint Mary's on the Madagascar mainland in April 1722, a boat from H.M.S. *Lion* 'brought off the sd. Liquors & the sd. Guard (to wit) a black Man & put them on board the Lyon'.[243] Magnus Dessen, a quarter-gunner on H.M.S. *Salisbury*, of 'Blackman Street, Southwark, Mariner & aged about fourty years', gave more information about the goods sold to Plantain and stolen from him: 'a Pipe of the Arrack in 2 or 3 Puncheons & about a hundred Weight of Sugar Candy in a Bag & several dozens of glass quart Bottles of Beer'.[244] These were 'conveyed from the Shoar' in the night by the *Salisbury*'s barge and an eight-oared boat from the *Lion* '& at break of Day the next Morning they sailed from Madagascar with the sd. Pipe of Wine & Arrack on board the Lyon'.[245]

Downing's description of the navy's dealings and double-dealings with Plantain, published some time later, in 1737, is thus corroborated in its basic, unadorned state, with the subtraction of 'several' blacks and the addition of a hundredweight of sugar candy, so that we can see and believe that Plantain's settlement on Madagascar was no Libertalia. Downing's plain tale of humble Plantain was, however, incongruously supplemented by a long account Downing supplied of Plantain's previous adventures on Madagascar, particularly his love for one Eleonora Brown, child of an English sailor and of a daughter of the King of Masselage, Deaan Toakoffu, 'King Dick'. The King refused Plantain his granddaughter and Plantain, aided by a man known as Mulatto Tom and supposedly a son of Every, attacked and captured Masselage and King Dick himself. Eleonora, however, had been impregnated by one of the local pirates at Masselage, and so Plantain horribly killed King Dick (targeted by lance-throwers while he danced on hot coals) and romantically married pregnant Eleonora. Although she nagged him with her persistent Christianity, he proceeded to make himself King of Madagascar, no less, aided as ever by Mulatto Tom.[246] Even the Madagascar historians who believe in Misson cannot credit all this, which seems to have grown out of proportion to its possible historical origins in a fleeting encounter with an ex-pirate's colonial settlement.[247] This tale of Plantain takes us, then, from a few mundane facts, supported by sailors ashore in riverside London, to the recurring legend of Every, or Avery: the pirate king and his exotic princess, an irrepressible fiction.

IV

Gow, the Pirate in Transit

'There was a laughing Devil in his sneer'

(Byron, *The Corsair*, I, ix.)

John Gow was taken on at Amsterdam as Second Mate aboard the *George Galley* by the commander, Oliver Furneau, in early June 1724. The principal business of their voyage was at Santa Cruz in the Canaries, where they took aboard a cargo of beeswax for shipment to Genoa. They sailed from Santa Cruz on 3 November 1724 and that night, at about ten o'clock, a mutiny took place. Gow's later account is vague about his own role. Although he was on deck at the time that some men were killed and tossed overboard, 'the night was so dark', he said, that he could not identify the murderers.[1] When it was immediately proposed that Gow 'should be the Commander' this was simply because 'there was not any Person on board who understood Navigation but him'.[2] Other sailors' testimonies were more detailed. The boatswain, James Belbin, had heard long ago at Amsterdam of 'a Design' to 'run away with the Ship' and a Swedish sailor, Peter Rollson, speaks of 'an Agreement' between Gow and others 'to kill the Master & his Clark & the cheif Mate & Surgeon'.[3] Rollson also heard cantankerous James Williams threatening young Michael Moor 'that if he the sd. Moor did not make the Sun & Moon shine through the sd Master Mate Surgeon & Clark he the sd. Williams would make the Sun & Moon shine through him the sd. Moor'.[4]

At ten on the night of the mutiny James Belbin was asleep 'upon the topsail Sheet Bitts before the Mainmast' when he was woken by cries.[5] Going aft to investigate, he saw Winter, Peterson, and others attempting to throw the Master, Furneau, overboard. Furneau was struggling

Figure 4.1. A graphic but imaginary depiction of 'Gow killing the Captain', from *The Pirates Own Book* (1837).

desperately to keep himself aboard the ship when the Mate, Bonad-venture Jelfs, came up on deck 'and asked what was the Matter', before running below for shelter.[6] Then Belbin saw Winter and Peterson use their knives on Furneau. In particular he 'saw the sd. Winter stab the Master & draw his Knife cross his Throat & John Smith [alias Gow] the 2d Mate fired a Pistol at him, the sd. Master & then they threw him over board' (see Figure 4.1).[7] During Furneau's struggle Rollson saw the ship's Surgeon run up 'upon Deck with his Throat cut'.[8] William Melvin saw the wounded Surgeon 'drop down' by the man at the helm, and he was subsequently thrown 'over board'.[9] Melvin, who had previously heard Williams threaten Moor, then 'saw Michael Moor…shoot the Cheif Mate', who had fled below in vain.[10] The Swede Peter Rollson (not an innocent party) witnessed the ship's Clerk 'lying wounded under a Hammock & begging of the sd Williams who stood by him with a Pistol in his hand to give him time to say his Prayers'.[11] Williams 'sayd Say your Prayers & be damned & then shot him'.[12] The Clerk then joined the others overboard. These disposals were immediately followed, according to Belbin, by Williams's call to Gow to fill the Master's role:

and then the said James Williams presented the Master's Watch & Sword to the sd. John Smith [Gow] & welcomed him to the Comand of the Ship & some of them called her the Revenge.[13]

Gow's own testimony confirms the presentation to him by Williams of the Master's watch and sword but states that 'all the Company in general' invited him to command a pirate ship: They 'imposed the Command...in order to proceed with her as a Pirate'.[14]

The *Revenge* did indeed so proceed, taking the *Delight*, a sloop from Poole, on about 12 November off Cape St. Vincent. There followed a number of other prizes, repetitively yielding prisoners and some more or less useful goods, 'Timber from New England', or 'fruit from Cadiz'.[15] At first Gow tended to sink the captured ships but then began to use them as vehicles for ridding himself of prisoners who did not care to become pirates, and ridding himself also of his own large cargo of beeswax from Santa Cruz. He had the sense to avoid a confrontation with one particular ship that outgunned the *Revenge*, but this enraged his fellow-mutineer, Williams, who protested by 'threatning to kill them all [his fellow-pirates] & snapping a Pistol three times...& swearing that he would blow up the Ship'.[16] He was overpowered and sent off aboard a captured and released ship, to meet his fate as a pirate.

The testimonies do not explain Gow's next decision, that 'then they went to the Orkneys', but the principal reason must have been Gow's familiarity with those islands, where he had lived and grown up since his merchant father moved from Wick in the north of Scotland.[17] The *Revenge* arrived in Gow's home port, the harbour of Stromness on the main island of Orkney, in mid-January 1725. They behaved as legitimate merchant seafarers, but a number of discontented men absconded in a longboat, reaching the mainland of Scotland. Some new men were taken on at Stromness: Robert Porrenger, for example, who later claimed to have been confined unwillingly on the ship.[18] He also later reported a night-time raid ashore on the house of a Mr Honyman, a

Sheriff of Kirkwall, Orkney.[19] The raiding party had particular instructions from Gow, as one of them, Alexander Rob, later divulged. Honyman himself was absent, as Gow probably knew, but a young lady of the house slipped past the pirates' guard with the money hidden on her person.[20] Gow had informed them 'they would certainly meet with some Thousands of Pounds', Rob told *Parker's Penny Post*, but 'they only found about 7l. as he knew of, and a few silver Spoons'.[21] When the pirates returned to the *Revenge* with this booty,

Gow was very angry that they had not taken the Diamond Ring off the young Lady's Finger, which he swore to his Knowledge, was worth above 50l. which Rob told him he had not the Heart to do, but Gow swore he ought to be hang'd then.[22]

Another subsequently captured pirate reportedly blamed the boatswain, Belbin, for leading the bungled burglary, and also for an associated villainy mentioned by Porrenger, that the burglars who brought so little loot 'returned on board & brought with them a Bagpiper & three Women'.[23] Rob later denied involvement 'in Ravishing and bringing on board the young Women'.[24] Nothing further is known of them but the accompanying piper voluntarily or involuntarily became a pirate.

A few days later Gow removed the *Revenge* from Stromness harbour and sailed for the smaller Orkney island of Eday. Porrenger testified that he was ordered by Gow 'to pilot the Ship into a proper place to take in Ballast' but Gow probably had other aims.[25] What certainly happened was that on 13 February the pilot Porrenger 'run her aground' (deliberately, he claimed) just off the Calf, a small uninhabited island close by the mainland of Eday.[26] James Laing, a merchant and friend of the local landowner, James Fea, declared later that Fea had received advance warning that Gow was planning 'to surprise the said Mr Fea', whose home was situated on the mainland opposite the Calf.[27]

A complicated but well-documented series of epistolary exchanges and tactical manoeuvres now transpired, the former inscribed in gentlemanly sentiments and the latter taking shape in trickery and bluff. About ten in the morning of the 13th, the expected ship was sighted. Signing himself as 'your old school commerad', James Fea immediately wrote to Gow asking him kindly to refrain from making a polite salute of guns, 'because of my wife's indisposition'.[28] When the *Revenge* went aground, Gow sent his only boat to the mainland requesting a boat to assist his men in getting the ship floated. In response Fea sent James Laing out to the ship with his letter requesting no gun salute and also to inform Gow that Fea's largest boat was unseaworthy, while meanwhile by Fea's orders that boat was staved in. Laing returned with a message from Gow that he requested boats for his assistance and promised what Laing termed 'a most generous present'.[29]

About five o'clock that evening, the pirates' boat came ashore again, with five armed men. Fea, unarmed, and two or three others met these visitors, who said they had requested help 'and now they would force it'.[30] They launched Fea's deliberately broken boat, which soon filled with water and was oarless. Fea then invited the pirates—the boatswain Belbin, Rob and three others—'to a change-house [a small inn], to drink their master's health'.[31] He secretly gave orders to his own men that meanwhile the oars should be removed from the pirates' own boat and that he should soon receive a call to attend to his ailing lady. When this appointed call came to the inn, he promised his pirate guests he would return and went away to arrange for four or five armed men to form an ambush. When he did return to the inn he persuaded the boatswain to accompany him as his timorous and indisposed wife 'was anxious to see one of them'.[32] Belbin was duly ambushed, bound and gagged with a napkin, whereupon Fea returned to the inn with his armed men coming in at two different entrances to surprise and disarm the pirates awaiting him. Rob later complained that, while 'he was guilty of no ill Manners, or Rudeness on his part', Fea's pirate-catchers 'were as great Pyrates as any of them, for they not only took their Money out of their Pockets, but strip'd them to the Skin, and if they could have made Money out of that, he believ'd they would have taken it also'.[33]

The next day, Sunday 14 February, the pirates on the *Revenge* set their sails but failed to free their ship. Then on Monday morning they sent a man ashore and Fea despatched another letter 'in friendship' to Gow, warning him fictitiously that frigates sent to catch him would

certainly be here to-morrow or the next day. I therefore, for the regaird I have to your father's son, being heartily sorry for you that ever you should be so ingadged with such a crew, desire you may expect better entertainment from me than any other; for if you doe surrender you can be evidence against the rest.[34]

The deliverer of this letter was given one from Gow to Fea, asking again for 'boats to assist me', offering himself as hostage for the boats, offering

'to pay you to the value of one thousand pound Sterling', and threatening otherwise 'to set fire to all, and all of us perish together'.[35] About
two o'clock that afternoon, Fea wrote again to Gow, saying that he had
a boat that needed repair and suggesting—somewhat implausibly—that
to this purpose Gow should come ashore with his carpenter. Gow's
answer rejected the previous proposals of surrendering and giving evidence against his men and renewed his request for 'a boat'.[36]

About five o'clock in the evening of 16 February, Fea (by means of
a speaking trumpet) spoke from the shore to Gow on the *Revenge*,
offering to talk to him if he would come ashore on the Calf, where the
ship was grounded. Gow agreed but Fea distrusted him and arranged
for Laing to keep a lookout on the mainland and signal him a warning
of any duplicity. Fea's distrust was warranted, as Laing saw four pirates,
out of Fea's sight, making for his boat. Although warned by Laing's
signal of danger, Fea stayed to receive a message from Gow brought by
a single man carrying a white flag and two letters, one for Mrs Fea,
with a present of a chintz gown, politely asking her to 'solicite' her
husband on Gow's behalf, and the other to Fea, refusing to come
ashore without having Laing in return as a hostage, repeating the
request for a boat—to make an escape this time—and promising in
return 'to leave the ship and cargo entire'.[37]

The next morning (of 17 February) Gow came ashore on the Calf
island, as previously suggested, but the armed men sent out to him by
Fea, under orders to take him, 'dead or alive', instead allowed him to
return to the *Revenge* with Fea's friend, William Scollay, as hostage.[38]
Fea, who had been watching from a distance, set out in another boat
and received Gow, returning to the Calf as arranged, but—somewhat
dishonourably—arrested him. Fea nevertheless managed to secure
Scollay's return to him, escorted by Winter and Peterson, who were
then seized by Scollay and Fea's men. With a pantomime of pretending
to mend a boat playing in full view of the *Revenge*—and other tricks
and inducements, apparently involving some collusion by Gow himself—Fea then persuaded the remaining pirates at about seven that
evening to come ashore, where 'they were all narrowly searched and
put in closs prison with strong guards set upon them'.[39]

The next instalment of this pirate story can be followed in the
newspapers. The murderous mutiny on the *George* had already been
noticed in February in *The London Journal*.[40] Then the London *Daily
Post* relayed news from 1 March, received at Edinburgh from Kirkwall,

Orkney, reporting the bloodless capture of all the pirates of the *Revenge* 'by the good Conduct and Management of Mr. James Fea'.[41] The pirates were being kept in irons awaiting the government's orders and their pirate ship was found to be 'richly laden' with figs, copper, and of course beeswax.[42] As it transpired, the pirates were fetched by H.M.S. *Greyhound*, which brought them up the Thames and deposited them at Marshalsea.[43] There they were joined by their former friend, Williams, whom they had sent off the *Revenge* as a captive to be tried as a pirate.[44]

On 2 April (and on the 10th) the prisoners were formally examined at the Admiralty court housed in the college near St Paul's known as 'Doctors' Commons'. On 2 April Gow pretended the night of the mutiny had been too dark for him to identify the murderers and maintained that he had 'voluntarily surrendered himself to James Fea' but his central role emerged from the various accounts of the mutiny and its aftermath.[45] On 26 May he and eleven others were put on trial at the Admiralty Sessions at the Old Bailey, but Gow refused to plead, as the newspapers reported.[46] The Court warned him of the consequences, which were duly put into effect, as *The Daily Post* explained: 'His Thumbs were ty'd and severely pull'd by the Executioner, assisted by another, at the bar of the Court as usual in such Cases'.[47] This legal procedure 'put him to most exquisite Pain', *The Daily Journal* added, but as he was 'still persisting in his Obstinacy, the Court order'd him to be press'd', to be pressed to death, in other words, his body gradually flattened with weights of iron and stone.[48] He was given the night to consider this prospect and when the Court convened again the next day 'the dread of the Press had put him into a better Temper', *The London Journal* reported, 'and induced him to enter on his Tryal, and plead not Guilty'.[49] He was nevertheless found guilty of murder, with seven others, and another four guilty of piracy, and all 12 men were sentenced to death.

The sentences were to be carried out without much delay but the newspapers reported that one man, Michael Moor, had been reprieved.[50] Also that Gow and Williams were to be afforded a posthumous distinction: 'the Captain and Lieutenant will be hang'd in Chains, the one over-against Greenwich, the other over-against Deptford'.[51] The prison chaplain attending Gow later reported in *A True and Genuine Account of the Last Dying Words of John Gow* (1725) that 'Some Days before he Dy'd, he was much vex'd, that he had read in some of the News-papers, that his Body was to be expos'd by being hung in Chains'.[52] Despite the title given to his work, the chaplain reported no 'Dying Words' of Gow but does inform us that 'He complain'd of one Fea, who apprehended him, contrary (as he call'd it) to his Word of Honour'.[53] Also that:

the gentleman who apprehended him, having been a school-comrade & an intimate acquaintance, had misrepresented him as barbarous, particularly in 'Debauching some Young Women in the Orkneys'... the Truth of [which] he absolutely deny'd.[54]

The Daily Journal of Wednesday 9 June carried an advertisement announcing that 'To Morrow will be published the 3d Edition of, a General History of the Pyrates', which would include an account of 'Smith, alias Gow, who is to be executed on Friday at Execution Dock'.[55] The following day the paper reported that 'four of the Pyrates, who had been Evidence against those who are to suffer to Morrow at Execution Dock, were discharged out of Newgate'.[56] *The Daily Post* of execution day informed its readers that the 'nine Malefactors' would be 'deliver'd up' from Newgate at about one o'clock and that, 'the Gallows being erected on the Shore, convenient Access will be had to it between two and three, upon the Reflux of the Tide'.[57] *The Daily Journal* of the day repeated its advertisement for the new edition of the *General History of the Pyrates*, 'Price 5s.', updated to include 'Smith, alias Gow, who is to be executed this Day at Execution Dock'.[58]

During the procession from Newgate to the place of execution, a dock at Wapping, the pirates (according to the next day's newspapers) 'behaved themselves... with an Air of Insensibility, and as under no Apprehension of Death'.[59] They were conveyed in three carts, preceded as usual by 'the Silver Oar' representing the authority of the Admiralty, and Gow and Williams, who were to share their fate in chains, shared 'the last cart, but none of them discover'd any Concern'.[60] *The Daily Post* recorded a brief interruption of Gow's hanging. He had requested

the Executioner to put him out of his pain as soon as posible; in Compliance therewith he pull'd him by the legs, but so hard that the Rope broke, and down he tumbled, but was immediately ty'd up again, and the Sentence of Death executed upon him.[61]

Mist's Weekly Journal recorded instead that the posthumous arrangements for Gow and Williams went ahead according to plan, and they 'were afterwards hung in Chains on the River Shore; the first over against Blackwall, and the other against Debtford, on Gibbets erected for the purpose'[62]

One of the 12 condemned men had been reprieved, Michael Moor, and another had been given a similar hope, Alexander Rob, who had come aboard the *Revenge* from one of her prizes. He was transferred at Newgate from 'out of the Condemn'd Hole into the Common side', but then 'Notice came to him to prepare for death' and he followed the silver oar to Execution Dock on 2 July.[63] Gow's final words were not recorded but Rob's were. He spoke in particular to other sailors among the spectators:

'Brother sailors, if ever it shou'd be your hard Fortune to be taken by the Pyrates, suffer yourselves to be shot, rather than joyn with them in their Villany, which has been the Cause of my Ruin. I forgive all the World, and God forgive me.'[64]

The account on sale in the *General History* on the day of Gow's death was in the main accurate and plainly derived from information given by the prisoners at Newgate, perhaps especially those who were released for giving evidence against those condemned. Some grounds for the mutiny were supplied by the description of the commander, Furneau, as 'a cross pevish old Man, [who] had pinch'd the Sailors in their Provisions', but the murders were unforgiveably horrible and factually correct, though Williams's words to the Clerk begging for time to say his prayers were more nasty than those quoted in the men's legal examinations.[65] In the *General History* Williams 'said "D—n you, This is no Time to say Prayers". And so shot him dead'.[66] Under examination Rollson had cited Williams as allowing time for prayers, and his quotation of 'Say your prayers & be damned' is corroborated by Moor's overheard 'Damn yr. Blood say your Prayers & be damned'.[67]

Gow in the *General History* explains his reasons for proceeding to Orkney, 'his own Country', in more detail—chiefly its potential safety—and these reasons are by implication supplemented by some new information, true or false, that, at Stromness:

Captain Smith [Gow] was acquainted and had long courted a young Woman of the Place, to whom he was fond of appearing a Commander, and there with told her a formal Story of his acquiring that Preferment, with other Gallantries, not worth taking Notice of here.[68]

The convoluted turns of events at Eday are somewhat simplified and also dramatized by the detail that after Gow's arrest the remaining men aboard the *Revenge* spent three to four days drinking all the wine and brandy aboard before drunkenly surrendering. Gow's initial refusal to plead at the trial is described as well as the treatment his thumbs received and also the threatened punishment of being 'press'd to Death' which he avoided to be condemned to a prospective hanging instead, on publication day.[69] There was no description of Gow in the *General History*. He has no particular appearance, no distinctive clothing, no individual mannerisms or locutions—and no characterization except by way of his courtship of the 'young Woman', which also supplies—potentially—some motivation. His story has no other explanation and its plot concludes simply because the whole 'Pyratical Crew' were 'so infatuated, as to Court, as it were, their own Ruin' by returning to their own country, where 'Providence wisely determin'd that strict Justice should suddenly be executed upon Villains'.[70]

The novelty in the *General History*'s story of Gow was indeed this romance with the young lady of Stromness, for which there is no supporting evidence—except, perhaps, for two letters, one written on 22 April 1725, a few days before the trial, to his captor, James Fea, by one Elizabeth Moodie. She has heard 'that there was letters found with Gou, which made som discovery of the correspondence held betwixt him and a sertan lady and her accomplises'.[71] If Fea had any such letters in his custody, or had heard any confession from Gow on that subject, Elizabeth Moodie was particularly anxious to be informed. Fea's answer, from London on 4 May, was that he had passed on (to the legal process, presumably) all the papers he knew of from the *Revenge*, and among them there were 'non at all of any lady's of my acquaintance'.[72]

On 1 July 1725 there appeared anonymously (from the publisher of an *Account* of the London master criminal, Jonathan Wild) *An Account of the Conduct and Proceedings of the late John Gow*, a work which has been attributed to Defoe, but for no convincing reason.[73] We should pause to consider the relation between these two publications, the *Account* of Gow and the *Account* of Wild. Both were advertised in *The Daily Post* in June 1725, and the *Account* of Gow, promising 'an account of all their Piracies, and the barbarous Murthers they committted', price one shilling, was advertised at the end of the first edition of the *Account* of Wild, price sixpence.[74] *The True and Genuine Account of the Life and Actions of the Late Jonathan Wild* has also been attributed to

Defoe, reasonably but not conclusively.[75] Jonathan Wild was enterprising and ingenious, a thief and pretended thief-catcher, acting respectably as well as feloniously, keeping a 'Compting House, or Office, like a Man of Business', a criminal acting as a detective, a folk hero for whom self-determination was the other side of the same coin as crime.[76] He was an astute businessman whose tricks of the trade and schemes were entertaining and thrilling, but he was also a criminal and worse, 'a Man turn'd into an incarnate Devil', requiring castigation by the author, as well as hanging at Tyburn, where 'a Life of horrid and inimitable Wickedness finish'd at the Gallows'.[77] An engaging story of illegal success and free-enterprise had to be condemned by moral judgement, the necessary hypocrisy shared with mutual satisfaction by writer and reader. Such criminal biographies emerged from the briefer newspaper stories of crimes, trials, and hangings and also from the sermonizing accounts of executions regularly written and sold by the ordinaries of Newgate.[78] 'When a notorious Thief was to be hanged, I was the Plutarch to preserve his Memory', wrote Richard Savage, poet (and sometime hack) in his satirical and realistic *An Author to be Lett* (1729).[79] A family resemblance between biographical accounts of pirates and criminals is apparent and they probably shared authors and readers as well as publishers.

Considerably longer than the Gow chapter in the *General History* (about five times so), *An Account of the Conduct and Proceedings of the late John Gow* is also more fully informed, particularly about events in the Orkneys. The initial mutinous murders are dramatic in their direct starkness—the victims with their throats cut crawling above and below decks, the stabbed and shot captain clinging to ropes and rigging for his life—and effective in their presentation also from the point of view of innocent sailors lying terrified in their hammocks, 'expecting Death every Moment; and not daring to stir'.[80] A vivid picture is also given of the frantic one-man rebellion of Williams, 'the most desperate and outragious Villain in the World'.[81] The pirates' pursuit of alcoholic plunder is made into a recurring motif, and also their tendency to make presents of beeswax to defeated and plundered ships.

Notably, there is no love story drawing Gow to the Orkneys, where the anonymous author situates well-sourced and amusing accounts of the bungled raid on Honyman's house and of Fea's activities, ambushing and duping the pirates with a performance of boat-mending, for example, when

Mr Fea order'd his Men to make a Feint, as if they would go to Work upon the great Boat which lay on Shore upon the Island, but in sight of the Ship; there they hammer'd, and knock'd, and made a Noise, as if they were really caulking and repairing her.[82]

Textual knowledge of Fea's letters to Gow is apparent between the lines of *An Account* and, in confirmation of this, one of Gow's letters to Fea is printed in full.[83] Indeed understanding of Laing's and Scollay's supporting roles in Fea's adventures is such that the author may even have seen Laing's and Scollay's Depositions (made at Kirkwall, Orkney, on 11 March 1725) or at least heard the substance of their contributions from his source for Fea's and Gow's correspondence. The anonymous author has knowledge, more easily acquired, of the trial and of the executions, which were subsequent to the publication of the third edition of the *General History*.

The story of *An Account* is told with attention to the supposed facts and the sequence of events rather than to characterization or explanation, but the author has made Williams more hyperbolically evil and less rational than Gow, whose 'Reasoning was Good' by contrast with Williams, 'a Fellow uncapable of any solid Thinking'.[84] We are informed that Gow 'was, indeed, a Superlative, a Capital Rogue', but he has no apparent character, no thought processes, no conversation, no psychological dimension.[85] The piratical deed spoke for itself and required no characterization of the pirate for explanation. There is no description of Gow, who is invisible in his own pirate life, as he was also in the narrative of the *General History*. Indeed, Williams is more fully and vividly characterized, when he mutinied against Gow, threatening him with a pistol, whereupon Gow and his crew decide to hand him over as a prisoner, 'in order to his being hang'd for a Pirate (so they Jeeringly call'd him)'.[86] For Williams

was the most inhuman, bloody, and desperate Creature that the World could produce; he was even too wicked for Gow and all his Crew, tho' they were Pirates and Murtherers, as has been said; his Temper was so Savage, so Villainous, so Merciless, that even the Pirates themselves told him it was Time he was hang'd out of the Way.[87]

So Gow was called a superlative rogue but was not characterized as a pirate, a role that was conferred on Williams. Gow himself had no particular character in *An Account*, not even as an aspirant gentleman and lover, and the plot does not depend upon him. He and his men were ultimately 'condemn'd by the visible Hand of Heaven' and therefore comprehensively 'outwitted', so that 'they dropp'd insensibly into Mr Fea's Hand'.[88] Thus the author balanced the parts played by morality on the one hand and Fea's 'perticular Bravery and Conduct' on the other, rendering the *Account* both entertaining and properly moral.[89] 'Well, Mr. Dash, have you done that Murder yet?' asks the publisher in Henry Fielding's satire of hackery, *The Author's Farce* (1730).[90] 'Yes, Sir', replies the hack, 'the Murder is done—I am only about a few moral Reflections to place before it'.[91]

The new (fourth) edition of the *General History* in 1726 contained a revised chapter on Gow and plainly derived some of its additional material from *An Account*. The geographical confusion in *An Account* of two islands both incorrectly called 'Calfsound' (at the first of which 'three Women' are kidnapped and 'used...Inhumanly') is echoed in the new *General History* chapter where the two islands are called 'the Calf' and 'Calf-Island' (and 'two young Women' from the former island are 'used in a most inhumane manner').[92] Both sets of mistreated women are probably derived from the three women abducted from the Honyman household, from where *An Account* and the *General History* of 1726 have both correctly derived the abducted bagpiper, whom the pirates employed 'to march along, Piping before them', when they returned to the ship, according to *An Account*, with 'a Bagpiper to play before them', according to the revised *General History*.[93] The wording of the weather information on 14 February, on which 'it blew very hard' in both versions and identically the wind 'shifted to W.N.W.', is a petty but suggestive example of textual borrowing, and combines with an error in both accounts about the timing of the *Revenge's* going aground, upon which Gow remarks in *An Account* that 'they were all dead Men' and in the new *General History* that 'We are all dead Men'.[94]

The accounts differ significantly, however, because Gow's romance, alluded to in the *General History* of 1725, is elaborated and promoted in 1726 into his main motive for sailing to the Orkneys, a motive he keeps to himself, 'a private View of his own':

The Case was this, Smith [Gow] had for a long Time courted a young Gentlewoman, the Daughter of one Mr. G-, in the Orkneys, where he was bred up, and was not ill received at his House, but as Smith's Circumstances in the World were not in any extraordinary Condition then, the Gentleman promised to consent to the Match, whenever he could obtain to be Master of a Ship.[95]

The 'young Woman' of 1725 has become in 1726 'a young Gentlewoman' and she now provides the real reason that Gow 'was resolv'd at
all Events to return to his own Country': to 'claim the Promise of
his intended Father-in-Law, but not to let him into the Secret of his
Adventures'.[96] This secret love, this 'private View of his own', is, however, 'very inconsistent with his present Affairs', according to the
General History.[97] A private love was in contradiction, therefore, was
incompatible with a pirate life, but real or fictional love would not be
'inconsistent' with future accounts of piracy. Love would become its
explanation (for the heart has its reasons, but piracy will have none).
Ashore at Stromness, Gow pursues this plot and, 'since he was visibly a
Captain of a Ship', the marriage was therefore 'agreed on' but receives
no further attention from Gow or his author, as Gow's fears of discovery to the authorities are aroused by the escapes of some of his men,
and the *General History* abandons its newly invented (but 'very inconsistent') love story.[98] In consequence Gow is propelled into carrying
out his plans for 'plundering the Gentlemen's Houses', and proceeds to
plunder Honyman's and, more succesfully, so he hoped, Fea's.[99] Returning to these actual events the *General History* of 1726 gives a much
fuller account of Fea's schemes than in 1725, with an 'Alehouse' and an
'Ambush'.[100] After Gow's capture the crew drink themselves into surrendering, as in the 1725 chapter, and the new edition, now on the
right side of history, can proceed beyond Gow's trial and condemnation to his being hanged at Execution Dock and 'afterwards hang'd in
Chains'.[101] The 1725 *Account* lacks the tale of romance enhanced in
the 1726 edition of the *General History* but the execution scene in the
Account is more careful and considered, concluding:

N.B. Gow as if Providence had directed that he should be twice Hang'd, his
Crimes being of a Two-fold Nature, and both Capital; soon after he was turn'd
off, fell down from the Gibbet, the Rope breaking by the Weight of some that
pull'd his Legs to put him out of Pain; he was still alive and sensible, tho' he
had Hung four Minutes, and able to go up the Ladder the second Time, which
he did with very little Concern'd, and was Hang'd again; and since that a third
Time (viz.) in Chains over-against Greenwich.[102]

John Gow was to be revived again, but not for nearly a century.

   In the summer of 1814, Scott, author of the recently published but
anonymous *Waverley*, cruised for about five weeks on a tour of inspection with the Northern Lighthouse Commissioners, spending about a

fortnight among the Shetland and Orkney islands. On his last day at Stromness, on 17 August, he encountered an old woman who 'remembered *Gow the pirate*'.[103] Scott and his travelling companions at Stromness climbed 'an eminence rising above the town, and commanding a fine view', according to his Diary:

An old hag lives in a wretched cabin on this height, and subsists by selling winds... She was a miserable figure; upwards of ninety, she told us, and dried up like a mummy... She told us she remembered *Gow the pirate*, who was born near the House of Clestrom, and afterwards commenced a buccanier. He came to his native country about 1725, with a *snow* [a type of two-masted vessel] which he commanded, carried off two women from one of the islands, and committed other enormities. At length, while he was dining in a house in the Island of Eda, the islanders, headed by Malcolm Laing's [the historian's] grandfather, made him prisoner and sent him to London, where he was hanged. While at Stromness, he made love to a Miss Gordon, who pledged her faith to him by shaking hands, an engagement which, in her idea, could not be dissolved without her going to London to seek back again her 'faith and troth', by shaking hands with him again after execution.[104]

Some of this old woman's tale can be assessed as accurate and some inaccurate: Gow was not dining in genteel fashion when taken by Fea on the island of Eday, for example. But some of the tale cannot be assessed. The Miss Gordon who pledged her faith to Gow, according to Scott's rendering in his Diary of the old lady's recollections, is perhaps connected—by more than a coincidental initial letter—with the 'Daughter of one Mr. G–' tantalizingly dangled in the 1726 edition of the *General History*.[105] The lapse of time between Gow's visit and Scott's is only a little less than the old woman's age, 'upwards of ninety', so her recollections are likely to be at second-hand, at best, but whatever their historical status they are certainly the real basis for the central love story of Scott's *The Pirate* (1821), some years in the future from Stromness in 1814.

In a letter of 25 December 1820, Scott's publisher Constable made a suggestion to his author: 'If you have not already resolved, might I presume to hint at a subject for the next, or for the Succeeding Work? "The Bucanier" is I think un-occupied ground.'[106] It could be argued that Byron had occupied some similar ground in 1814 with *The Corsair*, but its setting was Mediterranean not West Indian and it was a poem not a novel. *The Corsair* (1814) is one of Byron's Eastern tales, written in ten days, its Mediterranean location the mixed result of

fashionable orientalism and Byron's own passionate tourism.[107] His
hero, Conrad, roaming from his 'Pirate's isle', is a pirate in name more
than deed, defending his wild independence from the oppressive Turkish Pasha.[108] His complicated personality is the main plot, but in the
Mediterranean backdrop he is captured by the Pasha and rescued by a
doyenne of the Harim, playing the female role in what literary historians call the 'enamoured Muslim princess topos', in which a Muslim
lady falls in love with a captive (usually Christian) hero, whose escape
she arranges.[109] Conrad cannot reciprocate her love but returns on his
release to his pirate isle only to find that Medora, his own true love (to
whom he was faithful, for 'None are all evil'), has died.[110] Love is what
has freed him, however, not violent piracy, and love, including self-love,
is the preoccupation of Byron's pirate story, not violence, which is kept
out of sight.

In a note Byron added to the eighth edition in 1815 of *The Corsair*,
he sought to defend the credibility of his pirate hero's combination of
'virtue' and 'crimes' by citing an American newspaper report of an
early-nineteenth-century pirate, Jean Lafitte, whom Byron calls 'a
brother buccaneer', but who (in the Gulf of Mexico not the Boston
newspaper) engaged mostly in slaving and smuggling.[111] Byron's newspaper piece skipped over such unpleasant facts, explaining Lafitte's
supposed mixture of good and evil characteristics by likening him
twice to a fictional character, Schiller's Karl Moor, a principled but
violent noble outlaw, hero of *Die Räuber* (1781), an influential precursor of the Byronic hero.[112] According to the Boston *Weekly Intelligencer*
of 4 November 1814, as cited by Byron, Lafitte, 'like Charles de Moor
[i.e. Karl Moor], had mixed with his many vices some virtues'.[113] So
Byron's Conrad is like a real pirate who is like a fictional hero. The
resemblance between Byron's Conrad and Schiller's hero is a matter of
literary inheritance, but the supposed resemblance in the newspaper
story between Jean Lafitte and Schiller's hero is a more significant sign
of an incipient confusion between the conception of piracy and
Romantic ideology. The Boston *Weekly Intelligencer* is reading an
American pirate as a Romantic literary type. An appropriate sequel to
the career of this imaginary Jean Lafitte is his subsequent role as the
sub-Byronic hero of a popular novel, *The Pirate of the Gulf* (1837).[114]

Far from evil, Byron's Conrad is hardly evil at all. Although he
flies a 'blood-red flag aloft', he is not much of a pirate, more the
Byronic hero in gestation, though a bit early for the Elvis Presley

look, with curling lip.[115] He is not a pirate in the Mediterranean but in his mind, which is properly plotted, as he is a split but composite character, a 'laughing Devil', simultaneously Miltonic and Romantic, cynical and principled, his 'evil' psychologized, explicated—and thereby complicated:

> That man of loneliness and mystery,
> Scarce seen to smile, and seldom heard to sigh -
> …
> And oft perforce his rising lip reveals
> The haughtier thought it curbs, but scarce conceals.
> …
> There was a laughing Devil in his sneer,
> That raised emotions both of rage and fear.[116]

Byron's *The Corsair* was successful, selling 10,000 copies on publication day, but his corsair was more lover than pillager, more political than piratical, more noble outlaw, more feudal chief, than greedy, violent Kidd or Blackbeard.[117] Nevertheless, despite Conrad's obvious differences from 'our Heroe, Captain Thatch', the Satanic Blackbeard of the *General History*, that 'Fury, from Hell', Byron's Conrad has also some affinity with that dramatized Blackbeard, although Conrad is a more human Satan, 'a laughing Devil', his evil psychological, minimal, all too human. Indeed, Byron's hero is recognisably a prototype of the Romantic pirate, who becomes a Romantic type, and of course Byron's hero is abundantly characterized, by contrast with the Gow of the *General History* and *An Account*. Conrad is the pirate psychologized, internalized, his laughing and sneering split personality the mainspring of the poetical plot of Byron's poem, not to mention the longer, historical plot of Romanticism. Conrad himself does nothing much, certainly nothing distinctively piratical, but he is—extravagantly, narcissistically—himself. He is a new kind of pirate, a pirate in transit, from the high seas to the human mind, from the uncontrollable, unsociable oceans to the unfathomable depths—instead—of consciousness.

So the pirate was not quite the 'un-occupied ground' that Constable proposed late in 1820 for Scott's invasion, but by April the following year, 1821, John Ballantyne, Scott's former publisher, noted that Scott 'showed me the "Buccaneer" begun'.[118] On 27 September Scott wrote to William Erskine, his old friend (and travelling companion on the 1814 cruise), inviting him to Abbotsford and requesting informed conversation 'about the locale of Zetland [Shetland], for I am making my bricks with a very limited allowance of straw'.[119] Lockhart's *Memoirs* describes Erskine's delight at 'the progress of the tale' and no doubt (as a former absentee Sheriff of Orkney and Zetland) he gave advice, but Scott had other, printed sources and of course his own brief experience of the islands recorded in his diary.[120] The book was finished with a rush by the end of the year, and published at the very end of 1821, despite the date on the title page of 1822.

A symmetrical pattern shapes the characters and also the plot which is to reveal those characters' identities, concealed by the secrets of their births. Who is really related to whom is what is mysterious and awaits explanation. The central figure is Norna, a respectable and well-born version of the 'old hag' of Stromness, and the revelatory process has a love interest: which of two young men will marry which of two young women, Norna's cousins. One of the young men turns out to be her son and the other turns out not to be her son, and he marries one of the cousins. This family saga is set in a mysterious mist of Norse history and myth which are on the threshold of displacement by Scottish colonialism in the Shetlands and Orkneys, a process of enlightened progress but at the expense of the marginal and vulnerable Norse culture. Norna is the figurehead of the ancient ways and the dynastic outcome of the family saga is an indication of the ultimate defeat of her mystical notions in the face of the inevitable progress which would eventually bring, among other things, inspection of the scenery by Scottish Lighthouse Commissioners and Scott. The process of the novel itself is interfered with by the supposedly diverting comedy of two characters whose prolixity is merely tedious, and by the regular intervention of lumps of sung or recited verse.

The pirate of the title, Cleveland, is saved from drowning by his rival, Mordaunt, who is later saved from drowning by Cleveland, and they compete for the two sisters, Brenda who is practical and Minna who is mystical. This plot unrolls when Cleveland is shipwrecked spectacularly on the rugged scenery of Sumburgh Head, the southern tip of mainland Shetland, where he is saved by Mordaunt, who slides to the rescue down the 'abrupt and tremendous precipice', as did Scott himself more gently 'down a few hundred feet', for fun, in 1814, while the head of his expedition, Robert Stevenson, contemplated a site for a necessary lighthouse.[121] Restored to life, Cleveland becomes enamoured of Minna, who thinks a pirate is a gallant rebel, inspired by Viking-like principles. He is won over by her love, however, and rejects his pirate life (which seems to have been devoted mostly to saving lives and returning stolen property).

To locate his story on a chronological and cultural border, Scott has set his imaginary events back from Gow's time to 'the end of the seventeenth century', supposedly before indigenous Norseness had succumbed to colonial Scottishness.[122] Nevertheless the historical Gow—or Scott's idea of him—has inspired *The Pirate*. The encounter of 1814 with the 'old hag' on the heights over Stromness has been partly repeated in a Note to the book, in which she is made a little older, 'nearly one hundred years old'—perhaps to stretch her back to a potential encounter with Gow himself.[123] Some of her recollections and some additional Gow material are also made into the substance of an 'Advertisement' to the book which retells the story of Gow with the warning that the narrative of *The Pirate* will supersede the existing inadequate version of events:

The purpose of the following Narrative is to give a detailed and accurate account of certain remarkable incidents which took place in the Orkney Islands, concerning which, the more imperfect traditions and mutilated records of the country only tell us the following erroneous particulars.[124]

Scott's version of these 'particulars' is what immediately follows. Gow is said to have given 'dancing parties in the village of Stromness' and the old lady's love story is repeated: he 'engaged the affections and received the troth-plight of a young lady, possessed of some property'.[125] Fea's 'stratagems' to arrest Gow are mentioned (of which Scott had acquired some knowledge).[126] A description 'by an eyewitness' is quoted of Gow's judicial torture with whipcord twisted around his thumbs, a nastiness frequently perpetrated and reported at the time.[127] He is condemned and hanged and then Scott takes up again his own brief Diary account of the old lady's reference to Miss Gordon's dissolution of her troth-plight with Gow 'by shaking hands with him again after execution'.[128] This has naturally appealed to Scott's interest in the macabre and ritualistic, and he narrates and elaborates the story:

It is said, that the lady whose affections Gow had engaged, went up to London to see him before his death, and that, arriving too late, she had the courage to request a sight of his dead body; and then touching the hand of the corpse, she formally resumed the troth-plight which she had bestowed. Without going through this ceremony, she could not, according to the superstition of the country, have escaped a visit from the ghost of her departed lover, in the event of her bestowing upon any living suitor, the faith which she had plighted to the dead.[129]

The 'Advertisement' concludes Scott's story of the historical Gow by stating that:

the dates, and other particulars of the commonly received story, are inaccurate, since they will be found totally irreconcileable with the following veracious narrative, compiled from materials to which he alone has had access, by The Author of Waverley.[130]

This is a familiar authorial stance: what a century previously in Defoe's day would have been a claim for exclusive veracity has now become a conventional request for suspension of disbelief. We are to pretend that the fiction of *The Pirate* is a revelation of the real facts behind the erroneous received story of Gow.

Nevertheless, the received story and Scott's perception of it have permeated the fiction of *The Pirate*, in which the main initial event is the wreck of Cleveland's ship, the *Revenge*, named after Gow's, on the scenery of Sumburgh Head. The main concluding non-event of the book is Cleveland's not marrying Minna, a marriage much anticipated in the narrative by the description of the 'promise of Odin' which Minna proposes to Cleveland, explicated in the Notes as a 'troth-plighting' by couples who 'joined hands through a circular hole in a sacrificial stone, which lies in the Orcadian Stonehenge, called the Circle of Stennis', where the couple arrange their last and interrupted meeting, and where Scott himself visited in 1814.[131]

Scott reportedly obtained some personal sources of information about Gow. A manuscript of notes by Robert Stevenson, a companion on the 1814 cruise (and grandfather of R.L. Stevenson), states that he supplied Scott with details he in turn had learned from a friend, Dr Patrick Neill, who was distantly related to Fea (and was also the author of *A Tour Through Some of the Islands of Orkney and Shetland* (Edinburgh, 1806)).[132] Scott is also supposed to have seen an account of Gow prepared by Alexander Peterkin, a Sherriff-Substitute of Orkney and Zetland, which very probably contained or was derived from the Gow–Fea correspondence which Peterkin himself published shortly afterwards in a section of his *Notes on Orkney and Zetland* (Edinburgh, 1822).[133] Peterkin's manuscript account for Scott's benefit seems lost, but Robert Stevenson, who compared it with *The Pirate*, wrote of his 'astonishment' that there was little trace of it in Scott's book.[134] Indeed, judging by Peterkin's published account of Fea and Gow, Scott made little or no use of Peterkin's material, though occasionally there may be a trace. When Cleveland in *The Pirate* speaks of blowing up his ship as a last resort—'it is but snapping a pistol in the powder-room and as we have lived, so will we die'—he might be echoing Gow's similar threat in a letter to Fea, that 'I'm resolved to set fire to all, and all of us perish together', but the language is not close and the idea is somewhat conventional.[135]

Certainly Scott made use of some history or histories of pirates—of the *General History* itself (of which he owned a second edition, preceding the inclusion of Gow) and such works as the 1709 *Life and Adventures of Capt. John Avery*, which he also owned.[136] Some of Scott's pirates can be found in the *General History*. His Harry Glasby, for example, who betrayed his comrades, is presumably derived from the Harry Glasby of the *General History*, who also testified in court, after 'a Shot from the Man of War took off his Leg', appearing 'undaunted and rather solicitous, about resting his Stump, than giving any Answer to the Court'.[137] A shipmate of the historical Glasby, a 'waggish' pirate called Sympson, who signed himself 'Sim. Tugmutton' in jest, is copied by Scott's man Fletcher, who 'subscribed himself…Timothy Tugmutton'.[138] Predictably Scott's fictional pirates capture the two central ladies and one of the pirates asks them 'which of you would like to swing in a rover's hammock?'[139] Naturally: 'The terrified maidens clung close together, and grew pale at the bold and familiar language of the desperate libertine'.[140] Scott is conscious that pirates have a distinct tribal culture and has a Kirkwall magistrate complain to them that 'you have behaved in this town, as if you were in an Indian village at Madagascar'.[141] Cleveland follows the correct piratical manner of wearing extra pistols 'suspended over [his] shoulders in a sort of sling or scarf of crimson ribband', a mode particularly associated with Blackbeard, who wore in the *General History* 'a Sling over his Shoulders, with three Brace of Pistols, hanging in Holsters like Bandaliers', and was appropriately pictured.[142]

Nevertheless Scott has taken care to separate his titular pirate, Cleveland, from the cultural signs of piracy. To this effect Cleveland is contrasted with a rival captain, Goffe, who is fashioned more horribly in the image of Blackbeard. Goffe 'fired off his pistol under the table', for his amusement, 'and shot Jack Jenkins in the knee, and cost the poor

devil his leg'.[143] Scott's footnote attributes this 'exploit' to Avery but it
is particularly told of Blackbeard, who shot a man under the table 'thro'
the Knee and lam'd [him] for Life', a man described in the *General
History* in 1724 as 'alive at this Time in London, begging his Bread'.[144]
Cleveland does not practise gratuitous cruelty and Goffe is characterized, by contrast, as tastelessly dressed, 'like a boorish clown in the dress
of a courtier', drunken and foul-mouthed, given to repeated swearing
which Scott has to indicate with repeated dashes.[145] By this contrast
Cleveland is clearly piracy gentrified.

In a chapter headed by a quotation from *The Corsair*—

> There was a laughing Devil in his sneer,
> That raised emotions both of rage and fear

—Cleveland speaks of himself as having 'two different characters', in
effect the gentleman who loves Minna and 'the daring leader of the
bold band whose name was as terrible as a tornado'.[146] Cleveland's
duality—rather than duplicity—is meant to be a fundamental character trait, from his first appearance on emerging from the sea, when 'his
features shewed youth and comeliness, notwithstanding they were pal-
lid and disfigured'.[147] Minna's confusion of pirates with 'ancient heroes'
is similarly indicative of Romantic ambivalence about cultural mar-
ginals, displaced or distanced heroes, whether Viking or piratical.[148]
Cleveland is designed to register this ambivalence but does not have 'a
laughing Devil in his sneer'. He is not 'Byronic' because of a credible
characterization of moral ambivalence but because he is an authorial
muddle of good and bad, and his piracy, the other side of his double
character, is softened and sanctified to a point of nullity and absurdity.

The Corsair itself is not much concerned with piracy. It is indeed
at bottom an old-fashioned crusading romance. Nevertheless Conrad is a credibly complicated character whereas Cleveland is too
genteel for such a role, not simultaneously attractive and evil. As an
amateur anthropologist, Scott is more thrilled by weird Norseness
than by the aberrant behaviour of pirates, and the cultural border
he engages with is between Norse and Scots, not pirates and gentlemen. Ultimately, we learn that the 'pirate' of Scott's title was led
into piracy by the unfortunate circumstances of his well-born father
and was 'condemned' by his piratical colleagues for having 'too
much humanity', for which he was in punishment 'marooned'.[149]
Most of his previous and subsequent career consisted in nobly and

charitably saving lives and returning stolen property. 'I have borne a rough outside', he confides to a friend, 'but, in time of need, I can shew the number of lives which I have been the means of saving, the property which I have restored to those who owned it, when, without my intercession, it would have been wantonly destroyed'.[150] Even these good deeds he has renounced, for love of Minna, and he is officially pardoned for 'protecting, at the hazard of your own life, the honour of two Spanish ladies' who 'were persons of quality'.[151] Perhaps because he is revealed to be Minna's cousin's son, he is not allowed to marry Minna by their author, and dies a British naval hero.[152] His chest, which was saved with him from the wreck of the *Revenge*, turns out to contain not treasure but documentation, identifying him as of high descent, of 'quality', the son of Norna of Fitful Head, Scott's exalted rendering of Bessie Miller, the 'old hag' of Stromness. Cleveland's character in *The Pirate* left a literary legacy for many generations—of gentility (often secret or unknown), so that piracy was more like chivalry than piracy, a role played by a displaced or disinherited nobleman

Fourteen days after the publication of *The Pirate*, a play opened at the Surrey Theatre, Blackfriars Road, London, the work of Thomas Dibdin, actor, songwriter, playwright and all-round man of the theatre.[153] His play was entitled *The Pirate: A Melodramatic Romance, taken from the Novel of that Name*. The novel's encounter between Mordaunt and Cleveland is set at the climax of the first act of the play, and Mordaunt is ineffectually restrained from his heroism by his father, Mertoun, as in the novel. The drama does not lack spectacle, which must be imagined via the printed words:

A rocky shore, with breakers in motion, and a ship struggling with the surf, upon its beam ends. In the foreground, a cliff, upon which Mordaunt is seen agitated and observing the wreck, while a mariner is combating the waves, and thrown back as he approaches the shores.

MOR.   *[throwing off his coat]* Father! Father! I will die but I will save that man.
MER.   *[speaking as he enters in the cliff]* Stop! I command you! The attempt is death.
MOR.   Then I shall die with a sure pass to Heaven. *[Music. He leaps off the cliff.]*
MER.   My son! My son! *[falls on the cliff.]*

Music. Mordaunt disappears - rises - and is seen assisting the mariner to shore - faints at length from fatigue, over his body - recovers and sees the mariner give signs of life - kneels over him in thankfulness. The act drop falls.[154]

The information that these two young men are related by blood is revealed by Norna at an earlier stage of the play than the novel, forming a climax to the second act. The opening scene of the third act introduces some pirates and some scenery: 'a beautiful Bay at sun-rise, in which a handsome Privateer…is seen riding at anchor'.[155] Cleveland is captured by the Kirkwall authorities and in reprisal the pirates capture Brenda and Minna, who is surprised to discover Cleveland's profession: 'Cleveland a pirate!'[156]

The closing scene simplifies the novel's saga slightly, as the two central males are not half-brothers (as in the novel) but full brothers, both sons of Norna, Mordaunt as well as Cleveland. As Norna explains to their father, Cleveland's sea chest 'contained strong proof, the Pirate— is our son'.[157] Mordaunt and Cleveland enter together—'the Brothers'—and then Kirkwall officials enter with a naval captain to arrest Cleveland, but the captain asks: 'Did you not once preserve the honour of two Spanish ladies, when captured by your crew?'[158] 'I did', answers Cleveland.[159] His pardon is inevitable and he proposes a penitent patriotic future for himself in which Minna is forgotten by him and ignored by his author. On the back of the British Library copy of the play is a sticky label informing the reader: 'Love's Circulating Library, 81 Bunhill Row. The Reading of the Book is 2d. for each Day till returned.'[160] Meanwhile the theatrical production had its rivals, two other incarnations of Scott's *The Pirate* opening within days, at the Olympic Theatre off the Strand and at Drury Lane.[161] Scott's pirate, like Byron's, was popular.

Gow the violent and murderous pirate, the silent and impenitent prisoner tortured by thumbscrews, the convicted criminal publicly hanged and exhibited posthumously in chains, became an aspirant gentleman and lover as he moved from the law courts and newspapers to the novelized biographies in the *General History* and *An Account*, though otherwise devoid of character, with nothing to say for himself and nothing to think. Even then he was invisible in his impersonalized piracy and his plot was determined by 'Providence' and the 'Hand of Heaven', not by himself or by the imaginative twists and turns of an author. That eighteenth-century Gow was immoral and ambitious by implication of his supposedly verisimilitudinous actions rather than by way of any analysis or description of his character. Piracy was an alleged fact without any explanatory context, was a deed not a doer, a realistic act by a sailor not an artistic work by an author, an intrinsically evil crime, not an ambiguously fascinating literary performance—or so, at least, it was written to seem.

That eighteenth-century Gow was a blank, lacking any sensibility or interiority, by contrast with Cleveland, Scott's nineteenth-century sub-Byronic hero, who inhabited not an imitated reality but an invented, seventeenth-century history, set at a safe chronological distance, his plot representing, not the thrilling threat of upward mobility, but the reassurance of resurgent stability, the ultimate triumph of the true gentleman who is not a pirate after all, but an authenticated gentleman. Cleveland is a stranger in thought not deed, is mysterious not evil, his piratical acts charitable and chivalrous in essence, and his plot, not the brutal revolt with cut throats gushing blood, but the deserved reward of inheritance, a rediscovered and re-established status. Piracy itself is separated from violence and muddled with love, removed from the immediate present and the impending future, and relocated in an imaginary past. Scott's version of Gow had inherited little from factual piracy but left a literary legacy. The plot was not to acquire nobility in Madagascar but to rediscover it at home. Piracy was a role played by a displaced gentleman whose treasure chest contained 'strong proof' of his genuine—his gentlemanly—identity.

V

Buried Treasure

Now I remember those old woman's words
Who in my youth would tell me winter's tales:
And speak of spirits and ghosts that glide by night
About the place where treasure hath been hid.

(Marlowe, *Jew of Malta*, II, i, as quoted by Irving as
epigraph to 'The Money-Diggers')[1]

On 30 August 1817 Washington Irving called on Scott at Abbotsford, where he was welcomed by Scott himself, limping vigorously to greet him.[2] Like Coleridge, who had 'sate up the greater part of the night' over Irving's amusing *History of New York*, Scott had approved it, generously reporting it had made his sides 'absolutely sore with laughing'.[3] The American author was immediately given breakfast at Abbotsford and made at home for four days, during which Scott walked him around the locality, acting as guide to the scenery, local characters and history. At meals Scott was hospitably 'full of anecdote and conversation' and Irving noticed also Scott's 'book cases, well stored with works of romantic fiction in various languages, many of them rare and antiquated'.[4] Irving's father was born in the Orkneys and Irving shared Scott's Romantic enthusiasm for Scottish popular legends, superstitions and folklore, as well as following Scott's more scholarly curiosity about German writings of such romances and folktales.[5]

Irving's subsequent *Sketch Book* (1820) was dedicated to Scott who had been an inspiration and had secured its publisher, John Murray. The two most successful stories it contained, 'Rip Van Winkle' and 'The Legend of Sleepy Hollow', were combinations of European folk-tales and American settings, of the supernatural and the

picturesquely realistic.[6] Travelling in Germany and France during
1822–4 Irving experienced difficulty in repeating his literary successes
but eventually forced himself to produce another collection of tales,
Tales of a Traveller (1824), which included two he laboriously produced
in Paris during December and January, 1823–4, tales of buried pirate
treasure: a theme of many narratives to follow in the nineteenth century.[7] As with 'Rip Van Winkle' and 'Sleepy Hollow', he placed the
tales in relation to the comic mouthpiece for his burlesque *History of
New York*, Diedrich Knickerbocker. The two treasure tales, jointly
entitled 'The Money-Diggers', and described as 'Found among the
Papers of the late Diedrich Knickerbocker', were told by two companions on a convivial fishing trip enjoyed and described by Knickerbocker, who prefaced the tales with two sections of introductory
matter, the first entitled 'Hell-Gate', the name for a channel in the
East River of New York which was the site of a wreck, rumoured to
be that of a pirate ship sunk in a location which 'abounded with traditions about pirates, ghosts, smugglers, and buried money'.[8] The mundane American scene thus benefits from colourful and supernatural
popular 'traditions' which are given a historical excuse in Knickerbocker's second introductory section, entitled 'Kidd the Pirate'. This
provides a more-or-less accurate account of Kidd's career and fate but
brings this history into play as the source of reports and rumours of
'his having buried great treasures of gold and jewels before his arrest'.[9]
Indeed there were historically many such tales. Lord Bellomont, Kidd's
sometime partner and subsequent prosecutor as Governor of New
York, reported that 'a Committee of trusty persons' had 'searched
Kidd's Lodging and found hid and made up in two sea-beds a bag of
gold dust & Ingots of the value of abt. a 1000 l., and a bag of Silver'.[10]
He also reported the persistent rumours that Kidd admitted having
buried 'some Gold' on Gardiner's Island.[11] Irving himself heard 'stories about Kidd' in Paris and London, from the American consul-
general in London.[12] The Knickerbocker narrator of Irving's 'Kidd the
Pirate' brings such stories into his own experience of the leisurely
summer fishing party of New Yorkers, one of whom fished up an old-
fashioned pistol from the bottom of the river. Another of the party
speculates that 'it belonged to Kidd himself' and another is prompted
to sing the old ballad of Kidd which has acquired an extra American
verse (signalling Kidd's supposed abandonment of Christianity) since
its composition in 1701:

> I had the Bible in my hand,
>   As I sailed, as I sailed,
> And I buried it in the sand,
>   As I sailed.[13]

The singer then remembers 'a story about a fellow who once dug up Kidd's buried money', which he tells as the first tale of 'The Money-Diggers', entitled 'The Devil and Tom Walker'.[14]

His story's central concern is the supposed location, a 'few miles from Boston', of 'a great amount of treasure buried by Kidd the pirate'.[15] The story itself is set in 1727 and its principal character is a miser named Tom Walker who comes across the treasure site, which is presided over by 'a great black man' who 'was neither negro nor Indian' but the 'Devil' of the tale's title.[16] He makes the conventional Satanic pact with miserly and greedy Tom, to allow him the use of Kidd's treasure on condition that it is used in the Devil's service, in particular that Tom should become a usurer, which he does with success and satisfaction. He is somewhat troubled by the pact he has made but seeks to evade its consequences by zealously though insincerely practising Christianity. He does not desist from usury, however, and is typically 'foreclosing a mortgage, by which he would complete the ruin of an unlucky land speculator', when he hears 'three loud knocks at the street-door', where he finds the 'black man', who tells him: 'Tom, you're come for!'[17]

The fishing party goes ashore for a picnic and another one of them narrates 'a story of money-digging, which occurred in this very neighbourhood', thus providing the second tale of 'The Money Diggers', a second tale itself of two parts, both concerning a character named in the title of the first part, 'Wolfert Webber, or Golden Dreams'.[18] Again the story is set 'early' in the eighteenth century and its principal is Wolfert Webber, a cabbage-faced descendant of a Dutch cabbage-growing dynasty who inhabits 'a Dutch-built house' at the centre of his family land which is, unfortunately, in process of absorption into the spreading 'city of the Manhattoes'.[19] He has a comic wife forever comically knitting and a daughter who 'ripened and ripened' but is not cabbage-faced and has an admirer, Dirk Waldroon.[20]

Wolfert attends an inn on the East River, where tale-telling about piracy is the preoccupation, rather than piracy itself. The tale-telling in the inn, in contrast to the tale-telling of the fishing companions, is fiercely competitive and rudely sceptical. Tales of pirates have become tales within tales and pirates have become characters of fiction and legend, ghostly buriers of treasure rather than violent acquirers of it, gothic characters not historic persons, shoresmen, sailors adrift from the ocean wave, 'strangely cast upon dry land'.[21] A one-eyed English captain contradicts other tale-tellers at the inn, insisting that local treasures were not buried by Dutch colonists but 'were all buried by Kidd the pirate, and his crew'.[22] Wolfert Webber listened, thrilled: 'The soil of his native island seemed to be turned into gold-dust; and every field to teem with treasure'.[23] He returns home from the inn intoxicated by such tales of buried wealth and on three successive nights he dreams the 'Golden Dreams' of the tale's title:

He dreamt that he had discovered an immense treasure in the centre of his garden. At every stroke of the spade he laid bare a golden ingot: diamond crosses sparkled out of the dust; bags of money turned up their bellies, corpulent with pieces of eight, or venerable doubloons; and chests, wedged close with moidores [gold Portuguese coins], ducats, and pistareens [silver Spanish coins], yawned before his ravished eyes, and vomited forth their glittering contents.[24]

On awakening from the third of these repeated dreams, he frantically and futilely digs up his garden of cabbages, thus destroying his traditional fund of wealth and becoming shunned by his old acquaintances, with the exception of his daughter's suitor, Dirk Waldroon.

When disappointed Wolfert revisits his riverside inn, he finds it dominated by a new arrival, a 'strange sea-monster', a mysterious rum-drinking man who has come from the sea with a mysterious sea-chest and sleeps at the inn in a hammock not a bed, paying his bills with 'strange outlandish coinage': 'His face was dark and weatherbeaten; a deep scar, as if from the slash of a cutlass, had almost divided his nose, and made a gash in his upper lip'.[25] This stranger 'silenced' even the one-eyed English captain at the inn, dominating the tale-telling with 'talk of the exploits of the buccaneers', but another drinker at the inn, Peechy Prauw, starts another pirate story about a local black fisherman called Sam, which is again rudely interrupted by the scar-faced stranger who warns him to 'let the buccaneers and their money alone': 'They fought hard for their money; they gave body and soul for it; and wherever it lies buried, depend upon it he must have a tug with the devil who gets it!'[26] He then 'stumped upstairs to his chamber' at the inn and

the remaining men, including Wolfert, listen to the resumed story of
Sam, which concludes the Wolfert tale of 'The Money-Diggers', and is
called 'The Adventure of the Black Fisherman'.[27]

Black Sam had moored his boat one evening in the lee of Manhat-
tan Island when, unseen himself, he observed another boat approach
with six men whom he curiously followed ashore where they buried
what he took to be the body of a victim. 'The murderers!' he blurts out
and is chased and shot at before escaping.[28] 'And did Sam never find
out what was buried…?' asks Wolfert, 'whose mind was haunted by
nothing but ingots and doubloons'.[29] Further discussion at the inn of
the inconclusive 'Adventure of the Black Fisherman' is interrupted by
shots and shouts in the dark outside and the precipitate departure of
the scar-faced stranger, taking his mysterious sea-chest towards an
awaiting boat. As he loads his chest aboard, however, it falls into the
waves and he falls with it, to be 'hurried away by the rushing swiftness
of the tide', as we are informed by the narrator at Knickerbocker's fishing party.[30]

The evening's stories at the inn have further inflamed the avaricious
imagination of Wolfert, who locates old Sam, who guides him back to
the burial place Sam had observed in the tale told at the inn. Determined to return the next day for digging, Wolfert and Sam encounter
on their way home a figure in whom Wolfert 'recognised the grisly
visage of the drowned buccaneer', the scar-faced stranger of the inn.[31]
Wolfert and Sam flee in terror and some days of recuperation pass
before Wolfert confides in his doctor, who turns out to be a fanatical
expert in the lore and hocus-pocus of divining and obtaining buried
treasure. With much pedantic fuss and narrative padding to achieve
delay (and induce suspense), Wolfert and the learned fanatic accompany Sam back to the site where they uncover a buried chest but also
imagine the apparition of the drowned scar-faced pirate. The three
money-diggers run wildly in blind panic, Wolfert falls and is rescued
by his daughter's sensible admirer, Dirk Waldroon, and we are informed
that 'whether any treasure was ever actually buried at that place' was a
mystery never solved.[32]

Wolfert pines away gloomily, and all the more so when informed
'that the corporation were about to run a new street through the very
centre of his cabbage-garden'.[33] Grimly facing this fate, he bequeaths
his daughter to the faithful Dirk and calls for a lawyer to make his will.
The wise lawyer explains that the corporation's order has actually

made his fortune, and Wolfert revives to welcome the new street through his cabbage gardens where he had dreamed of finding treasure:

His golden dream was accomplished. He did indeed find an unlooked-for source of wealth; for, when his paternal lands were distributed into building lots, and rented out to safe tenants, instead of producing a paltry crop of cabbages, they returned him an abundant crop of rents.[34]

Kidd gave rise to treasure tales by starting them in his own defence, to buy his life, but his undiscovered treasure was thus discovered by Irving as a historical but indigenous backdrop for American rewritings of European folk-tales—moral fables, perhaps, demonstrating the consequences of neglecting the real world of impending progress in favour of illusory dreams of treasure buried and lost in the past. Irving's tales of Wolfert Webber are the first tales of buried treasure, and the first to associate the pirate not with terror at sea but with treasure on land. The nineteenth-century literary pirate is taking a variety of generic shapes. The gothic pirates of Irving's treasure tales are dead and buried, like their treasure, which they have bequeathed to readers, treasure which is unearned wealth but also unspent wealth, guarded by the ghosts of pirates past. Real pirates had buried their treasure in drink and dissipation but the nineteenth-century short story now made better use of it. When those real pirates had ceased to frighten, ghosts survived them who were congenial to the Romantic taste for folklore and popular superstitions, which gladly relished such ghouls and grotesques. We shall meet the descendants of Irving's disfigured guests assembling at another inn, later in the century.

In her recollections of her father, James Fenimore Cooper, his daughter Jane describes his conversation at table one evening with a friend, Charles Wilkes, and others about Scott's recently-published *The Pirate*. Cooper, who had sailed as a 17-year-old before the mast and subsequently as a midshipman in the US Navy from 1808–11, 'maintained the opinion that *The Pirate* was not thoroughly satisfactory to a nautical reader'.[35] Against the opinions of Wilkes and others that nautical technicality would be tedious to the general reader, Cooper argued that maritime fiction could be written with professional accuracy and still please shorebound readers lacking sealegs. Indeed, later that evening, he exclaimed that he would himself write such a book, 'a sea tale—to show what can be done in this way by a sailor!'[36]

The result of this table-talk was Cooper's *The Pilot; a Tale of the Sea* (1823), a novel that was properly nautical but not particularly piratical in its subject, which was to make a somewhat Byronic hero of a thinly-disguised portrayal of the American revolutionary figure, John Paul Jones. The Scots novelist Tobias Smollett had been a sailor as well as an author, as Cooper knew, and Smollett's *Roderick Random* (1748) had taken the novel authentically or at least credibly to sea, but with too much salty realism for Cooper's taste. In his Preface to *The Pilot* Cooper informed its reader 'that though he [the author] has navigated the same sea as Smollett, he has steered a different course'.[37] Cooper's model was Scott, his aim a more nautical Scott, and certainly *The Pilot* had more of the sea in it than *The Pirate* had, and was admired by Scott himself, who remarked in a letter to the novelist Maria Edgeworth that Cooper's novel 'is a very clever one, and the sea-scenes and characters in particular are admirably drawn'.[38]

In Paris a few years later, in the summer of 1827, and then in a country house on the Seine at the village of St Ouen, Cooper wrote another nautical novel, this time featuring a pirate, *The Red Rover*, published first in Paris and in London in 1827 and in Philadelphia early in 1828.[39] The novel's opening is set at Newport, Rhode Island, in 1759, the year Quebec fell to Britain. The opening scenes on land introduce a mysterious seafarer, named Wilder, with his two faithful sailor subordinates, Fid and Scipio, and an even more mysterious seafarer, the 'Rover' of the title, adept at disguises and the commander of a ship, with an intimate relationship with his cabin-boy, Roderick, and a preference for a red flag, like Byron's corsair's, when fighting. Two ladies are involved (who will later be captured, of course): a governess named Mrs Wyllys and her pupil Gertrude, who is accompanied by her black servant-woman, Cassandra.

The Rover takes Wilder into his employment but requests him to command a ship called the *Royal Caroline* on which the attractive Gertrude and Mrs Wyllys are to sail as passengers. They sail as arranged but the *Caroline* encounters a storm which unmasts it, whereupon the crew becomes mutinous and deserts the stricken ship in a pinnace. Wilder and the three women await the inevitable sinking of the *Caroline* and then successfully float off aboard a launch. On the ocean wave as in the American wilderness, Cooper's prose can confuse the reader at moments of excitement by the clash between the hypercivilized art of his genteel eloquence and the uncivilized nature of his sublimely

frightful wave or wilderness. As the ship sinks, the launch and its passengers float, but the thrilling marine effects of flowing, sinking, and
floating are not helpfully conveyed by such phrases as 'Still, as the water
rushed', 'darting down the declivity' and 'through the same gaping
whirlpool, to the bottom'.[40] The 'ship' is called 'vessel' and the 'launch'
is called 'boat' not by reason of nautical precision but for elegant variation, adding unwanted confusion to the reader's comprehension of
the flowing, sinking, and floating processes.[41] Nevertheless the description of the 'launch' as an 'ark' is significant, as we shall see, as well as
appropriate to its floating circumstance, and the poetic animation of
the ocean, which 'moaned' and 'slept', indicates Cooper's Romantic
infusion of metaphor into the alien watery world.[42]

The survivors of these fluid processes are rescued by the Rover's
ship, the *Dolphin*, where the Rover himself is more at home, more
himself and less disguised than formerly:

As though he disdained concealment, and wishing to announce the nature of
the power he wielded, he wore his pistols openly in a leathern belt, that was
made to cross a frock of blue, delicately edged with gold, and through which
he had thrust, with the same disregard of concealment, a light and curved
Turkish yattagan.[43]

The Rover with a Turkish dagger goes by the name of Captain
Heidegger and is hospitable to his female captive guests. They become
suspicious, however—especially because of the exotic and eclectic
trappings in his cabin, including typically a blue silk divan loaded with
'piles of pillows'—that their rescuers are... 'pirates!'[44] Wilder, previously employed by the Rover, takes a role as second-in-command, but
the pirate sailors resent him and he receives protection from his shipmates Fid and Scipio, who had shipped at Newport with the Rover's
crew. The Rover himself, instantly obeyed, restores good piratical
order.

In intimate conversation with Wilder he reveals that his piracy is a
form of protest against the unjust rule of Britain over the American
colonies, which he predicts will soon be independent with a national
flag. 'Had that flag been abroad, Mr Wilder, no man would have ever
heard the name of the Red Rover.'[45] In the course of another revelatory conversation, Mrs Wyllys and the Rover hear from Fid and
Scipio how they first met Wilder. Surviving the wreck of a boat in
the West Indies, the two sailors came across another wrecked but still

floating ship, deserted except for a dog, a dying woman and a boy they presumed to be her child. The starving Fid and Scipio ate the dog (in imitation, perhaps, of the treatment of 'Juan's spaniel' in the second canto of *Don Juan*) and saved the boy, Wilder.[46] They took the name of the ship to be the words they found printed on a horse-bucket aboard, which Scipio transcribed by tattooing them onto the arm of Fid, which bears the legend 'Ark, of Lynnhaven'.[47]

A ship appears in sight of the *Dolphin*, which Wilder admits is the *Dart*, the naval ship he served on before joining the Rover. A fight looms but the Rover out of sympathy for Wilder decides to avoid hostility. He therefore flies the British flag aboard the *Dolphin* which declares itself a naval ship. The Rover, as captain of this supposed naval ship, goes aboard the *Dart*, convincingly impersonates the aristocratic and well-connected officer he is purporting to be, 'the *honourable* Captain Howard, of his Majesty's ship *Antelope*', and obtains a list of the officers aboard the *Dart*, who include one Henry Ark, who was named after a wreck, the captain of the *Dart* informs him, and is at present absent 'on a most dangerous service'.[48]

Having thus confirmed Wilder's duplicity as a double agent and an inauthentic pirate, the Rover returns to his ship determined to fight the *Dart*. He confronts Wilder with his treachery but accepts Mrs Wyllys's plea not to punish him, and declares him free to rejoin the *Dart*, and take the ladies with him, and also Fid and Scipio. Aboard the *Dart*, the naval chaplain is by happenstance known to Mrs Wyllys, who introduces him as the one who married her to her deceased husband, who it now emerges was the son of one Rear-Admiral de Lacey, so Mrs Wyllys is in fact clandestinely Mrs de Lacy. Reluctantly but dutifully, Ark-Wilder informs the *Dart*'s captain that the ship in sight is the Red Rover's ship, and indeed that the visitor the *Dart* received was none other than the notorious Red Rover himself, a disclosure which astonishes the captain, who knew the Rover only by a reputation that reflects the public misconception of a pirate: 'I saw nothing, sir, of his shaggy whiskers, heard nothing of his brutal voice, nor perceived any of those monstrous deformities which are universally acknowledged to distinguish the man.'[49]

Ark-Wilder and the *Dart*'s captain decide to offer terms to the Rover, which Ark-Wilder conveys to him: a pardon in exchange for surrender and a promise to 'quit the seas and renounce the name of Englishman forever'.[50] The Rover refuses these terms and the two ships engage in battle with each other until the Rover and his men successfully board the *Dart* and 'crimson drops' on the Rover's yataghan betoken its 'fatal service in the fray'.[51] The men of the *Dart* are defeated, gallant Scipio is mortally wounded and breathes his last beside his surviving companion Fid. At this point some further revelations are required by Cooper's plot and the *Dart*'s chaplin notices the words tattooed on Fid's arm, 'Ark, of Lynnhaven', which he knows to be not the name of a ship, but of an estate, owned by a dear friend. Attention turns to a 'collar' mentioned by the dying Scipio, which he wears around his arm and which belonged to the nutritious dog found aboard the wreck with the boy Ark-Wilder.[52] Mrs Wyllys-de Lacey insists that the inscription on the collar be read, which declares 'Neptune, the property of Paul de Lacey'.[53] This information leads Mrs Wyllys-de Lacey to identify Ark-Wilder as her son, for whom she now requests mercy. The Rover responds and halts the proposed piratical hangings of the two-timing Ark-Wilder and Fid.

On the following day the *Dolphin* and the *Dart* are 'sailing in amity, side by side'.[54] On the *Dolphin* the Rover has spent the intervening night pacing 'the poop in brooding silence' and now addresses his crew and captives.[55] He dismisses his crew with the consolatory reward of his personal treasure of gold—'That you need have no grounds of reproach, I bestow my treasure'—and commands them to take the *Dolphin*'s coaster to shore.[56] He then bids farewell to Ark-Wilder-de Lacey and the two ladies and servant who are all restored to the *Dart*. As the *Dart* sails freely away, those aboard watch the diminishing figures of the Rover and Roderick, his cabin-boy, on the deserted *Dolphin* until they disappear in the distance. Then an explosion is seen and heard from the *Dolphin*, followed by a fire and finally 'an empty waste of water'.[57]

Twenty years later the British colonies of North America have successfully rebelled and at Newport a curtained litter is carried ashore, accompanied by a woman who enquires for Captain de Lacey. They are directed to his home where they meet Ark-Wilder-de Lacey, his wife Gertrude, son Paul and mother, Mrs Wyllys-de Lacey. The seaman in the litter is dying but Mrs Wyllys-de Lacey rather belatedly recognizes in his 'fading countenance' her brother, Ark-Wilder-de Lacey's uncle, none other than the Red Rover.[58] His female companion is plainly, by implication, Roderick. The Rover has been fighting anonymously for America, he explains, and in a final dying gesture he unrolls a package he has brought and 'let fall before him that blazonry of intermingled stripes, with its blue field of rising stars'.[59]

Cooper's narrative is more afloat than the narrative of Scott's *The Pirate*, and the Rover is more the centre of attention than is Cleveland, the reformed ex-pirate in *The Pirate*. Cooper, although unkindly called 'the Walter Scott of America', as if in colonial dependence, cultural debt, has benefitted from the fortunate historical coincidence between American literary independence and European Romanticism, which celebrated wildness, rebelliousness, and independence.[60] He has also recognized the ocean as a Romantic phenomenon, like the American wilderness of his frontier narratives featuring Natty Bumppo, and therefore the ocean mirrors the pirate role on it, unruly, threatening to social order, frightening, and sublime. Cooper has, however, paralleled his proper hero—Ark-Wilder-de Lacey of the latent love-and-marriage plot—and the proper pirate, the Red Rover. Wilder is potentially a pirate, is disguised as one for some considerable time, and is potentially also anomic and antisocial, calling himself Wilder, or 'Wild-one', as the Rover playfully remarks.[61] Of course he was only acting the role of a pirate, but then that is not unlike the behaviour of the Rover himself, who is a master of disguise and masquerade, as when he convincingly impersonates an aristocratic British naval officer. Indeed, the Rover is never obviously piratical himself, contradicting the public idea of a pirate—not shaggy-whiskered, brutal-voiced, or monstrously deformed, as the *Dart's* captain expects. His piratical role is balanced, even over-balanced, by his sense of honour. In proper Byronic mode, he engages in inscrutable brooding and exotic dress and décor, but never in dishonourable violence, and he nobly renounces his pile of treasure, which we see him giving away, not acquiring, treasure for which he seems to have little or no regard.

Indeed Cooper has disguised piracy in patriotism. The Rover's piratical role is motivated by the retrospectively romantic and admirable rebellion of Americans against British colonial power. His engagement with the antisocial marine world has been in quest of a nationality which he celebrates in his dying display of the stars and stripes. The rebellious ocean has been his medium for a voyage in search of political freedom. His anomic pirate role is not naturally his, however, for he is revealed to be the well-born and well-connected brother of Mrs Wyllys-de Lacey, and his behaviour has been in keeping with his high birth. The Rover's nephew, Ark-Wilder-de Lacey, has pursued a parallel quest on the ocean, whose sailors adopted him as a sea-borne found-ling, an apparent orphan. Ark-Wilder-de Lacey has indeed been on a quest for identity, successfully achieved in his recognition as well-born as well as non-piratical. Here again Cooper's plot resembles Scott's: the long-delayed recovery of family relationship. Piracy has been plotted as a search for identity and nationality, not loot. A cancelled passage in Cooper's manuscript has Mrs Wyllys identify herself with a different family than the de Laceys, indicating that his plot outcome was not planned originally, and reminding us of its artificiality.[62] What lies behind such contrivance, of course, is not only the precedent of Scott but the generic pattern of romance, evident in the Shakespearian plays from which Cooper has taken all but one of the epigraphs to his chap-ters, most of all from *The Tempest*. Indeed Shakespeare's late plays and romantic comedies are the literary model for the implausible plotting of *The Red Rover*: the quasi-magical rediscovery of the fractured family, the sea-changes provoked by the ocean, and even the cross-dressing of Roderick, the secretly female cabin-boy.

Wilder and the Rover are parallels, even doppelgängers, as well as nephew and uncle. Wilder seems to be a pirate but is instead a British naval officer, grandson of an admiral as well as nephew of the Rover, who is not so much a pirate as a patriot, and equally well-born. The artful and artificial revelations of Cooper's plot have this insistent ten-dency: that pirates are not pirates. This was the tendency also of Scott's *The Pirate*, about a pirate whose sea-chest contained not purloined treasure but legitimate proof of his gentlemanly pedigree. Literary pirates, then, were either Irving's grotesque ghosts who haunted comi-cally gothic and improbable tales of buried treasure or else they were Scott's and Cooper's gentlemen in disguise, heroes of romance disdain-ing treasure and undergoing magical transformation—protractedly, eventually, becoming the gentlemen they always really were in the first place. The two types have this much in common, however, considera-bly much, that both are literary beings, creatures of the imagination, insubstantial, unreal, at home where they belong, on the page not the ocean.

Scott grumbled into his journal that Cooper's *Red Rover* used 'too much of nautical language', but he respected Cooper's 'powerful con-ception of character and force of execution'.[63] When Eugène Sue launched the 'roman maritime' in France with *Kernok le Pirate* (1830), he prefaced it with praise not of Scott but of Cooper, the author of (in French translation) the *Corsaire Rouge*.[64] *The Red Rover* had some success with theatre-goers as well as readers. Indeed Scott had already enjoyed a London production of *The Pilot*, all the more because the adaptor had moderated the American nationalism of the novel.[65] The same adaptor was pleased that, although the London Adelphi theatre had received 'seventeen versions' of *The Red Rover* ('such was the rage for writing nautical pieces'), his own particular version was chosen for production and consequent public admiration.[66] Pirates were popular, obviously, on the stage.

Peripatetic Cooper meanwhile had produced another nautical novel, written mostly in Italy in 1829, in a study with a view of Naples and of a stretch of Italian coast. In *The Water Witch; or, The Skimmer of the Seas* (1830) the central piratical figure is the 'Skimmer' and his vessel is the *Water Witch*. Like the Rover, the Skimmer is an elusive, mysterious figure on shore as well as at sea. Rather than engaging in violent piracy, he is illegally free-trading exotic luxuries on the American coast in the first decade of the eighteenth century, a period, not long after Kidd, when colonial authorities and local traders were of questionable integrity.[67] The thrills of *The Rover* are to some extent repeated—the abduction of a beautiful heiress, battles, wrecks and rescues at sea. The Skimmer resents British colonial authority, but his revolutionary tendency is secondary to his fundamental decency. He evades the pursuing British naval ship by superior seamanship in the challenging navigation of Hell-Gate and other seaways in the vicinity of New York, but he then defends the British naval ship against a French attack, demonstrating strong principles of honour and rectitude. He is not, as is rumoured and believed, the son of a previous legendary and heroic Skimmer, who fled British 'tyranny' a generation earlier with an only daughter, but is instead an 'orphan' adopted and protected by the original Skimmer, as we learn in the wave of revelations that concludes the narrative.[68] The successor Skimmer's mysterious companion, Seadrift, alias Eudora, is female, not male, and is the original Skimmer's grand-daughter, not his daughter, and not the second Skimmer's sister. As the Skimmer explains to Alderman Van Beverout, who is abruptly revealed to be Eudora's father, she has only recently discovered who she is: 'It is now a year since she first learned she was not my sister. Until then, like you, she supposed us equally derived from one who was the parent of neither.'[69]

It is unfortunate that Cooper's thrilling if confusing dénouement is explained so clumsily that the reader, already drowning in the wave of revelations, must struggle to deduce that 'the parent of neither' is the original Skimmer, who was the 'parent' of 'neither' Eudora nor the second Skimmer. Cooper's books are sadly full of windbags, their awful verbosity—the tangled language in which they explicate his tangled plots—not a character trait but an authorial one. In conclusion the eligible abducted heiress, Alida de Barbérie, niece of Alderman Van Beverout, will marry the pursuing British naval captain, and Eudora, now in female clothing, decides to marry the Skimmer, who is not her brother after all, and they sail away together into the no-man's-land of the sea, aboard the *Water Witch*.

In 1827, while Cooper was writing *The Red Rover* on the Seine, Bellini's new opera *Il Pirata* opened in Milan. The librettist, Felice Romani, had as his source a Gothic drama by Charles Maturin, *Bertram; or, The Castle of St. Aldobrand; a Tragedy* (1816), a pirateless play performed at Drury Lane on the recommendations of Scott and Byron.[70] In Bellini's opera, Gualtiero, the Count of Montalto, has been pirating—that essentially aristocratic activity—until, as the opera opens, he is shipwrecked near the castle of the woman he loves, Imogene. Because his pirating stops when the opera starts, there are no scenes of pirate life, but he recalls those scenes and his thoughts at the time of Imogene. 'Nelle stragi del pirata', he sings, 'quell'imagine adorata si presenta al mio pensier?' ('Amidst the violence of a pirate's life, what adored image comes to my mind?') The adored image is unfortunately married to Gualtiero's enemy, Ernesto, the Duke of Caldora, so the piratical Count kills the marital Duke and is sentenced to death. In the climactic scene, the doubly loved and soon to be doubly bereaved Imogene loses her mind ('esser fuori di sé') but not her voice.

What this transposition indicates is that the pirate has a double, the Gothic hero, a noble outlaw again, Maturin's Bertram in this instance, who is himself in transition from the Gothic villain, a type with a dark and attractive—a Satanic—past. The Gothic Bertram of Maturin travels between London and Milan, drama and opera, but practises no piracy, even as the hero of *Il Pirata*. Maturin's Bertram, played at Drury Lane, London, by Edmund Kean, was not a pirate, but the stage pirate had been popular in England for many years.

Blackbeard; or, The Captive Princess, containing a blend of Blackbeard's theatrical character and Avery's imaginary Muslim Princess, opened and ran for many nights at the Royal Circus theatre in London in 1798. The first scene is set in 'The Pirates' Cabin', where they are carousing, playing cards, and singing jolly songs, when a sail is sighted 'and a vessel heaves in sight bearing Mogul colours'.[71] The second scene features a duet sung by Nancy, alias Anne, and William, a loving couple who do not like their captain—Blackbeard. Nancy-Anne explains in a ballad what she is doing 'disguised as a Piratical Seaman':

> In jacket blue, and trowsers neat,
>   Snow-white that play'd around my knee;
> I join'd the ship in Willy's fleet.[72]

Unfortunately, their naval idyll was interrupted when

> A Pirate's flag appall'd each heart![73]

So Willy and cross-dressed Nancy-Anne are now captives on Blackbeard's ship, the *Revenge*.

With this explanation out of the way, the suspended action proceeds:

> The Mogul's vaunting colours are torn to a rag,
> Triumphant above flies the Pirates black flag![74]

Another loving couple, Abdallah and 'Ismene (a Mogul Princess)', who is dressed in 'Crimson Turkish robe and trowsers, white turban ornamented', are taken captive.[75] Blackbeard, piratically costumed in a 'Black tabbed tunic trimmed with gold, sailor's petticoat trowsers [voluminous knee-length trousers], red leggings, black leather belt, black boots', is 'enamoured' of the Princess and orders William and Nancy-Anne to cast extraneous Abdallah into the hold.[76] A following scene is set at the 'residence of Blackbeard' at Madagascar, where he is awaited by his wife, Orra, wearing a 'Striped Indian dress, with beads, feathers, &c.', and accompanied by her retinue of slaves.[77] Blackbeard lands with Ismene, however, on whom his wife 'looks with a jealous eye'.[78] Meanwhile Abdallah has taken off his turban and William has recognized him as his saviour from slavery on some previous occasion. Gratefully he gives Abdallah his sword and releases him, pretending that he has escaped. Blackbeard's wife then escapes with Ismene, who has stolen Blackbeard's affection from his wife but also, confusingly, bribed her with jewels to aid the royal Mughal escape. Orra's motives are confusing but complementary in their result: abandoning faithless Blackbeard and removing the Princess at a profit.

The next scene is set with 'A West Indian View': 'Enter Orra and Ismene much agitated'.[79] They are not agitated by their abrupt transportation from the Indian Ocean to the Caribbean, but because females who are not cross-dressed have no other emotions or directions in the play. They characteristically flee and Blackbeard enters in pursuit with his faithful sideman, Caesar. They are not pursuing Ismene, however, but Abdallah, 'who has lost his way' (and not because he is unexpectedly in the West Indies).[80] Lieutenant Maynard and his crew now enter, in pursuit of Blackbeard. Agitated and confused, Orra decides to stab Ismene jealously but is stabbed herself by Blackbeard, who entertains the recaptured Princess to 'Cold Collation and Fruits' in his residence, where 'the piratical colours are pending'.[81] Unseen by him, Nancy-Anne slips a note to Ismene which reads—in letters legible to the audience—'Expect Friends'.[82] Blackbeard makes his move on the Princess: He 'extinguishes the lights; she becomes much agitated; he approaches her, drags her to the sopha, solicits, threatens, &c. when a groan is heard, and the Apparition of Orra rises!' (see Figure 5.1).[83]

Figure 5.1. Jack Helme 'in the character of Blackbeard', an engraving in which the incidental spectre of Orra is dimly visible, by C. Tomkins, after I.F. Roberts.

Interrupted, if not agitated, Blackbeard is now warned of Maynard's pursuit and reboards the *Revenge*, where he puts Ismene in charge of the faithful Caesar, with orders: 'Should the Enemy prove victorious, blow up the Ship'.[84] Caesar obediently drags Ismene into a scene set in the 'Interior of the Powder Magazine', furnished with 'barrels of gunpowder, cartridges, the powder trough, &c.'.[85] She is 'much agitated' but Abdallah 'rushes on', stabs Caesar, and rescues her.[86] In the climactic last scene, Blackbeard's *Revenge* and Maynard's *Pearl* are 'grappled together in close action' while the two leaders fight each other with pistols and cutlasses and Abdallah and Ismene join in, with the result that Blackbeard is 'overcome, and plunged into the sea'.[87] In triumphant conclusion, the slaves ashore and the victorious sailors at sea are somehow assembled on stage, 'the Curtain falling to their Huzzas of Victory'.[88]

A playbill for the Royal Circus, St George's Fields, an open space in London between Southwark and Lambeth, advertised *Blackbeard; or, The Captive Princess* and the other entertainments generously offered on the same evening, which included a 'Wire-Dancer, from Portugal', 'Tumbling', performed by 'Infant Pierrot and Modern Hercules', and concluded with a pantomime entitled *Harlequin Mariner: or, The Witch of the Oaks*.[89] The female pirate, we may note, is at home on the stage, if not the ocean wave, cross-dressing and going to sea amorously, and at least as popular as wire-dancers or tumblers. Pirates can be known, then, by the company they keep—popular entertainment as predictable as acrobats and pantomime, a variety act, part of a good night out in London. Yes, pirates can be known by the company they keep and, yes, Madagascar is in the West Indies. Blackbeard has become actually what he was latently in the *General History*, a theatrical villain, but his piratical qualities are diminished and indistinct, and he depends for effect on a fictitious leading lady, a captive princess, borrowed from the Avery legend. Hence the equivocating title: *Blackbeard; or, The Captive Princess*.

There were several American productions of *Red Rover* plays but pirates (and pirates-who-were-not-pirates) were popular with writers of popular fiction as well as drama. As Cooper noticed in a preface to his *Red Rover*, America lacked historical nautical events—such as those involving Avery or Madagascar—for fictional adaptation, with 'the exception of the well-known, though meagre incidents connected with the career of Kidd'.[90] So Kidd—though not a very historically accurate Kidd—was a favourite for many popularizers of pirates. J.S. Jones's *Captain Kyd or the Wizard of the Sea. A Drama* was first performed at Boston in 1830, one of multiple melodramas and farces by the popular Bostonian dramatist. The central character, Lord Lester, has been cradle-swapped at birth, it transpires, and he is actually Captain Kyd, the son of a paternal pirate called Hurtel of the Red Hand. At the ruined Tower of Hurtel, a sorceress, Elpsy, suggests Kyd should follow his real father's career. 'Wilt thou … become a pirate?—yesterday Lord of Lester, today a pirate?'[91] 'Yes!' says Lester.[92] 'I am wedded now to deeds of darkness. Through life I wade in blood.'[93] At sea he makes his victims walk 'the plank', an invention more fictional than piratical, apparently, with no recorded use in pirate practice of the eighteenth century.[94] When he is not wading in blood he is courting Kate Bellamont, the imaginary daughter of real Kidd's imprisoner at Boston, Lord Bellomont. After enough deeds of darkness to satisfy the audience, Kyd is informed that Elpsy, the sorceress, is actually his mother and—incredulous—he is 'overpowered with chains' and removed from the scene.[95]

Like Scott, the author of *Captain Kyd or the Wizard of the Sea* has muddled piracy and sorcery, and has made his plot a delayed disclosure of identity. In *Captain Kyd* the aristocratic Lester turns out to be a hereditary pirate, but this version of the more conventional pirate-to-aristocrat plot is no less contrived for reversing its direction. The play's Kyd is not really a wizard but the play's title requires him to be more than a pirate. Elpsy is indeed a sorceress of sorts, somewhat in the tradition of Scott's Norna, but melodramatic, not mysterious.

Jones's *Captain Kyd* was performed repeatedly in the 1830s, 40s and 50s, in Boston and New York.[96] It was so successful, indeed, that an energetic producer of historical romances decided to transform it into a novel. Hence *Captain Kyd: The Wizard of The Sea. A Romance* by J.H. Ingraham, published in America in 1839 and in London in 1842—with no apparent acknowledgement to any previous author or work, but repeating the same convoluted plot of contrived surprises, with a few extra twists and turns.[97] Captain Kidd, like Blackbeard and the Captive Princess, is a character in search of a plot, or a genre: *A Drama, A Romance*.

Frederick Marryat's *The Pirate* (1836) has accidentally become a kind of comedy—so much have thematic pirate characteristics subsequently changed in their effects from thrilling to silly. It concerns two respectable and well-born twin boys separated by a shipwreck in the Bay of Biscay, one surviving to be cared for by his uncle at Finsbury Square, London, and then pursuing a career in the Royal Navy, while the other, with his mother, is adopted by the evil and dreadful pirate Captain Cain, who characterizes himself by threatening a female captive so horribly that she jumps overboard into the jaws of sharks. This is thrilling. The regular naval twin, Edward, commands a naval schooner, coincidentally in search of Cain's coincidentally identical pirate schooner. The twin ships are a matching pair 'built at Baltimore'.[98] This is silly, as is the implausibly symmetrical plot, ruled by coincidence and predictability, with piracy as an undeviating voyage from suspended respectability to resumed respectability, from Finsbury Square all the way to Finsbury Square.

In 1839 Irving published a story in the *Knickerbocker Magazine* called 'Guests from Gibbet-Island'. His source was 'Gäste vom Galgen' ('Guests from the Gallows'), a tale in the Grimm Brothers' *Deutsche Sagen* (1816–18), a work Irving had acquired in Dresden in 1823 and had been reading in Paris later that year.[99] The Grimms' tale is brief. A drunken innkeeper on his way home encounters three hanged men on a gallows and in jest invites them to supper with him. When he reaches his home he finds them waiting for him and he collapses in horror and dies.[100] To Americanize and expand this tiny German tale Irving set it in the Dutch community of New York in the British colonial period, and he has given it a background of piracy: 'These were the times of the notorious Captain Kidd'.[101] Irving's title, 'Guests from Gibbet-Island', indicates the dependence of his plot on the German source, but he has used the Grimms' tale for what he calls 'the butt-end' of his story and stretched it to cover many years.[102] The central figure, Vanderscamp, is a young nephew of the innkeeper of a Dutch village in New York. The nephew, 'a real scamp by nature' as well as by name, forms a friendship with a black man, Pluto, who was found one morning cast ashore after a storm.[103] Together they misbehave locally, 'carrying on a complete system of piracy, on a small scale', and then disappear to practise on a larger scale, returning with a gang of 'noisy, roistering, swaggering varlets' who come ashore from 'a long, black, rakish-looking schooner'.[104] At their head is 'a rough, burly, bully ruffian, with fiery whiskers, a copper nose, a scar across his face', Vanderscamp, in other words, and at their rear was 'old Pluto, who had lost an eye, grown grizzly-headed, and looked more like a devil than ever'.[105] These 'boisterous men of the seas' take over the village inn which

Vanderscamp has inherited on his uncle's decease and they engage in
'such orgies' as 'drinking, singing, whooping, swearing'.[106] Thus they
terrify the community and come and go on piratical expeditions until
the British government becomes annoyed enough to hang 'three of
Vanderscamp's chosen comrades, the most riotous swashbucklers', on
the island in front of the inn, known as Gibbet Island.[107] The Grimm
Brothers' plot requires that Vanderscamp and Pluto have escaped this
fate, but the Grimms' ending is delayed in Irving's version by the
departure of his two characters on another voyage, from which they
return with a wife for Vanderscamp. One night the two men are rowing home by boat from some 'carousing' aboard a visiting ship, when
Vanderscamp sees the dead bodies of his former companions hanging
on Gibbet Island.[108] Somewhat drunk, he invites them to 'drop in to
supper' and finds them drinking at the inn on his return.[109] Horrified,
he falls downstairs and dies. The inn is thereafter shunned, 'pronounced
a *haunted house*', and Vanderscamp's wife and Pluto die horribly and
mysteriously, she apparently murdered and he washed up on Gibbet
Island 'near the foot of the pirates' gallows'.[110]

American literature of the early-to-mid nineteenth century felt in
need of a respectable historical dimension, and of legends of a supernatural kind, and pirates served such needs. Hence the attachment of
pirates to the macabre tales with ghosts, hauntings and grotesqueries.
Poe, however, had something more original to make of this recurring
material. He did rattle some skeletons but he took Irving's money-
diggers from mystification to explanation. The narrator of Poe's 'The
Gold Bug' (1843) had an acquaintance, Legrand, somewhat reclusive
and temperamental, who lived with a black servant on Sullivan's Island,
near Charleston, South Carolina. This Legrand found an unusual
weighty, gold-coloured beetle with a vicious bite, which his servant,
Jupiter, carefully wrapped in a piece of parchment he found sticking
out of the sand nearby. On the evening of the narrator's visit Legrand
has lent the beetle to a friend and was obliged, therefore, to describe it
by means of a sketch, which he made on the convenient piece of
parchment. The parchment is accidentally heated by the fire in the
room and in consequence a drawing of 'a skull, or death's-head',
appears on it.[111] Legrand becomes obsessed with discovering the significance of this death's-head, so much so that Jupiter and the narrator
are concerned for his state of mind. Jupiter fears Legrand has 'bin bit
somewhere bout de head by dat goole-bug'.[112]

Legrand insists that Jupiter and the narrator accompany him on an expedition to a secluded spot on the mainland, where he instructs Jupiter to climb a tall tree. At the end of a particular branch Jupiter finds a skull and is instructed to let fall the weighty bug through an eye-socket. Legrand marks the spot of its fall on the ground and calculates a certain distance from it and from the tree-trunk and there he insists they dig. After an apparent failure resulting from Jupiter's mistaking the left for the right eye-socket of the skull, with consequent miscalculation of the precise spot, the bewildered diggers and Legrand find two skeletons and then a chest containing 'a treasure of incalculable value' (see Figure 5.2).[113] In the chest the treasure was lying in confusion as well as profusion, 'heaped in promiscuously', but the narrator then takes a long paragraph to organise and enumerate the exact contents: gold coins 'of antique date'; 110 diamonds; 18 rubies; 310 emeralds; 21 saphires; solid gold ornaments such as rings, chains, and crucifixes; 197 gold watches, old but richly jewelled; all of which they valued (indeed 'undervalued') at 'a million and a half of dollars'.[114]

The treasure found and counted, Poe's tale is not complete, however, for the narrator 'was dying with impatience for a solution of this most extraordinary riddle'.[115] As with Poe's other 'tales of ratiocination' (his own term for the detective stories he originated), the pleasure of the story is not in the achievement of the desired result (the discovery of a murderer or recovery of stolen property) but in the explanation of the logical process by which the apparent mystery is solved.[116] Poe's originality—and modernity—was in the recognition of the complementarity of horrible Gothic mystery and rational, logical solution. The treasure possessed and assessed is abandoned by the narrative, therefore, and the thrilling plot repeated, this time with explanation.

There was method in Legrand's apparent madness, which he now reveals. Guessing that the death's head which appeared on the parchment must have been drawn with invisible ink, he heated the parchment methodically, revealing the figure of 'a kid'.[117] Knowing that 'the skull, or death's-head, is the well-known emblem of the pirate', he now 'looked upon the figure of the animal as a kind of punning or hieroglyphical signature', the signature, in effect, of Captain Kidd.[118] Recalling all 'the thousand vague rumours' about Kidd's treasure, and that 'the stories told are all about money-seekers, not about money-finders', he

Figure 5.2. Illustrations by Felix Darley for 'The Gold Bug', in the *Dollar Newspaper*, 28 June 1843.

reasoned that the multiplication of these stories implied that Kidd did indeed bury treasure, which he did not ever dig up, and which had never been found.[119] Further systematic heating of the parchment revealed a message in an impenetrable cipher, the very thing Legrand had expected and required: 'the text for my context'.[120] Again Poe's ingenuity is in recognizing the parallelism of the criminal and writer's mystifying process and the detective and reader's comprehending one. Legrand had now to decipher a textual mystery, a topic that had previously engaged Poe in writing a magazine piece called 'A Few Words on Secret Writing', in which he had promised to solve any ciphers that readers could devise.[121] Legrand solved the textual puzzle—by a process starting with the recognition of 'e' as the most frequently used letter in English—and was able to read the instructions for finding Kidd's treasure, after some further detective work deducing the geographical landmarks referred to and the method required for measuring the treasure's hiding place by means of the skull in the tree. A *memento mori* is introduced at the conclusion of the exciting treasure hunt and intellectual process: 'What are we to make of the skeletons found in the hole?' asks the narrator.[122] These also are explicable, replies Legrand, by Kidd's need to keep his secret to himself. 'Perhaps a couple of blows with a mattock were sufficient...?'[123]

Historical Kidd provided Poe with little more than an excuse for treasure-hunting, rewritten as a mental process. Certainly Sullivan's Island, South Carolina, had no connection with the historical Kidd— although it did with the young private Perry, alias Poe, of the United States Army, who was stationed there from 1827–8.[124] Legrand is a Romantic type, 'with unusual powers of mind' but misanthropic and of unstable mood, considered mentally ill even by his servant and the narrator.[125] His unusual ratiocinative process is Poe's real subject, not merely the treasure, and it is a process not ordered by moral or social goals so much as by an intellectual pleasure in puzzle-solving. It so happens that his obsessive puzzle-solving results in treasure-finding—a satisfactory result for a man whom 'misfortunes' had deprived of wealth—but the pursuit of treasure does not appear to be his governing motive, and Poe's narrative leaves it behind to reach for logical explanation, the rationale of the apparently irrational, an anticipation of Freudian explication.[126] The credible treasure is supplied by the Kidd legend, already used by Irving to Gothic effect, but pervaded by ghosts and the supernatural. Poe's tale retains a skull and two skeletons but, like his tales of ratiocination, takes its plot from a logical process: the creation of mystery is complemented by—indeed superseded by—the explication of mystery. Nevertheless, Poe's super-brained hero—the inspiration for Sherlock Holmes—is a man of perverse ingenuity, a counterpart of the Romantic pirate, Kidd, the supposed puzzle-maker, of whom Legrand, as puzzle-solver, is the mirror image.

When purportedly factual reporting—pseudo-biography and pseudo-history, the nascent novel—became literary fiction for the middle classes in the nineteenth century, then piracy, like crime, was stolen from the popular, plebeian villain, and rewritten as an essentially aristocratic practice. For the recently-risen middle classes, the criminal and the aristocrat were equally unreal, were marginal, were exchange-able even, almost identical, until discriminated by the surprising (because artificial and improbable) conclusion to the predictable, inev-itable plot. As the pirate was shadowed and doubled by the aristocrat whom he turned out to be, piracy, like crime, was subjected to a Romantic revaluation which celebrated the marginal man, the deviant, and aestheticized his deviance, rewriting it as an art, most obviously in De Quincey's 'On Murder Considered as One of the Fine Arts' (1827), in which the sailor-murderer is an artist, a natural aristocrat, transcend-ing the mundane, the middle class, the shore-bound world, by means of his imagination, his evasion of detection, and is treated artistically by his colleague, his accomplice, the author. The relation—perhaps literal, as a brother—between Poe's well-descended (well-born and fallen) detective, Dupin, with his 'diseased intelligence', and his arch-antago-nist, the nearly-anonymous 'Minister D-' in 'The Purloined Letter' (1845), anticipates Sherlock Holmes and Moriarty, but more immedi-ately parallels the relation between Poe's Legrand, the deserving, ingenious inheritor, and evil but ingenious Kidd, the piratical bequeather, who are united as the equally-ingenious solver and creator of the puzzle of the secret, encrypted pirate treasure, with Poe, of course, as their supremely-ingenious author, in collusion with the hyp-ocritical reader, his double, his . . . brother.[127] The pirate was one of the flowers, therefore, of evil.

Poe's tale involved him too in some treasure-hunting. Anonymously reviewing himself, he attributed the popularity of 'The Gold Bug' to the materialism of the public: 'The interest of the author was evidently to write a popular tale: money, and the finding of money being chosen as the most popular thesis'.[128] He had sold 'The Gold Bug' to *Graham's Magazine* for $52 but bought it back before publication (repaying the sum by writing some reviews) when he heard that the *Dollar Newspaper* was offering $100 as prize in a short story competition.[129] 'The Gold Bug' won the prize and was published and reprinted in June and July 1843, with consequent acclaim for its author.[130]

'The Gold Bug' demonstrated the ratiocinative pleasures of pirate treasure-hunting as well as the simpler thrill of treasure itself as material wealth. Kidd's treasure glittered in nineteenth-century literature, but other pirates provided other pleasures, as can be seen for example in *Fanny Campbell, The Female Pirate Captain* (Boston, 1845), authored supposedly by a Lieutenant Murray, but actually by pioneer of pulp, Maturin M. Ballou.[131] For her introduction to us Fanny has 'cast off her neat and becoming homespun dress' and is engaged in her evening prayers:

> Her limbs and person possessed that bewitching roundness, which, while it seemed to indicate a tendency to *enbonpoint*, yet is the furthest removed from an overfleshiness of habit; her full and heaving breast, her perfectly formed limbs, her round and dimpled arms, all spoke of a voluptuousness of person, and yet within the most delicate rule of beauty. A painter should have seen her there, her person modestly veiled yet displaying her form in most ravishing distinctness; her breast heaving with suppressed emotions, and her hands clasped and raised towards Heaven. Her features were after the Grecian school, with a coral lip that would have melted an anchorite. Where Fanny got those eyes from, Heaven only knows, they rivalled a Circassian's. Nature seemed to have delighted in ornamenting her with every gift it might bestow. Her teeth were regular and white as pearls, and her hair was a very dark auburn, worn parted smoothly across her brow, and gathered in a modest snood behind her head, while it was easy to see by its texture that if left to itself, it would have curled naturally. Such was Fanny Campbell.[132]

Such is the unambiguously feminine heroine of *The Female Pirate Captain*, in all her 'ravishing distinctness', with her 'heaving breast', and her 'breast heaving', on the brink of her author's plot, which is for her to capture and command a British ship, turn patriotic American revolutionary pirate, and rescue her lover from Spanish jail in Havana, all the while disguised as a 'manly sailor'.[133] *The Female Pirate* sold quickly: 80,000 copies in a matter of months.[134]

Properly male pirates also reached the emerging market for adventure stories, highbrow and low. After an apprenticeship as a hack writer,

writing to order for Maturin Ballou, Edward Judson, friend of buffalo-
meat supplier, William Cody, whom Judson reimagined and renamed
Buffalo Bill, paperback hero, wrote hundreds of dime novels under the
pseudonym Ned Buntline. One of these hundreds was *The Black
Avenger of the Spanish Main: or, The Fiend of Blood* (Boston, 1847), for
which Judson-Buntline was paid $100 by his former employer, the
author and publisher of *The Female Pirate Captain*.[135] Judson, who, as a
boy who ran away to sea, had read Scott, Irving, and Cooper, and then,
as a journalist, had criticized the sea fiction of J.H. Ingraham, author of
Captain Kyd: The Wizard of the Sea, because Ingraham 'did not know
the ropes', subsequently took to the popular press himself in Boston
and launched his career with *The Black Avenger*.[136] His hero, French-
born Francisco Solonois, 'el pirato pernicioso', is displayed in an illustration, cutlass in one hand and banner in the other, bearing his slogan
'Death to the Spaniards!'[137] The brief and swiftly-moving chapters are
prefaced with epigraphs from literary works such as Scott's *Lay of the
Last Minstrel* and Byron's *The Corsair*, from which Judson has taken the
name of Solonois's wife, Medora, whose death piratical Solonois is
keen to revenge: 'Blood for blood;—ay, for each drop of *her* precious
blood, rivers shall flow in revenge! Death to the Spaniards! Oh, my
Medora, thou shalt be avenged!'[138]

   This promise is made to the reader at the opening of the story and
is faithfully kept. The scenes and characters are more like Scott's work
than Byron's, more Gothic, indeed, than Romantic, more Monk Lewis
than Scott: palaces, gardens, ruined castles riddled with secret passages
and apparent phantoms, a 'hideous Ethiopian' hangman, his lost son
Quasey, who is a dwarf even 'more hateful to the eye', and—by
contrast—Luella, with delightfully small teeth, and lovely as the garden
she adorns:

as she laughed her voice seemed to mock the silvery fountain's clear dash,
while from between her lips as like a rose-bud-cleft, her small teeth glittered
like pearls in a lovely ruby set.[139]

Ships are not forgotten in favour of budding lips and glittering teeth.
There are cunning maritime manoeuvres and ropes are well understood by the vengeful pirate hero who gives knowledgeable nautical
orders: 'stand by to luff... Stand to the lee braces, men!'[140] Above all
there is the promised violence. The hero looks so 'fiendish' that his
own men 'shuddered with horror', although they themselves obediently

emerge from a Spanish frigate at Havana with 'stained and reeking hands' and 'weapons from which the clotted blood dropped in huge lumps'.[141]

This is romance with a difference, then, romance with nasty violence, but the plot, supposedly 'founded on historical fact', resolves in a reconstituted and reconciled family whose fragmented parts are, as it were, reanimated, each having thought the others dead or lost forever.[142] The black avenger and fiend of blood loses the characteristic 'cold haughtiness of his look' and 'the firm compression of [his] chiselled lip' and becomes as nice as pie, reunited with his wife, Medora, and his son, Juan, who has his paternity and identity revealed and explained.[143] Solonois is even at peace with his evil Spanish father-in-law, the Governor of Cuba, who—it transpires—did not kill Solonois's wife and son. As the nice-as-pie ex-fiend-and-avenger explains: 'if Medora lives, then once more will Solonois learn how to smile—and how to spare a Spaniard!'[144] Even the 'hideous Ethiopian' rediscovers his surviving, long-lost son, the even more hideous dwarf, and lovely Luella of the tiny teeth can climatically marry Don Juan, who is not her cousin after all.

Edward Judson, alias Ned Buntline, followed this success, reprinted and reprinted, with *The Red Revenger; or, The Pirate King of the Floridas* (1847) and only later found William Cody slumbering under a wagon in Nebraska and turned him into the Western hero—Natty Bumppo for a new age—*Buffalo Bill: The King of the Border Men* (1869). Buntline was so proud of his inferior writing that we should perhaps be suspicious of his boasts, when asked if his plots were planned:

I never lay out plots in advance. I shouldn't know how to do it, for how can I know what my people may take it into their heads to do? First I invent a title. When I hit a good one I consider the story about half finished. It is the thing of prime importance. After I begin I push ahead as fast as I can write...[145]

So says the author of pirate heroes, who are not plotted at all, but produced by the heroic author at top speed: the pirate as pulp hero, address Gleason Publishing, Grub Street, USA.

A locked and mysterious chest from the waves had already penetrated Cooper's distant woods in *The Deerslayer* (1841), in which Deerslayer (one of Natty Bumppo's many names) is informed about its owner, Floating Tom Hutter, that he was once reputedly 'a companion of a sartain Kidd, who was hanged for piracy,... and that he [Floating

Tom] came up into these regions, thinking that the king's cruisers could never cross the mountains, and that he might enjoy the plunder peaceably in the woods'.[146] As it transpires over many pages, the chest contains no treasure but 'documents', which confirm that Floating Tom was indeed a pirate, so we can be sure that an authentic pirate had indeed reached the frontier of Cooper's Leatherstocking (Natty Bumppo) novels.[147]

Cooper's last nautical novel, *The Sea Lions* (1848/9), also used a chest as a narrative device and had a treasure map for a plot—for the beginning and end of the book, at least, if not for its expansive middle. At its opening, in the district of Oyster Pond, Long Island, in 1819, a 'worn-out and battered seaman' named Tom Daggett comes ashore, equipped with 'a substantial sea-chest'.[148] He had not long to live, he knew, and communicated to the greedy local Deacon Pratt that he possessed two valuable secrets, the location of an island abundant with seals in the Antarctic Ocean, and the location of an islet in the West Indies, where a pirate treasure was buried—a treasure island, no less. The old seaman will not reveal the precise latitudes and longitudes of these two locations, but they are marked on charts in his chest, which the Deacon opens on Daggett's death, to find 'two old, dirty, and ragged charts'.[149] Greedily, the Deacon arranges for his niece's potential husband, a sailor named Roswell Gardiner (a relation of the owners of Gardiner's Island, supposed hiding place of Kidd's treasure, as Cooper knew) to undertake a voyage to these two secret places, in the Antarctic and the West Indies.[150] To appreciate the romantic subplot, we should know that the niece, Mary, loves Gardiner but will not marry him because he does not believe in the divinity of Christ.

The large bulk of *The Sea Lions* is about the rival pursuit of the sealing island by Gardiner and a relative of Daggett, who has heard rumours of the seals and the treasure. The Daggett relative is captain of a ship called the *Sea Lion*, named after Gardiner's ship, the *Sea Lion*—hence Cooper's plural title. Captain Daggett perishes of cold in the Antarctic winter and Captain Gardiner survives, learns to believe in the divinity of Christ, and escapes the Antarctic with a cargo (worth more than $20,000) of sealskins from the secret island.[151] On his return to Oyster Pond, he immediately informs Mary of his new faith in 'Christ as the Son of God', but finds that his employer, the Deacon, is dying.[152] Impatiently (and characteristically) the Deacon asks after the pirate treasure, and young Gardiner tells him what has been deliberately but rather crudely omitted from the preceding narrative, that he located the West Indian treasure islet and found the indicative tree and the significant 'hillock of sand', which concealed a box containing 143 doubloons (worth 'a little more than 2000 dollars').[153] He hands this loot to the dying Deacon, who grasps it and dies. He has, however, bequeathed his property to Mary, who happily marries the properly Christian and consequently prosperous Gardiner. The dying sailor and his chest containing a treasure map will have some literary future, of course, rather more than the adventures of Antarctic sealers.

Boys as well as men can have adventures. When the three boys on Ballantyne's Pacific island in *The Coral Island* (1857) have exhausted their author's stock of desert island topics, they sight a schooner approaching but 'observed that the flag at the schooner's peak was black, with a Death's head and cross bones upon it'.[154] The boys' response is as predictable as their visitors, one of whom makes himself at home at the boys' rudimentary shack by 'swinging the poor cat round his head by its tail': 'As we gazed at each other in blank amazement, the word "pirate" escaped our lips simultaneously'.[155]

Meanwhile the poetry of Byron's *The Corsair* was still popular in the English Victorian novel, as the characteristic reading of suspicious and pretentious ladies, such as the Hon. Blanche Ingram of Charlotte Brontë's *Jane Eyre* (1847). 'Know that I doat on Corsairs', she tells Mr Rochester and his drawing room.[156] Another, later in the century, is Lady Eustace of Trollope's *The Eustace Diamonds* (1873), who seeks 'a peer, unmarried, with a dash of the Corsair about him!', while recognizing that the attractions of the Corsair can be impractical for his wife:

To be hurried about the world by such a man, treated sometimes with crushing severity, and at others with the tenderest love, not to be spoken to for one fortnight, and then to be embraced perpetually for another, to be cast every now and then into some abyss of despair by his rashness, and then raised to a pinnacle of human joy by his courage—that, thought Lizzie, would be the kind of life which would suit her poetical temperament. But then, how would it be with her if the Corsair were to take to hurrying about the world without carrying her with him, and were to do so always at her expense? Perhaps he might hurry about the world and take somebody else with him. Medora, if Lizzie remembered rightly, had had no jointure or private fortune.[157]

So a pirate lover was thrilling but also worrying for a wife without a private fortune. The volatile Byronic pirate was comical in his effects on the excitable emotions of well-born ladies in Victorian novels.

But imaginary pirates could excite older boys as well as titled ladies by provoking emotional responses, as Douglas Stewart demonstrated in *The Pirate Queen: or, Captain Kidd and the Treasure* (London, 1867), in which 'the fine and superbly developed bust of the beautiful girl heaved tumultuously'.[158] Two young men, Jack and Fred by name, are captives on a pirate island, with Flora, the sister of one and loved-one of the other. The female with the tumultuously heaving bust is not Flora, however, but Inez, who is one of the pirates, but reluctantly, and arranges the escape of Jack and Fred. They find themselves in a place crowded with skeletons, by which they identify 'Dead Man's Hollow', and are recaptured by 'a tall, dark, handsome, but ferocious-looking man' who is not only tall, dark, and handsome but also 'the dreaded pirate, Captain Kidd'.[159] Jack and Fred are about to be hanged and join the skeletons when they are saved again. 'A female form of surprising beauty bursts in among the pirates':

And who is this female, who boldly, with flashing eyes, stands amidst the pirate horde, from whom she has snatched their prey? It is the beautiful Elmira, the *Pirate Queen*![160]

Elmira, the main character of Douglas Stewart's triple-titled *The Pirate Queen: or, Captain Kidd and the Treasure*, is another reluctant piratess with another tumultuously heaving bust, very like the traditional simultaneously good and bad reluctant pirate types, but with some natural differences which are emphasized, not disguised:

Somewhat above the medium height, her figure was lithe, supple, and admirably formed; her richly developed bust heaved tumultuously beneath a tight-fitting bodice of velvet, richly laced with gold; her arms, bare to the shoulders, were plump and beautifully rounded; her face, of the true Spanish type, was of the utmost beauty; her complexion, tinted with the dark olive of her country-women, and masked with a rich rosebud hue on either cheek, contrasted well with her fine piercing black eyes, which, when not lit up by fierce anger, shone with a bright glance of liquid languour and love. A vest of satin, richly trimmed with gold lace, set off to advantage her exquisitely moulded figure; her feet, encased in red Spanish boots, also edged with gold fringe, exposed a neat and well-turned ankle; and her beautifully rounded limbs were left fully exposed by a rich tunic, the skirt of which reached only to the knees. A lovely woman was Elmira, the Queen of the Buccaneers, and in the flower of her youth, numbering only some twenty summers.[161]

Elmira, the Queen of the Buccaneers, is in no danger of being mistaken for a man. Formerly Kidd's mistress, she plays the by-now-familiar role of the good pirate, while Kidd himself is unregenerately bad. The plot of the novel is an unremitting series of captures and escapes but the third item in the title—treasure—is not forgotten. After a number of escapes by the interesting characters—from Kidd's lusts and, for variety, from sharks and a snake—Elmira's own anti-piratical ship is wrecked on a reef and the assembled interesting ones—Jack, Fred, Flora, Inez, and Elmira—join a few surviving supposedly reformed pirates to escape (again) on a raft which reaches an uninhabited (and unlocated) island. Here, in an abandoned hut, they find two skeletons, one clutching 'a slip of paper or discoloured parchment'.[162] This parchment is 'blank' until Elmira makes use of it in lighting a fire, whereupon, to her surprise (if not the reader's):

The piece of old, yellow, worn parchment, blank, and without characters, of any description, when thrust in among the burning embers, now, under the heat, began to appear covered with writing, the words coming out stronger and stronger to the eyes of the beholder as the fire grew fiercer.[163]

The parchment reveals the secret instructions for digging up a treasure. Once again, then, writing reveals treasure, but Elmira has another surprise when she notices in addition 'a figure which appeared suddenly revealed at the top'.[164] This was none other than 'the rude outline of a kid' while, 'at the foot of the parchment, the signature consisted of a skull and crossbones'.[165]

Pestered by their company of supposedly reformed pirates, who are led by a black named Scipio, the interesting characters follow Kidd's instructions to a huge cedar tree, which Jack climbs to find, at the end of a branch, 'firmly nailed down the grim and ghastly head of a skeleton, with two pieces of glass thrust, in hideous mockery, into the space which should hold the eyes'.[166] Dropping a bullet from the skull to the ground and measuring a prescribed distance in the prescribed direction, they then mark the spot. That night they return and dig, discovering a skull and 'two gigantic skeletons', plus 'a huge coffer'.[167] Immediately they are attacked and captured by Scipio and his gang, who open the coffer and enjoy the treasure—huge quantities of jewels. They intend also to enjoy the three women 'dis night', as Scipio plans, but that night Scipio's men hear a ship's bell and decide to conceal the treasure all over again.[168] Having hidden the treasure somewhere new, Scipio is lustfully grabbing Elmira when he is shot and she is saved by Captain Kidd. They are all captured again and taken aboard Kidd's ship, the

Rattlesnake, where Kidd ogles 'the beauteous figures' of Inez and Flora.[169] Inez calls out in horror 'Father, father!' but Kidd explains that, to her surprise, he is not her father, with unfortunate consequences. Jack and Fred escape and rescue Inez and Flora from Kidd's lust.[170] Kidd is then about to execute Elmira when he is interrupted by news that the *Rattlesnake* is leaking badly. Somehow the interesting ones escape to Kidd's island home where the narrative began and where they soon see Kidd's ship approaching. Elmira vengefully burns his house down but is captured by one of his worst men, a 'sinewy Italian' who is about to rape her when struck down by Jack.[171] Fortunately, Kidd's *Rattlesnake* is opportunely 'surprised by an English ship of war' and soon flies the Union Jack, not the 'ominous black flag'.[172] Kidd himself escapes but the interesting ones are saved by the British navy. Elmira continues to seek Kidd's still missing treasure while Fred marries Flora and Jack marries Inez. A week later the happy couples hear that Kidd, who has rejoined history, has been captured at Boston. He is duly hanged at Wapping in London and Elmira witnesses his death. Her four friends hope that some day in the future they will 'hear again of Elmira, the Pirate Queen'.[173] Fortunately, they did not.

In 1870 Harriet Beecher Stowe published a story called 'Captain Kidd's Money', one of a series set in a nostalgic New England background, later collected as *Oldtown Fireside Stories* (1871). Like the other *Oldtown* stories, 'Captain Kidd's Money' is narrated by drawling, folksy Sam Lawson, who tells it to boys in a barn furnished with a 'soft fragrant cushion of hay', gently clucking hens, and an irremediably cheerful, chortling black servant, who supplies a note on his fiddle for Sam to sing some verses of the Americanized ballad of Kidd, including the one in which Kidd abandons the Bible his father gave him:

> And I sunk it in the sand
> Before I left the strand,
> As I sailed, as I sailed.[174]

With this introduction Sam then explains Kidd to the boys, as a pirate who 'got no end o' money,—gold and silver and precious stones', but who 'couldn't use it, and dar'sn't keep it; so he used to bury it in spots round here and there'.[175] Many have dug for Kidd's treasure, but none has 'ever got a cent'.[176] 'You see, boys, *it's the Devil's money*, and he holds a pretty tight grip on't.'[177] Sam himself remembers an attempt here in

Oldtown, where there was a rock with 'queer marks', 'sort o' lines and crosses', said to be 'Kidd's private marks'.[178] A local family of hick layabouts decided to dig there for Kidd's treasure and Sam accompanied the expedition, warning of a superstition that the discovery of the treasure should be made without a word being spoken. Sure enough, about five feet underground, they uncover 'a gret iron pot' which they heave up until one of them calls out triumphantly *we've got it!*', whereupon the pot falls back into the earth which closes over it, 'and then they heard the screechin'est laugh ye ever did hear'.[179] Sam pronounces the mysterious but blatantly obvious meaning of all this: 'It shows the vanity o' hastin' to be rich'.[180] The listening boys prefer a more material, less moral, conclusion, asking Sam 'what do you suppose was in that pot?'[181] 'Lawdy massy! boys: ye never will be done askin' questions. Why, how should I know?'[182]

Harriet Beecher Stowe's story is derivative of Irving's 'Money-Diggers' to the point of plagiarism, but the comically gothic tale has become the firmly moralising fable. The narrative frame remains cheerily sociable and convivial, a farmyard party replacing a fishing one, and tale-telling remains part of the tale, with money-digging as well as pirating quaintly and comfortably lost and buried in the past. The audience in the tale is now, however, boys.

In *The Adventures of Tom Sawyer* (1876) Harriet Beecher Stowe's next-door-neighbour, Samuel Clemens, alias Mark Twain, took up the pirate topic for boys.[183] Tom daydreams of escaping his Missouri village. Perhaps he could 'join the Indians' in 'the far West'?

But no, there was something grander even than this. He would be a pirate! That was it!...How his name would fill the world, and make people shudder!...And, at the zenith of his fame, how he would suddenly appear at the old village and stalk into church all brown and weather-beaten, in his black velvet doublet and trunks, his great jack-boots, his crimson sash, his belt bristling with horse-pistols, his crime-rusted cutlass at his side, his slouch hat with waving plumes, his black flag unfurled with the skull and crossbones on it, and hear with swelling ecstasy the whisperings: 'It's Tom Sawyer the Pirate! the Black Avenger of the Spanish Main!'[184]

It is in pursuit of this fiction that Tom takes his cohorts, Huck and Joe, alias 'Huck Finn the Red-handed, and Joe Harper the Terror of the Seas', to live on Jackson's Island in the Mississippi.[185] Tom is well informed about pirates by 'his favourite literature'.[186] Huck asks warily 'What do pirates have to do?' and Tom explains:

'Oh, they have a bully time – take ships, and burn them, and get the money and bury it in awful places in their island where there's ghosts and things to watch it, and kill everybody in the ships – make 'em walk a plank.'[187]

The boys get bored and homesick, however, and are not enthused even by Tom's suggestion that they find hidden treasure: 'a rotten chest full of gold and silver'.[188]

Back home at the village on the riverbank Tom revives this prospect and does succeed in interesting 'Huck Finn the Red-handed' in digging 'for hidden treasure'.[189] 'Where'll we dig?' asks Huck.[190] Again Tom explains:

'It's hid in mighty particular places, Huck – sometimes on Islands, sometimes in rotten chests under the end of a limb of an old dead tree, just where the shadow falls at midnight; but mostly under the floor in ha'nted houses.'[191]

Why don't the buriers of the treasure dig it up 'and have a good time'?[192] Tom responds patiently to Huck's ignorant question. The treasure-buriers usually forget the clues they need in order to find the hiding places:

'they generally forgets the marks, or else they die. Anyway it lays there a long time and gets rusty; and by-and-by somebody finds an old yellow paper that tells how to find the marks – a paper that's got to be ciphered over about a week because it's mostly signs and hy'rogliphics.'
  'I lyro-which?'
  'Hy'rogliphics – pictures and things, you know, that don't seem to mean anything.'[193]

Tom, 'the Black Avenger', has been reading 'The Gold Bug' or its literary derivatives, as well as Buntline's *The Black Avenger*, but Twain's *Adventures of Tom Sawyer* is ultimately a fiction itself and concludes with Tom and Huck's 'real' discovery of hidden treasure. Twain's fiction plays games with boys' games derived from literary fictions—and incidentally indicates that pirates are well-established in childish imaginations of the 1870s or earlier. Piracy was childish; thrilling for young boys but increasingly ridiculous.

The pirate types in Irving's 'The Money-Diggers', like the scar-faced 'sea monster', were gross and ghostly caricatures; the other pirate types, Scott's and Cooper's, were implausible, unpiratical gentlemen. The two corresponding genres, of comical gothic and historical romance, both literary but generically distinguishable, were superseded by a kind of blend, a composite, combining comedy and implausibility: the pirate ridiculous.

At the Strand Theatre, London, a play by Francis C. Burnand was performed in 1877 with a deliberately silly title: *An Entirely New and Original Burlesque, Being the very latest edition of a Nautical Tradition told by one of the floating population to the Marines who entitled it The Red Rover; or, I Believe You, My Buoy!*[194] A Prologue invites the audience to return to the 'nursery days' of plays made with 'a toy Theatre' and to a particular 'favourite—the Red Rover!'[195] The plot itself begins at Newport, where the Red Rover enters in disguise and requests the audience's complicity by means of a song called 'Keep it Dark':

> I am the Red Rover, as all of you know,
> > Keep it dark!
> But out of disguise on land I don't go,
> > Keep it dark!
> Of drama romantic, the hero I've been,
> The idol of little boys under fourteen;
> But in truth I am cowardly, cruel, and mean.
> > Keep it dark![196]

He is in love, he informs us confidentially, apparently with Gertrude. This is, of course, to be expected and no cause for alarm. As Tom Sawyer knew, pirates 'don't kill the women—they're too noble. And the women's always beautiful, too'.[197]

Wilder enters, to inform us that he too is in love with Gertrude, but sadly beneath her.

> What does her aunt say? Oh, the usual tale!
> That I'm below her in the social scale.

Gertrude enters—'by the meerest accident', she says—and he dares to embrace her but confesses he is an orphan with no family connections.[198] She congratulates him, however, on being 'a *self-made man!*' and bereft of relations: 'Heavens! what a blessing!'[199]

She and her melancholy aunt, Madame de Lacey, still mourning her 'long-lost boy', must sail to Carolina, however, aboard the Rover's ship, which Wilder and his men board also, as spies, in disguise as pirates ('Petticoat skirts, the Pirate dress I know', remarks Fid).[200] Aboard the Rover's 'bad ship *Dolphin*', the Rover sings autobiographically:

> When I was a bit of a lad,
> > I stayed with my father at Dover.

> On nautical pirates quite mad,
> > I wanted to be a Red Rover.
> My father he frowned upon me,
> > With a very unpleasant expression,
> And said, 'My dear boy, don't you see,
> > A Red Rover is *not* a profession?'[201]

He has followed this unsuitable profession, but

> One day, I'll my wickedness cease,
> > When none of my schemes are effective.
> I'll enter the London police,
> > And be a most careful detective.
> When middle aged I may be,
> > Of fun I'll have had a satiety.
> I'll get myself made an M.P.,
> > And live in the highest society.[202]

He orders the arrest of Wilder, explaining

> I'm going to hang you – I will tell you why;
> Because I rather think that you're a spy.[203]

Gertrude suggests the Rover is jesting: 'Oh, 'tis your fun!'[204] But he seriously shows his hand:

> I'll let him off on one condition,
> That Gertrude shall be mine…[205]

Wilder, in an aside to Gertrude, advises temporizing rather than refusing. Meanwhile 'the good ship *Dart*' is sighted.[206] Guinea (alias Scipio) proposes swimming to inform the *Dart* and in preparation rolls up a sleeve, revealing he is wearing a 'dog collar on his arm'.[207] Fid explains that long ago he and Guinea were wrecked and found a dog and a child whom they gave to the captain of the *Dart*. Wilder responds by '(*melodramatically gasping*) I was that child-er! The Captain gave to me the name of Wilder'.[208] Madame de Lacey also cries out: 'My boy! My child! I am your long lost mother'.[209] The Rover cheerily holds a tea party, with muffins and crumpets.

The *Dart* is in pursuit in the next scene, however, and the Rover, equipped with a telescope and speaking trumpet, barks out nautical orders: 'Gaff the jibboom!'[210] He orders a flag to be flown but 'Not our own flag of course', not the 'Red Rover's flag, with skull and cross-bones', which Guinea waves in pretended error.[211] The Rover desperately seizes Gertrude:

> Ha! you shall be my wife.
> You're mine! and dearly will I sell my life.[212]

Wilder and the Rover fight for Gertrude and for principle, no doubt, but one of the Rover's pirates is mutinous and shoots him. Unremittingly dastardly, he shouts out:

> ...The shot I can't survive,
> But none of you shall leave the ship alive![213]

He proposes to explode his ship but the *Dart* has rammed the *Dolphin* and the right people are able to escape to the 'good ship'.[214] The Rover achieves his explosion but 'falls', to the concluding airs of 'Rule Britannia' and a hornpipe, to which the audience are sung an entreaty that

> You will give to our Red Rover
> Some encouragement by promising to come again.[215]

This Rover does not survive to discover himself Madame de Lacey's brother, so Burnand's plot is not quite so contrived as Cooper's original, but the burlesque indicates, of course, that familiarity and predictability had brought literary pirates from historical romance to ridicule and comedy. Cooper's Red Rover has become a figure of fun.

Francis Burnand was a future editor of *Punch* and a past and future collaborator on work with Sullivan and Gilbert.[216] *The Pirates of Penzance* (which opened in 1879 in New York to foil the American copyright pirates) has a less famous subtitle, *The Slave of Duty*, which indicates the work's satire of the public muddle of piracy and principle. The central character, Frederic, has been mistakenly apprenticed (because of a mishearing) as a pirate instead of a pilot. He has met no females except Ruth, the nurserymaid who made the mistake, until he encounters 'a bevy of beautiful maidens' on the shores of Cornwall, the daughters of a Major-General.[217] He wants to marry one of them, Mabel, and indeed all the pirates would like to marry any of them. In order to save his daughters from this social catastrophe, the Major-General pretends to be an orphan, a circumstance that always moves the tender-hearted pirates to mercy. The Major-General considers his lie an 'innocent fiction' not a 'terrible story' but his daughters are not so certain.[218]

Because Frederic is now 21 he is 'out of his indentures', free of his apprenticeship, and has a duty to oppose piracy which overcomes his former duty to follow it.[219] He will lead the local constabulary on a raid on his former colleagues, he decides, but is prevented by the Pirate King, who sees a loophole in the small print of Frederic's apprentice-ship contract: Frederic was born on 29 February (in a leap year) and has reached the age of 21 but only his fifth birthday. His 21st birthday must await 1940. Frederic must revert to his pirate duty, although he abhors piracy. It is his duty, therefore, reluctantly to inform the pirates that the Major-General is not truthfully an orphan.

Frederic explains his circumstances to Mabel, singing that 'when stern duty calls, I must obey', and swearing to be hers in 1940.[220] 'It seems so long', she says.[221] The police enter, sternly marching, and Mabel informs them that Frederic's duty obliges him to return to piracy. The police complain that their own duty does not make them happy:

> When constabulary duty's to be done – To be done,
> The policeman's lot is not a happy one.[222]

The opposing pirates sing as they approach:

> A rollicking band of pirates we,
> > Who, tired of tossing on the sea,
> Are trying their hand at burglaree . . .[223]

And indeed there are no shipboard scenes and no piracy in *The Pirates*, and the opposition to the pirates is provided by the constabulary not the royal navy (perhaps because *H.M.S. Pinafore* had just preceded).

The Major-General enters in his nightwear, with a candle, sleepless with sorrow at his 'falsehood'.[224] His daughters also enter, similarly attired and equipped, singing of their concern at their father's new behaviour, he who was formerly 'the most methodical of men'.[225] The police and pirates fight and the police are defeated but order the pirates to 'yield, in Queen Victoria's name!'[226] Dutifully, the pirates 'yield at once': 'Because, with all our faults, we love our Queen'.[227] As Ruth declares:

> They are no members of the common throng;
> They are all noblemen who have gone wrong![228]

The Major-General delightedly renders his daughters to such well-bred pirates.

This conclusion is the logical one to the plot Scott started in *The Pirate*, 58 years previously, but it is more significantly a joke at the ultimate exhaustion of the Romantic pirate, unable to be piratical and condemned to be dutiful and noble, even comically sentimental. In an obituary we should notice that the nineteenth-century afterlife of the eighteenth-century pirate is principally an Anglo-American story, or Scots-American, passing in instalments from Scott to Cooper, Irving, and back again. Under the influence of both transnational Romanticism and Romantic nationalism, in which both Scott and Cooper played creative parts, the pirate becomes a safely historical character, not a living threat or thrill, and finds himself a congenial home in literary romance, as a mysterious but predictably unpiratical hero, disdaining treasure and fighting chivalrously to protect women and to assert his personal or national identity: the pirate as a hero in search of himself. In another aspect, also pervaded by Romanticism, he is a character in search of a genre and a role, finding both by surviving as a caricature, a scar-faced man more grotesque than frightening. A damaged man with a macabre past at sea, but now washed up on land, out of his natural element as well as his historical period, he becomes a gothic ghost of himself, more ridiculous than mysterious, more comic than gothic. His self-defining aim in life, his reason for being and for being himself, his ill-gotten, never-expended treasure, violently acquired, never pleasurably spent, stored and wasted instead in a buried chest, protected by a cryptographic mystery, has been inherited by readers and its mystery solved by textual exegesis, so that his treasure—all that he left of himself apart from a skull and some bones—has been found, counted and sold, by the writers who are keeping him—barely, vestigially—alive.

These two roles for the survival of the pirate—as the genteel and unpiratical hero of romance and as the scar-faced haunter of his buried treasure—are then superseded by his popularization as a reliable stereotype, a provider of inoffensive entertainment, in competition with acrobats and harlequins, the Kidd or Blackbeard of the stage, desperately made into a wizard and sent in futile pursuit of aristocratic ladies and exotic princesses. Meanwhile in prose the pirate sailed into the popular novel, itself flowing from the previous Grub Street source of the eighteenth-century pirate, although now the nineteenth-century pirate, 'el pirato pernicioso', is a blood-dripping, swashbuckling substitute from the high seas for the buckskinned, long-rifled Natty Bumppo or Buffalo Bill of that other frontier, the far, wild West, or else is a gender-bended, tender-hearted, heaving-breasted piratess. By way of these various routes, the literary back streets, the pirate of the high seas became a hero—or, rather, an alter-ego—for boys, Tom Sawyer (the Black Avenger) and others, and then a farcical villain, as Cooper's Red Rover emerged from the oceans via the toy-cupboard onto the stage of children's pantomime to serve muffins and crumpets. Exhausted by this spreading popularity and diminishing seriousness, confused by his descent from romance to burlesque, exiled from the unfathomable ocean, emerging from his mist of mysteriousness and distance, ruling the matinée audience not the ocean wave, the pirate of romance was deservedly parodied by Gilbert and Sullivan, portrayed as sentimental, patriotic and—most comical of all—aristocratic: 'They are all noblemen who have gone wrong!' The poor pirate certainly had gone wrong, tumbling from romance to the pulps, then the nursery and burlesque: a laughing stock. What future would the pirate face?

VI

Treasure Neverland

'My dearest people, I have a great piece of news. There has been offered for *Treasure Island* - how much do you suppose?... A hundred pounds, all alive, oh! A hundred jingling, tingling, golden, minted quid.'

(Stevenson, to his parents, 5 May [1883], *Letters*, IV, 119.)

The story of the genesis of *Treasure Island* in 1881 was told some years subsequently by Stevenson in 'My First Book', published in *The Idler* in August 1894, and can be supplemented by his correspondence at the actual time of the genesis. Stevenson, his wife Fanny and stepson Lloyd, aged 13, were renting a cottage in Braemar, Scotland, and were accommodating also Stevenson's mother and father. To amuse himself Lloyd made use of 'pen and ink and a shilling box of water colours' and 'turned one of the rooms into a picture gallery'.[1] Stevenson sometimes joined in this playful artistry and on one occasion, he remembered, 'I made the map of an island' which he called 'Treasure Island'.[2] This map stimulated his imagination:

as I paused upon my map of 'Treasure Island', the future character[s] of the book began to appear there visibly among imaginary woods; and their brown faces and bright weapons peeped out upon me from unexpected quarters, as they passed to and fro, fighting and hunting treasure, on these few square inches of a flat projection. The next thing I knew I had some papers before me and was writing out a list of chapters.[3]

Lloyd's own retrospective account, written even longer afterwards than Stevenson's, lays claim to the inspirational map but leaves the actual inspiration to Stevenson. Lloyd remembers himself with his paintbox, tinting the map of an island I had drawn. Stevenson came in as I was finishing it, and with his affectionate interest in everything I was doing, leaned over my shoulder, and was soon elaborating the map, and naming it. I shall never forget the thrill of Skeleton Island, Spy-Glass Hill, and the heart-stirring climax of the three red crosses! And the greater climax still when he wrote down the words 'Treasure Island' at the top right-hand corner![4]

What is striking in this creation tale is that a map was the inspiration and that 'Treasure' was the name for the island of the map. The apparent theme of the creation tale is that the famous story itself began accidentally and as a result of childish play.

In 'My First Book' Stevenson places the inspirational event in September, but in a letter he wrote from Braemar which has been credibly dated at 24 August 1881 he told his friend W.E. Henley that he had made no progress 'with our crawlers', stories he had earlier called 'creepers', ghoulish stories, 'but', he reported,

I am on another lay at the moment, purely owing to Sam [Samuel Lloyd Osbourne], this one; but I believe there's more coin in it than any amount of crawlers: now, see here.
The Sea Cook
or Treasure Island:
A Story for Boys.
If this don't fetch the kids, why, they have gone rotten since my day. Will you be surprised to learn that it is about Buccaneers, that it begins in the *Admiral Benbow* public house on Devon Coast, that it's all about a map and a treasure ... ?[5]

He added that two chapters were already written and had been 'tried on Sam with great success' and the following day he reported three chapters which had been read aloud:

All now heard by Sam, F. [Fanny], and my father and mother, with high approval - it's quite silly and horrid fun, - and what I want is the *best* book about the Buccaneers that can be had - the later B.'s above all, Blackbeard and sich, and get Nutt or Bain to send it skimming by the fastest post.[6]

Nutt and Bain were London booksellers and what Stevenson was requesting was historical information about pirates (not buccaneers) such as Blackbeard. Although he wanted to be supplied with historical facts, he knew very well the generic fictional form and the prospective readership—boys. In 'My First Book' he remembered that 'I had counted on one boy, I found I had two in my audience. My father

caught fire at once with all the romance and childishness of his original nature'.[7] The creation story was of a collaboration, a collective
'childishness' across three generations. Stevenson's father 'not only
heard with delight the daily chapter, but set himself acting to collabo-
rate', providing a name for a pirate ship, the *Walrus*, and 'an inventory'
of the contents of a pirate chest.[8] The collaboration was possible
because of a shared generic sense, which Stevenson cheerfully acknowledged when signing his letter to Henley 'R.L.S. Author of Boys' Stories'.[9] Henley would share this generic expectation also, and would not
be 'surprised to learn' that a work about pirates would feature 'a map
and a treasure'.

Stevenson lacked historical information (while he awaited 'the *best*
book' on pirates) but he knew very well the literary tradition. In a letter to Henley the previous month Stevenson had mentioned Scott's
The Pirate as a beneficial influence.[10] He had known for many years of
Scott's presence on the Stevensons' lighthouse-inspecting voyage
which had resulted in the old lady's recollection of Gow and the inspiration for *The Pirate*, a voyage Stevenson wrote about many years later
in Samoa to introduce his grandfather's 'Reminiscences of Sir Walter
Scott'.[11] Some of his literary sources he readily acknowledged in 'My
First Book'. 'No doubt the parrot once belonged to Robinson Crusoe',
he admitted unashamedly.[12] Thus he traces Long John Silver's pirate
parrot to Defoe's or Robinson Crusoe's, which Crusoe at one point
imagines may still be on his island 'calling after "Poor Robinson
Crusoe" to this Day' and at another point, with Defoe's characteristic
combination of inconsistency and verisimilitude, reports removing
with him on his departure from the island.[13] Stevenson does not, however, record a more substantial debt to *Robinson Crusoe*, in the form of
his marooned man on Treasure Island, Ben Gunn. Stevenson's father
was alert to the debt, we know, and wrote to Stevenson protesting at
the clothing of Ben Gunn as he originally appeared in the serial publication of *Treasure Island* in *Young Folks* magazine:

I object to the goatskin dress and hat which is merely R. Crusoe and his running down goats which is the same. He ought to have some tattered naval
uniform for a coat and ragged canvas trousers.[14]

It hardly matters that Crusoe's fictional goatskins, improbably worn on
his tropical island, were borrowed from Defoe's own source, 'a Man
cloth'd in Goat-Skins' rescued from Juan Fernandez, Alexander Selkirk.[15]

Stevenson accepted his father's advice and Ben Gunn's 'kilt of goatskins' in *Young Folks* was changed for book publication into 'tatters of old ship's canvas and old sea-cloth', although Stevenson did forget to adjust consistently a subsequent reference to 'the marooned man in his goat-skins' which survived the reclothing of the Ben Gunn of *Young Folks*.[16]

'No doubt the skeleton is conveyed from Poe', Stevenson acknowledged casually in 'My First Book', remarking more explicitly that 'I broke into the gallery of Mr. Poe and stole Flint's pointer'.[17] He thus refers to his pirate captain's use of a skeleton to point to the location of the treasure on Treasure Island, by which Stevenson recognizes a slight debt, perhaps, to Poe's use of a skull as indicator of Kidd's treasure, or merely to Poe's placing of skeletons in its vicinity, but perhaps more generally to 'The Gold Bug' as the originator of treasure puzzle narratives. These debts to Defoe and Poe, the parrot and the skeleton, Stevenson pronounced mere 'trifles and details' but, as he wrote in 'My First Book':

> It is my debt to Washington Irving that exercises my conscience, and justly so, for I believe plagiarism was rarely carried farther. I chanced to pick up the *Tales of a Traveller* some years ago with a view to an anthology of prose narrative, and the book flew up and struck me: Billy Bones, his chest, the company in the parlour, the whole inner spirit, and a good deal of the material detail of my first chapters – all were there, all were the property of Washington Irving.[18]

Stevenson overstates the case, perhaps, for the benefit of the autobiographical story of 'My First Book', but the debt is significant and marks another instalment in the continuing Scots-American story of the pirate. In Irving's *Tales of a Traveller*, Wolfert Webber's futile treasure hunting is inspired partly by the scar-faced old sea-dog with a sea-chest who imposes his presence at an inn from which he scrutinizes the local nautical activities. This character of Irving's does indeed resemble the person and circumstances of scar-faced Billy Bones, 'The Old Sea Dog at the "Admiral Benbow"', whose chest is more significant in Stevenson's story than Irving's.[19] But Stevenson's old sea-dog and chest have another literary precedent. In his verses 'To the Hesitating Purchaser' of *Treasure Island* Stevenson acknowledged the generic tradition of his book in more general terms than the specific debts registered in 'My First Book':

If schooners, islands, and maroons
    And Buccaneers and buried Gold,
And all the old romance, retold
    Exactly in the ancient way,
Can please, as me they pleased of old,
    The wiser youngsters of to-day:

- So be it, and fall on! If not,
    If studious youth no longer crave,
His ancient appetites forgot,
    Kingston, or Ballantyne the brave,
Or Cooper of the wood and wave:
    So be it, also! And may I
And all my pirates share the grave
    Where these and their creations lie![20]

These verses are more a claim to belong to a literary family tradition, more a claim to an inheritance, than an admission of specific indebtedness, but—leaving aside Kingston and Ballantyne for the moment—we may surmise that the naming of Cooper is in recognition of a particular influence. The phrase 'wood and wave' neatly signals the nautical Cooper as well as the better-known Cooper of the frontier, and we may recall the old seaman of Cooper's *The Sea Lions* (1848) as well as Irving's of *Tales of a Traveller* (1824). Indeed the old seaman of Cooper's narrative is in some respects more like Billy Bones than is Irving's old seaman, in particular because of Cooper's man's sea-chest, which contains the map which starts the treasure-hunting voyage, as does the chest of Stevenson's Billy Bones.

Stevenson's connection to Ballantyne was personal as well as professional. At 15 Stevenson had introduced himself to Ballantyne and declared himself an admirer of *The Coral Island*, which he had read twice, he said, and hoped to read twice more.[21] He knew the book, then, and acknowledges Ballantyne in the prefatory verses as the author of boys' adventures such as *Treasure Island*, but there may be a more particular parallel between Stevenson's book and Ballantyne's, or at least a coincidence, for Ballantyne's character Ralph, one of the three manly boy heroes of *The Coral Island*, is kidnapped by the cat-swinging pirate visitors to the Coral Island, and eventually finds himself single-handedly sailing their ship with the help only of a good pirate who has been wounded and is cared for by Ralph, circumstances similar to those of young Jim in *Treasure Island*, who also finds himself sailing the pirates' ship alone, with the help only of a wounded bad pirate, Israel

Hands. The debt to Kingston is principally a general generic one, a recognition of his precedence as an author of boys' adventure stories, but in 'My First Book' and in a letter in 1884 Stevenson acknowledges a more specific if tiny debt to Charles Kingsley, for the phrase 'dead man's chest' in Stevenson's fictitious sea-shanty in *Treasure Island*, which comes from the name 'Dead Man's Chest', given to one of the Virgin Islands by a buccaneer, according to Kingsley's travel book, *At Last: A Christmas in the West Indies* (1871).[22]

Those are some of the literary relations of *Treasure Island* but what of its historical sources? What came of Stevenson's request from Braemar to Henley in London for 'the *best* book about the Buccaneers' (as he loosely called the pirates, 'Blackbeard and sich')?[23] The answer comes in another letter from Stevenson at Braemar to Henley in early September 1881: 'My dear Henley, A thousand thanks for Johnson who is a brick. The tale advances a chapter a day.'[24] He thus refers of course to Captain Charles Johnson, the supposed author of *A General History of the Pyrates*, which is indeed 'the *best* book' on its subject.

The plot of *Treasure Island* was well under way by the time of Stevenson's earlier letter to Henley of 24–5 August, with three chapters already written, establishing the Irving-Cooper opening with the old sea-dog at the Admiral Benbow, and the fourth chapter for the following day, presumably, the 26th, no doubt to be entitled (as it was) 'The Sea Chest'. No matter how quickly the *General History of the Pyrates* was posted, Stevenson's progress of 'a chapter a day' (as he measured it at the time) would have meant that literary tradition and Stevenson's imagination were more responsible for the plot of *Treasure Island* than was the *History*. Indeed, Stevenson has used the *General History of the Pyrates* principally to authenticate two speeches by Long John Silver providing historical piratical background in two consecutive chapters, first for his parrot and then for himself. The first of the two speeches is made by Silver to Jim and outlines the career of the parrot:

'She's sailed with England, the great Cap'n England, the pirate. She's been at Madagascar, and at Malabar, and Surinam, and Providence, and Portobello. She was at the fishing up of the wrecked plate ships. It's there she learned "Pieces of eight," and little wonder; three hundred and fifty thousand of 'em, Hawkins! She was at the boarding of the Viceroy of the Indies out of Goa, she was...'[25]

The parrot's career is an authentic pirate's career. Like Silver, she has sailed with Captain Edward England, who visited Madagascar, Malabar,

and Providence, if not perhaps Surinam and Portobello, where Captain
Taylor, Edward England's partner in piracy, took the *Cassandra* for
Spanish pardons. The salvaging of the coins from the hurricane-
wrecked Spanish plate fleet in the Gulf of Florida was done by the
Spaniards themselves, but '350000 Pieces of Eight in Silver' of those
coins, according to the *General History*, were stolen by English pirates,
although England himself is not named as 'one of those, who stole
away the Silver which the Spaniards had fished up from the Wrecks of
the Galleons'.[26] But Captain England probably was one of those who
captured and ransomed the Vice Roy of Goa in actual history, although
not in the *General History*, which leaves him out of that story.[27] So
Stevenson has mixed episodes from different pirate lives in the *General
History*, but plausibly.

Silver's next historical speech is overheard by Jim hiding in the ship's
apple barrel (in imitation of Stevenson's father as a young boy, who
thus overheard a previously sycophantic sailor revealing himself as a
'truculent ruffian').[28] The pirate career this time is Silver's not his
parrot's:

'It was a master surgeon, him that ampytated me - out of college and all - Latin
by the bucket, and what not; but he was hanged like a dog, and sun-dried like the
rest, at Corso Castle. That was Roberts' men, that was, and comed of changing
names to their ships - *Royal Fortune* and so on. Now, what a ship was christened,
so let her stay, I says. So it was with the *Cassandra*, as brought us all safe home
from Malabar, after England took the Viceroy of the Indies; so it was with old
Walrus . . .'[29]

The surgeon who amputated fictional Silver's leg was the real pirate
Peter Scudamore, taken prisoner after the defeat and death of Captain
Bartholomew Roberts, who was dressed for the occasion by the *General History* 'in a rich crimson Damask Wastcoat, and Breeches, a red
Feather in his Hat, a Gold Chain ten Times round his Neck, a Sword
in his Hand, and two pair of Pistols hanging at the End of a Silk Sling,
which was slung over his Shoulders (according to the Fashion of the
Pyrates)'.[30] In this equipment Roberts received his death from 'a
Grape-Shot' which 'struck him directly on the Throat' but Scudamore
survived and was taken prisoner aboard the last incarnation of the
name *Royal Fortune*.[31] Despite 'his Employ and better Education'
Scudamore tried to incite his fellow prisoners and their Angolan slaves
to retake the ship, arguing 'that it was better venturing to do this, . . . than

to proceed to Cape Corso, and be hang'd like a Dog, and Sun dry'd'.[32] He was indeed hanged, nevertheless, at Cape Corso (Cape Coast Castle, on the Gold Coast) and his corpse 'hung in Chains' subsequently, in the West African sun.[33] Roberts called two different ships, both prizes he took over as his own, the *Royal Fortune*. The *Cassandra*, which kept her name, was the prize taken by Captain England, with Captain Taylor, at the island of Johanna, near Madagascar, and the *Walrus* was named at the 'particular request' of Thomas Stevenson.[34]

Pirate history was thus credibly mixed with the requests and recollections of Stevenson's father, but Stevenson made some other more whimsical borrowings from the *General History of the Pyrates*. Long John Silver, Stevenson's principal legacy to literary piracy, was inspired largely by his wooden-legged friend W.E. Henley, as Stevenson confessed in a letter to him: 'It was the sight of your maimed strength and masterfulness that begot John Silver in *Treasure Island*'.[35] The maimed but masterful Silver had piratical precedents, nevertheless, such as, for example, the unexpected protector of the defeated captain of the *Cassandra*, Captain Macrae, in danger during his subsequent negotiations with Captain England, when, according to the *General History*,

a Fellow with a terrible Pair of Whiskers, and a wooden Leg, being stuck round with Pistols, like the Man in the Almanack with Darts, comes swearing and vapouring upon the Quarter-Deck, and asks, in a damning Manner, which was Captain Mackra: The Captain expected no less than that this Fellow would be his Executioner; - but when he came near him, he took him by the hand, swearing, Damn him he was glad to see him; and shew me the Man, says he, that offers to hurt Captain Mackra, for I'll stand by him.[36]

The resemblance to John Silver is perhaps coincidental, merely, but the coincidence is to Stevenson's credit, as the creator of a credible fictional pirate. The pirate in the *General History* (see Figure 6.1) is also realistic and credible, but probably as fictional as Stevenson's Long John Silver. The vivid and dramatized passage does not derive from either of the two sources used in the *General History* for the *Cassandra* episode, Macrae's own published letter and his crewman Richard Lasinby's unpublished account, both written in plain, sailorly language, not the language of professional fiction, like Stevenson's. Other characters in *Treasure Island* have their names from the *General History*. The pirate Captain Davis, admired as 'a man' by Silver, who 'never sailed along of him', was Captain Howell Davis, who was killed by the Portuguese Governor of

Figure 6.1. 'Captain Mackra, and the Pirate with a wooden leg', from *The Pirates Own Book* (1837).

Principe.[37] Benjamen Gunn appears in the *General History* in 'A List of the White-Men, now living on the high Land of Sierraleon', as well as in *Treasure Island*.[38] Israel Hands, who sails alone with Jim on the *Hispaniola*, to his death, appears previously in the *General History*'s chapter on Blackbeard, where we have already met him.[39] Israel Hands was not killed or captured in Blackbeard's final defeat, because he was ashore, 'having been sometime before disabled by Black-beard, in one of his savage Humours'.[40] To make himself memorable, Blackbeard had discharged his pistols under the table as he sat carousing with his companions, according to the *General History*, and Israel Hands had been 'lam'd for Life'.[41] He had escaped execution by pardon, reportedly, 'and is alive at this Time in London, begging his Bread'.[42] The lame beggar caught Stevenson's eye in the *General History*, and left his name forever in *Treasure Island*.[43] Some characters have names with other, more playful connections, such as the captain of the respectable ship, the *Hispaniola*, Captain Smollett, a nod from Stevenson to his fellow Scot and nautical author, Tobias Smollett.

Although based on Irving's and Cooper's narratives, the opening of *Treasure Island* is more artfully arranged to build suspense. Stevenson's pirates are horribly Gothic, not comically, like Irving's, and especially so to the youthful Jim, Stevenson's narrator. The menace of piracy is introduced to Jim's father's respectable Admiral Benbow inn by a series of injured but intimidating figures: scar-faced Billy Bones, the fierce guest with the mounting debt to Jim's father; Black Dog, missing two of his fingers; and sinister Blind Pew. They are, of course, preparatory for the one-legged Long John Silver, the sea cook, the central character of Stevenson's original title, as given to Henley almost immediately:

The Sea Cook
or Treasure Island:
A Story for Boys.[44]

In Wycherley's *The Plain-Dealer* (1677) there is a running joke about wooden legs for sailors—'Raillery upon wooden legs'—and we should remember, although he is better known today than in Stevenson's day, Melville's Gothic Captain Ahab, with his 'ivory leg' of whalebone.[45] Injuries were suffered by real seamen, of course, especially those who chose to achieve 'either a golden chain or a wooden leg', like John Morris, and ships' cooks were commonly chosen from sailors who were no longer able-bodied (see Figure 6.2), so Silver and Stevenson's other maimed men are realistic, as well as Gothic, like the one-eyed sailor and scar-faced pirate of Irving's 'Money-Diggers'.[46]

The injured figures of *Treasure Island* connect Jim to piracy but also to treasure, a connection supposedly legitimized by Jim's burglary of Billy Bones's sea-chest to secure payment of the dead pirate's bill at the inn. Billy Bones's death looms larger in the narrative than the nearly simultaneous death of Jim's innkeeper father, whose legacy to Jim takes the form, in narrative practice, of Billy Bones's Treasure Island map, taken from his sea-chest. The pirates are potential father-figures. As keeper of the Spy-glass inn, Long John Silver is clearly a parallel to Jim's own deceased father. But, although Jim is inheriting the wealth of the pirates, he sanctions his inheritance by securing more socially respectable father-figures, the doctor-magistrate Dr Livesey and the Squire Trelawney, who begin *Treasure Island* by authorizing Jim 'to write down the whole particulars'.[47]

Treasure Island is essentially a competition between two groups for possession of treasure, a commodity vaguely defined but consisting, in its most attractive light, of unearned wealth. The respectable and

Figure 6.2. Thomas Rowlandson, portrait of a nautical cook, *c.*1799.

unrespectable groups are differentiated principally by class, indicated by education and by pre-existing wealth. Both groups are motivated by greed for the treasure, the unearned wealth. 'What were these villains after but money?' asks the Squire rhetorically, before rejoicing with childish glee in the prospect, as possessors of the treasure map, of 'finding the spot, and money to eat—to roll in—to play duck and drake with ever after'.[48] This competition for loot which forms the plot, with its acquisition as the plot's resolution, is not very different from the creaking machinery in previous nineteenth-century novels with events and outcomes that turn on inheritances—Dickens's *Great Expectations* and *Bleak House*, to cite two well-known examples. The distant colonial world—Australia in *Great Expectations* or Africa in *King Solomon's Mines*, for example—is often the mysterious source of such expected or unexpected 'treasure' (*King Solomon's Mines* having been written in deliberate emulation of *Treasure Island*).[49] Crusoe's unexpected wealth, after his years of economic unprofitability on his island, is derived from the accumulated profits of his Brazilian plantation of toiling slaves, but *Treasure Island* combines island solitude with the acquisition of treasure—by Ben Gunn, Crusoe's heir in Stevenson's story. The treasure of *Treasure Island* is not just unearned wealth, but stolen.

Some individuals are able to move between the two competitive teams in *Treasure Island*, chiefly young Jim, whose class is an open question, and also Long John Silver, who is socially mobile and plans a financially secure future with his savings and his wife (the only one in *Treasure Island*, apart from Jim's bereaved mother), a prospect more respectable than the Squire's of rolling around in money and playing ducks and drakes with it. Ben Gunn is another pirate who changes sides, but Long John's side-switching, his keeping 'a foot in either camp', is an essential component of his ambiguous character.[50] Silver is duplicitous, a good actor of his roles, as subordinate sailor and pirate leader. When Stevenson later borrowed Blackbeard (anachronistically) from the *General History* for *The Master of Ballantrae* (1889), the frightful pirate is comical with his blackened face and multiple pistols, 'a perfect figure of fun', manfully defeated by the Master, who scornfully—and accurately—accuses him of 'play-acting'.[51] Blackbeard is melodramatic in the *General History* and comic in *The Master*, but Silver's acts are sinister and convincing, as well as duplicitous.

'So you've changed sides again', says Jim to Long John, in a whisper necessitated by his own difficult position, as simultaneously Long John's captive, tied to him by a rope, and his accomplice in treasure hunting.[52] Jim's movements between the two sides are not so morally questionable as Long John's, and Jim's are necessary for the narrative, which needs its narrator to perceive events from both respectable and unrespectable points of view (the latter excusable by Jim's youth). Nevertheless Jim's evading the respectable gentlemen's adult authority is recognized by him as 'truantry'.[53] He deserts the *Hispaniola* to go ashore on Treasure Island with the pirates and later he slips surreptitiously away from the stockade, the redoubt of the respectable party. These escapes or escapades have beneficial results—his encounter with Ben Gunn (who has possession of the treasure) and his rescue of the *Hispaniola* from the pirates—as well as beneficial results for the excitement of the narrative, and are explained as childish notions: 'I was only a boy, and I had made my mind up.'[54] But his 'truantry' is a form of misbehaviour, mitigated by his youth and the reader's opportunity to engage directly with the pirates, whose own misbehaviour has complementary aspects of childishness (naivety, drunkenness, untidiness, and squabbling). Jim's boyhood allows him to behave as a marginal, a maverick, as Silver does, ultimately escaping from the *Hispaniola* and its hierarchy with a stolen share of the (stolen) treasure. Jim's disobedience is sanctioned by his liminal boyhood status, and thus separated from the criminal disobedience of the pirates themselves, who form an alternative subculture as 'gentlemen of fortune' (a concept borrowed from the *General History*), governed by their own 'rules' as we are repeatedly reminded, particularly by Silver, who is their principal ruler—and betrayer.[55]

Jim's own latent ambivalence about piracy is a function of Silver's own ambiguity. He is bad but attractive—the former quality being Stevenson's main contribution to the long—increasingly ridiculous— literary tradition of impeccably behaved pirates who are obviously well born and mistakenly displaced heirs to legitimate titles and wealth. Silver cruelly kills an innocent man before Jim's eyes (and the reader's) but still retains some charm and, above all, literary immortality. For a boy, Stevenson remarked, 'a pirate is a beard in wide trousers and literally bristling with pistols', but of course Silver is much more and thereby memorable.[56] Although he is not as dandified as Captain Bartholomew Roberts, Silver has four guns and a cutlass as well as one leg and a parrot 'perched upon his shoulder and gabbling odds and ends of purposeless sea-talk', Crusoe's parrot with a larger vocabulary and made into an indelible and characteristic mark of piracy.[57]

As a boys' book, *Treasure Island* inevitably and properly rewards adventures with wealth. Jim could potentially have achieved both by joining the pirate gang. As an inn-keeper, like Jim's father, Silver is an obvious substitute father. But instead Jim identifies himself with the respectable hierarchy—the Doctor-Magistrate and the Squire—who receive the burgled treasure map and its burgled rewards. Jim's narrative potential—as 'a noticing lad'—is to overhear and observe the pirates (from an apple barrel, from undergrowth on the island, as a captive in their camp, and as a boarder of their vessel) and to escape the stultifying authority of the respectable party, thus encountering Ben Gunn, who actually possesses the treasure, and recapturing the vital *Hispaniola*, from which he immediately hauls down 'their cursed black flag'.[58] Some of the implicit ethical questions—about stealing, or killing—are evaded by his childhood status, more innocent than the piratical one. When Jim steals Billy Bones's map he is owed money; when he shoots Israel Hands it is in retaliation and almost by accident ('I scarce can say it was by my own volition').[59]

While siding Jim with the authorities as narrator, Stevenson as author allows Silver to succeed also, escaping the Squire and doctor and taking with him some of the treasure (to which, as a pirate, he is perhaps more entitled than Jim or Squire Trelawney). Silver's future—and perhaps a sequel—is envisaged in the book.[60] As he tells his fellow pirates, he will rejoin his black wife to enjoy his prospective wealth.[61] We can see why Stevenson originally called his book 'The Sea Cook', placing the ambiguous Silver at its centre, although he agreed, at the request of the *Young Folks* editor, to substitute the original subtitle, *Treasure Island*, thus signalling the plot and its profitable resolution (in exotic wealth) as the dominant attraction of his work.[62] Stevenson was not a mercenary author but he needed money. 'My dearest people', he wrote to his parents, 'I have a great piece of news. There has been offered for *Treasure Island*—how much do you suppose?... A hundred pounds, all alive, oh! A hundred jingling, tingling, golden, minted quid.'[63]

The story behind *Peter Pan, or The Boy Who Would Not Grow Up* traditionally begins with a terrible event in the life of its author, J.M. Barrie, aged six when his older brother David, aged 13, died in a skating accident. In Barrie's book about his mother, *Margaret Ogilvy* (1896), he described the consequences, particularly for his mother who was bed-ridden with grief. His sister told the young Barrie to 'go ben [within] to my mother and say to her that she still had another boy'.[64] Timidly he entered his mother's dark room and she asked 'Is that you?' to which he could make no answer. So she asked

more anxiously 'Is that you?' again. I thought it was the dead boy she was speaking to, and I said in a little lonely voice, 'No, it's no him, it's just me'.[65]

After this incident he began to comfort his mother by imitating his dead brother in an attempt to replace him by impersonating him, learning his whistle and wearing his clothes. Nevertheless David's life had stopped, as Barrie knew: 'When I became a man...he was still a boy of thirteen'.[66]

Role-playing came early to Barrie, then, and as a basis for mother–child relations. As he grew (which he could, unlike his brother) other fictions engaged him in imitation. 'We read many books together when I was a boy, *Robinson Crusoe* being the first (and the second)'.[67] R.M. Ballantyne's subsequent Robinsonade for children inspired a schoolboy Barrie to play as well as write: 'Ballantyne was for long my man', he declared in a preface he later wrote for *The Coral Island*.[68] He awaited Ballantyne's new books eagerly, 'but they all lagged behind *The Coral Island*', which 'egged me on, not merely to be wrecked every Saturday for many months in a long-suffering garden, but to my first work of fiction, a record of our adventures'.[69] This garden was at Dumfries, where he attended secondary school and, he remembered, he and some friends

crept up walls and down trees, and became pirates in a sort of Odyssey that was long afterwards to become the play of *Peter Pan*. For our escapades in a certain Dumfries garden, which is enchanted land to me, were certainly the genesis of that nefarious work. We lived in the tree-tops, on cocoanuts attached thereto, and that were in a bad condition; we were buccaneers and I kept the log-book of our depredations... That log-book I trust to be no longer extant, though I should like one last look at it, to see if Captain Hook is in it.[70]

These nineteenth-century boys' island adventures took shape in Barrie's adult writings. The author of *Peter Pan* was already a successful London playwright—of theatrical Robinsonades such as *The Admirable Crichton* (1902), for example, which inverted the civilized English hierarchy by wrecking an aristocratic family and its servants on a Pacific island.

Of course the biographical explanations of *Peter Pan* have a wider literary-historical context—in the legacy of *Robinson Crusoe*. By imitating the distant world of travel literature, the many Robinsonades presented a more believable geographical relocation of the increasingly unbelievable historical world of romance and adventure. In the course of the nineteenth century, however, realistic *Robinson Crusoe* and the subsequent fantastic Robinsonades were the points of departure for a further literary subgenre—boys' adventure stories, such as *The Coral Island* and *Treasure Island*, that increasingly presented the idealized Romantic conception of childhood as another, irreversibly distanced, utopian lost world. Like the world of romance, which had been sent beyond verification into geographical distance, the Romantic ideal of childhood was distanced and separated—not from history, however, but from manhood. The boy was no longer father to the man: they were set apart, unrelated. The narratives of nineteenth-century manly boys—shipwrecked on *The Coral Island*, for instance, to undergo rites of passage—represent the Romantic conception of childhood as remote, separate, a lost world. Peter Pan is of course a manly boy with a difference, an unmanly boy, 'the boy who would not grow up'. Neverland is a childhood that depends on youth and faith. 'Do you believe in fairies?' Peter Pan famously asks his audience, whose faith saves Tinker Bell's life.[71] Flying is also an act of faith, not a suspension of disbelief, of faith not just in fairies but in fantastic children's fiction. 'You just think lovely wonderful thoughts and they lift you up in the air', Peter explains (flight not erection).[72] A remote island is a location for utopian fiction—such as *The Admirable Crichton*—and also for children's fiction. Neverland, like Alice's wonderlands, is accessed by way of a voyage, as hers are by voyages down a rabbit-hole or through a looking-glass. Literary pirates have their role in this literary-historical otherworld, this utopian nowhere. A historical novel such as Scott's *The Pirate*, for instance, is an early nineteenth-century fiction of late seventeenth-century history. This imaginary past of historical but dead and ghostly pirates, fictionally brought to life again, was then further displaced by children's literature of the later nineteenth century, reanimating pirates who were no longer frightening but silly, melodramatic, artificial, ridiculous, creatures for childish fantasy.

It should be recognized that the biographical 'explanation' of the *Peter Pan* fiction is itself a kind of story, seen through the words of its author, Barrie, who describes his relationship with his mother and his dead brother as performed by means of role-playing and dramatic dialogue. In some ways this story of the origins of Peter Pan in Barrie's childhood is a kind of Romantic fable, a celebration of the special imagination attributed to children in the nineteenth century, a matter of invention and presentation by Barrie, not altogether unlike Stevenson's story of the invention and discovery of *Treasure Island* in childish play. The more immediate biographical context for *Peter Pan* is usually supplied from the facts of Barrie's adult life, however, and his adult fascination with other people's children (a circumstance analogous to Dodgson-Carroll's, of course, with the same attendant suspicion of unchildish sexuality as the possible motivation and ultimate explanation) but Barrie's adult fascination with children is not in contradiction or competition with his childhood experience of his brother's death and mother's love. Rather the Barrie childhood and adulthood are compatible and indeed complementary. The more immediate if not initial facts in the case of *Peter Pan* are Barrie's encounters in Kensington Gardens, London, with young George Llewelyn Davies and his brother, Jack, and baby brother, Peter, and at a New Year's Eve dinner party, 1897–8, with the boys' mother Sylvia, a beauty with a lopsided smile.[73] She explained to Barrie that her son Peter was named after the central character and narrator in her father George du Maurier's novel, *Peter Ibbetson* (1891), a character who had a dog named Porthos, after the character in *Les Trois Mousquetaires*, a dog after which Barrie had named his own dog Porthos, as Barrie explained to Sylvia.[74]

Bearing the real Peter's name, the fictional Peter Pan took shape in stories Barrie told to the eldest boy, George, featuring the real Kensington Gardens and fictional fairies which came out when its gates were closed to the public at night. Some of these fairy tales then found their way into Barrie's *The Little White Bird* (1902), an episodic series of stories somewhat loosely connected as a narrative (for adults) about a relationship between the adult narrator and a boy David, to whom the various stories or fables are told. This framing narrative culminates in the creation of a book, an imaginative birth, *The Little White Bird*, which is contrasted with a natural birth to the boy's mother, who is called Mary A—, apparently in reference to Barrie's wife, Mary Ansell, although the fictional character was actually based on Sylvia, just as the boy, David, was based on George. The boy David's birth is told as a kind of fairy tale or fable about birds on an island in the Serpentine Lake in Kensington Gardens who subsequently become boys and girls. Six chapters of the book are about Peter Pan, however, and were later published (after the success of the play) as an independent work called *Peter Pan in Kensington Gardens* (1906). Peter Pan is a bird-boy who reversed the bird-to-boy process and 'escaped from being a human…by the window and flew back to the Kensington Gardens'.[75] On the birds' island in the Serpentine he is unable to revert to his bird condition and can no longer fly, becoming neither bird nor human but 'a Betwixt-and-Between'.[76] He is able to escape his island captivity and ship-wrecked condition, however, by sailing a thrush's nest from the island to the surrounding Gardens, which are frequented at night by the fairies. These fairies grant his wish to be able to fly back to his mother but he decides at first not to relinquish his familiar pleasures in the Gardens, only to find later that the window to his mother has been closed and she has another baby. Back in the Gardens Peter encounters

Mamie, a girl who has played in the Gardens past closing time and been built a protective house by the fairies. He and she romantically muddle kisses and 'thimbles' (anticipating Peter and Wendy) but Mamie cannot bring herself to abandon her mother to play with Peter in the Gardens.[77] Instead she makes him a present of a toy goat, which the fairies obligingly turn into a real goat, on which Peter can ride around the Gardens at night while playing his flute (thus indicating two signs of his remote classical ancestry in Pan, the goat-legged and pipe-playing Greek god).[78]

Peter Pan is not the only anticipation of *Peter Pan* in *The Little White Bird*. The imaginative map of Kensington Gardens that formed its frontispiece pronounced in its top right hand corner that 'The shade of Pilkington is over all the Gardens'.[79] What loomed thus was the eponymous headmaster of Wilkinson's preparatory school in Orme Square, at the north-west corner of the Gardens, where George was beginning in May 1901 and his brothers to follow.[80] In the book itself the real Herbert Wilkinson lurks behind the dreaded Pilkington.[81] According to *The Little White Bird* (which is not strictly consistent or systematic in its myth-making):

On attaining the age of eight, or thereabout, children fly away from the Gardens, and never come back... Where the girls go to I know not,... but the boys have gone to Pilkington's. He is a man with a cane.[82]

Pilkington's anticipation of another character is unmistakable. Here is Pilkington:

Abhorred shade! I know not what manner of man thou art in the flesh, sir, but figure thee bearded and blackavised, and of a lean, tortuous habit of body, that moves ever with a swish... 'Tis fear of thee and thy gown and thy cane, which are part of thee, that makes the fairies to hide by day... How much wiser they than the small boys who swim glamoured to thy crafty hook. Thou devastator of the Gardens, I know thee, Pilkington.[83]

Pilkington's connection to Hook is clearer in an original draft of *Peter Pan* than in the play as first performed. Ending *Peter Pan* was difficult even at its manuscript beginnings and a 'first draft' (quoted extensively in Roger Lancelyn Green's *Fifty Years of 'Peter Pan'*) sets a final scene in Kensington Gardens, where Peter and Wendy, dressed as clown and columbine, catch sight of Hook 'dressed as schoolmaster in cap and gown and carrying birch'.[84] Hook meets a park-keeper who is Starkey,

one of his former pirate crew, now in disguise, to whom Hook explains
that he escaped the crocodile in Neverland with the help of his hook:

STARKEY (cringing). Times are so hard. T'was those boys did for us.
HOOK. That's why I'm a schoolmaster - to revenge myself on boys! I hook
    them so, Starkey, (indicating how he lifts them by waist) and then I lay on
    like this! When it was found out what a useful hook I had every school in
    merry England clamoured for my services.[85]

Hook and 'assistant masters' attempt to capture Peter Pan, but the
Crocodile emerges from the Serpentine and swallows Hook before
itself being swallowed back in the Serpentine.[86]

In 1900, well before the writing of *Peter Pan* in 1903–4, Barrie's wife
Mary found a house in Sussex called Black Lake Cottage, attractively
surrounded by pines and a lake.[87] Here the fictions of fairies in Kensington Gardens (beside Barrie's London home) were replaced for the
growing Llewelyn Davies boys (George eight in August 1901, Jack six,
Peter four) by pirates and desert islands, games acted out in humorous
acknowledgement of popular fictional formulas and photographed by
Barrie. The fictional prototype was principally *The Coral Island* but also
the boys' Robinsonade in general, as exemplified also in Marryat's
Masterman Ready (1841). Barrie produced a book of his photographs
with captions, *The Boy Castaways of Black Lake Island*, printed in only
two copies, one for the boys' father, Arthur, who immediately lost it
on a train.[88] According to the listed chapter headings, which outlined
the plot implied by the photographs and captions, the boys are wrecked
on Black Lake Island where they hunt and build a hut before making
the 'Startling Discovery that the Island is the Haunt of Captain Swarthy
and his Pirate Crew'.[89] The photographs depict the ensuing adventures: a picture of Barrie's dog Porthos is punningly captioned 'The
dog of a pirate had seen us'.[90] The pirate captain Swarthy prefigures
Hook, as Barrie recognized in the 'Dedication' to the Llewelyn Davies
boys that introduced the belatedly published text of *Peter Pan* (1928):

In *The Boy Castaways* Captain Hook has arrived but is called Captain Swarthy,
and he seems from the pictures to have been a black [swarthy-faced] man. This
character, as you do not need to be told, is held by those in the know to be
autobiographical.[91]

One of the photographs by Barrie features a dummy of the autobiographical Swarthy being punished by the boys: 'We strung him up'.[92]

Peter Pan opens at bedtime in a nursery in a house in Bloomsbury (where Barrie lived on arrival in London).[93] The Darling children are playing at being adults and having a baby. The adults, in particular Mr Darling, are behaving childishly. Peter Pan has come from Neverland to the nursery window in Bloomsbury to hear stories.[94] He tells Wendy Darling he no longer lives with fairies in Kensington Gardens but with the Lost Boys in Neverland. Barrie's character Wendy is named in memory of the daughter of W.E. Henley (himself the model for Long John Silver) who couldn't pronounce her 'r's and called Barrie her 'fwendy', but Wendy's brothers John and Michael are named after the Llewelyn Davies boys, as is Peter, after Peter Llewelyn Davies (himself named for du Maurier's *Peter Ibbetson*).[95] Peter invites the Darling children to fly with him to Neverland, a prospect made particularly enticing to John by Peter's promise that 'There are pirates': 'JOHN. Pirates! (He grabs his tall Sunday hat.) Let us go at once!'[96]

Neverland is a land of children's fictions come true—featuring fairies (notably Tinker Bell), redskins (notably Tiger Lily), and pirates (most notably Captain Hook). The redskins are the inhabitants of Fenimore Cooper's frontier novels (which had gravitated to the nursery) and the pirates are again the conventional ones from nineteenth-century popular fiction, notably *Treasure Island*, which, as a significant prototype and analogue for Neverland, is deliberately evoked.[97] Cordial relations had been established between Barrie and Stevenson, who wrote often from Samoa (sometimes in Scots dialect) repeatedly inviting Barrie to meet him in Samoa and also recognizing their fellowship as Scots authors: 'There are two of us now that the Shirra [the Sheriff of Selkirkshire, Walter Scott] might have patted on the head'.[98] Neverland is not Samoa, however, nor is it Treasure Island, which—Stevenson told a newspaper reporter—'is not in the Pacific'.[99] Neverland is a relocation of piracy to the imagination. Treasure Island is somewhere supposedly real, at a geographical and historical distance, but Neverland is explicitly nowhere and never. The pirate survives, but is in exile from the real world.

One of *Peter Pan*'s pirates is called Bill Jukes and playfully described as 'the same Jukes who got six dozen on the *Walrus* from Flint', identifying him as a man who had sailed on the pirate ship of Flint, Long John Silver's pirate captain.[100] Peter Pan himself has a sword 'the same he slew Barbicue with', so he is supposedly the slayer of Long John Silver (called Barbecue by his fellow-pirates in *Treasure Island*).[101]

Another of Barrie's pirates is called Mullins, which commentators have noticed as a sign that Barrie had been researching in the *General History* and had taken the name of Darby Mullins, Kidd's man who was hanged with his captain at Execution Dock in 1701. But Barrie's pirates are more fictional than historical, as the jesting references to *Treasure Island* plainly demonstrate. Most of his minor pirates were named after Barrie's literary friends (Alf Mason is the novelist A.E.W. Mason; Chay Turley is Charles Turley Smith, another writer) or their sons (Cecco, 'who cut his name on the back of the governor of the prison at Gao', is the son of the novelist Maurice Hewlett).[102]

His most successful pirate, Hook, is a piratical type of perfect conventionality as well as distinct originality, the hook being Barrie's rejoinder, perhaps, to Long John Silver's crutch. The text of the play contains a full verbal portrait:

> Cruelest jewel in that dark setting is Hook himself, cadaverous and black-avised, his hair dressed in long curls which look like black candles about to melt, his eyes blue as the forget-me-not and of a profound insensibility, save when he claws, at which time a red spot appears in them. He has an iron hook instead of a right hand, and it is with this he claws. He is never more sinister than when he is most polite, and the elegance of his diction, the distinction of his demeanour, show him one of a different class from his crew, a solitary among uncultured companions. This courtliness impresses even his victims on the high seas, who note that he always says 'Sorry' when prodding them along the plank.[103]

Hook is a rendering of the nineteenth-century well-bred pirate, hyper-civilized almost to the point of foppery, with even 'a touch of the feminine' as Barrie remarks, 'as in all the greatest pirates', a construction artfully artificial and conventional, not real or historical, and—with all his artificial parts in harmony—the last great contribution to the literary gallery of pirate types.[104]

Gerald du Maurier, Sylvia's brother, played Hook (and Mr Darling) in the first production. His costume (with those of the other pirates) was designed by the artist William Nicholson, whose wife (and biographer) reports that 'One of the points on which Barrie was most insistent was that the pirates should be *real* pirates, not Gilbert-and-Sullivan travesties'.[105] For Gerald du Maurier, Nicholson produced 'a superb wig of purple chenille, arranged to look like snakes', but du Maurier 'refused to wear it because his wife said it was unbecoming', making him look 'like a cross between Charles II and a fourteen-year-old schoolgirl'.[106]

Gerald's own biographer, his daughter Daphne, was not alone in celebrating her father's performance, from which 'children were carried screaming':

How he was hated, with his flourish, his poses, his dreaded diabolical smile! That ashen face, those blood-red lips, the long, dank, greasy curls; the sardonic laugh, the maniacal scream, the appalling courtesy of his gestures...Gerald *was* Hook; he was no dummy dressed from Simmons' in a Clarkson wig [London's theatrical costumier and its wig-maker], ranting and roaring about the stage, a grotesque figure whom the modern child finds a little comic. He was a tragic and rather ghastly creation who knew no peace, and whose soul was in torment; a dark shadow; a sinister dream; a bogey of fear who lives perpetually in the grey recesses of every small boy's mind.[107]

He was gothic rather than comic, then, a Byronic descendant of Milton's fallen angel, but descended to a childish level nevertheless. Nicholson's sketch for Hook does show a sinister face between the frock coat and three-cornered hat (see Figure 6.3) and a photograph of Gerald on stage does confirm his capacity to send children screaming.[108]

We should pause to consider why the two most distinctive pirates in the English language, Long John Silver and Captain Hook, should turn up in literature written specifically for children. As we have seen, pirates had in the course of the nineteenth century become children's characters (heroic alter-egos for Twain's Tom Sawyer and many other real boys), more ridiculous than thrilling, more comic than horrible, but in a period around the turn of the century when children's literature—only recently come into its own—was flourishing and when ideas of childhood in relation to adulthood were under post-Romantic investigation and reimagination, two classics of literary piracy were written and were immediately popular. One, Stevenson's, was fully informed by the significant Scots-American literary tradition—that continuing story from Scott, via Irving, Cooper and Poe—and the other, Barrie's, was fully aware of Stevenson's book, with the latest instalment of that story. The two pirate works were the most successful works their authors ever wrote, and are still successful, but both authors, it should be remembered, wrote for adults as well as children, and their ideas of childhood—particularly Barrie's—were contemporaneous with the emerging consciousness of psychology, an emerging discipline aspiring to science, especially in relation to a hypothetical, semi-fictional, sexuality of childhood—the myths and truths of psychoanalysis, for example, concerning the growth, as it were, of sexual

Figure 6.3. William Nicholson, design for costume of Captain Hook.

organs in the mind, myths and truths rooted in Romantic ideology but outgrowing it.[109] Both Stevenson and Barrie were imbued in youth with the Robinsonade, the fictional colonial adventure which had travelled regressively from men to boys, from *Robinson Crusoe* to *The Coral Island*, but Stevenson's imagination of sexuality was shy and blank, while Barrie's was sharp and insinuating, coy and knowing, and—crucially—Neverland has female inhabitants, entirely absent from Treasure Island. 'No women in the story' was Lloyd's request to Stevenson, which he was 'blythe to obey', knowing the rules of 'boy's stories'.[110]

Of course the principal originality of *Peter Pan* is its whimsical engagement with the ambiguities of nineteenth-century ideas of gender and childhood (particularly in relation to the crucial, definitional sexless-ness of childhood) and Hook is, although permanently popular and a canonical pirate type, nevertheless a fundamentally conventional element in the play. The embarrassment potentially provoked in adults by the coy charm of *Peter Pan* is the consequence not of Bar-rie's sickly or ungovernable sentimentality or paedophilia but of his full and humorous comprehension of the ambiguity and mystery of his main subject: the sexual difference between childhood and adult-hood.[111] The Romantics' invention of childhood—as a separate con-sciousness, a kind of subculture, not an inferior and pejoratively primitive physical and mental condition—had entailed a cult of the conceptions of childhood imagination and, above all, innocence, the perfect ignorance of sexuality, the knowledge of which brought a fall. This early nineteenth-century perception of childhood was fol-lowed by a celebration of it as a paradisal state and one lost, therefore, by 'growing up'. Childhood and adulthood were thus fatefully divided, and ambiguously, becoming states of mind, not body, and depending for distinction on states of innocence or consciousness, ignorance or knowledge.

Certainly all references in *Peter Pan* to houses and entrances are for adult imaginations obviously vaginal references—including the Bloomsbury nursery window, by which the Darling children escape, and also their underground house in Neverland with its multiple entrances, one each for all the Lost Boys, and of course its extra room for Tinker Bell, 'a lovely hole, the size of a band-box [proverbially small], with a gay curtain drawn across so that you cannot see what is inside'.[112] The females of the play, Tinker Bell, Tiger Lily, and princi-pally Wendy, pose the central question of *Peter Pan*: the distinction between childhood and adulthood which is the sexual frontier tra-versed by growing up—by way of a tumescence—and thus becoming, in an infinite plotless circle, mothers and the sexual partners that pre-cede mothers. The question is continually latent in the play but can be illustrated by its most explicit surfacing in the following exchange between Peter, Wendy, and Tinker Bell about the facts of life of the family of Lost Boys:

PETER (scared). It is only pretend, isn't it, that I am their father?
WENDY (drooping). Oh yes.
(His sigh of relief is without consideration for her feelings.)
    But they are ours, Peter, yours and mine.

PETER (determined to get at facts, the only things that puzzle him).
   But not really?
WENDY. Not if you don't wish it.
PETER. I don't.
WENDY (knowing she ought not to probe but driven to it by something within).
   What are your exact feelings for me, Peter?
PETER (in the class-room). Those of a devoted son, Wendy.
WENDY (turning away). I thought so.
PETER. You are so puzzling. Tiger Lily is just the same; there is something or other she wants to be to me, but she says it is not my mother.
WENDY (with spirit). No, indeed it isn't.
PETER. Then what is it?
WENDY. It isn't for a lady to tell.[113]

At this, Tinker Bell, 'who has doubtless been eavesdropping, tinkles a laugh of scorn', before the dialogue resumes:

PETER (badgered). I suppose she means that she wants to be my mother.
   (Tink's comment is 'You silly ass.')[114]

The leading females of Neverland persist in their ambiguous relation to Peter, *The Boy Who Would Not Grow Up*, and his main antagonist is Hook, whom he impersonates. Tiger Lily has been piratically marooned by the pirates on Marooners' Rock (where there is incidentally and irrelevantly buried 'treasure') and Peter gives orders in Hook's voice—play-acting the pirate—for her release and escape.[115] Confused, Hook questions the imposter hidden in the dark mermaids' lagoon:

HOOK (addressing the immensities). Spirit that haunts this dark lagoon to-night, dost hear me?
PETER (in the same voice). Odds, bobs, hammer and tongs, I hear you.
HOOK (gripping the stave [marking the 'hidden treasure'] for support). Who are you, stranger, speak.
PETER (who is only too ready to speak). I am Jas Hook, Captain of the *Jolly Roger*.
HOOK (now white to the gills). No, no, you are not.
PETER. Brimstone and gall, say that again and I'll cast anchor in you.
HOOK. If you are Hook, come tell me, who am I?
PETER. A codfish, only a codfish.
HOOK (aghast). A codfish?[116]

   The climactic encounter in Neverland is between Hook and Peter (who has already—before the play's beginning—severed Hook's arm and fed it as an appetizer to the play's Crocodile, ever-lurking and remorselessly ticking with the sound of a swallowed clock). Hook has captured the lost boys and the Darling children and will make them walk the plank from his pirate ship. Peter comes to the rescue, fights Hook valiantly but ultimately defeats him by nonchalantly 'sitting in the air still playing upon his pipes':

At this sight the great heart of Hook breaks. That not wholly unheroic figure climbs the bulwarks murmuring 'Floreat Etona', and prostrates himself into the water, where the crocodile is waiting for him open-mouthed. Hook knows the purpose of this yawning cavity, but after what he has gone through he enters it like one greeting a friend.[117]

With Hook's demise the Darling children can return from Neverland to Bloomsbury, bringing the Lost Boys for adoption and education, which Peter refuses, because 'I want always to be a little boy and to have fun'.[118] Peter can never grow, as Wendy must and does, and the play can never properly conclude, except by a return to the nursery of its beginning. The childhood world of fairies, redskins, and pirates is in reality a Neverland.

A principled authorial indecision kept *Peter Pan* in a state of textual flux and indeterminacy. An extra final scene was played once in 1908, entitled 'When Wendy Grew Up: An Afterthought'. Wendy 'is now a grown-up woman' attending to 'her little daughter Jane' in 'the same nursery',[119] After a long absence Peter comes again through the window and is distraught when convinced that Wendy is an adult and that Jane is her daughter. Wendy rushes from the room, also distraught, and Peter asks Jane 'Will *you* be my mother?'[120] Wendy returns, grants her maternal permission for Jane to visit Neverland with Peter, and then concludes the extra scene by expressing her hope that Jane will have a daughter who will continue the process 'for ever and ever'.[121]

Since the first performance of *Peter Pan* in 1904, the part of Peter has traditionally been played by an actress, not an actor. Perhaps Peter Pan has always been played on stage by a female for the good reasons that have been suggested: that such practice is a common pantomime convention, that the first producer favoured a particular actress for the part, or that females are naturally smaller than males, so the role of a child could be performed more plausibly by someone who was not a minor.[122] Perhaps, but there is a reason that comes closer to the play itself: that Peter Pan should be played by a female because she can never grow up, never tumesce.

A prose narrative of the play, entitled *Peter and Wendy,* was published in 1911. Once again 'pirates' are promised at Neverland and tempt the Darling boys with prospective adventures.[123] Michael and John Darling already 'knew Hook's reputation'.[124] He was 'Blackbeard's bo'sun' and 'the only man of whom Barbecue was afraid'.[125] His reputation pertains to both fact and fiction, therefore. Allusions to *Treasure Island* are elaborated and multiplied. Hook was said to be 'the only man that the Sea-Cook had feared', the Sea-Cook and Barbecue being names for Long John Silver, whom we are informed that 'Hook had brought…to heel'.[126] Peter later thinks that he has himself killed Long John Silver, seizing 'his [Peter's] sword, the same he thought he slew Barbecue with', the element of uncertainty being added to the sword of the play, which was simply 'the same he slew Barbicue with'.[127] In his swordfight with Hook, Peter is able repeatedly to turn aside Hook's 'favourite thrust, taught him long ago by Barbecue'.[128] Barrie even makes a nod of acknowledgement to Stevenson when remarking mock-philosophically that mothers practising self-abnegation will be taken advantage of by their children 'and they [the mothers, presumably] may lay to that', a favourite locution of Long John Silver's.[129]

In *Peter and Wendy* Neverland is provided with a 'Kidd's Creek' to match the 'Capt. Kidd's Anchorage' of *Treasure Island*.[130] The Llewelyn Davies boys having proceeded (all but one of them) to Eton from 1907 on, *Peter and Wendy* makes more of Hook's education and his inability to grow out of it. He has evolved from headmaster of Pilkington's (or Wilkinson's) to old boy of Eton. Hook 'still adhered in his walk to the school's distinguished slouch. But above all he retained the passion for good form'.[131] A ghostly voice remonstrates with him about his lack of 'good form', to which Hook replies:

'I am the only man whom Barbecue feared…and Flint himself feared Barbecue.' 'Barbecue, Flint - what house?' came the cutting retort.[132]

He uses the derogatory school slangword 'scugs' for his pirate subordinates and ponders the form required for being in 'Pop', the select Eton boys' society: the supreme form of having 'good form without knowing it'.[133]

Wendy's female response to captivity aboard the pirate ship is telling: 'To the boys there was at least some glamour in the pirate calling; but all that she saw was that the ship had not been scrubbed for years.'[134] When Hook loses the fight on his ship his mind rises above his enemies and regresses: 'his mind was no longer with them; it was slouching on the playing fields of long ago, or being sent up for good [sent to the housemaster for commendation], or watching the wall-game [the Eton wall game] from a famous wall'.[135] As he walks the plank he achieves one last triumph—by provoking Peter to kick him overboard improperly rather than send him at the point of a knife. ' "Bad form", he cried jeeringly, and went content to the crocodile.'[136]

Peter's identification with Hook is more pronounced than ever after Hook's exit to the crocodile. The victorious Peter requires Wendy to make him a new suit

out of some of Hook's wickedest garments. It was afterwards whispered among them that on the first night he wore this suit he sat long in the cabin with Hook's cigar-holder in his mouth and one hand clenched, all but the forefinger, which he bent and held threateningly aloft like a hook.[137]

Whether or not Peter's behaviour is strictly Oedipal, there is no doubting that Hook is an alter-ego, much more attractively so than the alternative adult male, childish Mr Darling. Barrie has thus dramatized a child's ambivalence about pirates, admirable and reprehensible, charming and frightening.

Barrie had not yet completed Hook or his formative education, however, for in about 1920 (probably) he prepared a 'Scenario for a proposed film of Peter Pan'.[138] In this 'Scenario' Hook is introduced as 'Jas. Hook, the Pirate Captain (Eton and Balliol)' and some remarks are made about 'the playing of this part':

Hook should be played absolutely seriously, and the actor must avoid all temptation to play the part as if he were conscious of its humours ... He is a bloodthirsty villain, all the more so because he is an educated man. The other pirates are rough scoundrels, but he can be horribly polite when he is most wicked. He should have the manners of a beau. But above all the part should be played with absolute seriousness and avoidance of trying to be funny.[139]

So piracy must be played sans irony. Barrie's authorial interpretation here is quite consistent with the textual history of his character Hook, but it is explicit in placing the character in relation to the conventions of literary piracy. Here we see Barrie separating his conventionally gentlemanly pirate from the subsequent (and partly consequent) nineteenth-century convention of attendant comedy. The earlier nineteenth-century pirate, educated and cultured, must be distanced from his comic consequences in the latter part of the nineteenth century. We may notice also that in the gentlemanly pirate there lurks also, as ever, the potential for satire—the insinuation that gentlemen are politely piratical. Barrie's mention of the 'beau' may be an indication that Hook is perhaps touched by the tradition of the great Restoration stage fops, in plays such as *The Man of Mode* (1676) or *The Relapse* (1696). But, above all, the children's pirate must not be 'funny'.

The 'Scenario' affords an intimate view of Hook's cabin:

We see Hook's cabin with no one in it at first. This cabin is largely furnished like a boy's room at Eton. It has a wicker chair and a desk with a row of books as in an Eton room. On the wall besides weapons are the colours he won at school, the ribbons, etc., arranged in the eccentric Etonian way, and the old school lists, caps, and also two pictures, which when shown in close-ups are seen to be (1) Eton College, (2) a photograph of an Eton football eleven; the central figure is Hook, as he was when a boy, but distinguishable, with a football in his hands and the prize cup between his knees. He and the other boys must wear correct colours. The cat-o'-nine tails also hangs up prominently.[140]

Obviously Hook is a pirate who cannot grow up. When he enters his cabin, 'He lies in bed smoking and reading the *Eton Chronicle* (of which a real copy must be used)'.[141] Paramount Pictures did not use a real copy of the *Eton Chronicle*, nor Barrie's 'Scenario', but at the real school Michael Llewelyn Davies had already been co-editor of the real *Eton Chronicle*.[142]

Years later, on 7 July 1927, long after Michael had drowned while a student at Oxford, Barrie made by arrangement a speech at Eton. His topic was 'Captain Hook at Eton' and his aim to prove that Hook had been 'a good Etonian though not a great one'.[143] He wished 'to have Hook, so to speak, sent up for good'.[144] At Eton Hook had been 'a dry bob' (not a 'wet bob', a practiser of water sports, because, 'boy or man, he hated the touch of water').[145] He had borrowed books from the library which could still be found on second-hand bookstalls, inscribed with his name, exclusively works of 'poetry and mostly of the Lake school'.[146] A search of his cabin after his death revealed hundreds of well-thumbed copies of the *Eton Chronicle*: 'throughout the years of his piracy he had been a faithful subscriber'.[147] Moreover, Barrie could prove that Hook had been elected—whether legitimately or not—a member of Pop, although the page recording his election had been 'mysteriously destroyed'.[148] This mystery Barrie could now solve. He had been reliably informed by a chronically nostalgic and underdeveloped

Old Etonian, unable to leave Windsor, that Hook had been seen back at Eton one night, after his piratical career on the Spanish Main, dressed 'in the incomparable garb of Pop', 'the handsomest man' the informant had ever seen, 'though, at the same time, perhaps slightly disgusting', and sitting on a particular college wall 'on which none may sit save Pops'.[149] He was challenged by a policeman: 'Are you a Pop, Sir?' 'After an agonizing struggle', Hook replied 'No'.[150] He thus displayed perfect good form. Rather than bring dishonour to his old school, he denied that he was ever in Pop, or even at Eton. Later that night he broke into the premises of Pop in the school buildings, where he destroyed the evidence in the records that 'he had once been a member'.[151] 'In that one moment', Barrie asked, 'was he not a good Etonian?'[152] Satirically, gentlemen were pirates. Romantically, pirates were gentlemen. Now, simply, pirates were gentlemen who would not grow up.

VII

Hollywood Lemons

'Hollywood was a place where they grew lemons.'

(Leslie Baily, *Gilbert and Sullivan*)[1]

On 31 October 1912, Barrie informed his agent that he had been offered '£2,000 in advance of royalties for *P. Pan* in cinematograph'.[2] He refused this offer but others followed. On 4 December 1918 Barrie wrote to his agent again: '*P. Pan* film I'm not having done at present. Was offered £20,000 in Paris the other day, advance sum!'[3] As it happened Jesse L. Lasky, former medicine show cornet player and subsequent movie mogul, acquired the rights to *Peter Pan* and other Barrie plays, and Barrie decided to write his own 'Scenario', while receiving visits from Hollywood executives in 1920 and 1921. Paramount asked him to watch auditions by many actresses for the part of Peter Pan, informing him that 'there are 200 applicants of note in the movie world'.[4] Nico, the youngest Llewelyn Davies boy, remembered viewing these clips with Barrie: 'I don't know how many people he and I saw together—who shall we have for Peter Pan? We went to shot after shot.'[5] The movie men also visited Nico's room at Eton, as Barrie recommended, to measure and draw it as a model for Hook's cabin.[6] Barrie himself was invited to attend the 'shooting' at Hollywood in September 1924 and his attractive and aristocratic secretary, Lady Cynthia Asquith, was asked if her son, Simon, would play one of the Darling boys, and if she would 'come too, and play Mrs Darling'.[7] 'Long dormant ambition flared', she remembered.[8] 'I started to pack', but Barrie changed his mind.[9] He would not go to Hollywood and, as for Lady Cynthia and her son 'going without him? Out of the question!'[10] Nico favoured his namesake Marion Davies (William Randolph

Hearst's girlfriend) for Peter Pan. Mary Pickford was mentioned, and Lillian Gish, but Paramount chose an unknown, Betty Bronson, and filming went ahead at Paramount's Vine Street studios in Los Angeles (for the Darling house) and at Catalina Island (for Neverland and the pirate ship).[11] Barrie heard that the island location (in November) was 'cold and harsh'.[12] 'Think if you had gone with Simon!' he told Lady Cynthia.[13]

Barrie's 'Scenario' had required original cinematic effects, 'novel cinema treatment', scenes 'not in the acted play'—effects which the experienced director, Herbert Brenon, mostly avoided.[14] The imaginary growth at speed of Peter Pan into a man was not portrayed, nor the faithful, doglike pursuit of him by devoted flowers.[15] Real dogs and crocodiles were not mixed with costumed actors.[16] (Instead the talented animal impersonator, George Ali, played the Darling's dog-nanny, Nana, with strings to waggle her ears and tail, and—multitalented—he also performed the ticking crocodile.) Peter Pan's flattening out and reshaping of John and Wendy Darling with a rolling pin was omitted.[17] No football was played, as Barrie had suggested, by actors 'flying about over the tree-tops', but Peter does tip mischievous fairies out of a leafy pillow and sweep them 'away with a broom'.[18] Barrie had planned for the flight to Neverland from London to take in, en route, views of the House of Commons and of an animated, 'mothering' Statue of Liberty, both of which were left out.[19] Barrie's request that Mr Darling be seen to read 'a London paper, not an American one', was ignored and indeed the Darlings' Bloomsbury, London, house is not located anywhere.[20] The 'redskins' in Neverland belong to the authentically fictional Fenimore Cooper tribe, as stipulated (and they feature a young Anna May Wong as Tiger Lily).[21] Multiple mermaids flop and wallow in the shallows of a real Pacific sea, awkwardly breaststroking, but the dramatic fun begins with the capture of Wendy and the Lost Boys by the pirates.

Hook, played by Ernest Torrence, former Scot and operatic baritone, turned Hollywood 'heavy', is more comic than horrifying, despite Barrie's direction in the 'Scenario' that 'Hook should be played absolutely seriously'.[22] He does not read the *Eton Chronicle*, as Barrie had stipulated, but a manual entitled *Gems of Deportment and Hints of Etiquette*. Aboard the pirate ship the two captive Darling boys are recruited by Hook as cabin boys. 'Didst ever want to be a pirate, my hearty?' Hook's written caption asks the elder Darling boy, who consults the younger eagerly, and replies: 'Oh, yes, Sir! But shall we be faithful to the Stars and Stripes?'[23] 'NO!' thunders Hook.[24] 'Then I refuse!' replies the elder boy. 'AND, I REFUSE TOO!' shouts the younger.[25] 'That seals your doom!' pronounces Hook and calls for captive Wendy to be brought from below decks.[26] He then calls for 'Silence all, for a mother's last words to her children', consulting his etiquette book.[27] Wendy feels that she has a message for the Lost and Darling boys from their 'real mothers', who would say: 'We hope our sons will die like American gentlemen'.[28]

This patriotic sacrifice will not be required, however, as Peter Pan and the ticking crocodile have come to the rescue, Peter lurking in Hook's cabin and stabbing pirates who venture there. (The cabin is dark but not Etonian, which would have been appropriately un-American, perhaps, but also, unfortunately, beyond American comprehension, doomed to be lost in the cultural translation.) Peter arms the captive boys with pirate cutlasses and they fight the pirates on the decks and in the rigging, sending them splashing into a real sea. Hook and Peter fight man-to-man. Hook is skewered but descends below to blow up the whole ship, which Peter prevents (as in the play).[29] Victorious and piratical, he insists that Hook walk the plank. Defeated Hook takes the walk but does not heroically and arrogantly dive into the crocodile's jaws with Etonian 'dignity', as proposed by the 'Scenario'.[30] Peter Pan hauls down the Skull and Crossbones from the pirate masthead and breaks out the Stars and Stripes in its place. To travel from stage to screen was also—almost inevitably, with the global dominance of Hollywood—to travel transatlantically, to Americanize as well as colonize Neverland.

The pirate ship speeds impossibly fast through the sea and cinematically and magically through the air to London (unidentified) where Peter and Tinker Bell conspire to close the Darling nursery window (as in the play and 'Scenario') so he can keep Wendy in Neverland, but he is moved by supremely motherly Mrs Darling playing 'Home Sweet Home' on the piano (as outlined in the 'Scenario'), so he flings open the nursery window for the Darling children to return to their moping mother, contrite father, and doting Nana, of the eloquently wagging tail and waggling ears. Peter watches the rapturous reunion from the liminal windowsill, that symbolic site of transition between adult and child, the birth-passage of Barrie's imagination, releasing children but also excluding them—sexual imagery and implications which

are invisible in the film. The excluded Neverland Lost Boys are introduced, dressed as pirates, for adoption by the Darlings. Peter refuses
adoption because it would entail school and then working in an office
(the reasons given in the play) and (additionally) because he does not
'want to be president!'.[31] Neverland is still a utopian noplace, lost in
space as well as time, but is naturally placed in relation to America
rather than Britain. What Peter does want is to return to Neverland
with Wendy. Mrs Darling grants him an annual visit by Wendy (as envisaged in the play and 'Scenario'): 'I will let Wendy go to you one week
each year as your mother to do your Spring cleaning'.[32] But Barrie's
circular time-bending ending (as indicated in his 'Afterthought' and in
the 'Scenario') which has Peter flying away with Wendy's daughter,
Jane, is not enacted.

Filming finished in December and pre-publicity began immediately.
Betty Bronson was displayed in person across the United States and
greeted at New York by a disciplined mob of children dressed as Peter
Pans and fairies.[33] The film itself opened at Grauman's Million Dollar
Theatre in Los Angeles on Boxing Day, 1924, and then simultaneously
in theatres across the country, receiving 5,825,260 customers and
$2,155,346 in the first week.[34] *Variety* welcomed Betty Bronson as 'the
find of the year', 'for she is a delight'.[35] Ernest Torrence 'as the famous
Captain Hook, the pirate leader, is another delight'.[36] Scenes in Neverland 'were exceedingly well handled, but the real thrill came with
the pirate ship and the battle on its deck'.[37] When the film opened in
London in January, 1925, the *Times* was somewhat more analytical,
pronouncing that the director had 'sensibly' been faithful to the play,
'rigidly following his original':

instead of making a film of *Peter Pan*, he has merely taken the play as it was on
the stage and photographed it. He could not have done it better.[38]

Barrie, who had been more cinematically adventurous in his 'Scenario', took an opposite view when he saw some previews in November 1924. Yes, the film was faithful to the play, but that was because the
director had not used the new medium to best effect: 'so far it is only
repeating what is done on the stage, and the only reason for a film
should be that it does the things the stage can't do'.[39] The transition
between old medium and new had not been made, according to Barrie, and was still for him an unanswered question. More simply but no
less thoughtfully, Nico conceded on viewing the film that Betty

Bronson was 'quite good' as Peter Pan, but 'the thing that broke my heart', he remarked coolly, 'was my wonderful room at Eton not being used as Hook's cabin—that was a heartbreak'.[40]

Peter Pan was more a children's film than a pirate film and it left the question of the cinematic pirate open. What was the cinematic pirate, then, and how would he distinguish himself from his literary precursor? To this open question a regular answer was that a pirate film was one made from a pirate book, especially a Sabatini book. Made the same year as the film of *Peter Pan*, *The Sea Hawk* (1924) was an American silent film of the popular novel of the same name, written by Rafael Sabatini, and published in 1915.[41] Born in Italy of an Italian father and an English mother, Sabatini was educated internationally in Portugal and Switzerland before coming to England, where he worked on a Liverpool newspaper and at other jobs until he was able to publish fiction and survive and then thrive by it. In his *The Sea-Hawk* a late sixteenth-century Cornishman, Sir Oliver Tressilian, knighted by Queen Elizabeth for patriotic seafaring services (including some buccaneering), is in love with Rosamund, a neighbouring lady who quaintly inhabits a 'bower'.[42] Her relatives refuse him her hand in marriage, accusing him of being a pirate because of his patriotic buccaneering: 'I'll not have my sister wed a pirate'.[43] The accusation is merely an excuse for local political and commercial rivalry and Rosamund loves Sir Oliver nevertheless, but unfortunately his younger half-brother kills Rosamund's brother and Sir Oliver is suspected of the crime. Treacherously, the half-brother ('that dastard') has Sir Oliver captured by a local captain, unscrupulous, piratical Jasper Leigh, who will sell him as a slave to the Barbary corsairs, the Muslim pirates who operated from ports in North Africa.[44] Sir Oliver reappears in the book turbaned, baggy-trousered, and 'shod in a pair of Moorish shoes of crimson leather, with up-curling and very pointed toes'.[45] Promoted from galley-slave to corsair leader, right-hand man of the Basha of Algiers, Sir Oliver is now Sakr-el-Bahr, the Sea Hawk, a renegade and a Muslim.

When he hears that Rosamund—who believes that he killed her brother—is to wed the real killer, his own half-brother, the Sea Hawk takes his corsair ship to Cornwall and kidnaps both Rosamund and his half-brother, removing them to Algiers. The brother confesses to the killing, so Sir Oliver's name is cleared, but Rosamund is horrified instead by his new role: 'Are you not—you that were born a Cornish

Christian gentleman—become a heathen and a robber, a renegade and a pirate?'[46] It is the 'pirate' problem again, exacerbated by his cultural transformation, his new religion as well as his Moorish shoes with 'up-curling and very pointed toes'. To add to the Sea Hawk's difficulties, his leader, the Basha, wants Rosamund. By marrying her as a Muslim and by heroic and gallant efforts, the Sea Hawk contrives to escape with her onto a convenient Christian ship, so the loving couple can return to Christendom, Cornwall, and happiness. A Sabatini pirate is evidently not so different from a Scott pirate, but a Sabatini plot is less convoluted and has a lady at the beginning and the end, its cause and effect. Sabatini's best-selling novels were historical novels, after all, in the continuing and developing tradition of Scott's novels, but Sabatini's were briefer, with less description, less digression, and more of a story.

The film of *The Sea-Hawk* was directed by Frank Lloyd for First National, and follows the novel's plot, predictable and simple, but winding, for some two hours. Gallant Sir Oliver is in love with Rosamund, who reciprocates, but her relatives insult him by calling him 'a pirate!' and therefore denying him her hand (and land). Sir Oliver's brother kills Rosamund's brother and allows Sir Oliver to be blamed, arranging for him to be kidnapped by comical seafaring rascal Jasper Leigh, played by Wallace Beery as a loveable rogue.

Kidnapped Sir Oliver becomes the fearsome Sakr el Bahr, the Sea Hawk, a Muslim Barbary pirate, who kidnaps Rosamund and his dastardly brother ('Ye dastard!') who are about to be married and enjoy the Tresillian lands and manor, but are shipped instead as slaves to Algiers (see Figure 7.1). There Sakr-el-Bahr outwits his leader, the piratical Basha, by marrying Rosamund as a Muslim. His brother has confessed to the killing of her brother, so Sir Oliver's name is cleared and he can escape his role as Sakr-el-Bahr to live happily with Rosamund in his Cornish manor house. The reviewer in *Variety* enthusiastically described the film of *The Sea-Hawk* as 'a work of art' that had cost $800,000 to make but would recoup that sum and 'a lot more'.[47] Viewing the film was 'just as thrilling and gripping as reading one of Sabatini's novels', but 'the real kick' on the screen came with 'the sea stuff', particularly the 'sea fights'.[48] These were indeed to be the climactic set-pieces of pirate films, visual spectacles no longer left to a reader's imagination. The word 'pirate' did not occur in the review, however. Certainly there are

Figure 7.1. Rosamund at auction in Algiers, ogled by the Basha (centre) and his wily factotum, while Sir Oliver looks on in his pointed helmet (still from the silent *The Sea Hawk*, 1924).

some fierce sea-battles with 'action aplenty' before Sir Oliver resumes his rightful gentlemanly identity, and certainly Sakr-el-Bahr, his piratical alter-ego, is played by Milton Sills as a manly pirate as well as an Elizabethan gentleman, but for the pirate part he is dressed as a Hollywood Arab, distinctive not just in his Moorish shoes but as a chivalric version of the Valentino Sheik, in chain mail, robes and a tur-baned helmet, not in the costume of a pirate of the golden age.[49] That costume—headscarf and three-cornered hat, with beard—is worn by comical rogue Jasper Leigh, not by the film's hero. So *The Sea Hawk* was not perhaps the perfected cinematic rendering of the pirate of public expectations.

The film *Captain Blood* was made a little later the same year (1924) from another novel by Rafael Sabatini, *Captain Blood: His Odyssey* (1922). This Sabatini story concerns an Irish doctor who is unjustly punished for giving medical aid to a rebel in Monmouth's failed rebel-lion of 1685 against James II. The victim of this injustice, Peter Blood, is shipped to Barbados, where he is bought as a slave by the tyrannical planter, Colonel Bishop, but gains some independence by relieving the Governor's chronic gout. He is befriended by Bishop's spirited, principled—and beautiful—niece, Arabella, although his scenes and dialogue with her are marked by his charming but unacceptable impudence.

Blood's insubordination leads to rebellion and he escapes with his fellow slaves aboard a Spanish ship which has captured the harbour at Barbados but is defeated by his trickery and bravery. Renaming his Spanish prize the *Arabella*, he becomes Captain Blood instead of Dr Blood and begins a career of piracy—about halfway through the book, previously a captivity narrative. Blood's piratical exploits are borrowed—as Sabatini playfully acknowledges—from the buccaneer-author Esquemeling's *Bucaniers of America* (in English translation, 1684), particularly Esquemeling's account of Captain Morgan and his taking of Spanish Maracaibo, Venezuela, which Blood copies exactly, so it becomes 'Blood's buccaneering masterpiece'.[50]

Raised to heights of notoriety, he forms a partnership with a more typically piratical and evil French pirate, Levasseur, but then defeats him in a duel which Blood fights to save a Mlle d'Orgeron from being ransomed—or worse—by Levasseur and also, we are told, because Blood hopes Arabella Bishop might approve of his gentlemanly conduct. In a separate and coincidental series of events, Blood defeats a Spanish admiral who has captured both Arabella and an English emissary, Lord Julian Wade. Ungrateful Arabella calls her rescuer a 'thief and pirate', but Lord Wade is empowered to offer Blood a commission in the Royal Navy, by analogy with 'Morgan, who had been enlisted into the King's service under Charles II'.[51] Because Arabella has called him a 'thief and pirate' Blood refuses the commission. Again the plot turns on the implications of 'pirate', especially in conjunction with 'thief'. As Lord Wade tells her: 'Your words have rankled with him. He threw them at me again and again. He wouldn't take the King's commission'.[52] Later he accepts the commission as a matter of expediency, merely, but with some hope, as he tells Arabella, 'that this honourable service might redeem one who was a pirate and a thief'.[53] She still thinks him a 'murderer', however, misunderstanding his chivalrous and honourable killing of evil, piratical Levasseur.[54] In consequence he resigns the commission and reverts to the high seas of piracy—until luckily he rescues another English envoy, Lord Willoughby, who brings him up to date with the national news. Bad King James—held responsible for Blood's wrongful conviction and enslavement—has been replaced by good King William and, additionally, England and France

are at war. Willoughby offers Blood service under King William and so
Blood defeats the French ships which have taken Port Royal, Jamaica.
Bettering Morgan, who became Deputy Governor of Jamaica, Blood
becomes Governor. Arabella assures him that she 'no longer' thinks
him 'a thief and a pirate'.[55] Moreover she is not engaged to Lord Wade
but in love with Governor Blood:

'There was never, never anybody but you, Peter.' They had, of course, a deal to
say thereafter, so much indeed that they sat down to say it, whilst time sped
on, and Governor Blood forgot the duties of his office. He had reached home
at last. His odyssey was ended.[56]

Sabatini's plot has more action than the old Scott plot, more dialogue, and less psychological complication, but it works in basically the
same way, demonstrating how a good man can become a pirate: by not
really being one. Piracy is knight-errantry, a gentlemanly rite of passage, a deviation with a good sense of direction. For half the book
Blood is unjustly a slave, not a pirate. When he does become a pirate
he does so in response to the injustice he has suffered, and his piracy
consists in fighting the English national enemies, the French and Spanish. The Frenchman Levasseur is really the pirate and is killed skilfully
and chivalrously by Blood, who is motivated much more by love for
Arabella than greed for treasure. The Odyssean progress of Dr Blood
to Governor Blood is only briefly interrupted by Captain Blood, a
mere deviation from the true course of the personal voyage home.

Vitagraph, the makers of the silent *Captain Blood*, were a New York
and California company consisting mostly of members of an English
family called Smith. David Smith was the original director of *Captain
Blood*, but was replaced by his brother Albert Smith, while the cameraman, presumably throughout the filming, was Steve Smith Junior.[57]
The Smiths tried to buy the real ships used for *The Sea Hawk*, but were
refused, so bought and hired their own real ships and constructed miniature models.[58] Their silent film of *Captain Blood* has potentially a
more promising pirate hero than the Sea Hawk, the principled doctor
Peter Blood, who is wrongfully sold as a slave to a sadistic landowner
in Barbados, Colonel Bishop, who has—thanks to best-selling
Sabatini—an attractive niece, Arabella. The film follows the novel's plot
with some simplifications but quite closely, so Dr Blood the slave does
not become Captain Blood the pirate for some time. Eventually he
leads a slave revolt which coincidentally and patriotically results in the

Figure 7.2. Captain Blood and an appreciative Arabella (still from the silent *Captain Blood*, 1924).

capture by the slaves of a Spanish ship which has invaded the main port of Barbados. Victorious Blood makes nasty Colonel Bishop walk the plank, a scene derived from the novel, and Bishop is not drowned, merely humiliated by the 'ducking'.

Despite this rebellion and insubordination, Blood is thanked for saving the British colony by attractive Arabella (see Figure 7.2), before setting sail with his freed slaves as Captain Blood, the pirate. Although a pirate, to Arabella he 'doesn't look like a pirate', manifesting 'the soul of a gentleman not a pirate', so his ambiguity in the novel is minimal in the film. He is chivalrous and patriotic, as well as in love with Arabella, and is appointed a British naval captain, bringing the film to a fierce and exciting conclusion with a battle between his ship, romantically named the *Arabella*, and some French ships attacking Port Royal, Jamaica. These climactic scenes feature real ships firing brightly flashing broadsides, as well as real and also model ships exploding, and those subsequent staples of pirate film, scenes of ships in collision being overrun by boarding hordes of leaping and slashing extras.

An article by the cameraman Steve Smith Junior in the *American Cinematographer* in 1924 describes the difficulties of filming from a rolling boat on 'the open sea', the camera operators flung alternately into 'waist deep water' and then 'high and dry' in the air, while desperately 'panning' (turning the camera) to keep the other boats that they were filming in camera shot.[59] The 'gigantic sea battle' at the film's conclusion was also perilous for the film-makers, particularly the spectacular elimination of a 169-foot 'French' ship with '3,600 pounds of 100 per cent dynamite' off Catalina Island (formerly Neverland) at mid-afternoon.[60] As Steve Smith Junior reminds us: 'There could be no retake the next day'.[61] Fortunately, skilfully, the intrepid film-making was successful, although hazardous: 'with the terrific explosion...came a rain of wood and bits of iron that made the most hardened of the crew seek shelter under the tripods [the camera supports]'.[62] (The *Daily Graphic* admired this spectacular climax of *Captain Blood*: 'the biggest and rowdiest thing yet seen on the silver screen'.[63]) The pirate ship *Arabella* was also exploded and sunk in the action, a 'shot...taken at ten in the morning' to get the right light (see Figure 7.3), but Captain Blood survived, victorious again, was made Governor of Jamaica and will certainly marry Arabella—now that he is no longer the pirate captain but the colonial governor, Governor Blood.[64]

Figure 7.3. The exploding *Arabella*, during the filming of *Captain Blood*, 1924.

The reviewer of the film in *Variety* agreed with the *Daily Graphic* that 'the aquatic warfare is eye-filling', 'well staged and pictured', providing 'the high point of the presentation, culminating in the blowing up of two of the ships', but some of the film's ships had 'a decided smack of miniatures' and in any case none of the spectacular maritime excitements compensated for the poor casting and acting.[65] J. Warren Kerrigan was a known 'name' but played the title role 'without rising to any heights'.[66] Significantly, the word 'pirate' was not used in the review. The novel *Captain Blood* was considered by the reviewer to be 'the most adaptable for the screen of all Sabatini's historical romances' but on the screen Sabatini's hero did not seem to embody or evoke the ideal 'pirate' type.[67]

Sabatini's Captain Blood is nearer than his Sir Oliver to the pirate character of popular imagination, but in the film the actor J. Warren Kerrigan, elegant and almost foppish in extravagant lace cuffs and long ringlets, is neither muscularly swashbuckling nor even dramatically masculine. The director Albert Smith considered him 'a little too effeminate for the role', intended for the unobtainable John Barrymore, and Smith (Albert) got the girl in the end, marrying the actress who played Arabella, Jean Paige, before Vitagraph itself foundered and sunk.[68] We shall return to these Sabatini novels in their later Hollywood incarnations as sound films, noticing meanwhile that cinematic piracy is motivated mostly by love, for Rosamund and for Arabella, the lady not the pirate ship.

Two years after the films of these Sabatini novels came another answer to the question of the proper pirate film. Bursting with capitals and italics, an opening caption announced the attractions of *The Black Pirate* (1926):

Being an account of BUCCANEERS & the SPANISH MAIN, the *Jolly Roger*, GOLDEN GALLEONS, bleached skulls, BURIED TREASURE, the *Plank*, dirks and cutlasses, SCUTTLED SHIPS, *marooning*, DESPERATE DEEDS, DESPERATE MEN, and—even on this dark soil—ROMANCE.[69]

We have heard all this before, of course, but we have not seen it—seen it cinematically, that is. As Hollywood extended its reach and repertoire from slapstick comedy to thrilling crime and to the nineteenth-century novel, serious and popular (Hugo, Dickens, Eugène Sue, Marie Corelli), Douglas Fairbanks moved from films with contemporary settings to historical ones. The plot of *The Black Pirate* was concocted by

Fairbanks himself and consisted of the simplest Scott plot of a respect-able aristocrat for the best possible reasons appearing to play the role of a pirate—only to be disclosed as an aristocrat, a suitable mate for a captive princess. This plot outline Fairbanks simply crammed with all the necessary pirate items, as promised in his opening caption.

The pirate ingredients were well-established and what was new was to enact them on the screen and with cinematic spectacle and the physical talents of Fairbanks himself, an acrobat as much as an actor, who could perform stunts, leaping, bounding, swinging through the air, flashing his smile and his sword. His characterization was less important than his gymnastics. He had to play the role of a pirate who could out-pirate real pirates while keeping the audience's confidence that he was no such thing and could defeat pirates at their own game, by tricks, stunts, and sheer effrontery. Pirates were sea-faring outlaws and gangsters, characters in search of a genre, but were obviously his-torical, probably European, and no longer American national heroes like the frontiersman or his successor—on a horse and with a shorter gun—the cowboy. So a pirate film was not a Western, not a Gangster or Detective film, not a Screwball Comedy or a Musical, but was per-haps a 'Swashbuckler', a poor relation, a kind of cinematic subgenre.[70] On those mean seas a man must sail who was not himself mean—the anti-pirate, a hardboiled but turned-around gangster. Not that the seas were evil. That Puritan ocean, those seventeenth-century 'great Deeps', not only of 'the Sea, but of Hell also', had been rediscovered in the nineteenth century as Gothic.[71] From the Paris flat of Isidore Ducasse his character Maldoror addressed the ocean with rhetorical questions. 'Dis-moi donc', he asked:

Tell me then if you are the dwelling of the Prince of Darkness. Tell me . . . if the breath of Satan makes these tempests which lift your salt waters up to the clouds. You must tell me, because I would rejoice to know Hell so close to man.[72]

The cinematic ocean was pleasingly demonic, not horribly, was wild— as wild as the West—and the anti-pirate was in his natural element. The role required 'swashbuckling', an onomatopoeic term derived from the sound of swords striking shields (bucklers). Signifying a dramatic swag-gerer and thence a book or film portraying such a dashing character, the term applied to the theatricality and daring swordplay of historical novels' central figures, designed by Scott, Dumas, and Stevenson (and copied by Sabatini) to thrill with skill and potential evil, while triumphing ultimately on the side of right and at the side, probably, of some delicate and eligible beauty.

Words were beside the point of such a plot, such a spectacle, and no specific literary source was necessary. Fairbanks's film needed everything, not anything in particular. 'It always takes a certain combination to produce a definite result', he explained to an attentive writer for *Picture-Play Magazine*:

> That is the way it was for us in working out *The Black Pirate*. We started with the idea of pirates as A. Pirates? What are they? What do they act like? How do they look?... We felt that they had never really been shown properly on the screen. *The Sea Hawk*, for example, was a great picture but not a pirate picture.[73]

Certainly Sir Oliver in his baggy trousers and Moorish shoes was not properly costumed and his film lacked the pirate essentials listed in Fairbanks's opening caption. *The Sea Hawk* did feature '—even on this dark soil—ROMANCE', but it lacked 'the SPANISH MAIN, the *Jolly Roger*, GOLDEN GALLEONS, bleached skulls, BURIED TREASURE, the *Plank*'.

To correct the generic inadequacy of *The Sea Hawk*, then, and perhaps also of *Captain Blood*, the idea of pirates had to be defined for the new medium, according to Fairbanks: the idea 'A', as he called it. Next it was necessary to add B to the pirate idea A. 'When it came to visualizing them, it became necessary to add B to A, but for a long time we didn't know what B was, and that was the reason for the delay.'[74] Some time passed in contemplation of this mysterious B, 'that would make pirates look as they should look'.[75] 'But', as Fairbanks continued to explain,

> the thought that kept intruding all the time was that pirates demand color. Stories of modern life, war stories, even romances like *Robin Hood* and *The Thief of Bagdad* [his previous swashbucklers] might be told in black and white, but what pirates needed was something more vivid. It was impossible to imagine them without color.[76]

Experiments with colour had been made before in film. As Fairbanks acknowledged, 'We were familiar with the technicolor camera', but he was determined to achieve improved results and these required, in these early days, the painting of the studios and the colour coordinating of the actors' costumes and makeup to ensure the filmed results would achieve the desired effects by way of the 'two colour' Technicolor process then available.[77]

That pirates were not merely a matter of colour seems to have been recognized in the advance publicity for *The Black Pirate*. There was consideration, also, of the pirate 'idea', which was outlined by an article in *Picture-Play Magazine* (1923) prophetically entitled 'The Pirates Are Coming':

> On with the pirates! The screen needs their swaggering braggadocio, their gun play, and flashing broadswords…Last year the sheiks had everything their way…No doubt pirates will enjoy a similar rage.[78]

This forthcoming rage (involving some generic uncertainty: braggadocio, gun play) called for a learned expert:

> The coming of pirates to the screen means the coming into motion-picture production of the man who knows most about pirates—Dwight Franklin, a sculptor whose miniature models of pirates have invaded even the sacred precincts of staid art museums and universities. Hardly had the wave of interest in making pirate pictures begun when producers began to seek out Mr. Franklin and bid for his services…He is second to none as an authority on their customs and clothes and manners.[79]

His expertise was so wide-reaching as to be ungraspable, ineffable. He had been for some years 'connected with' the Museum of Natural History in New York as 'wild-animal photographer, field collector, taxidermist, sculptor, artist, and general naturalist'.[80] Also, the 'lives of prehistoric man, Vikings, American Indians, and Eskimos as well as pirates are all an open book to him'.[81] Such were his attractions and talents that Douglas Fairbanks and his wife Mary Pickford 'were visitors at the Franklin studio during their recent trip to New York, and it was shortly after that that he [Fairbanks] announced his plan to play a pirate'.[82] Indeed in an interview to promote *The Black Pirate* Fairbanks mentioned that he had engaged Mr Franklin, whose vague affiliations had apparently shifted from the New York Museum of Natural History, as he was now billed as 'a research expert formerly connected with the Metropolitan Art Museum, who probably knows more about pirates than the pirates ever knew about themselves'.[83] The credits to *The Black Pirate* do list Dwight Franklin as a 'consultant' but no signs of his omniscience can be deduced from the finished film. The combination of supposed historical authenticity and successful saleability was not new, of course, but perennially the story of the popular pirate.

Film historians have surmised a more likely influence than Franklin's on the depiction of Fairbanks's pirates, though this other influence has not been demonstrated by any firm evidence. The authors of a study of *The Films of Douglas Fairbanks, Sr.* state nevertheless that the art directors of *The Black Pirate* 'were bowing to the ... work of the book illustrators of the turn of the century—Howard Pyle and N.C.Wyeth'.[84] The supposition is reasonable. Howard Pyle was celebrated for his pictures of pirates, as well as other picturesquely historical subjects, and had written his own extremely predictable pirate stories to accompany his illustrations, tales mixing the legends of Kidd, Blackbeard, and other famous names, with the narrative strategies of Poe and Stevenson— tales and pictures published in American magazines of the 1890s and collected posthumously in *Howard Pyle's Book of Pirates* (1921). The child star Jackie Coogan, an enthusiast for *Howard Pyle's Book of Pirates*, claimed to have inspired Fairbanks to make a pirate film during a backstage conversation at an awards ceremony in 1922.[85] Pyle's successor as a popular illustrator of pirate stories was his pupil, N.C.Wyeth, whose illustrations in 1911 for *Treasure Island* were thrilling, dramatic enactments and immediately successful. Wyeth's modern biographer states—without providing evidence—that in the 1920s 'Wyeth refused offers to work in Hollywood, repeatedly turning down Douglas Fairbanks's and Mary Pickford's enticements to direct pirate pictures'.[86] Certainly Pyle and Wyeth shaped the popular imagination of pirates, even if it is improbable that Fairbanks wished Wyeth to 'direct pirate pictures' for him.

The Black Pirate was directed by Albert Parker, an experienced professional and an old friend, but Fairbanks supervised and played the role of producer-director as he did all roles. 'It was like watching him on the screen', according to a journalist granted an audience '—same panther-like activity, same piercing eyes—same everything'.[87] Beach scenes were filmed on the back lot of the Pickford-Fairbanks Studios at Formosa Avenue, West Hollywood, and a marine scene off Catalina Island, although a tank on the back lot held 700,000 gallons for other sea-scenes, churned into waves by aeroplane propellors.[88]

Beyond the connection of A and B, the creative processes of Douglas Fairbanks are not documented. The implications of his opening caption, quoted above, are that he proceeded not by way of a plot, nor a particular (narrative) source of fact or fiction—but by accumulation. His film *The Black Pirate* was by his definition piratical—unlike *The Sea Hawk*—presumably because it collected every typical piratical circumstance (and something, too, of *Robinson Crusoe*, a desert island classic). His film was therefore—deliberately, by design—a predictable picture. As he told *Picture-Play Magazine*:

We have gone at the film in quite the old-fashioned way, putting something sensational right at the beginning to take the audience's mind off the color photography and center it on the picture. We have a smashing series of opening shots showing the destruction of a merchantman by the pirates. A big explosion—men boarding the decks—plenty of excitement. It is the old recipe, but it seemed to us absolutely necessary for use again, since we are dealing with a brand-new medium.[89]

The 'big explosion' is the destruction of a ship of which the Fairbanks character and his father are the sole survivors, reaching a tropical island where the father expires and Fairbanks vows revenge against the pirates responsible. Their captain conveniently arrives on the island with some companions to hide the loot from the destroyed ship in an underground 'Secret Hiding Place'. Fairbanks bravely offers to join them (to achieve his revenge and also to escape his Crusoe-like solitude) and proves himself by challenging the captain to a duel, which Fairbanks wins when the captain clumsily falls onto a sword cunningly placed for that purpose by Fairbanks—one of a number of clever tricks to come. The captain's deputy is sulky at Fairbanks's promotion but another, more amusing, one-armed pirate, played by Donald Crisp, is sympathetic to the new pirate recruit, who proves himself to the whole pirate crew by another stunt, the spectacular feat of capturing a ship single-handed. This arrangement of acrobatic heroics is achieved by his clambering aboard the vessel in question and nimbly swinging up by a rope to the mast (a reversed film of Fairbanks swinging down) where he inserts his knife into the spread sail and slides precipitately down, slicing the sail in two (assisted by a concealed and secure board behind the sail into which the knife was slotted, as Fairbanks told David Niven).[90] He then takes control of two cannons and trains them on the ship's crew, sailors who make an improbably late appearance on deck and immediately surrender en masse. The pirates have been watching this spectacle, like the film's audience, and are impressed.

Aboard the captured ship a princess, played by Billie Dove, is discovered and Fairbanks proposes to the pirates that, instead of exploding the ship, they should send it with a message demanding a ransom for the princess, who would be kept safe and alive meanwhile aboard the pirate ship. Fairbanks composes the ransom note, which he signs

'The Black Pirate', but secretly sends another note to the captain of the captured ship, requesting that soldiers be sent to capture the pirate ship, from which he plans to release the princess by surreptitiously taking her ashore in a boat. The sulky pirate, however, who desires the princess for himself, arranges to prevent her being ransomed by planning instead the explosion of the captured ship carrying the ransom note.

This sulky pirate, Sam de Grasse, an actor practised at villainous roles, witnesses the explosion as planned and happens to notice also the elopement of Fairbanks and the princess, who are showing many signs of love (what the comical pirate in his comically Scots-accented caption calls 'an affleection of the heart'). Fairbanks and the princess are apprehended and Fairbanks is put on trial for his treachery and sentenced to 'walk the plank' (one of the promised pirate essentials). Instead of perishing by this process, however, Fairbanks escapes by swimming underwater and then to the shore, where he finds a convenient horse and rides off along beautiful beaches. The sulky pirate knows the ransom will never come and grapples with the princess in a sequence that alternates with footage of the 'rescue' approaching: a galley filled with soldiers from the shore and with Fairbanks at the prow. He dives and swims underwater to the pirate ship, followed by his soldiers in uniformed swimming costumes, who swim in formation underwater—a spectacular effect, filmed 'without any water', with 120 breast-stroking extras hanging by piano wires against a blue-green painted ocean, embellished with 'wisps of tissue paper...giving the illusion of seaweed'.[91] Fairbanks, his muscular arms and legs displayed by his swimming costume, saves the princess by fighting with the sulky pirate. His swimming soldiers reach the pirates, engage them victoriously, and rescue Fairbanks, hoisting him up by hand from deck to deck in gymnastic celebration. A boat arrives from shore containing 'His Excellency, the Governor', who congratulates Fairbanks, whom he addresses as 'My Lord Duke'. The princess is surprised and repeats 'Lord Duke?' The Governor introduces the happy couple: 'Your Highness—His Grace, the Duke of Arnoldo'. Fairbanks flashes his big smile and proposes marriage. They draw apart from the throng and kiss (for which act Billie Dove was replaced by Mary Pickford, uncredited but jealous).[92] The attendant comical pirate suggests—presumably without innuendo—'The treasure in the Secret Hiding Place—a wedding gift', but Fairbanks and the princess—whom Fairbanks has already called his 'treasure'—are blissfully oblivious and the pirate ship—restored to legality—sails into 'THE END'.

'The Black Pirate' was only a role, then, and he is revealed as a Duke after all, twice rewarded, with a princess and the pirate treasure. Reviews of the film were complimentary, although *Variety* complained that 'the tale that it spins [is] the weakest Fairbanks ever had. [He] should have done Sabatini's *Captain Blood*'.[93] The plot of *The Black Pirate* is indeed the old Scott contrivance, a voyage from gentleman to pirate and back again, not unlike *Captain Blood*, but the film has been made from the necessary pirate staples—treasure, as well as walking the plank—with the effect of cinematic spectacle—more acrobatic stunts than acting—and is now a classic of a new genre, the pirate film, while seeming to be a continuation of the old, literary legacy, as the reviewer of the American premiere in New York City noticed in the *New York Times*:

> The audience was ushered into the realm of piracy by the singing of 'Fifteen Men on a Dead Man's Chest' and afterward by a ghost-like voice that asked everyone to go back to the days of bloodthirsty sea robbers. With its excellent titles and wondrous colored scenes this picture seems to have a Barriesque motif that has been aged in Stevensonian wood...As for Mr. Fairbanks, he seems more active than ever...This is a production which marks another forward stride for the screen.[94]

A speeded-up film of film's commercial history, its forward strides, would show Kinetoscopes and Mutoscopes in penny arcades turning into picture theatres, nickleodeons, then cinemas, movie-houses, dark spaces where growing audiences crowded in to sit in flickering light that showed them faces as big as houses, trompe l'oeil simulations of distant or non-existent times and places, illusions of all shapes as well as sizes, including—of course—pirates, who came to life again to lighten those dark spaces, penny arcades turning into million-dollar businesses. As Fairbanks said of *The Black Pirate*, it was 'the old recipe', the literary pirate, but transferred now to the 'brand-new medium'. The silents were regenerating the literary pirates: 'Pirates? What are they?' asked Fairbanks. Answer: not pirates, but antipirates, displaced gentlemen. The cinematic pirate had been in rehearsal in books and was ready now for the big screen.

All is well at the Admiral Benbow inn on some Californian coast until the arrival of a sinister seaman with a seachest, Billy Bones, imposing his presence and language on the customers—'Rum for all hands, say I!…Clear the decks for pleasant action!…Belay there!…Rum!'—telling bloodthirsty yarns and leading compulsory singalongs of 'Fifteen men on a dead man's chest'.[95] A pirate has come to the Admiral Benbow and sound has come to the pirate film, *Treasure Island* (1934). Dr Livesey will not stand for such piratical behaviour. 'Are you addressing me, Sir?' asks Livesey, promising as a magistrate that Billy Bones will hang if he does not behave. Thus the two teams for the treasure hunt are displayed in action: the gentlemen and the pirates—and also the two go-betweens: young Jim Hawkins and Long John Silver. Black Dog and Blind Pew fail to get their hands on the treasure map in Billy Bones's seachest, which is taken by young Jim, who shares it with the respectable party, Dr Livesey and Squire Trelawney, who set sail from eighteenth-century Bristol, reconstituted in Oakland, California, with a crew of pirates recruited by Long John Silver.

The relation between Jim and Long John Silver is at the heart of the film. Twelve-year-old Jackie Cooper is more irritating than charming as Jim, but former circus performer, female impersonator and silent-film actor Wallace Beery made a likeable rogue in a conventional mould out of one-legged, parrot-carrying Long John Silver, who flatters gullible Jim, 'Matey, you're just as smart as paint!' and gives him spitting lessons (not to spit into the wind) and nautical instruction at the wheel: 'Starboard a bit, matey, she's luffing.'[96] Treasure Island is sighted: 'Gadzooks!' cries Squire Trelawney, delighted and comically English. Treasure Island is Catalina Island, formerly Port Royal, Jamaica, in *Captain Blood*, as well as Neverland, and abounds in palms, banana trees and exotic birds borrowed from the private collection of William Wrigley Jr, chewing-gum millionaire.[97] Hostilities break out between the respectable party at the stockade ashore (built of pine logs shipped from Canada) and the pirates aboard the *Hispaniola* (reconstructed from a whaling ship used in a previous film, *Eskimo*).[98] At the stockade the Union Jack is hoisted while the soundtrack plays 'Rule Britannia'. Correspondingly, the Skull and Crossbones is raised to the masthead of the ship. Maverick Jim discovers marooned Ben Gunn and captures the *Hispaniola* from Israel Hands. Jim hauls down the Skull and Crossbones from the mast and sails the ship ashore, but Hands pursues him up the rigging, knife in mouth. 'One more step, Mr Hands, and I'll blow your brains out!' Jim warns, using Stevenson's own words, but Hands takes no heed of Jim's pair of pistols, flinging the knife, which narrowly misses.[99] Simultaneously Jim fires his pistols and Hands falls with a splash into a real sea. The experienced director, Victor Fleming, proudly described the 'difficult scene' with young Jackie Cooper (or a stand in): 'Jackie's perch sixty feet above the deck was precarious. The roll of the boat made it hard to maintain the balance of the cameras built on parallels over the edge of the boat'.[100]

Fleming stresses the cinematic methods rather than the artistic effects but the Art Director of the film had been influenced by N.C. Wyeth's illustrations of the book.[101] Stevenson told his American publisher Charles Scribner that he wished in retrospect that Howard Pyle had illustrated *Treasure Island*, but the British edition published by Cassell's in 1899 had illustrations by Walter Paget.[102] In 1911, however, Scribner's asked Pyle's former pupil, N.C. Wyeth, to produce a new illustrated edition of *Treasure Island*. Wyeth enthusiastically set to work, beginning with the illustrations by Paget, whose frontispiece, in black and white, depicted Jim in the rigging of the *Hispaniola* firing his pistols at the falling Israel Hands (see Figure 7.4). Wyeth's colour illustration is plainly derived from Paget's but Wyeth's is more dramatically foreshortened, so Jim and Hands are closer and we look up to Jim, firing his pistols down between his legs at Hands, whose knife is poised for throwing at Jim (see Figure 7.5).

The Wyeth painting is more exciting because of this foreshortening, which more directly confronts the two figures, and because of the tension of the suspended action: Jim and Hands are in armed confrontation, and the outcome is not shown. The scene in the film is not so tightly framed as Wyeth's painting, so we do not see Jim and Hands in direct confrontation (perhaps Jackie was replaced by a stand-in, and could therefore only appear in close-up) but the dramatic action is clearly influenced by Wyeth's painting and Jim shoots his pistols down between his legs as Wyeth had imagined.

After taking the *Hispaniola* Jim returns to the stockade and is captured by Long John Silver and the pirates who have occupied it. Long John saves Jim from the pirates' wrath and indeed he and Jim are somewhat in alliance as the pirates go treasure-hunting with the map. This is piracy with clues and mystery, as Stevenson, after Poe, had conceived it, not piracy with violence, but the treasure is not in the assigned spot. Violence results: another pirate mutiny against Long John and Jim ('It's only a cripple and a boy!') who are saved by the intervention of the

Figure 7.4. Walter Paget, frontispiece to *Treasure Island* (1899).

respectable party and conducted to Ben Gunn's cave, where he has carried the glittering piles of treasure.[103] "Pon my soul!' says Jim.[104]

Accompanied by the treasure and Long John Silver as a prisoner, the respectables sail for Jamaica but encounter a British ship on which Silver can be tried and hung. The respectables go aboard this ship, leaving irresponsible, cheese-guzzling Ben Gunn on guard aboard the *Hispaniola*. Meanwhile Long John has stolen a share of the treasure,

Figure 7.5. N.C. Wyeth, illustration to *Treasure Island* (1911).

hidden under his coat. By miming his pitiable death from hanging, he then arouses Jim's sympathy and, in this deviation from Stevenson, Jim unlocks Silver's cell. A tearful farewell follows as Long John gives Jim his parrot, and rows in a ship's boat to a prosperous future and a potential sequel, smiling and waving to Jim and the viewers.

The result was satisfying to the public taste. *Kinematograph Weekly* praised Wallace Beery's 'strong study of genial villainy', not unlike his performance as Captain Jasper Leigh in the silent *The Sea Hawk*, and found Jackie Cooper 'courageous and venturesome', not annoying, as young Jim.[105] The *Monthly Film Bulletin* praised the 'trouble and expense' that were evident in the preparation of the Admiral Benbow and the *Hispaniola* and admired the fidelity to Stevenson's novel, apart from 'the very last, tearful scene of parting between Jim Hawkins and Long John Silver'.[106]

Fairbanks had invented his own silent pirate plot, credited pseudonymously to 'Elton Thomas' (Fairbanks's two middle names for Roman Catholic confirmation, aged 12), but the significant sound films that followed depended on historical romances for their swashbucklers—in particular the novels of Rafael Sabatini.[107] One of his greatest successes, filmed in 1923 and 1952, was *Scaramouche:A Romance of the French Revolution* (1921).The 1952 film, starring Stewart Granger, has reputedly the longest swordfight in cinema history (six and a half minutes) but the action stays on dry land. Sabatini's continued popularity, in combination with Hollywood's repetitive tendency, meant that the silent *Captain Blood* of 1924 was filmed again with sound in 1935, in imitation of the preceding film as well as the book, although the new film, the remake, followed the generic model of Fairbanks, who had established the 'swashbuckler' genre in films, featuring sharply distinguished heroes and villains who engaged in battles and duels and—incidentally, but necessarily—in romance.The film genre has its origins in Scott's historical novels (frequently dramatized) and in the novels of Dumas *père* (dramatist as well as novelist) and his successors (including Stevenson) who transformed historical events into duels and japes, escapes and chases, conducted by gentlemanly outlaws and adventurers, translating the Romantic psychology of duality—combined nobility and piracy, for example—into melodrama and adventure.

The Smiths of Vitagraph had purchased the rights to Sabatini's *Captain Blood* for $20,000 and these rights passed to Warner Brothers when they acquired Vitagraph in 1925. Warners then renegotiated those rights with Sabatini in 1930, paying him a further $10,000, but it was not until 1935 that the company set to work on a remake of the novel. 'What was the nickel for?' a character asks Monroe Stahr, the Hollywood film producer in Fitzgerald's last novel *The Last Tycoon* (1941).[108] ' "I don't know," said Stahr. Suddenly he laughed. "Oh, yes—the nickel was for the movies." '[109] Period costume films came in waves as studios swayed to the breeze of fashion or commercial success.Warners were keenly watching the Hollywood weather. Historical costumes disguised popular rebels against English authority, such as Robin Hood or Fletcher Christian, and disguised the sex and violence prohibited by the Motion Picture Code of 1930, its rulings reinforced by the Catholic

Legion of Decency in 1934. In January 1935 the cinema trade paper
Variety remarked on the popularity of historical films and the reason,
that 'the files of history' provided material with less risk 'of offending
the Church and other busybody factions from a censoring stand-
point'.[110] Warners soon cast the English actor Robert Donat as Captain Blood, and Jack Warner cabled Randolph Hearst on 20 February
1935, wondering 'would Miss Marion Davies be interested in playing'
the role of Arabella, 'an excellent feminine part'.[111] Although Hearst's
Cosmopolitan Productions had merged with Warner Brothers, his girlfriend did not like the role, for some reason, and neither did Robert
Donat want his. A Warner producer, Harry Joe Brown, wrote wondering aloud to the top Warner producer, Hal Wallis, about somehow
getting Leslie Howard, or Clark Gable, or Ronald Colman. Brown was
convinced 'that no man in the business is too big to go after for *Captain Blood*' and 'confident that it is one of the best stories of its kind
ever written'.[112]

Nothing seems to have come of these speculations and Jack Warner
himself considered taking a risk with an unknown actor. A script had
already been completed by Casey Robinson, an experienced screenwriter, Michael Curtiz had been appointed to direct and sets were
under construction for studio sailing ships, but the main roles were still
not cast when, on 11 June 1935, Hal Wallis requested screen tests on
'George Brent and Errol Flynn for the part of Captain Blood in the
picture of that name'.[113] Thus did Errol Flynn get his chance for a
major role, thanks to Jack Warner (as they agree in their two rather
different autobiographies).[114] For the 'feminine part' Warner also chose
an unknown, 'a girl with big, soft brown eyes', as he described her,
'a fresh young beauty' with a 'name nobody can spell'—Olivia de
Havilland.[115]

In his scenario for the film, Casey Robinson, with the approval no
doubt of Michael Curtiz and Hal Wallis, had simplified (and thereby
improved) Sabatini's plot, most economically by removing the distrac-
tions provided in the novel by apparent possible alternative mates—red
herrings—for Blood and Arabella, in the persons of Mlle d'Ogeron,
daughter of the French Governor of Tortuga, and Lord Julian Wade.
Further simplifications followed in consequence, beneficially. Blood is
not offered a commission twice, by Wade as well as by Willoughby,
with an intervening reversion to piracy, but once only, by Willoughby. The
elimination of Mlle d'Ogeron allows the duel between Levasseur and

Blood to be about Arabella instead of her French counterpart, an obvious convenience. The villains are reduced to two, merely, the cruel, slave-owning Bishop and the piratical pirate Levasseur.

The main action scenes, as planned and in the result, were the duel between Blood and Levasseur and the final maritime battle between Blood's ship and those of the French occupiers of Port Royal. Cinematic piracy meant swordfights and explosions. The duel was shot at Laguna Beach, south of Los Angeles, and was choreographed by Fred Cavens, the fencing master who had worked with Fairbanks on *The Black Pirate*. Curtiz insisted that the protective tips be removed from the points of the swords, in case they might be visible, and the actors proceeded unprotected, against Cavens's advice, but all was well, nevertheless, Levasseur's prone body being washed by a Californian wave in place of a Caribbean one.[116] The battle at Port Royal was fought in the Warner studios by about 400 extras and stuntmen, with 50 cannons, 350 cutlasses, and 300 daggers, for more than two weeks.[117] Most of the film was made thus in the studio rather than on location, with studio sailing vessel sets, enormous studio cabins, model ships manoeuvred in studio tanks, and even old stock footage, some apparently from Warner's inherited property, the silent *Captain Blood*.[118]

Behind the scenes, Hal Wallis's missives to Curtiz insisted that telling the story—narrative—was more important than artistic effects such as 'the composition of a candle-stick and a wine bottle on a table'.[119] Because, 'if you don't tell a story, all the composition shots and all the candles in the world aren't going to make you a good picture'.[120] Curtiz is not considered a great 'auteur' by film historians, more an obedient cog in the Warners wheel, but he sometimes disobeyed the orders sent him by studio bosses, and the finished film shows he kept his candle and bottle in the shot and still told the necessary 'story'. Hal Wallis kept his eyes on the daily rushes and fulminated to Curtiz regularly, particularly about Blood's costume, which he had decided, even at the test shootings of Flynn, should be plain and simple, not spangled and braided. 'Yet tonight, in the dailies', Blood was wearing lace cuffs (as he did in the silent version) and collar:

What do I have to do to get you to do things my way? I want the man to look like a pirate, not a molly-coddle. You have him standing up here dealing with a lot of hard-boiled characters, and you've got him dressed up like a God damned faggot...Let him do a little swashbuckling, for Christ sakes! Don't always have him dressed up like a pansy! I don't know how many times we've talked this over.[121]

Genre depended on characterization, then, and characterization on manly clothing. Errol Flynn was not to wear the lace of 'effeminate' (and homosexual) J. Walter Kerrigan, nor the wig of long ringlets. It was essential also that Curtiz apply himself to directing Flynn 'and give him a little confidence':

the fellow looks like he is scared to death every time he goes into a scene. I don't know what the hell is the matter. When he has confidence and gets into a scene, he plays it charmingly.[122]

Flynn was quickly confident, it appears from the completed film, and played Blood charmingly, as Wallis knew he could.

Although the pirates carouse at Tortuga with prostitutes thinly disguised by historical costumes, the scenario and its direction by Curtiz kept piracy motivated by love, as Sabatini had arranged it. The film retains the Scott pirate plot concerning a gentlemanly outlaw who finds his merited place at the top and gets his well-deserved girl. She is independent, somewhat 'boyish' as Sabatini indicated, and is played with spirit as well as allure by Olivia de Havilland.[123] The film enhances the parallels between Arabella and Blood, who was her uncle's captive as she becomes his (when he has defeated Levasseur). She remains his inspiration and guiding light. In a scene in his cabin after he has won her, he sits with Arabella beside an open treasure chest of his accumulated loot. While shadows sway on the background to simulate the motion of a ship on the waves, he shows her this loot, including some pearls, but speaks wistfully: 'I often wondered why I bothered to save all these things. Tonight I know it's because... one day you'd be here in this cabin to wear them'.[124] 'I'll never wear them—never—those nor any other plunder gotten by a thief and pirate', she replies indignantly.[125] 'Thief and pirate', he repeats in close-up, stung.[126] Love, not greed, was what had moved him, and the film is intent to show this. Like Sabatini's hero—and silent Hollywood's—Flynn's Captain Blood is no pirate.

Flynn was even more successful and popular than de Havilland, and his smile and sword made him the top swashbuckler of Hollywood, the successor of Douglas Fairbanks. Hollywood's sound film of *Captain Blood* was released for Christmas on 24 December 1935, to good reviews and publicity, such as appeared in the *Film Daily*, which promoted the film as a

Smashing drama to please all...Every type of imaginable appeal to lure the femmes as well as the men and boys...An outstanding production...Moves with surging suspense from one stirring episode to another. Errol Flynn is splendid. A superlative job.[127]

The *Variety* review complained at the slight 'romantic interest' and at the logic of Blood's being a likeable pirate who contradicts and opposes piratical practice: 'Here is a gallant, engaging, young blade who, under pirate's colors, repels the very aspects which first cement his brave appeal'.[128] This quibble about the inconsistency and ambiguity—the unpiratical character—of the screen pirate was somewhat sophisticated, however, and *Variety* recognized correctly that, even if it lacked adequate 'romantic interest', or logical consistency, nevertheless

Captain Blood, from the Sabatini novel, is a big picture. It's a spectacle which, had it a bit more romance, or marquee values, could well be a smash. And it is, it will do very well and establish both Errol Flynn and Olivia de Havilland.[129]

It 'could well be a smash' if it were not for its flaws, but also, somehow, 'it is' a smash. *Variety*'s logic is not clear but its judgement about the two stars was prophetic and history has been kinder to Warner's *Captain Blood*, a classic of pirate cinema, even if it lost the Oscar for best picture to *Mutiny on the Bounty*, which featured American Clark Gable as rebellious Fletcher Christian, with Englishman Charles Laughton as authoritarian William Bligh...and real ships.

Warners had acquired some rights to Sabatini's earlier novel, *The Sea-Hawk* (1915), via their acquisition of another film company, First National, which had made the silent version of the book in 1924. Sabatini had received $10,000 for the silent rights to *The Sea-Hawk* and Warners considered a remake a popular prospect, negotiating a further price of $25,000 for the 'talking motion picture rights'.[130] ('Put another nickel in the nickelodeon.'[131]) What they had purchased was Sabatini's story combining romance and piracy, quite faithfully followed by the silent *The Sea Hawk*, which had kept closely to Sabatini's plot. A screenwriter was set to work on the novel, while the film of *Captain Blood* was still under production, and he decided to enlarge the Elizabethan historical side of *The Sea Hawk*, developing the patriotic buccaneer and removing the Muslim corsair. On 14 December 1935 Hal Wallis asked Harry Joe Brown, who had been working on *Captain Blood*, for his opinion of the reworked *Sea Hawk* material 'as a possible follow-up on *Captain Blood*'.[132] Another Warners writer was assigned, who restored the Barbary corsair but found Sabatini 'florid and unbelievable'.[133] Thus *The Sea Hawk* continued through the wheels of studio machinery, Muslim corsairs coming and going and also Hollywood writers—'schmucks with Remingtons', as Jack Warner is supposed to have called them.[134] In 1938 another writer was assigned, Seton Miller, who departed freely from Sabatini's plot in favour of a buccaneering raid by a Captain Geoffrey Thorpe, not a Sir Oliver Tressilian, on a Spanish treasure convoy en route from Panama on the Pacific to Nombre de Dios on the Caribbean, a raid modelled on Drake's similar one in 1573.[135] So the pirates of the novel, the Barbary corsairs of the Mediterranean, were to be translated into Elizabethan pillagers of the Spanish Main—problematic Muslims turned into patriotic Elizabethans. The Warners writers were working with some stirring biographies of Drake and a jolly account of *Elizabethan Sea-Dogs*, so the idea of 'sea dogs' suitably stood in for the Sea Hawk, Sakr-el-Bahr.[136] As Miller acknowledged: 'I based Thorpe's character on Drake, Hawkins and Frobisher . . . The raid on Panama is from Drake, but otherwise Thorpe's adventures vary . . . widely from Drake's history'.[137]

Indeed, although Geoffrey Thorpe is sometimes Francis Thorpe in drafts, Geoffrey Thorpe did deviate from Drake in Miller's plot, being captured by the Spanish and sentenced to galley-slavery (like Sabatini's hero, Sir Oliver).[138] As a slave Thorpe learns that the Spanish are planning to back Mary's accession to Elizabeth's throne. He therefore leads a rebellion of the galley slaves who take the Spanish ship to England with a warning of this Spanish plan. Miller called his outline 'Beggars of the Sea', though 'sea-dogs' would have been a more historical term if 'sea hawk' had to go. He had worked as a writer on Flynn's latest swashbuckler, *The Adventures of Robin Hood* (1938), and the producer Henry Blanke, who had also worked on *Robin Hood*, was designated producer of the *Sea Hawk* project. He approved 'Beggars of the Sea' and told Hal Wallis 'I think it offers twice the possibilities of a *Captain Blood* and will make a sequel to *Robin Hood*'.[139]

Miller continued work on his 'Beggars', drafting and redrafting a script, which Henry Blanke then sent to a newly-contracted studio writer, Howard Koch. Michael Curtiz was now involved and he and Hal

Wallis considered some potential economies, re-using some footage from the sea battles in the sound film of *Captain Blood*, and also they decided to rename the 'sea beggars' the 'sea hawks'.[140] Koch reworked Miller's plot, started Thorpe's romance with the Spanish ambassador's niece a little earlier than Miller had planned, and added the Spanish Armada and its loss to Elizabethan forces, an addition he later subtracted in his screenplay. The writing credit for *The Sea Hawk* was later disputed between Miller and Koch, Miller protesting that he should rightfully share the credit with Koch, who had used Miller's story not Sabatini's as the basis for the final script. 'There is not one word of Sabatini's novel in the script', he pointed out.[141] Koch had used Miller's story (based largely on historical Drake) and thus the 'characters and characterizations are the same from the heroes to the heavies'.[142] In the end the screenplay was credited to both Koch and Miller. Neither of them felt that Sabatini deserved any credit, though Miller recognized 'the sales value the studio places on the Sabatini name', and indeed Warners had purchased the right to use the Sabatini title even though Sabatini refused the use of his name in relation to the studio product that had wandered so far from his own.[143] Unlike the silent film of 1924, the sound version of *The Sea Hawk* (1940) was of Warners's story, then, not Sabatini's.

In preparation Warners built a huge 'maritime' stage on their lot. This construction, Stage 21, could be filled with water, sluiced with pipes and drains, and in this water, only a few feet deep, a full-scale British man-of-war and a Spanish galleas were constructed, with a pit of deeper water between them, to allow stuntmen to fall from the ships spectacularly but safely. Beneath the ships were wheels on rails and around them a painted cyclorama representing sea and sky. Hydraulic systems rocked the ships when required and the art director invented a 'ripple machine' that simulated different kinds of waves, from normal to rough, by moving sheets of 'wave silhouettes' across the lights behind the ocean-painted part of the cyclorama.[144] 'Miniature' ships were also constructed, to represent ships at a distance. They were not tiny, however, but about 18 feet long, concealing inside a supine man who could steer them and operate their concealed motors and small-scale cannons.[145] This was all state of the cinematic art and enabled a sea-and-ship film to be made under completely artificial and controlled circumstances.

The finished film marked a peak of the studio-made film era. Such a film would later be made much more on location, but little on *The Sea*

Hawk was filmed beyond the Burbank Warners lot. Some shots of Venta de Cruces on the Isthmus of Panama were filmed at a Warners ranch at Calabusas, a few miles from Burbank, where Mexican sets remained from a previous film, and a beach at Point Magu, up the Californian coast, briefly represented the Caribbean coast of the Isthmus.[146] A studio property a few blocks from Warners's Burbank lot was turned into a Panamanian jungle by the film's art director: water was installed to provide a swamp, tropical vegetation featured creepers, and a fog machine provided the illusion of steaming heat.[147] All other scenes were rendered on the Warners lot, at Barham Boulevard, Burbank: the Spanish and English royal palaces, Dover, and, of course, the sea and ships.[148]

In November 1939 casting for *The Sea Hawk* was considered. Flynn was to be lead, of course, and Curtiz to direct, but Olivia de Havilland was not to play the 'feminine part', the role of Donna Maria, the Spanish ambassador's niece, who was replacing Rosamund, dumped by Warners's rewrite. Flynn had been in love with Olivia and showed his feelings with pranks she may not have appreciated. 'There was the time', Flynn remembered, when 'she found a dead snake in her panties as she went to put them on'.[149] Perhaps also, as Flynn speculated more sympathetically, she became 'sick to death of playing "the girl"' in his films.[150] For whatever reason, Olivia de Havilland was either not offered or declined the female role in *The Sea Hawk*, the part of Donna Maria, which went to Brenda Marshall, a new and more forgettable Warner actress. Flora Robson was to play Queen Elizabeth, Claude Rains the conniving Spanish ambassador to England (and uncle of Donna Maria) and Henry Daniell to play the treacherous (and imaginary) Lord Chancellor, Lord Wolfingham.

Filming began in February 1940 and Wallis protested to Curtiz about departures from the script, in particular during a scene livening up Elizabeth's court with Thorpe's pet monkey, a piece of business invented by Koch. 'The added lines about a lot of monkeys already living in the palace and the pulling the tail line are ad lib cracks put in on the set and have a tendency to make the scene phoney because they are colloquialisms'.[151] The ad libs stayed in, however, and the monkey business too. In March Curtiz moved on to film the opening battle scene of fighting between Thorpe's *Albatross* (named by Koch) and the Spanish galleas carrying the Spanish ambassador (Claude Rains) and his interesting niece. The producer Henry Blanke told Wallis what film footage from *Captain Blood* he hoped to use for *The Sea Hawk*: shots of men swinging on ropes between ships, of guns firing and their effects: 'wreckage, masts falling, etc'.[152] Some of this old stock was apparently used, but of course most of the battle would be acted out on the new 'maritime' Stage 21. Curtiz was concerned to construct an effective battle sequence and (rather than resort to *Captain Blood*, saving time and money) he went on filming 'battle scenes' for some time, to the further annoyance of Wallis viewing the rushes the following month.[153]

Apart from the sea battle of the ships, the other essential action (for a swashbuckler) was a duel near the conclusion of the film, featuring gallant Thorpe fighting and finally defeating and killing Elizabeth's fictitious Lord Chancellor, Lord Wolfingham (Henry Daniell), treacherously in league with Spain. There was initially some difficulty and delay caused by Daniell's incompetence at swordplay. A unit manager reported that 'Mr. Daniell is obviously helpless and his closeups in the duel will be mostly from the elbows up'—closeups which would exclude from view his fumbling foot-work and wrist-work.[154] Daniell was doubled (by Olympian swordsman Ralph Faulkner, for instance) and is frequently seen from the back, with 'elbows up' closeups inserted. After triumphing over those difficulties, the two actors and their doubles, choreographed by that foremost specialist of cinematic swordplay, Fred Cavens, burst through the glass of a window into a brief balcony scene. Flynn then retreats, pursued, through a door and down a corridor, tumbling down a flight of stairs, but then advancing as Lord Wolfingham retreats, across an enormous stateroom, Thorpe dominating and perfidious Wolfingham succumbing, until at last run through, lifeless on the palace floor.

Thorpe's victory is England's and the final scene of the film is provided by his knighthood conferred aboard ship by the grateful Queen, a spectacle performed in front of his adoring lady, the niece of the Spanish ambassador, and his cheering sailors in the rigging. In the British release the Queen (Flora Robson) makes a stirring speech not included in the American release (in which its implication is nevertheless quite clear, of contemporary events in the World War):

And now, my loyal subjects, a grave duty confronts us all: to prepare our nation for a war that none of us wants...We have no quarrel with the people of Spain or of any other country, but, when the ruthless ambition of a man threatened to engulf the world, it becomes the solemn obligation of all free men to affirm that the Earth belongs not to one man, but to all men.[155]

The Muslim and Christian rivalries in the Mediterranean, rewritten as Spanish and English rivalries on the Spanish Main, were thus updated to accommodate the Second World War. Piracy was neither here nor there, but Flynn was on the right side.

He was more bashful with Donna Maria than with Arabella, but his suave charm is the film's main attraction, set against Curtiz's presentation of the action set pieces, the sea battles and the duel. The maritime effects are dramatic and the acrobatics of the fighters thrilling, even if the nautical material is sometimes inauthentic to the point of apparent pastiche. Thorpe begins a series of orders which is taken up by officers and crew: 'Aloft there, clear your lease-lines!' 'Do away your mizzen banks!' 'Tuck your halyards!' 'Take away your true-lines!'[156] This is as far removed from historical Drake as Thorpe is from fictional Sakr-el-Bahr, and of course Thorpe's piracy is transparently patriotic and polite. When pillaging the Spanish ambassador's captured ship, he returns Donna Maria's personal jewels to her, with a note to say 'Only a pirate would deprive you of these jewels'.[157] Pirates must prove they are not pirates, despite dashing and glamorous appearances. 'Plus ça change', perhaps, but the nineteenth-century literary pirate is now at home in the twentieth-century cinema. Books set the scenes, the characters, and the plots, but films have taken—have overtaken—the stage and page.

Some audiences may have felt that the court scenes and intrigues detracted from the more athletic action in *The Sea Hawk*, but Warners had no doubt their sound film was an ideal Flynn vehicle to follow-up his *Captain Blood* and *Robin Hood* performances, as an advertisement poster clearly signalled: 'Adventure Bound! O'er the Spanish Main sails a lone pirate ship, hunting for gold and glory...captained by the feared "Robin Hood of the Sea"!'[158] Warners' publicity office—part of the whole collaborative cinematic process—ensured sketches in *Vogue* of practical and attractive redesigns of the film's costumes, a *Sea Hawk* model to build from a kit, a comic book in colour of the story—all the signs of success.[159] Another nickel for the nickleodeon, paid by those crowds in the darkness watching the flickering light? Perhaps, but Grub Street depended on money too, as pirates did on diamonds in their day. We may note in conclusion—and anticipation—that women were esssential for this successful celluloid pirate. In the words of the opening caption to *The Black Pirate*: 'even on this dark soil—ROMANCE'.

VIII

Something for the Broad

'Well, is there anything for the broad to do?'

(Jack, a film producer at Universal)[1]

'As for the loss to himself of his share of the Spanish gold, what was all the treasure of Spain to him compared with this other treasure which lay here ready to his hand, tormenting him with its irresistible allurement?'[2] Such is the dilemma facing loathsome pirate captain, Tom Leach, and firmly at the heart of Rafael Sabatini's *The Black Swan* (1932). Which of these treasures, then, is more alluring, the treasure of unimaginable wealth or the other, tangible treasure, the daughter of the Governor of the Leeward Islands, Miss Priscilla Harradine, who 'displayed an outward grace of body that was but the reflection of an inner grace of mind', the former aspect particularly evident to Tom Leach when she swam naked in a tropical Caribbean pool, 'a nymph of an incredible whiteness'.[3] The treasure of Miss Priscilla is perhaps more alluring also to suave, dandified Monsieur de Bernis, who seems to be another pirate, despite his prominently obvious breeding and education. But perhaps the civilized, sweet-voiced, and chivalrous Monsieur, who pretends that Miss Priscilla is his wife, is only playing a role ('I have a part to play', he says) to protect alluring Miss Priscilla from the repulsive real pirate, Tom Leach?[4] Perhaps Monsieur de Bernis is not a pirate, after all, and perhaps Miss Priscilla finds him alluring too? The answer to low-browed Tom Leach's question is that Miss Priscilla is more alluring than Spanish treasure and more significant to her author, Rafael Sabatini, and to his readers. Romance matters more than swashbuckling, and the plot of *The Black*

Swan turns on the acquisition of captive, tangible Miss Priscilla, not Spanish gold. The outcome is unsurprising: Monsieur de Bernis duly defeats Tom Leach in a duel and it is revealed that he never was a pirate, just pretending, so now he can happily marry Miss Priscilla.

The hero of the film of *The Black Swan* (1942) is named Jamie Waring, not Monsieur de Bernis, and is played by Tyrone Power, at the peak of his swashbuckling appeal. The director was Henry King, perhaps better at Westerns. Jamie falls in love with Margaret Denby, who is not called Priscilla, and is played by Maureen O'Hara, fiercely feminine and red-haired in Technicolor. A large part of the film is set in colonial Jamaica, where saucy Jamie and petulant Margaret replay more roughly and toughly the interplay of Flynn and de Havilland in the sound film of *Captain Blood*. Jamie calls Margaret a hell-cat but insists she will marry him, although she calls him a 'nasty, vulgar rogue'.[5] Perhaps he is worse, a pirate? He kidnaps her to sail with him in his pursuit of evil, piratical Captain Leech (George Sanders), whom he pretends to join, hauling up the skull and crossbones, to the disgust of Margaret, who thinks Jamie is showing his true colours. As the film joins the book, Jamie Waring pretends to Captain Leech that Margaret is his wife, so they must share a cabin to keep up the pretence and show O'Hara to advantage, alluringly abed in lacy night attire, though not naked. Chivalrously, roguish Waring hangs a hammock for himself to sleep chastely apart, but he is forced to join Margaret in bed for Captain Leech's inspection.

Leech sees through this acting, that Waring is pretending to be her husband and pretending to be a pirate, so he ties him inextricably into his hammock, from which he escapes, alluringly shirtless, to skewer Leech athletically and gallantly rescue Margaret. So Jamie Waring was not a pirate, after all, and he and Margaret conclude the film by kissing against a Technicolor setting sun, representing—in the words of the concluding line, delivered by Sir Henry Morgan—'the end of the Spanish Main'. Ladies are essential in pirate films but cannot marry pirates, only those playing pirate roles.

RKO did not think the pirate sun had set and responded to Twentieth Century-Fox's *The Black Swan* with *The Spanish Main* (1945), directed by Frank Borzage, whose Hollywood career had probably peaked with an Oscar in 1927 and another in 1931. Innocent Dutch captain Van Horn (unexcitingly portrayed by Paul Henreid) is imprisoned by dastardly Don Alvarado, Spanish Viceroy of New Grenada, from whom he escapes to become a notorious pirate, the Barracuda, who attacks only Spanish shipping, in a remorseless vendetta against Alvarado. So the Barracuda is not really a pirate and indeed the main plot of the film concerns his capture of the intended bride of Alvarado, the proud, haughty daughter of the Viceroy of Mexico, the Countess Francisca de Guzman Angandora (performed by Maureen O'Hara, who had an annual picture commitment with RKO). Obviously the Barracuda is motivated by revenge against Don Alvarado, and presumably that is also why he insists on marrying Alvarado's intended. Francisca consents reluctantly, lest he carry out his threat to attack another Spanish ship if she does not. On the wedding night in the Barracuda's cabin, Francisca clutches a knife behind her back to protect herself but she lets it fall when he kisses her. This promises well but then he tucks her into bed and bids her goodnight. As he exits, she 'folds arms indignantly', according to the script.[6] Is he perhaps chivalrous or does this prove that he has married her out of hatred for Alvarado, not any feelings for her?

At Tortuga haughty Francisca meets her match in Anne Bonny (Binnie Barnes), who is really a pirate, not pretending, and is flagrantly female. As such, she loves Van Horn, the Barracuda, and is fiercely jealous of his new wife, Francisca, whom she calls 'a powdered prissy trollope!'[7] A pirate should know a trollope when he or she sees one, but Francisca does not fit this bill. In a Tortuga tavern the two tough women agree to duel with much protocol, in obedience to the correct piratical rules for settling disputes. The tension builds as the pistols are prepared for them and the Barracuda shouts 'Fire!' but the outcome is merely two blackened female faces, because the Barracuda has loaded the pistols with chimney soot.

For all Francisca's supposedly piratical chivalry, the real pirates, Anne and the Barracuda's comrades, want rid of her, fearing reprisals from the Spanish, and sail with her to return her to Alvarado, treacherously leaving the Barracuda behind on Tortuga. Anne Bonny flies Francisca's nightdress, which she believes has enchanted the Barracuda, as the ship's colours. But the dastardly Don Alvarado breaks Francisca's promise of safe conduct for Anne Bonny and the other pirates who delivered her. When his men invade the pirate ship to imprison the pirates, Anne strikes its colours, that significant nightdress, and resists manfully, kicking out at Alvarado, who exclaims: 'Bless me, it's a woman!'[8] 'So I am', says captured Anne. 'But what are you?'[9] Unmanly Alvarado wants to marry

Francisca immediately but she protests at the prospect of having two husbands. Alvarado points out that the Barracuda does not count. 'A pirate
can never be regarded as a husband', he says, but Francisca does not want
to marry Alvarado.[10] 'He's fat!' is what she thinks.[11] Fortunately the
Barracuda sails to the rescue—of Francisca and of the wrongfully imprisoned pirates. With her collusion he helps the pirates fight their way out
of Alvarado's jail. The escape involves exciting duelling and unfortunately the death of brave Anne Bonny, but the happy couple are free to
be together, she no longer proud and he no longer piratical.

The cinema reviewers were pleased with the formulaic shape of *The
Spanish Main*. 'It represents all that is best in time-honored "skull and
crossbones" pantomime', was the verdict of *Kinematograph Weekly*.[12]
'Love and piracy on the high seas—that is the ever popular theme',
remarked *Today's Cinema*.[13] The combination of 'hearty work with the
cutlass' and 'a near-naughty cabin sequence' made 'the picture a really
peppy stimulant for the populace'.[14] Near-naughtiness was female,
then, by contrast with hearty cutlasswork, which was male, but even
further from naughtiness, hardly evil at all. The reviewer of the film of
The Black Swan in *Kinematograph Weekly* considered it 'immensely
thrilling adventure entertainment', 'vigorously adapted from Sabatini's
swashbuckling romance', but the reviewer in the *Motion Picture Herald*
regretted that pirates were not what they were in the days of Douglas
Fairbanks: 'some of the high gusto has been lost'.[15] The Sabatini novel
had provided the film of *The Black Swan* with some proper pirates 'in
the old tradition of unregenerate scoundrels' but Tyrone Power, as 'a
landed, law-abiding squire', was not properly piratical.[16]

Anne Bonny's manful role in *The Spanish Main* is indicative of the
direction of imaginary piracy in the twentieth century. As we have
seen, piracy was becoming a love story, and by the middle of the century pirates were increasingly becoming piratesses. This feminization
of the pirate was quite obviously in keeping with the emancipation of
the film-going public, female as well as male, and was also in keeping
with the exhaustion of the male pirate as a significant character type,
except perhaps for children. The male pirate became, indeed, not just
a false pirate and genuine gentleman, but emasculated, marginalized in
the pirate plot. The popular pirate of the twentieth century was increasingly female, then, despite the minimal historical basis for female
pirates in the golden age, the supposed source of the popular pirates'
historical reality.

Anne Bonny, openly female but nonetheless manful in *The Spanish Main*, is not in male disguise in the film *Anne of the Indies* (1951), one of director Jacques Tourneur's more unusual B movies, but she is cross-dressed and is characterized principally by a gender crisis. The historical Ann or Anne Bonny was the inspiration for *Anne of the Indies*, in which Anne, played by Jean Peters, former Miss Ohio, future Mrs Howard Hughes, is freely fictitious. She dislikes the English and makes a captured English captain walk the plank, but welcomes his prisoner, a Frenchman, into her crew. She is herself half-French, but orphaned early, called Anne Providence after her birthplace on Providence Island, and trained and raised by Blackbeard, who was her 'father and mother', raising her as a pirate not a woman. She wears trousers and is tough but is not in disguise. The French recruit Pierre (Louis Jourdan) politely calls her 'Mademoiselle' but she slaps him, requiring to be called 'Captain' instead. He is perhaps a spy but claims to be a genuine pirate and has a treasure map. Allowed to choose an item from captured pirate loot, he chooses a dress, for some reason. While the crew of the *Sheba Queen* careens the ship, Anne tries on this dress in the privacy of her tent ashore, where Pierre interrupts her. 'May I help, Captain?' he asks. 'Bear a hand with these lines astern', she orders him, referring to the laces at the back of the dress. 'They won't clew up properly.' 'Wenches are mad', she says. 'How can they move clewed up like this?' 'They don't', he explains, smoothly removing her pirate headscarf. 'They wait for the men to make the moves.' She looks at herself in a mirror. 'Do men like this?' He answers affirmatively: 'It's the nature of men.' 'You mean, a man sees a woman like this—and he wants to make love to her?' He nods. 'Yes.' 'How?' 'Surely you've seen them in Nassau', he replies, embarrassed. But the sailors at Nassau are vermin, she protests. 'How does a Frenchman make love—a gentleman?' He puts his arms around her and kisses her passionately, but they are interrupted. A sail has been sighted. It is the *Revenge*, Blackbeard's ship. She turns to Pierre for assistance in removing the dress. 'Help me out of this', she asks, laughing. 'What's the jest?' he asks her. 'Blackbeard', she explains. 'He'd tear the hide off me if he ever caught me in such a thing.'

Ashore Blackbeard is large and his well-researched beard is correctly braided and beribboned. He is suspicious of the Frenchman, flinging a cupful of rum at him, a 'traitor scum'. Perhaps Pierre is not really a pirate—only pretending? Blackbeard has found out that Pierre is Lieutenant Pierre François La Rochelle of the French Navy, which he admits was once true but is no longer: he has been dismissed in disgrace. Anne takes his word, asserting her authority over Blackbeard with a slap to his face, an insult he will 'never forgive'. The happy couple with the treasure map sail for Jamaica, where Pierre goes ashore to find the missing half of the map, supposedly, but actually to see his wife and to report to the British navy that the notorious Captain Providence (Anne) is at hand and can be attacked and captured. Anne discovers Pierre's double treachery—that he was not a pirate after all, and is married—so she kidnaps his wife before escaping the punitive British ships. Ashore, properly unpiratical Pierre is refused his reward, the return of his confiscated ship, because Anne was neither defeated nor captured, so he turns pirate himself. He promises gold to his men, but he is not sincerely a pirate, aiming to free his wife from Anne's ship, which—he tells his men deceptively—'carries a rich treasure...a treasure for which I would gladly lay down my life'. We may note that women have replaced treasure in the cinematic pirate world, a switch anticipated in Sabatini's novels and in Fairbanks's *The Black Pirate*. Once again, repetitively, this is not treasure, nor treasure island, but treasure woman.

At an improbable Arab slave market at Maracaibo, Anne throws a dress at Pierre's wife—that same significant one that Anne tried on before. 'Here. Put that on. I'll cheat the Arabs and sell you for a lady.' Pierre's wife questions cruel Anne's own gender: 'Do you consider yourself a woman?' Undeterred, Anne starts her pitch for the sale of Pierre's wife but is stopped by her conscientious ship's doctor, who protests, and by guns from Pierre's ship. Anne fights and defeats Pierre's ship, which is handicapped because he will not endanger his wife, tied up and on exhibit aboard Anne's ship, the *Sheba Queen*. Dragged dripping from the sea for more dialogue about gender—and genre—he begs her to spare his wife. 'Why should I spare her?' Because 'You're a woman', he suggests. 'You've taught me to be a *sort of* woman', she replies. He apologises for that: 'It was no part of the plan.' But he would do anything to save his wife. 'Anything for her', Anne repeats, 'and nothing for me!'

She maroons them on an isolated desert islet called 'Dead Man's Cay', where Pierre dabs cooling sea water on the brow of his wife, supine under a protective canopy, made of that significant dress. All is lost, but then he sees the *Sheba Queen*. Anne has returned and sends the conscientious doctor to the cay, with a boat, provisions, and a map.

Unfortunately another sail is sighted, the *Revenge*, Blackbeard's ship. He has not forgotten Anne's insult to his honour. She could outsail him and escape but she chooses to fight, to protect the innocents on the cay. Her ship is destroyed by his superior gunpower and she stands, alone but defiant on the burning deck, calling to Blackbeard, 'Come on board, if you dare!' He orders his men to hold fire but too late. A shot ends her female pirate career and gender ambiguity. Back on the cay, Pierre speaks the epitaph: 'She's home at last. Let the sea keep her.' Metaphorically she may be a sea creature but that did not answer her gender question. Anyway, the tale is told. A woman can be a fiercer pirate than a man but not if she discovers her gender. Romance is more powerful than wealth, the real treasure is love not gold, and piracy is gender ambiguity.

In *Against All Flags* (1952), directed unremarkably for Universal by George Sherman, Errol Flynn is a British naval officer who infiltrates the pirate republic of Libertalia on Madagascar, that fiction from the *General History*. He pretends to have been dismissed from the navy with two other supposedly disloyal British sailors and wishes to join the pirate community, with authentic British lashings scarred on his back as proof—proof for the pirates, that is, not the viewer. The essential inauthenticity of the pirate hero has been inherited from Scott and a collective Romantic sensibility, but is increasingly emphatic in the twentieth century. The pirate must be authenticated as a spy, not a real pirate, as an antipirate, indeed, beneath his thin disguise as a pirate. His act, his performance of the role of pirate, must not convince us— crucially not, because his definitional essence, his audience appeal, is his reliable inauthenticity. In order to convince the pirates that he is not a spy, Flynn must pass further tests, including participation in the capture of a ship of the Grand Khan—the legend that grew out of Every's original exploit—and of the Grand Khan's daughter, that further development of the Avery legend. Pirate captain Roc Brasiliano, alias Anthony Quinn, is suspicious of pirate recruit Flynn and is enamoured of the other pirate captain, called Spitfire, piratess Maureen O'Hara (now working for Universal) who has feelings for Flynn not Quinn.

Flynn had nothing to say about *Against All Flags* in his memoirs and neither did Maureen O'Hara in her anodyne ghosted equivalent, except to reveal that Flynn was drinking continuously while working, though never forgetting his lines. When alcohol was banned on set, 'Errol would inject oranges with booze and eat them during breaks'.[17]

To attract Flynn's character in the film itself, O'Hara wears a dress instead of her usual piratical trousers and draws him into a dialogue about how civilized ladies behave. The scene is of a kind with the dress scene between Pierre and Anne in *Anne of the Indies*. Flynn explains to Maureen O'Hara how to wear a beauty patch to enhance her attractions, how to reveal her leg seductively when boarding a sedan chair, how to curtsey low, to pout winsomely, and thus proceed successfully through an evening's gallantry in London. While miming and demonstrating these female arts of love, Flynn's spying eye is on a map of the pirate harbour's gun emplacements which is hanging in her room. O'Hara, who is apparently charmed as well as educated by his lesson in female coquetry, smiles seductively and asks innocently 'And what then?' He is unsure how to proceed politely and truthfully, but moves to answer her with a kiss, when he is abruptly stopped by her pistol in his ribs. 'I kiss when I feel like kissing', she tells him. 'And see that you remember that!' Apparently naive as a woman, she is nevertheless the man in charge. She has the drop on him.

Despite this assertion of her superiority, O'Hara's relations with Flynn develop romantically, and she asks him to assist her escape from the pirate community at Madagascar. While still believing in his pirate credentials, she for herself has decided to quit piracy, as she frankly reveals to him. Meanwhile the supposed pirate Flynn has spiked the protective pirate guns with the help of his two British subordinates, dressed in blue-striped T-shirts and also masquerading as pirates. When the expected British man-of-war enters the pirate harbour, the sabotaged guns blow themselves up. Quinn makes an escape on his ship with O'Hara, but we have already seen Flynn's head bobbing up stealthily aboard Quinn's ship. He and his two men, with valiant, trousered O'Hara on their side, attack Quinn and his pirate crew. O'Hara fights manfully, killing several pirate men, and Quinn is engaged in duelling by Flynn, who leaps and bounds for some reason up the mainmast, with Quinn at his heels, and then fearlessly out onto the top of the sail. What is Flynn doing? He (or a stand-in) is emulating Douglas Fairbanks, of course, and acrobatically slices the mainsail in two by sliding down it with his sword. Safely back on deck after his slide, Flynn eliminates Quinn with superior swordsmanship and soon the victorious survivors are assembled aboard the British man-of-war, where Flynn secures official British forgiveness for ex-piratess O'Hara. But how is he going to explain his duplicity to her? He has pretended to be a pirate and perhaps also to be in love with her. Was his love just another pretence, part of his patriotic British plot? 'Appearances are sometimes a little difficult to explain', he says evasively to her, but her response is simply—and fiercely, of course—to tug his collar so that they end the film with a kiss. He was only pretending to be a pirate, acting a role, and she, who was a better pirate than a man, has found a man to make a woman out of her. Piracy is not piracy, of course, but a love story.

The female pirate had a long career in fiction as well as film. We may recall the leading character who 'bursts in among the pirates' in Douglas Stewart's *The Pirate Queen* (1867): 'And who is this female, who boldly, with flashing eyes, stands amidst the pirate horde, from whom she has snatched their prey? It is the beautiful Elmira, the *Pirate Queen!*'[18] Elmira is much like the conventional nineteenth-century male pirate, more silly than terrifying, but with some natural differences, emphasized not disguised, so that 'her richly developed bust heaved tumultuously beneath a tight-fitting bodice of velvet'.[19]

A few years later Bret Harte's *The Queen of the Pirate Isle* (1886) followed another recourse of the late-nineteenth-century male pirate, as a character in a children's book, in which the Queen is the ladylike little Polly, whose 'royal duties...consisted in putting the Pirates to bed after a day of rapine and bloodshed'.[20] Pirates and children were indeed so imaginatively interdependent that they were in combination the subject of Richard Hughes's *A High Wind in Jamaica* (1929). The nineteenth-century children in Hughes's twentieth-century historical novel wonder at night how to conceive of their captors, pirates of the high seas but also of the mind:

'Emily Emily may I ask you a question, please?' 'Go to sleep!' There was a moment's whispered confabulation. 'But it's very important, please, and we all want to know.' 'What?' 'Are these people pirates?' Emily sat bolt upright with astonishment. 'Of course not!' Harry sounded rather crestfallen. 'I don't know...I just thought they might...' 'But they *are*!' declared Rachel firmly. 'Margaret told me!' 'Nonsense!' said Emily. 'There aren't any pirates nowadays.' 'Margaret said', went on Rachel, 'that time we were shut up on the other ship she heard one of the sailors calling out pirates had come on board.' Emily had an inspiration. 'No, you silly, he must have said *pilots*.' 'What are pilots?' asked Laura.[21]

The children have not read or heard *The Pirates of Penzance* or *Peter Pan*, but their author plainly has.

That pirates were lost in the past, that 'There aren't any pirates now-adays', as Emily confidently pronounces, is amusingly implied in the conclusion to a spoof publication in 1935 of a 'Letter' in eighteenth-century French from the pirate captain Louis-Adhémar-Timothée Le Golif, known as Borgnefesse (One-eyed-bum, or Single-buttock), who ends his tale of West Indian buccaneering adventures in the foreign land of modern France, being driven in 'une de leurs voitures sans chevaux' ('one of their horseless carriages'), to a lunatic asylum at Charenton.[22] This pirate belongs to the past and the madhouse.

In *Le Flibustier mysterieux: Histoire d'un trésor caché* (1934), scholar and maritime historian Charles de La Roncière attempted to bring the pirate up to date by telling a tale of an anonymous lady who came to La Roncière's office at the Bibliothèque Nationale with a crypto-gram, a puzzle which she believed would reveal, if deciphered, the site of a treasure buried on some island in the Indian Ocean. After a long and undiscriminating account, derived mostly from the *General History*, of various factual and fictional pirates in the eighteenth-century Indian Ocean, La Roncière connects the cryptogram to what he des-ignates a 'tradition', for which he provides no evidence of any kind. This 'tradition', of which La Roncière himself may be the origin, is that the eighteenth-century pirate La Buse, the Buzzard, on the day of his hanging on the beach at Réunion in 1730, flung a written puz-zle into the attendant and expectant crowd, shouting to them: 'Pour celui qui la découvrira' ('For whoever will discover it').[23] La Roncière is either the gullible dupe of the lady at the Bibliothèque or more probably the cunning perpetrator of a hoax (and, yes, he has read 'Le Scarabée d'or', 'The Gold Bug', in Baudelaire's translation) but in either case the hidden treasure, supposedly bequeathed by La Buse to the most ingenious spectator of his execution, is—deliberately or not—a fiction.

A few years later, in 1936, the Surrealist poet Robert Desnos com-posed a 'Lament for the Pirate'. The pirate had a dramatic past, he wrote ('un passé plein de drame'), and was a kind of knight with a heart of stone ('une espèce de chevalier au coeur de pierre'), who cruelly raped his victims while pathetically imagining his long-lost love, and for him (and on him) we should shed a tear: 'Versons un pleur sur le pirate'.[24] This refrain, repeated at the end of each stanza, leaves the pirate sopping wet ('tout mouillé') with tears, and deserv-ing a big kick:

To awaken him from his absurd dream
He should see himself with his silken sleeves
His sunken stomach, his sparse hair—
A man, an enslaved man, a sleeper awakened—
Shed a tear for the pirate
For the pirate and for piracy.[25]

The male pirate was drowned in tears of derision but the historical
Mary Read and Ann Bonny were not forgotten. In *Les Femmes pirates*
(Paris, 1934), Henri Musnik reported that, although detailed information is lacking about Read and Bonny, he had no doubt of 'l'authenticité
de leur existence'.[26] He proceeded to provide the missing details,
novelizing the accounts in the *General History*, supplying descriptions,
characterization and imaginary scenes and dialogues.[27] The historians'
female pirates are indistinguishable from the novelists' female pirates,
not to forget the dramatists' female pirates. That same year the playwright James Bridie put Mary on stage, acted by Flora Robson, in a
play called *Mary Read*, based on what he no doubt believed were the
historical facts of the *General History*. He did not neglect the theatrical
conventions that the *General History* was probably based on. Ann
Bonny, the consort of Jack Rackam, and openly female, takes a fancy
to Mary Read, disguised as Will, and asks him to 'Kiss me'.[28] Will
responds that 'I love you in my way, but it's not the way you think'.[29]
'What way is that?' asks Ann indignantly, answering herself: 'It is no
way at all. If you love me in any way, why don't you take me, and to
hell with Jack Rackam?'[30] 'Because I'm a woman', is Mary's simple
reply.[31]

Frank Shay's *Mary Read: The Pirate Wench* (London, 1934) is a fanciful
but predictable story about Mary Read, based loosely on the fanciful
General History, on the published account of the *Tryals* of Mary Read
and Ann Bonny, and on pirate history more generally and vaguely.
Successfully disguised as a man, Mary rises through the pirate ranks,
delicately swigging bumbo and encountering Calico Jack Rackam and
his manifestly female mistress, Anne Bonny, 'tall, blonde and fully
developed', as well as Woodes Rogers at New Providence and others
such as Bartholomew Roberts, Blackbeard and Stede Bonnet.[32] She is
provided with a father, a Captain Skinner supplied from the *General
History*, who is horribly killed with broken glass bottles, like the original Captain Skinner in the *General History*.[33] Disguised as a young male
sailor, she is teasingly kissed by Anne Bonny, whose feminine intuition

has seen through Mary's pretended gender: 'I knew you for a wench the minute I laid eyes on you'.[34]

Rising above the unambitious pirate life of Calico Jack, who enjoys 'loafing' and swinging low in a hammock with Anne 'singing to him in her throaty contralto', Mary captures and captains a Spanish 'treasure ship' and marries above her humble social status, the 'Honourable Edwin Brangwin', whom she has taken hostage.[35] A return to the facts requires her, somewhat artificially, to rejoin Rackham and Bonny so that she can be captured with them by British authorities, but her author separates her from the published *Tryals* and *General History* by describing her as refusing to plead her belly, as Anne Bonny does. Instead she dies of some illness, influenza perhaps, in jail at Port Royal, Jamaica, 'clothed not in the habiliments of her sex', a 'pile' of once looted but now rejected dresses, petticoats, silken stockings and embroidered slippers, which she had hoarded like treasure in a 'precious chest', but instead 'in her old leathern breeks, her old shirt and cotton hose, a gay bandanna about her head'.[36]

Philip Rush, novelist and maritime historian, author of *Mary Read, Buccaneer* (1945), explains in a Note that his 'story of Mary Read is based on a foundation of known truths' which he has 'filled out by a liberal use of imagination'.[37] He has sometimes closely followed the narrative and even the wording of the *General History* but he has indeed filled it out to accommodate his fulsomely fictional heroine. Like Mary Read in *Mary Read: The Pirate Wench*, Mary Read in *Mary Read, Buccaneer* joins up with pirates in order to preserve her male disguise under threat of being stripped 'to the buff' in *Pirate Wench* or 'stripped naked to the waist' in *Buccaneer*.[38] Ann Bonny, voluptuously female, invites cross-dressed Mary to a tyrst in a room at an inn, where Ann makes her advances: 'slipping off the bed and lifting her dress above her knees, Ann sat on Mary's knee and put her arms around her neck'.[39] 'Panic-stricken, Mary jumped to her feet and pushed the woman away', but 'Ann smiled'.[40] She has recognized Mary's secret gender 'By instinct!'[41] Rackam has become emasculated 'through self-indulgence and running after a woman', spending 'his time in Ann Bonny's cabin, drinking and making love', so the liberally-imagined, manly Mary surpasses him in piracy and attracts a lover, an imaginary, unhistorical American sailor.[42] Her success as a manly pirate is measured in accumulating loot but her love affair cannot proceed because—in a recurring metaphor—'Mary's sex was dormant'.[43] Even with her accumulated loot—'the richest cargo one vessel's ever carried'—and with her gender eventually revealed, she is still recognized by the pirate crew as 'the best man amongst us', dresses as a man and remains 'a sleeping woman'.[44] Even as an acknowledged female with a recognized gender, she cannot be translated generically from pirate adventure into pure romance. Her conventional story-book treasure is represented by the usual icon:

Her own treasure chest was a large one, kept in her cabin, filled to the brim with golden coins and precious stones but she never looked at it and only lifted the lid to throw in more jewels and coins. There was also another chest. It was full of clothes taken from the women on the ships she captured: an amazing elegance of silken gowns which had graced the boudoirs of many a Spanish and French lady of society. Mary never opened this chest either and was secretly ashamed of its presence, regarding it as an inexplicable weakness, but she often added to its contents, cursing herself as she did so.[45]

The treasure chest of piratical success is rivalled, therefore, by the chest of womanly awakening. At the height of her piratical career, in the cabin of her captured Spanish prize,

Mary had a strange tranced feeling upon her. First of all, she went to the full-length mirror and regarded herself. The mirror showed her a young man, sturdy and vigorous with the health of youth. He was dressed in a white cotton shirt, breeches of rough texture with thin silk stockings coming to the knee and shoes carrying large silver buckles.[46]

In quick succession she takes off the male clothing of this young man, plunges into a 'perfumed bath', emerges and lets her hair down, examines herself 'naked in front of the mirror', and then runs 'to the despised clothes-chest':

She selected the daintiest of the underclothes and put them on slowly, making her movements almost a ritual. Deliberately she turned over the pile of dresses and finally chose a simple gown of white satin, cut low at the front and back.[47]

She makes up her face, arranges her hair and returns to the full-length mirror:

Instead of the young man, there was a beautiful girl. This girl was tall, the flowing lines of the satin gown dispelling any tendency to stockiness that the young man had had. This girl had sweeping nut-brown hair; a wide-browed but delicate face; red, full lips and deep brown eyes. Mary Read stared at herself, lips half-parted, eyes shining.[48]

There is a knock at the door. Her lover enters, suddenly attractive to her, to be welcomed by Mary, 'holding out her arms to him like a sleep-walker'.[49] In response he takes up the authorial metaphor: '"You've come to yourself at last", he said. "Before, you were sleeping…"'.[50]

In recognition of this new discovery of femininity she decides to abandon piracy and the couple board a ship's boat, into which the pirate crew 'shipped the treasure chest, together with a chest of clothes Mary was taking'.[51] The lovers bury the irrelevant treasure chest on a desert island, as conventional fictional pirates should, and then decide to pay a visit to Rackam and Bonny's ship, an odd decision which awkwardly lurches the fictional plot back towards the necessary historical circumstances for Mary's capture in company with Rackam and Bonny, who are respectively and historically hanged for piracy and reprieved for pregnancy. Mary, however, refuses to plead her belly, as she is unhistorically not pregnant, but has caught 'gaol-fever' and dies in female dress, 'strangely happy' to have discovered her gender and with it her genre—romance.[52] All's well that ends well for the plot, if not the piratess.

In 1945 Hergé produced *Le Trésor de Rackham le Rouge*, a distant relation of Calico Jack. If piracy was operatic in 1827, why not a comic strip in 1945? 'Tout est bien qui finit bien!' is Hergé's concluding line.[53] In 1952 the male pirate Borgnefesse re-emerged from the madhouse with the discovery in 1944, in an old sea-chest (oh, yes), of the eighteenth-century manuscript of his memoirs, published as *Cahiers de Louis-Adhé-mar-Timothée Le Golif dit Borgnefesse* (Paris, 1952), containing his pirate maxim, that 'La fortune est sur la mer, où il faut savoir l'aller quérir' ('Fortune is on the seas, for those who know how to fetch it').[54] This spoof by the author and artist Gustave Alaux, with its frontispiece photograph of the tattered, inky, fake manuscript, did not fail to fool. The maxim of Borgnefesse is cited in 1996 (with an attribution to Louis Le Golif, French Buccaneer, 1734), as an epigraph to a chapter by a historian of the buccaneers.[55] In that same year as the return of Borgnefesse, 1952, Ann Bonny hammed manfully, without Mary Read but with Captain Kidd (performed by Charles Laughton), in the all-singing, all-dancing, all-hamming Hollywood production of *Abbott and Costello Meet Captain Kidd*. A treasure map and a love letter are swapped and muddled by a plot that thus contrives to mix loot and love, until—none too soon—Costello (the small, fall guy) defeats Captain Kidd (left hanging, hamming, from the yard-arm) and wins Ann Bonny.

So far in literary fiction Mary Read had done most of the pirating, but now Ann Bonny came into strong competition. John Carlova's *Mistress of the Seas* (New York, 1964), described by the modern editor of the *General History* as 'a popular history based on documents in the Caribbean archives', features a 1960s Anne Bonny, the anachronisms explained by the author as historical accuracies when properly viewed 'in the framework of her own times—the early 18th century'.[56] As an eighteenth-century woman Anne 'anticipated her emancipated sisters of the 20th century', Carlova explains.[57] This properly historical woman has been thoroughly researched, we are assured by the author, who investigated 'original material' in the London Public Records Office, the British Museum Library, and the Admiralty Court Records, as well as in archives in seven or more cities across the world.[58]

There are frequent quotations from these fake 'records', 'logs of ships', and 'contemporary accounts', but the circumstantial and perhaps historical details of the *General History* and the *Tryals* of Read and Bonny are few in *Mistress of the Seas* and treated freely.[59] More frequently Anne's role in *Mistress* is imaginary. Her best friend is 'the pansy pirate' Pierre, who captains her ship with his 'mincing and prancing' crew.[60] She has an affair with Stede Bonnet but rejects the advances of Blackbeard, who 'shattered the kneecap of Israel Hands' (as he did in the *General History*) in a vain attempt 'to attract her attention'.[61] With the help of her childhood American Indian friend, Charley Fourfeathers, she gallantly attempts to save Stede Bonnet from his historical captivity and hanging. She both inspires and dominates Rackam, who sinks to a drunken stupor as she sails to piratical supremacy, captaining a captured 36-gun ship. Like the novelized Mary Read before her, this Anne Bonny is required by her author to excel her original as a pirate: 'By now, Anne was really living as an empress of the seas. Her lavish quarters in the aftercastle of the *Queen Royal* became a throne room, luxuriously decorated'.[62] Here 'she stretched out on a large four-poster bed', surrounded by 'fine furniture, magnificent paintings, exquisite tapestries, colorful artificial flowers and rich draperies', while 'designing and making gorgeous costumes', including 'her many and varied "action" outfits'.[63] Here, too, she was accompanied by her 'pets—a monkey, a cat and two parrots', and entertained by the cavortings of her 'court jester...a dwarf seaman'.[64] 'In quieter moments', however, 'Anne would read books and periodicals taken from plundered ships'.[65] Doubtless, like her author, Anne is a keen researcher.

Whenever she wished, she would romp amorously with any of her crew she chose. Only one had resisted her, a 'handsome young seaman' named Mark Read.[66] Remorselessly, piratically, Anne 'flung him on the bed', despite his fierce resistance:

Anne struggled no less strenuously. She ripped her victim's shirt loose, tore off the buttons of his trousers, and worked her hand between his legs. Then Anne abruptly drew back and exclaimed, 'Good Lord, lad, you've got no parts!'

At least, Mark had no male parts, for 'he' was a she. The torn shirt and a tight binding of cloth beneath had parted to reveal a pair of small, firm, female breasts. Anne gasped, 'Good Lord, who are you?' 'Mary Read,' sobbed the woman on the bed.[67]

This is not history, of course, but it is written in the spirit of the *General History*, in which fiction is also mixed with fact.

After these fictional heights there is a rude return for Anne Bonny to circumstances closer to historical reality, enabling Anne Bonny, Mary Read, and Rackam to be humbled, captured, and tried at Port Royal, Jamaica. Rackam is historically hanged and Bonny and Read both plead their bellies. Read soon dies, however, and the heroine, Anne, reformed by an imaginary man of principle, Michael Radcliffe, is freed to marry him and retire genteelly, happily, and fictionally to Virginia.

At breakfast 'with a radical feminist friend' Steve Gooch was inspired to write his play *The Women Pirates Ann Bonney and Mary Read* (1978) by a 'tiny booklet' which 'fell out of the shredded wheat packet' and briefly told the stories of Bonny and Read.[68] In a prefatorial statement to the published play he recognizes that his historical play is actually a reflection of the feminism and anti-imperialism of his own times in 'the late 1970s'.[69] He has been inspired by the *General History* version of Bonny and Read as well as the shredded wheat version, and also by the novelizations, principally but not solely Carlova's *Mistress of the Seas*. Ann's father is called William Cormac and her mother Peggy Brennan, after Carlova's characters. In Carolina Ann is trained and mentored by an Indian like Carlova's Charley Fourfeathers and in Nassau she visits Carlova's 'House of Lords' tavern, which Gooch has merged with the 'combination coffee shop, tailoring salon, and hairdressing establishment' managed by Carlova's Pierre.[70] The result in Gooch's play is a scene set in 'Pierre's Cafe', which is 'The House of Lords in New Providence'.[71] Gooch's Pierre is as gay as Carlova's, and Gooch follows Carlova—or one of Carlova's followers—in calling Mary 'Mark Read'.[72] Gooch's Ann is not disguised as a man but his

Mary is disguised as a man and Ann 'Reaches for Mary's crotch' in a stage direction, only to be repelled and informed 'I'm a woman'.[73] Rackam is jealous and has to be let into the secret. The two women resist the capture by Barnet's ship while the male pirates hide down below decks, making suggestive male remarks to the women—'I'm up!'—so Ann can righteously tell Rackam in court: 'If you'd fought like a man, you wouldn't have to die like a dog'.[74] As seventies feminists, the two women triumphantly plead the exclusively female condition of their bellies to the court, where 'all the judges are men'.[75]

George MacDonald Fraser's *The Pyrates* (1983) is a pastiche and burlesque of all the piratocracy of page and screen. His hero is Captain Benjamin Avery, who 'was everything that a hero of historical romance should be; he was all of Mr Sabatini's supermen rolled into one', as well as being 'the young Errol Flynn, only more so', former 'head prefect at Uppingham', with a 'First from Oxford', 'R.A.D.A.-trained', irresistibly attractive as well as impeccably educated, valiant, patriotic, and faultlessly chaste—as well as excessively superlative—his duty to restore the stolen crown of the King of Madagascar and to defeat the pirate Brotherhood of the Coast (the buccaneer 'frères de la côte') and also the rival might of the Spanish Main.[76] In these multiple missions he is beset, not only by an alliance of all possible piratical characters, speaking fluent and 'authentic Mummerset' (' "Aaargh!" cried the burly captain, twice for emphasis'), and by caricature Spaniards of the Main, but by hyperbolically beautiful women: Sheba, 'the black pirate queen', Donna Meliflua, the sultry and Latin-accented Spanish teenager, and—supremely—Lady Vanity, 'tennis captain o' Cheltenham Ladies', with Swiss Finishing School credentials, a perfectly pouting mouth and other parts—'practically everything about Lady Vanity pouted, including her shapely figure'.[77]

Avery is entrusted by Pepys at the Admiralty with his secret mission, to ensure the safe delivery to Madagascar of the local King's bejewelled crown. Aboard the ship on the voyage are Lady Vanity and also, imprisoned below, the piratess Black Sheba, whose pirate comrades have signed on in disguise as loyal sailors and will inevitably take possession—to Avery's excruciating shame—of perfect Lady Vanity and the priceless Madagascar crown. To regain these prizes Avery must fight off the amorous advances of Donna Meliflua and the evil schemes of her ridiculously repulsive intended, Don Lardo, Viceroy of the Indies, 'Spain's answer to Billy Bunter', but aboard the soon-to-be-captured ship on its way to never-to-be-reached Madagascar is Avery's principal enemy, the leader of the pirate Brotherhood, in a give-away disguise of 'neatly-pressed white calico': Calico Jack Rackam, whose ambition is to acquire enough loot 'to start a modest pub'.[78] As Robert Desnos lamented, the pirate

> ... était devenu un pauvre bougre
> Employé de banque ou représentant de commerce.[79]

(The pirate 'has become a poor bugger, a bank clerk or a sales rep'.) Avery's ship is duly taken by the pirates and the Madagascar crown is scrupulously divided among them, multiplying Avery's difficulties in regaining it in its pristine entirety. Rackam's portion, for instance, is prudently sent 'by registered post to his faithful paramour, Anne Bonney, on their shark-infested island retreat'.[80]

By means of the impossible twists and turns of Fraser's plot, irresistible Avery is sold as a slave and despatched, like the missing piece of the crown, to Anne Bonney, as a treat. Avery thus finds himself, dressed in 'a huge pink tinsel bow', in the pirate palace of Anne Bonney, with 'priceless rugs and flying ducks'.[81] On the walls, 'among the Van Dycks and Arthur Rackams (work that one out sometime)' were 'group paintings' of crews and captains sitting gravely with piles of treasure, paintings 'labelled "Caracas '67" or "Nombre de Dios '71" and the like'.[82] The joke is made at the expense of the piratical yearning for tasteless chic and respectability. Rackam's overwhelming regret, at the prospect of the doom and destruction of the pirate fraternity, is that he 'hadn't listened to his parents' advice and taken that office job with Somerset County Council'.[83] In this dubious splendour, gift-wrapped Avery awaits Anne Bonney, who drawls 'like a wanton Lady Bracknell'.[84] 'You may have seen the picture, in Johnson's *Historie*', Fraser addresses his learned readers, but 'that was ages ago':

Nowadays the bra-burning buccaneerette had become an exquisitely languid young matron who ate far too much creamy food, dieted self-indulgently, read popular novels in bed, crammed herself into fashionable creations, and couldn't have roused herself to scuttle or slit a paper bag, although she remained passionately addicted to young men, innocent or not, because (she maintained) it took her mind off slimming.[85]

From its hiding place inside Bonney's mattress—precisely indicated on a useful treasure chart, 'a parchment which had fallen out of a fashionable sea-boot'—Avery retrieves the last missing piece of the Madagascar crown and then leads the pirates ('You always knew they were going to get together, didn't you?') against their mutual (Spanish) enemy, disgusting Don Lardo, from whose nasty foreign clutches are rescued: Donna Meliflua, Black Sheba, in her favourite 'leopard-skin tracksuit', and—supremely, superlatively—Lady Vanity, her 'blonde hair elegantly shampooed and set' after an 'all day' post-captivity makeover.[86] In an authorial 'Afterthought' about his sources, Fraser names 'Every, or Everie', Blackbeard, and of course the original, historical Rackam and fantastical-historical Ann Bonny of the *General History*.[87] Fraser's characters and plot are burlesque with hyperbolic excess but, he protests, what of the supposed historical truth of the account given of Rackam and Bonny in the *General History* (which Fraser thinks was written by Defoe)?

...no fiction-writer in his senses would accept it as a credible plot for a moment. But the one difficulty about dismissing it as far-fetched nonsense is that, so far as can be judged from the evidence, it appears to be true. Records of the trial are said to exist, and no one has ever cast convincing doubts on the detailed account given in Defoe.[88]

This is said tongue-in-cheek, of course, but pirate fiction is not more implausible than supposed pirate fact—so Fraser slyly and reasonably argues. The pirate is now a parody in prose, as he was in song, in Gilbert and Sullivan's comic opera, a century earlier.

Carlova's *Mistress of the Seas* was comedy and Pamela Jekel's *Sea Star: The Private Life of Anne Bonny, Pirate Queen* (New York, 1983) would seem to be kitsch—perhaps, as an artistic effect, the ultimate pirate shipwreck. The relationship between Carlova and Jekel is close, however. Here in *Sea Star* are Carlova's fictional characters—Charley Fourfeathers, for instance, Anne's Indian sidekick, with whom she attempts to rescue her former lover Stede Bonnet from execution, according to Carlova's imaginary plot. But Anne in *Sea Star* reads 'Molière, Milton, Boccaccio and Boileau', by contrast with Anne in *Mistress*, who preferred periodicals.[89] As Rackam succumbs to drink and opium in *Sea Star*, Anne rises to luxurious success 'as a pirate queen', furnishing her cabin with 'an intricately carved French royal chair' and 'a small four-poster bed with a damask canopy', reading 'books plundered from other ships', but keeping only one pet parrot, not two as Carlova told us.[90] She is attracted to Mark Read and one dark night on deck she 'moved her mouth to his' but he does not reciprocate.[91] '"My God,"' she whispered. "Who are you?"'[92] 'Mark Read, of course', he replies, but Anne has found him out.[93] 'You're a woman! Say it. You're a woman as I am.'[94] Later, in somewhat reduced circumstances, Anne, like Carlova's Anne, rejoins history for capture, and is then restored to fictitious morality and true love by Carlova's imaginary Michael Radcliffe, with whom she escapes Jamaican jail as a free, reformed, and happily married woman. There are some variations and additions to Carlova's dialogue and the love scenes with Michael are more poetical: '"Your breasts are like warm moons", he said softly and lowered his mouth to her erect nipples, tugging at them gently. "So soft", he murmured.'[95]

Sea Star is plagiarized from *Mistress*, then, and—like Carlova—Jekel claims to have researched her novel's (or his novel's) facts in records kept in libraries and archives. Indeed, she acknowledges a particular debt to one previous researcher: 'I am especially indebted to John Carlova whose excellent biography of Anne Bonny, *Mistress of the Seas*, was my principle [sic] source of research.'[96] *Sea Star* is not plagiarized, therefore, but researched. The source of its fiction is acknowledged as a historical source—a work of fact, not a joke.

In a Preface to Mace Taxco's *Anne Bonney and Mary Read: Women Buccaneers* (1998), the author informs us that Daniel Defoe 'was present at their trials and recorded his observations of the events at the time'.[97] Taxco himself has spent 'two years on my own independent investigation'.[98] His book follows the two women's lives imaginatively, with some occasional relation to the supposed facts in the *General History*. It is written with an illiteracy that characterizes Taxco himself, not his characters. During her military career on the continent, Mary Read, disguised as 'Leftenant Mark Read' (her Christian pseudonym derived from Carlova's *Mistress*), meets the Dutch or Flemish husband mentioned in the *General History* and reveals her female gender by disclosing her bosom, 'bearing it for all to see', and announcing: 'My name is not Mark Read. T'is Mary Read.'[99] She insists on her military rank and status, nevertheless. 'I may be a woman but I can still cut any man to pieces with me blade and put a whole in his head with me pistol.'[100]

A separate narrative describes the life of Anne Bonney and her piracy with her lover, Rackam. In a duel fought precariously on the top yard of the mainmast of Blackbeard's ship, Andrew (Anne) Bonney defeats Captain Tew (of Madagascar fame) by removing her blouse, so that 'her bosom fell free to his gaze'.[101] Distracted, he is fatally stabbed by the owner of the unexpected bosom and falls dead to the deck below. Despite her passion for Rackam, Anne becomes in love with

Mark when their two stories connect. Mark, alias Mary, is astonished when Andrew Bonney reveals she is Anne 'and her bosom burst forth'.[102] Mark is not seduced by this sight, however, and 'at last her own bosom blossomed forth'.[103] They become friends, not lovers, and successfully notorious as pirates: 'Their names out reputed even their own captain, Calico Jack Rackam'.[104]

When they are all captured—Anne and Mary resisting valiantly—by historical Captain Barnet, whose role is unhistorically stretched through the book—Rackam is properly hanged and Anne's lawyer father, William Cormac (named by Carlova in *Mistress*, and copied by others such as Jekel in *Sea Star*), appears in Jamaica to defend the two women pirates by staging another simultaneous revelation for the courtroom: 'Anne and Mary pulled aside their own clothing as their bared bosoms came into view.'[105] This is all true because it was witnessed by 'Daniel Defoe, Clerk of the Court. He would scribe the events'.[106] As further proof of his story Mace Taxco prints a false version of the title page of the Jamaican *Tryals* (1721), in which his two 'pyrateses' are named as 'Andrew Bonney and Mark Read', and also a portrait of himself, captioned 'Mace Taxco at the gravesite of Mary Read in Jamaica, in his hand a cutlass from the Frank Freiderhoff collection believed to have belonged to Anne Bonney.'[107] During his two years of 'independent investigation', no doubt, Mace Taxco ascertained what he tells us, that Anne's cutlass was given to her by Captain Kidd.[108]

Jacqueline Church Simonds's *Captain Mary, Buccaneer* (2000) is about an Anne Bonny called Mary, who has a similar background on a plantation in Carolina, but is better read than Carlova's Anne or Jekel's. Mary's cabin has 'walls full of books' by Milton, Shakespeare, and Machiavelli, as well as Raleigh's and Marvell's poems, 'Ben Johnson's essays' (perhaps Ben Jonson's?) and 'a treasure she valued more highly than . . . gold', namely Spenser's *The Faerie Queene*.[109] Such erudition is stimulating for Captain Mary and her crew. After 'reading the further adventures of the Redcrosse Knight', Captain Mary's French doctor 'nibbled the tops of her breasts and pinched her stiff nipples'.[110] Her lesbian lover does better: 'Elaina squeezed Mary's nipples, not pinching them, like men had, but with a firm, teasing grip that made Mary feel as if she were melting'.[111] Ultimately, however, piracy and promiscuity do not pay. The French ship's doctor prefers Elaina, the blonde lesbian lover, telling Mary in his flawed eighteenth-century English that Elaina 'is lovely and almoste as welle read as You'.[112] Mary loses both of these lovers, to each other, and also her pirate ship, sunk by a storm, but ends up happily, suckling her child by her one true lover, a retired black pirate, with whom she is rich, faithful, and running a colonial gold mine.

Most of the novelizations of the lives of the two women pirates contain more love-making than sailing, more naming of body parts than ships' parts. The characters are not convincingly at sea and inhabit circumstances of privacy and secrecy rather than the close proximity of real sailors who slept in hammocks slung a few inches apart, excreted more or less publicly into the sea, and lived and breathed in an environment that was cramped, damp, smelly, and stifling below decks, as well as potentially terrifying on deck, or in the rigging, circumstances not conducive to romance, circumstances neither romantic nor erotic.[113] Lacking realism on the one hand, the authors do not seem on the other to have read and followed the nineteenth-century fictional tradition collectively formed and shaped by Scott, Irving, Cooper, and Stevenson. There is no buried treasure, for example, except in Rush's *Mary Read, Buccaneer*, and treasure chests contain female clothing. The twentieth-century novels have more dalliance than violence, are generically closer to romances than adventure stories, and have used each other as much as they have used the *General History*, forming their own fictional tradition. They are presumably popular, to judge by their proliferation, and have little literary merit, to judge by their repetition.

Have the fictions of these novelizations been dispelled by the twentieth- and twenty-first-century historians? How does the academic pirate appear, stripped of the myths? What have historians to say about Bonny and Read, for example? The two women have over the years become part of the pantheon of piracy, the piratocracy, providing romance and lending variety to the tedious prevalence of males on the oceans. A popular conduit for the diffusion of pirate lore, *The Pirates Own Book, or Authentic Narratives of the Lives, Exploits and Executions of the Most Celebrated Sea Robbers* (1837), could not omit Bonny and Read, repeating (without acknowledgement) the inventions of the *General History*— including the disguised Bonny's love for the disguised Read—but adding a suitably feminine characterization of Read, who was 'susceptible of the tenderest emotions, and of the most melting affections. Her conduct was generally directed by virtuous principles'.[114] The aim here

Figure 8.1. 'Mary Read killing her antagonist', from *The Pirates Own Book* (1837).

was patently to produce a thrilling paradox—piracy in conjunction with supposedly typical female psychological and moral traits, as well as violence and breasts (see Figures 8.1 and 8.2).

Philip Gosse, in *The History of Piracy* (1932) did what most pirate historians do, which is to pirate the *General History*. He quotes the author of the *General History*'s proof of the veracity of his stories about Bonny and Read—the public trial in Jamaica—and declares himself satisfied. 'With any lurking doubts thus dispelled', Gosse proceeds to repeat the stories of the disguised female pirates but adds some original remarks of his own, informing us that 'both Anne Bonney and Mary Read were very fair to look upon', and also of John Rackam's characteristically piratical ways with women: 'Jack's methods of courting a woman or taking a ship were similar—no time wasted, straight up alongside, every gun brought to play and the prize boarded'.[115] Gosse's opinion about Rackam's methods has been influential, turning up repeatedly in the novelizations, such as Carlova's *Mistress*, in which Rackam speaks Gosse's words for himself.[116] Although he believes in the *General History* without any doubts, Gosse does not seem to have

Figure 8.2. Mary Read reveals her gender to her defeated antagonist, from P. Christian, *Histoire des pirates et corsairs* (1846).

read it carefully—or he read it in a poor edition, perhaps—as he adds some errors as well as remarks. Thus Anne Bonny's execution was 'postponed because of the condition of her health'—presumably her pregnancy is meant—but the court, we are told, decided about Mary Read 'that no exception could be made in her case, and she was condemned to death'.[117]

John Robert Moore was not particularly interested in female pirates or in male ones. His aim in the 1930s was to assign the *General History* to the canon of Defoe. This aim led him to assess the work's considerable influence on subsequent historians and to make an accurate observation: 'that the author of the *History* has created the modern conception of pirates'.[118] His method of assigning this influential work to the author who was his major concern—Defoe—was, however, to weave a web of conjectures and then to show that Defoe's supposedly distinctive vocabulary and turns of phrase—such as 'parcel of rogues', 'whose name I have forgot', 'mighty well pleased', 'in short', 'in a word', etc.—were used in the *General History*.[119] The method is self-evidently unconvincing and was systematically discredited in 1988, but has been successful, as the best modern edition of the *General History* is ascribed to Defoe on its title page, as are all editions of the work in many libraries, which Moore kept firmly in touch with his scholarly discoveries.[120]

Fanny Campbell, the comically implausible piratess of the symmetrically 'heaving breast' and 'breast heaving', was neither comic nor implausible to historian Linda Grant De Pauw, who retold Maturin Ballou's *Fanny Campbell, The Female Pirate Captain* (1845) as pure and simple history. In De Pauw's study of *Seafaring Women* (1982) Fanny is welcomed aboard in all seriousness, as a seafaring, cross-dressing woman, not as a pioneering, pulp marketing success, together, of course, with the Bonny and Read of the *General History* and of Carlova's *Mistress of the Seas*, which provides historian De Pauw with the fictional names of Bonny's father and mother, William Cormac and Peg Brennan.[121] De Pauw has, however, imagined for herself the historical fact that Calico Jack Rackam wore 'striped trousers'.[122]

The truth of Moore's remark that the *General History* created the modern idea of pirates, which he demonstrated by listing the many historians who had used it as a primary source, is still evident in recent times.[123] David Cordingly's serious but readable *Life Among the Pirates* (1995) makes use of other primary sources for his account of Bonny and Read, for example, as well as some secondary sources. He repeats Gosse's remark that Rackam applied his piratical processes to women—'no time wasted, straight up alongside, every gun brought to play, and the prize boarded'—a quotation he ascribes to another historian, Clinton Black, who presumably copied it from Gosse or from another copier of Gosse.[124] Cordingly knows the rare Jamaican pamphlet of the *Tryals* but nevertheless repeats the stories in the *General History* that a disguised Bonny became enamoured of a disguised Read and that the two of them provided the 'only resistance' to their ship's capture by Barnet.[125]

In a chapter of *Bold in Her Breeches: Women Pirates Across the Ages* (1995), Julie Wheelwright is more sceptical of the discrepancies between the *Tryals* and the *General History*, noting that Bonny and Read were not disguised as men and were not braver and more resolute in defending the *William* than the male pirates on board.[126] In *Women Pirates and the Politics of the Jolly Roger* (1997), however, Ulrike Klausmann and Marion Meinzerin are much more gullible about Bonny and Read, although they do not seem to have read the *General History*. Their chapter on Anne Bonny introduces her standing in moonlight at the bow of her ship, using 'a grappling hook dripping blood...to strike repeatedly at a human form'.[127] The crew of a menaced merchant ship 'is frozen with terror' at this sight and immediately surrenders.[128] Klausmann and Meinzerin explain that the 'idea for this scenario was Anne Bonny's' and that she had 'planned the attack together with her friend, Pierre Vane, a homosexual hairdresser from New Providence'.[129] This statement is not quite correct. The idea was John Carlova's in *Mistress of the Seas*, although a grappling hook has been substituted for the axe in Carlova's novel, and Carlova's gay hairdresser was called Pierre Bousquet and other names, not surnamed after the historical pirate, Charles Vane.[130]

David Cordingly naturally revisits Bonny and Read in his *Heroines and Harlots: Women at Sea in the Great Age of Sail* (2001). He introduces them by quoting the author of the *General History* acknowledging that the story of Bonny and Read might seem 'no better than a novel or romance', but Cordingly makes the same defence as the author of the *General History*, that the trial in Jamaica provided proof of his story. Cordingly says that the 'transcript of that trial' and 'several other contemporary documents' provide 'enough evidence' about Bonny and Read 'to confirm the events which they experienced at sea'.[131] There is no such evidence, however, to confirm the stories Cordingly retells from the *General History* of the births and backgrounds of the two women, including the 'complex saga involving the theft of some silver spoons', before their meeting on Rackam's ship.[132] When at sea they 'were both dressed as men', says Cordingly, 'and Anne Bonny took such a liking to the handsome Mary Read that she let her know she was a woman'.[133] There is of course no evidence that the two women were 'disguised as men', as Cordingly says, nor that they were so well disguised that they deceived each other.[134] Woodes Rogers named them as 'two Women', so there is no reason to believe that the two women did not know what Woodes Rogers did. Cordingly also states that, when Barnet captured the *William*, Bonny and Read 'were the only two members of the pirate crew to remain on deck and put up any resistance'.[135] In spite of the evidence of the *Tryals* that Cordingly knows, he thus persists in preserving what we can deduce to be the essential features of the myth: that Bonny and Read were disguised as men and fiercer than men. The historians are recycling the same romances that are the stock in trade of the historical novelists. Cordingly concludes by mentioning 'some evidence' that Bonny's father, named William Cormac, rescued her from Jamaican jail, and that she married respectably and had eight children, dying aged 84 in 1782.[136] This 'evidence' is described as 'family papers in the collection of descendants'.[137] It is not available for inspection and cannot be assessed, therefore, but the name Cordingly gives to Bonny's father, William Cormac, was invented by John Carlova, in his influential *Mistress of the Seas*, and copied by many other novelists, who probably came to believe it as a documented historical fact.[138] The next year, 2002, the French historian Gilles Lapouge repeated in his *Pirates, boucaniers, flibustiers* the myth of Bonny and Read, adding for good measure that Calico Jack wore red trousers.[139] Grub Street is an address in Paris as well as London.

In 2004 *The Oxford Dictionary of National Biography* published new biographical entries for Bonny and Read. David Cordingly wrote these new biographies and they contained the perennial myths from the *General History*: that Mary Read was disguised as a man and so was Ann Bonny, who was attracted to Mary while believing her to be a man. Also that both women valiantly resisted Barnet's capture of the *William* and 'were the fiercest members of the crew'.[140] In *Villains of All Nations: Atlantic Pirates in the Golden Age* (2004), Marcus Rediker introduces his Bonny and Read chapter with the response of the Jamaican 'jury', as he calls it, to their pleading their bellies. 'The jury inquired into the matter', says Rediker, and 'discovered that they were indeed women, pregnant ones at that'.[141] Although he has consulted and quotes the *Tryals* and comes to the correct conclusion in consequence, 'that Bonny and Read did not cross-dress all of the time aboard the pirate ship', he cannot resist the myth promulgated by the *General History*, that the two women were disguised as men until the jury 'discovered that they were indeed women'.[142] He repeats without question the stories in the *General History*, even when contradicted by the *Tryals*, including the defiant last stand of Bonny and Read at the capture of the *William*, when 'the rest of the pirates scuttled down into the hold in cowardice'.[143] He chooses to believe that the women were successfully disguised as men and that they were also braver, more manly, than men. So the mythical eighteenth-century pirate is still surviving, curated by the twentieth and twenty-first-century historians.

In discussing the two women Rediker treats as factual their pre-birth and pre-piratical backgrounds as narrated in the *General History*.[144] On the evidence of the *General History* Rediker argues that Bonny and Read are working class heroines, champions of denied rights, and he deduces—again, from the *General History*, not the *Tryals*—that 'they clearly exercised considerable leadership aboard their vessel'.[145] Their transgressive lives are echoed, he argues, in novels such as Defoe's *Moll Flanders* or in a drama such as Gay's *Polly*, whose respective heroines, Moll and Polly, sometimes dressed as men. What Rediker does not consider is whether the influence might be in the reverse direction, that the features of Bonny and Read that Rediker singles out from the *General History* may be the result, not the cause, of literary fiction. Rediker suggests 'that Gay knew of and drew on the adventures of the real women pirates', Bonny and Read.[146] The similarity is actually rather less than Rediker indicates, as Gay's Polly did not cross-dress and go to sea as a pirate, as Rediker tells us. She is cross-dressed in the wild West Indies to protect her from the 'continual dangers' to which a 'woman so young and so handsome must be expos'd'.[147] Moreover, Gay would not have been influenced by what Rediker calls 'the real women pirates', because the Bonny and Read whom he is characterizing— on the evidence of the *General History*—were themselves largely fictional, like Gay's Polly.

The more the pirate changes, the more he or she stays the same. The pirate story from the eighteenth to the twenty-first century has two essential continuities: it depends for its authenticity on its sup-posed golden age, in the early eighteenth century, and it depends for its appeal on fiction. The pirate of the eighteenth-century golden age was imagined for the rising reader and purchaser by the Grub Street writers, and that pirate has persisted as an authentic fiction ever since, in poetry, drama, pseudobiography, and, especially, in history, or pseu-dohistory, where the pirate persists under many disguises: sensational

Satanist, radical proto-Marxist, ethical Feminist, transgressive Sodomite. The pirate would seem infinitely plastic, but actually he or she depends on his or her supposedly real originals, the written characters in the *Bucaniers of America* and the *General History of the Pyrates*. History is the supposed home of the pirate but the novel of the same golden age is his or her real historical template, and fiction is where he or she properly and historically belongs—above all in realistic and credible eighteenth-century London writings, purporting to be biographical and historical, in particular the *General History*, a fiction for all time.

The pirate was fake when he was imagined in the early eighteenth century, but that fake pirate was a real folk-hero, a rebel who sailed for the reader on the no-man's land of the ocean, escaping the boundaries of society, in search of self-discovery. The nineteenth-century pirate was also a folk-hero, but rebelled against his eighteenth-century paternity, asserting himself as a double, an alter-ego of the gentleman, a wrongfully displaced member of polite society who would be rightfully reinstated by the reliable, predictable authorial plot. From this Romantic type would in turn emerge the emasculated twentieth-century pirate, retired to the margins of historical romance, a historical genre, in a plot consigning him to his former maverick role and status, but as an uncelebrated and pathetic figure, worthy perhaps of our sympathy, but not receiving it. This twentieth-century pirate is apparently sanctified, harmless as well as emasculated, moribund, but he survives nevertheless, is read, is seen on the screen, and believed. Should we shed a tear for him?

The historians, it seems, are continuing the fictions of the novelists and still believing them. The twentieth-century novelists were reclaiming as their own—as fiction—the pseudohistory of the *General History*, the literary inventions in which we should no longer suspend our disbelief. 'Do you believe in fairies?' asks Peter Pan, desperate to save Tinker Bell.[148] Should we believe in fictional pirates as well as fairies? The historians, it seems, are professionally continuing the fictions of Neverland, as are the film-makers. In the second of the film series featuring swashbuckling Johnny Depp, *Pirates of the Caribbean*, films that began as a 'ride-through' Pirate Wax Museum at Disneyland, a supporting actor (or a stunt man) goes up to the top of the mast and slides significantly down, slitting the mainsail with a knife from top to bottom, 'referencing', as it is called, Douglas Fairbanks in *The Black Pirate* and Errol Flynn in *Against All Flags*, the swashbuckling cinematic dynasty.[149] From Captain Kidd to Johnny Depp is a long dissolve, but pirates are postmodern now and self-referential—except perhaps, at the time of writing, in Somalia, not Hollywood, where post-colonial disorder rules, as precolonial disorder did in its time, a political condition that entails, of course, what we call robbery at sea: piracy.

Notes

CHAPTER I

1. 'A Copy of Verses Composed by Capt. Henry Every now gone to Sea to Seek his Fortune', 388/4, fo. 59, PRO. There is a printed copy in *The Pepys Ballads*, ed. W.G. Day (5 vols; Cambridge, 1987), V, 384.

2. David Creagh, testimony, *The Tryals of Joseph Dawson, Edward Forseith, William Day, William Bishop, James Lewis, and John Sparkes. For several Piracies and Robberies by them committed, in the Company of Every the Grand Pirate* (London, 1696), 15.

3. Creagh, testimony, *Tryals*, 15.

4. Creagh, testimony, *Tryals*, 15

5. Creagh, testimony, *Tryals*, 15.

6. Creagh, testimony, *Tryals*, 15.

7. Creagh, testimony, *Tryals*, 15.

8. Creagh, testimony, *Tryals*, 15.

9. James Houblon, 10 August 1694, 388/4, fo. 55, PRO. Houblon's MS copy presumably predates the printed copy of the ballad in Pepys's collection (see *The Pepys Ballads*, ed. W.G. Day, V, 384). The petitioning wives were led by Jane May, whose husband William was one of the two 'Sports-men' referred to by Every, and one of the few of the crew who were later tried and hanged.

10. John Dann, testimony, *Tryals*, 18; Dann, Examination, in J.F. Jameson, ed., *Privateering and Piracy in the Colonial Period: Historical Documents* (New York, 1923), 166; William Phillips, account, Dublin, 8 August 1696, SP 63/358, fo. 127v, PRO; Phillip Middleton, Narrative, 4 August 1696, MS, British Library, IOR/H/36, 199.

11. Phillip Middleton, testimony, *Tryals*, 20.

12. Middleton, Narrative, 199; and see Dann, Examination, 167.

13. William Phillips, account, fo. 128v.

14. Governor Fletcher, quoted by Jameson (from *New York Colonial Documents*, IV, 447) in J.F. Jameson, ed., *Privateering and Piracy*, 167, n. 16.

15. Dann, Examination, in Jameson, ed., *Privateering and Piracy*, 168.

16. See Dann, Examination, 168, and also William Phillips, account, fos. 128v–129r.

17. Dann, Examination, 168; John Elston, Deposition, 27 May 1698, in *Archives of the State of New Jersey*, First Series, II, 225. Elston, a young cabin

boy, estimated £20,000 as the worth of the 'slight ship' but Dann's esti-
mate is probably better informed. The Indian historian, Kháfi Khán,
speaks of 'eighty guns and four hundred men on board', but he was not
an eye-witness. (See Kháfi Khán, 'Muntakhabu-l Lubáb', in *The History of
India, as Told by its Own Historians*, ed. H.M. Elliot and John Dowson (8
vols; London, 1867–77), VII, 350.) William Phillips speaks of '70 Guns and
700 Men' (account, fo. 129r.); Elston of 'forty or fifty Gunns mounted and
others in hold' (Deposition, *Archives*, 225).

18. Dann, testimony, *Tryals*, 18.

19. See: Kháfi Khán, 'Muntakhabu-l Lubáb', *History of India*, VII, 350; William
Phillips, account, 129r.

20. William Phillips, account, 129r.

21. William Phillips, account, 129r.; Adam Baldridge, Deposition, 1699, in
Jameson, ed., *Privateering and Piracy*, 184.

22. *General History*, II [1728], 109.

23. Kháfi Khán, 'Muntakhabu-l Lubáb', *History of India*, VII, 350.

24. Kháfi Khán, 'Muntakhabu-l Lubáb', *History of India*, VII, 350–51.

25. Middleton, Narrative, 199.

26. William Phillips, account, fo. 131v.

27. Abstract, E.I.Co. Letters from Bombay, 12 October 1695, quoted by
Jameson, *Privateering and Piracy*, 158–9. See also Abstract, E.I. Co. Letter
from President and Council, Surat, 21 April 1697, where agents 'were all
put in Irons' because of the 'takeing' of the 'Gunsway' (MS, British Library,
E/3/53, fo. 27).

28. Despite the agreement 'to share and share alike' (William Phillips, account,
fo. 128v), there were some inequalities, for various reasons, in the distribution of the loot. (See Dann, in Jameson, ed., 169; and William Phillips,
account, fo. 129v.)

29. Dann, Examination, in Jameson, ed., *Privateering and Piracy*, 169 (and see
William Phillips, account, fo. 129r).

30. Thomas Phillips, 'A Journal of a Voyage made in the Hannibal of London,
Ann. 1693, 1694', in A. Churchill, ed., *A Collection of Voyages and Travels*
(6 vols; London, 1732), VI, 179.

31. R.P. Labat, *Nouveau Voyage aux isles de l'Amerique* (8 vols; Paris, 1742), VII,
333. The timing of Labat's visit to St. Thomas, in April 1701, makes the
identification of the English pirate ship with the *Fancy* somewhat improbable, but the tale Labat heard in relation to the Grand Mughal is distinctive, even as myth.

32. Labat, *Nouveau Voyage*, 336.

33. Dann, in Jameson, ed., *Privateering and Piracy*, 170.

34. Middleton, Narrative, 201.

35. Middleton, Narrative, 201.

36. Middleton, Narrative, 201.

37. Dann, in Jameson, ed., *Privateering and Piracy*, 170, 171.

38. See Dann, in Jameson, ed., *Privateering and Piracy*, 171.

39. *Tryals of Joseph Dawson*, 6, 4, 28.

40. *An Account of the Behaviour, Dying Speeches, and Execution of... William May, John Sparcks, William Bishop, James Lewis, and Adam Foreseith, for Robbery, Piracy and Felony; at the Execution-Dock: On Wednesday the 25th of November, 1696* (London, 1696).

41. *An Account of the Behaviour, Dying Speeches, and Execution.*

42. *An Account of the Behaviour, Dying Speeches, and Execution.*

43. Dann, in Jameson, ed., *Privateering and Piracy*, 171.

44. William Phillips, account, fo. 130v.

45. William Phillips, account, fo. 131r.

46. Baldridge, Deposition, in Jameson, ed., *Privateering and Piracy*, 184.

47. See Baldridge, Deposition, in Jameson, ed., *Privateering and Piracy*, 184.

48. Samuel Perkins, Deposition, 1698, in Jameson, ed., *Privateering and Piracy*, 176; Baldridge, Deposition, in Jameson, ed., *Privateering and Piracy*, 181. A careful 'Plan du Port de l'isle Ste Marie' can be seen in British Library, Add. MSS, 15319, fo. 34.

49. Henry Watson, Narrative, *CSP, CS, A&WI, 27 October 1697–31 December 1698*, ed. J.W. Fortescue (London, 1905), 108.

50. Watson, Narrative, 108.

51. Baldridge, Deposition, in Jameson, ed., *Privateering and Piracy*, 183.

52. Baldridge, Deposition, in Jameson, ed., *Privateering and Piracy*, 183.

53. Baldridge, Deposition, in Jameson, ed., *Privateering and Piracy*, 183.

54. Edward Randolph, 'To the Honourable Commissioners of his Majesty's Custom', 10 November 1696, *Colonial Records of North Carolina*, ed. William L. Saunders, I (Raleigh, North Carolina, 1886), 463.

55. Baldridge, Deposition, in Jameson, ed., *Privateering and Piracy*, 184.

56. Perkins, Deposition, in Jameson, ed., *Privateering and Piracy*, 178.

57. See Baldridge, Deposition, in Jameson, ed., *Privateering and Piracy*, 186–7, and Perkins, Deposition, in Jameson, ed., *Privateering and Piracy*, 176–7.

58. See Baldridge, Deposition, in Jameson, ed., *Privateering and Piracy*, 186–7. Kidd told Lord Bellomont when under examination that Baldridge was responsible for the 'insurrection of natives in St. Mary's near Madagascar', which was in revenge for Baldridge's capturing many Malagasy and shipping them as slaves to the French island of Réunion (Governor the Earl of Bellomont to the Council of Trade and Plantations, Boston, 24 August 1699, *CSP, CS, A&WI, 1699*, ed. Cecil Headlam (London, 1908), 404).

59. *Reasons for Reducing the Pyrates at Madagascar: And Proposals humbly offered to the Honourable House of Commons, for effecting the same* [London, 1707], 1.

60. *Reasons for Reducing the Pyrates at Madagascar*, 2.

61. [Defoe,] *A Review of the State of the British Nation*, 18 October 1707, in Defoe's *Review*, ed. A.W. Secord, Facsimile Book 10 (New York, 1938), vol. IV, no. 107, 425.

62. 'The Asiatic Campaigns of Thut-mose III', *Ancient Near Eastern Texts*, ed. James B. Pritchard (Princeton, 1955), 239.

63. Lionel Casson, *Ships and Seafaring in Ancient Times* (London, 1994), 48.

64. See Philip de Souza, *Piracy in the Graeco-Roman World* (Cambridge, 1999), 3.

65. Homer, *The Odyssey*, 9.252–5, transl. A.T. Murray (Loeb edition, 1919).

66. See de Souza, *Piracy*, 2.

67. Homer, *The Odyssey*, 14.223–33, transl. Murray (Loeb edition).

68. Homer, *The Odyssey*, 14.223–33.

69. Paul, Titus, 1: 12, *The New English Bible* (New York, 1971).

70. Longus, *Daphnis and Chloe*, transl. Paul Turner (Penguin edition, 1968), 41. Cf. Longus, *Daphnis and Chloe*, ed. J.M. Edmonds (Loeb edition, 1916).

71. Giovanni Boccaccio, *Il Decameron*, Giornata quinta, Novella seconde, ed. Aldo Rossi (Bologna, 1977), 282.

72. Boccaccio, *Il Decameron*, Giornata seconda, Novella decima, 141.

73. François Villon, *Le Grant Testament* (Paris, 1489), [7–8].

74. Augustine, *The City of God*, transl. Henry Bettenson (Penguin edition, 1972), 139.

75. For the anecdote, see Cicero, *De re publica*, III, xiv (Loeb edition, 1988), 202.

76. Cicero, *De officiis*, III, 107 (Loeb edition, 1913), 384.

77. See Daniel Heller-Roazen, *The Enemy of All: Piracy and the Law of Nations* (New York, 2009), particularly 192.

78. Miguel de Cervantes Saavedra, *El Ingenioso Hidalgo Don Quixote de la Mancha* (Lisboa, 1695), 360, 361.

79. Cervantes, quoted in William Byron, *Cervantes: A Biography* (London, 1979), 186.

80. [Voltaire,] *Candide, ou l'optimisme* (1759), [Ch. XI,] 79, 80.

81. John Stow, *A Survay of London* (London, 1598), 347. Accounts of the 'outragious searovers' and of Clinton Atkinson, whose father was a minister, are provided in Raphaell Holinshed [and others, including John Stow], *The First and second volumes of Chronicles* (London, 1587), 1354.

82. John Stow, *The Annales of England* (London, 1605), 1175.

83. Stow, *Annales*, 1175.

84. Thomas Heywood and William Rowley, *Fortune by Land and Sea. A Tragi-Comedy* (London, 1655), V, i. Walton is called Purser in the play, another name for Walton, as explained in *A True Relation, of the Lives and Deaths of the two most Famous English Pyrats, Purser, and Clinton* (London, 1639): 'Purser, so commonly cald because he had beene Purser of her Majesties Ships Royall, whose name was Thomas Walton'. On the conjectured date of the play, see Herman Doh, *A Critical Edition of Fortune by Land and Sea* (New York and London, 1980), 32–7.

85. Heywood and Rowley, *Fortune by Land and Sea*, V, ii.

86. Heywood and Rowley, *Fortune by Land and Sea*, V, ii.

87. *A True Relation, of the Lives and Deaths of the two most Famous English Pyrats, Purser, and Clinton* (London, 1639).

88. Robert Daborn, *A Christian turn'd Turke: or, The Tragicall Lives and Deaths of the two famous Pyrates, Ward and Dansiker* (London, 1612), stage direction, Scene 2.

89. Daborn, *A Christian turn'd Turke*, Scene 4.

90. 'The Seaman's Song of Captain Ward, the Famous Pirate of the World, and an Englishman Born', in Daniel J. Vitcus, ed., *Three Turk Plays from Early Modern England* (New York, 2000), Appendix 1, 345–8.

91. William Lithgow, *The Totall Discourse, of the Rare Adventures, and painefull Peregrinations of long nineteene Yeares Travayles* (London, 1632), 358.

92. *Ward and Danseker, Two notorious Pyrates, Ward an Englishman, and Danseker a Dutchman* (London, 1609).

93. *Ward and Danseker.*

94. François I, quoted in S.E. Morison, *The European Discovery of America: The Northern Voyages* (New York, 1971), 435, 456.

95. On 'boucaner', see Jean de Léry, *Histoire d'un voyage fait en la terre du Bresil* (La Rochelle, 1578), 152–4; on the etymology of 'buccaneer', see, e.g., *Le Robert. Dictionnaire historique de la langue française* (3 vols; Paris, 2000).

96. See Jean Baptiste du Tertre, *Histoire generale des Antilles* (4 vols; Paris, 1667–71), III, 141.

97. See du Tertre, *Histoire*, 142, and Pierre-Francois-Xavier de Charlevoix, *Histoire de l'Isle Espagnole ou de S. Domingue* (2 vols; Paris, 1730), II, 44.

98. See Le Pers, MS, printed in Pierre Margry, *Relations et mémoires inédits pour servir à l'histoire de la France dans les pays d'Outre-mer* (Paris, 1867), 282–9, at 282.

99. For clothing, see Le Pers, in Margry, *Relations et mémoires inédits*, 284, and Labat, *Nouveau Voyage*, VII, 233–4.

100. See du Tertre, *Histoire*, III, 141–2.

101. See: Le Pers, in Margry, *Relations et mémoires inédits*, 285; Charlevoix, *Histoire*, II, 44; Pierre de Vaissiere, *Saint-Domingue: La Société et la vie créoles sous l'ancien regime (1629–1789)* (Paris, 1909), 13.

102. See Le Pers, in Margry, *Relations et mémoires inédits*, 285.

103. Le Pers, in Margry, *Relations et mémoires inédits*, 285. On crossing the line, see Peter Earle, *Sailors: English Merchant Seamen 1650–1775* (London, 1998), 96–7, and description, Woodes Rogers, *A Cruising Voyage Round the World* (London, 1712), 23–4.

104. See Le Pers, in Margry, *Relations et mémoires inédits*, 287.

105. See Le Pers, in Margry, *Relations et mémoires inédits*, 286, 288.

106. See Le Pers, in Margry, *Relations et mémoires inédits*, 288.

107. Le Pers, in Margry, *Relations et mémoires inédits*, 288.

108. Basil Ringrose, 'The Dangerous Voyage and Bold Attempts of Captain Bartholemew Sharp, and others', in John Esquemeling, *Bucaniers of America: or,*

a true Account of the most remakable Assaults committed of late upon the Coasts of the West Indies, by the Bucaniers of Jamaica and Tortuga, both English and French (2 vols; London, 1684), II, 31.

109. Ringrose, 'The Dangerous Voyage', in Esquemeling, *Bucaniers*, II, 31.

110. Ringrose, 'The Dangerous Voyage', in Esquemeling, *Bucaniers*, II, 31.

111. William Dampier, *A New Voyage Round the World* (London, 1697), 271.

112. Dampier, *A New Voyage*, 271.

113. Esquemeling, *Bucaniers*, Part III, 68. On correlation between Esquemeling and other sources, see Peter Earle, *The Sack of Panamá* (London, 1981), 265–6. I have compared my quotations from the English edition of the *Bucaniers* (London, 1684) with the Penguin translation from the original Dutch edition (Exquemelin, *The Buccaneers of America*, transl. Alexis Brown (Penguin Books, 1969)) and found only one discrepancy, which I notice in a following note.

114. Esquemeling, *Bucaniers*, Part I, 43.

115. See Esquemeling, *Bucaniers*, Part I, 81, and Le Pers, in Margry, *Relations et mémoires inédits*, 286.

116. Esquemeling, *Bucaniers*, Part II, 38.

117. Esquemeling, *Bucaniers*, Part II, 116–17.

118. Esquemeling, *Bucaniers*, Part II, 124.

119. Esquemeling, *Bucaniers*, Part I, 106, and Part II, 33.

120. Esquemeling, *Bucaniers*, Part I, 106.

121. Esquemeling, *Bucaniers*, Part I, 106.

122. See Esquemeling, *Bucaniers*, Part I, 107–8.

123. Esquemeling, *Bucaniers*, Part II, 56.

124. Esquemeling, *Bucaniers*, Part I, 86. There is no equivalent to this slogan in the wording of the Penguin translation of the original Dutch edition, *Buccaneers* (Penguin Books, 1969), 71.

125. Esquemeling, *Bucaniers*, Part I, 87.

126. Morgan's biographer disputes Esquemeling's complaints about Morgan. See Dudley Pope, *Harry Morgan's Way: The Biography of Sir Henry Morgan 1635–1684* (London, 1977), 246, 243, for Morgan's cheating on the proceeds of Panama and his unscrupulous passion for a captive Spanish lady.

127. Henry Morgan, 'A True Accompt and Relation of this my last Expedition agst the Spaniards by vertue of a Comission given unto mee by his Excy Sr Tho: Modyford', 31 January 1671, MS, British Library, Add. 11268, fo. 78.

128. Sir Thomas Lynch, to Sec. Lord Arlington, 17 December 1671, *CSP, CS, A&WI, 1669–1674*, ed. Noel Sainsbury (London, 1889), 299.

129. John Evelyn, *The Diary*, ed. E.S. de Beer (6 vols; Oxford, 1955), IV, 46.

130. Hans Sloane, *A Voyage to the Islands madera, barbados, Nieves, S. Christophers and Jamaica* (2 vols; London, 1707), Introduction, I, xcviii.

131. John Flavel, 'To all Masters, Mariners, and Seamen', *Navigation Spiritualized: or, A New Compass for Seamen* (eighth edition, London, 1760), v.

132. James Boswell, *Journal of a Tour to the Hebrides*, ed. F.A. Pottle and C.H. Bennett (New York, 1936), 104.

133. Boswell, *Journal*, 211.

134. On European ideas of the sea as well as the shore, see, e.g., Alain Courbin, *Le Territoire du vide: L'Occident et le désir du rivage 1750–1840* (Paris, 1988).

135. Flavel, 'To All Masters, Mariners, and Seamen', iii.

136. Edward Barlow, *Journal of his Life at Sea*, ed. Basil Lubbock (2 vols; London, 1934), I, 60.

137. Jeremy Roch, Journals, in *Three Sea Journals of Stuart Times*, ed. Bruce S. Ingram (London, 1936), 104; Barlow, *Journal*, I, 214.

138. Richard Brathwait, 'A Sayler', *Whimzies: Or, A New Cast of Characters* [1631], in *A Critical Edition of Richard Brathwait's 'Whimzies'*, ed. Allen H. Lanner (New York and London, 1991), 213–17, at 217.

139. John Morris, letter, Liverpool, 6 November 1739, in J.H. Davies, ed., *The Letters of Lewis, Richard, William and John Morris, 1728–65* (2 vols; Aberystwyth, 1907, 1909), I, 13.

140. Morris, letter, in Davies, ed., *The Letters of Lewis, Richard, William and John Morris*, I, 13.

141. On the fate of John Morris, see Frank R. Lewis, 'John Morris and the Carthagena Expedition, 1739–1740', *Mariner's Mirror*, XXVI (1940), 257–69, at 265.

142. See William Phillips, account, fo. 128v.

143. John Dann, Examination, in Jameson, ed., *Privateering and Piracy*, 167.

144. Middleton, Narrative, 199.

145. Middleton, Narrative, 199.

146. Dann, testimony, *Tryals of Joseph Dawson*, 18.

147. See John J. Richetti, *Defoe's Narratives: Situations and Structures* (Oxford, 1975).

148. *The Life and Adventures of Capt. John Avery* (London, 1709), iv. A briefer version of *The Life and Adventures*, without the Van Broeck authorial frame, was published in *The Monthly Miscellany: or, Memoirs for the Curious*, November, 1708, II (London, 1708), 344–53.

149. *The Life and Adventures*, 18.

150. *The Life and Adventures*, 20.

151. *The Life and Adventures*, 25.

152. *The Life and Adventures*, 28.

153. *The Life and Adventures*, 30.

154. *The Life and Adventures*, 30.

155. *The Life and Adventures*, 31.

156. *The Life and Adventures*, 31–2.

157. *The Life and Adventures*, 32.

158. See *The Life and Adventures*, 37, but the chief French East-India Company's resort on Madagascar, somewhere supposedly 'in the North part of that Island', is named 'Port St. Mary' (*The Life and Adventures*, 57).

159. *The Life and Adventures*, 39.
160. *The Life and Adventures*, 40, 41.
161. *The Life and Adventures*, 43.
162. *The Life and Adventures*, 45.
163. *The Life and Adventures*, 46.
164. *The Life and Adventures*, 55.
165. *The Life and Adventures*, 56.
166. See *The Life and Adventures*, 58.
167. *The Life and Adventures*, 64.
168. *The Life and Adventures*, 39.
169. There are many instances but, for example, the descriptions of Every in Douglas Botting, *The Pirates* (Amsterdam, 1979), 80, and in David Cordingly, *Life Among the Pirates: The Romance and the Reality* (London, 1995), 33, are derived from *The Life and Adventures*.
170. Rogers, *A Cruising Voyage*, 125, 419.
171. Charles Johnson, *The Successful Pyrate* (London, 1713), Prologue.
172. Johnson, *The Successful Pyrate*, 3.
173. Johnson, *The Successful Pyrate*, 6.
174. Johnson, *The Successful Pyrate*, 27.
175. John Dennis, 'To the Master of the Revels. Writ upon the first acting of a Play call'd *the Successful Pyrate*', *The Critical Works*, ed. E.N. Hooker (2 vols; Baltimore, 1939–43), II, 398. 'Flip, Sea Drink, of small Beer (chiefly) and Brandy, sweetened and Spiced upon occasion' (*A New Dictionary of the Terms Ancient and Modern of the Canting Crew* (London, 1699)).
176. Dennis, 'To the Master of Revels', *The Critical Works*, 398.
177. Furbank and Owens dispute the attribution, but their reasons are not conclusively persuasive. (See P.N. Furbank and W.R. Owens, *Defoe De-Attributions: A Critique of J.R. Moore's 'Checklist'* (London and Rio Grande, 1994), 122.)
178. *The King of Pirates: Being an Account of the Famous Enterprises of Captain Avery, The Mock King of Madagascar. With his Rambles and Piracies; wherein all the Sham Accounts formerly publish'd of him, are detected. In Two Letters from himself; one during his Stay at Madagascar, and one since his Esape from thence* (London, 1720), iii.
179. *The King of Pirates*, iv.
180. *The King of Pirates*, iv.
181. *The King of Pirates*, vi.
182. *The King of Pirates*, vi.
183. *The King of Pirates*, l.
184. Joel H. Baer has detected traces of Every's maritime career (though the facts of his birth are less reliable). See Joel H. Baer, ' "Captain John Avery" and the Anatomy of a Mutiny', *Eighteenth-Century Life*, 18 (1994), 1–26.
185. *The King of Pirates*, 28.
186. *The King of Pirates*, 57.

187. *The King of Pirates*, 57–8.

188. *The King of Pirates*, 58.

189. Barlow, *Journal*, 472.

190. Alexander Hamilton, *A New Account of the East Indies, Being the Observations and Remarks of Capt. Alexander Hamilton, Who spent his Time there from the Year 1688 to 1723* (2 vols; Edinburgh, 1727), I, 43.

191. *The King of Pirates*, 63.

192. *The King of Pirates*, 71.

193. *The King of Pirates*, 73, 74.

194. *The King of Pirates*, 74.

195. *The King of Pirates*, 44.

196. *The King of Pirates*, 93.

197. John Stow, *A Survey of London*, corrected [etc.] by John Strype, in 6 Books (London, 1720), Book III, 93. For the conjectured etymology of Grub Street, see Pat Rogers, *Grub Street: Studies in a Subculture* (London, 1972), 24.

198. Samuel Johnson, *A Dictionary of the English Language* (2 vols; London, 1755). For Defoe and Grub Street, see Rogers, *Grub Street*, 311–27.

199. See Frank W. Chandler, *The Literature of Roguery*, I (London, 1907), 139ff.

200. Freeman is named in the *Atlas Maritimus* (which may or may not be written by Defoe) and he has been found in the archives of the Royal African Company. See *Atlas Maritimus* (London, 1728), 252, and Peter Knox-Shaw, *The Explorer in English Fiction* (London, 1987), 51, 62–3.

201. [Daniel Defoe,] *The Life, Adventures, and Pyracies, of the Famous Captain Singleton* (London, 1720), 179.

202. [Defoe,] *Captain Singleton*, 180.

203. [Defoe,] *Captain Singleton*, 217, but cf. 201, where such things are received as 'Stories'.

204. See Part IV of Robert Knox, *An Historical Relation of the Island Ceylon, in the East-Indies: Together, With an Account of the Detaining in Captivity the Author and divers other Englishmen now Living there, and of the Author's Miraculous Escape* (London, 1681); [Defoe,] *Captain Singleton*, 292–3.

205. [Defoe,] *Captain Singleton*, 238; William Dampier, *A New Voyage Round the World* (London, 1697), 497.

206. [Defoe,] *Captain Singleton*, 316.

207. [Defoe,] *Captain Singleton*, 317.

208. [Defoe,] *Captain Singleton*, 319. (Cf. repentance in *Moll Flanders*.)

209. [Defoe,] *Captain Singleton*, 327, 337.

210. [Defoe,] *Captain Singleton*, 344.

211. [Daniel Defoe,] *A New Yoyage Round the World, by a Course never sailed before* (London, 1725), 62.

212. See P.N. Furbank and W.R. Owens, *The Canonisation of Daniel Defoe* (New Haven and London, 1988), 100–9.

213. Charles Johnson, *A General History of the Robberies and Murders of the most notorious Pyrates* (first edition, London, 1724), 25.

214. Johnson, *A General History*, 25.
215. Johnson, *A General History*, 26.
216. Johnson, *A General History*, 31.
217. Johnson, *A General History*, 31.
218. Johnson, *A General History*, 35.
219. Johnson, *A General History*, 35–6.
220. Johnson, *A General History*, 36.

CHAPTER II

1. 'Captain Kid's Farewel to the Seas', reprinted in Jameson, ed., *Privateering and Piracy*, 254.
2. Claude Lévi-Strauss, 'Le Champ de l'Anthropologie', in *Anthropologie Structurale Deux* (Paris, 1973), 38.
3. Lévi-Strauss, 'Le Champ de l'Anthropologie', 38.
4. Stuart Beattie, '*Pirates of the Caribbean*: The True Story', Channel 5, UK, 29 May 2011.
5. Kidd's Scots birth and his approximate age are from Paul Lorrain, *The Ordinary of Newgate* (London, 1701); Greenock and the minister father are from Robert C. Ritchie, *Captain Kidd and the War Against the Pirates* (Cambridge, Massachusetts, and London, 1986), 27.
6. See Robert Culliford, Examination, 2 October 1701, ADM, 1/3666, fo. 255, PRO.
7. See Ritchie, *Captain Kidd*, 36, 37.
8. See Kidd, 'Narrative', 7 July 1699, in Jameson, ed., *Privateering and Piracy*, 206. This 'Narrative' is constrained by the need to clear its author of piracy, but is a usable source, with care.
9. In his unreliable 'Narrative' Kidd declares that 'about fifty men died there in a weekes time' ('Narrative', in Jameson, ed., *Privateering and Piracy*, 206).
10. Barlow, *Journal*, 484.
11. Barlow, *Journal*, 485. Robert Bradinham describes the encounter with Barlow's *Sceptre* from the *Adventure Galley*'s point of view in his Examination, 25 April 1701, HCA, 1/15, PRO.
12. See Bradinham, Examination, 25 April 1701.
13. See Barlow, *Journal*, 491.
14. See testimony of Robert Bradinham, ship's doctor, *The Arraignment, Tryal, and Condemnation of Captain William Kidd, for Murther and Piracy, upon Six several Indictments, at the Admiralty-Sessions, held.... at the Old-Baily, on Thursday the 8th. and Friday the 9th. of May, 1701. Who, upon full Evidence, was found Guilty, receiv'd Sentence, and was accordingly Executed at Execution-Dock, May the 23d.* (London, 1701), 9. Much the same exchange is recorded in the Examination of Joseph Palmer, 25 April 1701, HCA, 1/15, PRO.
15. Bradinham, testimony, 19.

16. On the lease of the *Quedah* to a member of Aurangzeb's court, see Ritchie, *Captain Kidd*, 127.
17. Bradinham, testimony, 27. Similar dialogue recorded in Joseph Palmer, Examination, 25 April 1701, HCA, 1/15, PRO.
18. Bradinham, testimony, 27.
19. Bradinham, testimony, 27.According to the testimony of Joseph Palmer, bumbo 'is made of Water, and Limes, and Sugar', but surely he omits the alcohol (*The Arraignment, Tryal* (1701), 58). 'Bumbo is a liquor composed of rum, sugar, water and nutmeg', according to Tobias Smollett, *The Adventures of Roderick Random* (2 vols; London, 1748), footnote, I, 301.
20. Theophilus Turner, Deposition, 8 June 1699, CO, 5/714, 70 iv, PRO, and in Jameson, ed., *Privateering and Piracy*. For the piloting of the *Adventure Galley*, see Joseph Palmer, Examination, 25 April 1701, HCA, 1/15, PRO.
21. Abel Owen and Samuel Arris, crewmen of the *Adventure*, Deposition, 4 July 1699, CO, 5/860, 64 xxiii, PRO.
22. For the number of absconders, see Kidd, 'Narrative', 210.
23. Edward Buckmaster, Examination, 6 June 1699, in Jameson, ed., *Privateering and Piracy*, 198.
24. Kidd, 'Narrative', 209.
25. Kidd, 'Narrative', 209–10.
26. Kidd, 'Narrative', 210.
27. Kidd, 'Narrative', 210.
28. Kidd, 'Narrative', 210.
29. Kidd, 'Narrative', 210.
30. Kidd, 'Narrative', 211
31. See Kidd, 'Narrative', 211.
32. Primary sources differ. See Jameson, ed., *Privateering and Piracy*, 218, n.11.
33. See Ritchie, *Captain Kidd*, 167, for these details, which are not mentioned in Kidd's 'Narrative'.
34. See Kidd, 'Narrative', 211–12.
35. See Ritchie, *Captain Kidd*, 176.
36. Bellomont, to the Board of Trade, Boston, 8 July 1699, CO 5/860, PRO; Bellomont, to Council of Trade and Plantations, Boston, 26 July 1699, *CSPC, CS, A&WI, 1699*, ed. Cecil Headlam (London, 1908), 374. For Kidd's acquisition of the boy and girl, see information of Joseph Palmer, Minutes of Navy Board, 15 April 1700, quoted in Harold T. Wilkins, *Captain Kidd and His Skeleton Island* (London, 1935), 153; for Bellomont's rejection of the gift, see Bellomont, to the Council of the Board of Trade, undated, quoted in Wilkins, *Captain Kidd*, 125.
37. See, e.g., John Gardiner, 'Narrative', 17 July 1699, CO, 5/860, 64 xxi, PRO, and in Jameson, ed., *Privateering and Piracy*, 220–3.
38. Gardiner, 'Narrative'.
39. Kidd, 'Narrative', 213. See also Gardiner, 'Narrative'.

40. Bellomont, to the Board of Trade, 8 July 1699, CO 5/860, PRO.
41. Kidd, Declaration, CO 5/860, 65 xix, PRO.
42. Joseph Palmer, Examination, 25 April 1701, where his age is given as 'abt 32 yeares', HCA, 1/15, PRO.
43. Joseph Palmer, Examination, 29 July 1699, CO, 5/15, PRO.
44. Bellomont, to the Council of Trade and Plantations, 24 October 1699, CO 5/860, PRO.
45. Bradinham, Examination, *CSP,CS, A&WI, 1700*, ed. Cecil Headlam (London, 1910), 277.
46. Bellomont, to the Council of Trade, Boston, 25 May 1700, *CSP,CS, A&WI, 1700*, ed. Cecil Headlam (London, 1910), 269; William Penn, to Mr Secretary Vernon, 26 February 1700, *CSP,CS, A&WI, 1700*, 83.
47. Kidd, MS letter to the Earl of Orford, 11 April 1700, British Library, Add. MSS, 70036, fo. 104.
48. Undated record, quoted in Wilkins, *Captain Kidd*, 153.
49. See Examinations of Bradinham and Palmer, 25 April 1701.
50. Palmer, in *The Arraignment, Tryal*, 8; Cf. Bradinham, in *The Arraignment, Tryal*, 9.
51. Bradinham, in *The Arraignment, Tryal*, 9.
52. Kidd, in *The Arraignment, Tryal*, 8.
53. Kidd, in *The Arraignment, Tryal*, 12.
54. *The Arraignment, Tryal*, 14.
55. *The Arraignment, Tryal*, 14.
56. Bradinham, in *The Arraignment, Tryal*, 18.
57. Palmer, in *The Arraignment, Tryal*, 23; Bradinham, in *The Arraignment, Tryal*, 39.
58. Palmer, in *The Arraignment, Tryal*, 23. Bradinham gave the same account in his Examination, 25 April 1701. Kidd's use of beating to extract information about hidden money is repeatedly mentioned. See, e.g., Depositions by Nicholas Alderson, Benjamine Franks, Jonathan Fredway, MSS, British Library, E/3/53, fos. 147, 153, 200v.
59. Bradinham, in *The Arraignment, Tryal*, 21.
60. Palmer, in *The Arraignment, Tryal*, 23, 25.
61. *The Arraignment, Tryal*, 58.
62. Palmer, in *The Arraignment, Tryal*, 58.
63. Bradinham, in *The Arraignment, Tryal*, 21.
64. Kidd, in *The Arraignment, Tryal*, 25.
65. Kidd, in *The Arraignment, Tryal*, 28.
66. Kidd, in *The Arraignment, Tryal*, 48.
67. Sir Charles Hedges, undated, HCA, 15/1, PRO.
68. *The Arraignment, Tryal*, 60.
69. Kidd, *The Arraignment, Tryal*, 60.
70. Kidd, New Gate, 12 May 1701, to Robert Harley, in Jameson ed., *Privateering and Piracy*, 253.

71. Paul Lorrain, *The Ordinary of Newgate his Account of the Behaviour, Confession, and Dying-Words of Captain William Kidd, and other Pirates that were Executed at the Execution-Dock in Wapping, on Friday May 23 1701* (London, 1701).

72. Lorrain, *The Ordinary*.

73. Lorrain, *The Ordinary*.

74. *A True Account of the Behaviour, Confession and last Dying Speeches, of Captain William Kidd, and the rest of the Pirates, that were Executed at Execution Dock in Wapping, on Friday the 23d of May 1701* (London, 1701).

75. Lorrain, *The Ordinary*.

76. Lorrain, *The Ordinary*.

77. Lorrain, *The Ordinary*.

78. See Jo. Clerke, 'The Marshalls farther Account of Charges', ADM, 1/3666, fos. 210–11, PRO.

79. For 'Captain Kid's Farewel', see Jameson, ed., *Privateering and Piracy*, 253–7, and for treasure diggers and authors see Willard Bonner, *Pirate Laureate: The Life and Legends of Captain Kidd* (New Brunswick, 1947), in particular 137, about the confusion of Kidd and Avery, on which see also Wilkins, *Captain Kidd*, 297.

80. *The Pirates Own Book, or Authentic Narratives of the Lives, Exploits and Executions of the Most Celebrated Sea Robbers* (Philadelphia, 1837), 188.

81. 'An Account of some of the Traditions and Experiments respecting Captain Kidd's Piratical Vessel' (New York, 1844), quoted in Wilkins, *Captain Kidd*, 297–8; *The Pirates Own Book*, 188.

82. Mrs H.P. Spofford, quoted in Wilkins, *Captain Kidd*, 281.

83. Wilkins, *Captain Kidd*, 316, 317, and see photographs, facing 180, 181, 337.

84. See Ritchie, *Captain Kidd* and Peter Earle, *The Pirate Wars* (London, 2003).

85. For evidence of Trott's bribery, see, e.g., William Phillips, account, fo. 130r.

86. *Piracy destroy'd: Or, A short Discourse shewing the Rise, Growth and Causes of Piracy of late... In a letter from an Officer of an East-India Ship lately arriv'd in the River* (London, 1701), 2.

87. [Defoe,] *Captain Singleton*, 226.

88. [Defoe,] *Captain Singleton*, 265.

89. *The Boston News-Letter*, 18 July to 25 July 1723.

90. *The Boston News-Letter*, 25 July to 1 August 1723.

91. See S. Charles Hill, *Notes on Piracy in Eastern Waters* (Bombay, 1923), 147–8.

92. John Vickers, Deposition, enclosed in Lt. Governor Spotswood to the Council of Trade and Plantations, *CSP, CS, A&WI, January 1716–July 1717*, ed. Headlam (London, 1930), 140–1.

93. Vickers, Deposition, 141.

94. Capt. Mathew Musson to the Council of Trade and Plantations, received London 5 July 1717, *CSP, CS, A&WI, January 1716–July 1717*, ed. Headlam (London, 1930), 338.

95. Capt. Mathew Musson to the Council of Trade and Plantations.

96. David Herriot, 'The Information of David Herriot and Ignatius Pell', Appendix, *The Tryals of Major Stede Bonnet, and other Pirates* (London, 1719), 45.

97. The first edition of the *General History* stated that 'Edward Thatch, (commonly called Black-beard,) was born in Jamaica' (1724), 86, which was revised in the second edition to 'Edward Teach was a Bristol Man born' (1724), 70.

98. Governor Hamilton to Council of Trade and Plantations, received London 6 January 1718, *CSP, CS, A&WI, August 1717–December 1718*, ed. Cecil Headlam (London, 1930), 149.

99. Stede Bonnet's background is uncertain but Robert Ritchie writes in *The Oxford Dictionary of National Biography* that 'he is probably the Stede Bonnet who married Mary Allumby in the parish of St. Michael's, Barbados, on 21 November 1709'.

100. *The Boston News-Letter*, 4 November to 11 November 1719.

101. *The Boston News-Letter*, 4 November to 11 November 1719.

102. *The Boston News-Letter*, 4 November to 11 November 1719.

103. *The Boston News-Letter*, 4 November to 11 November 1719.

104. *The Boston News-Letter*, 4 November to 11 November 1719.

105. *The Boston News-Letter*, 4 November to 11 November 1719.

106. *The Boston News-Letter*, 4 November to 11 November 1719.

107. Archives nationales, Paris, Colonies, C9 A5, fo. 27, quoted by Jean-Pierre Moreau, *Une Histoire des pirates des mers du Sud à Hollywood* (Paris, 2007), 206.

108. Henry Bostock, master of the sloop *Margaret*, Deposition, 19 December 1717, enclosure with Governor Hamilton to the Council of Trade and Plantations, in *CSP, CS, A&WI, August 1717–December 1718*, ed. Cecil Headlam (London, 1930), 150.

109. Bostock, Deposition.

110. Bostock, Deposition, 150–51.

111. Stephen Godin, 13 June 1718, with Extracts of several letters from Carolina, *CSP, CS, A&WI, August 1717–December 1718*, ed. Cecil Headlam (London, 1930), 337.

112. Evidence from one of the marooned men, *The Tryals of Major Stede Bonnet*, 46.

113. *The Tryals of Major Stede Bonnet*, v. See also Mr Gale to Thomas Pitt, junr., Carolina, 4 November 1718, enclosed with Mr Secretary Craggs to the Council of Trade and Plantations, *CSP, CS, A&WI, March 1720–December 1721*, ed. Cecil Headlam (London, 1933), 10.

114. *The Tryals of Major Stede Bonnet*, 7.

115. *The Tryals of Major Stede Bonnet*, 13.

116. *The Tryals of Major Stede Bonnet*, 19.
117. *The Tryals of Major Stede Bonnet*, 40.
118. *The Tryals of Major Stede Bonnet*, 40.
119. *The Tryals of Major Stede Bonnet*, 43.
120. Governor Woodes Rogers to the Council of Trade and Plantations, *CSP, CS, A&WI, August 1717–December 1718*, ed. Cecil Headlam (London, 1930), 372. For a description of Nassau at the time of Rogers and a painting of it dated 1729/30, see Michael Craton, *A History of the Bahamas* (London, 1962), 111–12 and illustration facing 193.
121. Rogers, to the Council of Trade and Plantations, 376.
122. Rogers, to the Council of Trade and Plantations, 377.
123. For the French ship, see, e.g., Governor Spotswood, to Secretary of State James Craggs, 22 October 1718, *The Official Letters of Alexander Spotswood*, ed. R.A. Brock (2 vols; Richmond, Virginia, 1882 and 1885), II, 305.
124. Governor Spotswood, to the Council of Trade and Plantations, 22 December 1718, *CSP, CS, A&WI, August 1717–December 1718*, ed. Cecil Headlam (London, 1930), 431.
125. Spotswood, to the Council of Trade and Plantations.
126. 'Abstract of a letter from Mr. Maynard, first Lieutenant of His Majesty's Ship the Pearl, the Station-Ship at Virginia, to Mr. Symonds, Lieutenant of His Majesty's Ship the Phoenix, the Station-Ship at New York', *The Weekly Journal or British Gazetteer*, 25 April 1719.
127. *The Boston News-Letter*, 23 February to 2 March 1719.
128. *The Boston News-Letter*, 23 February to 2 March 1719.
129. *The Boston News-Letter*, 23 February to 2 March 1719.
130. *The Boston News-Letter*, 23 February to 2 March 1719.
131. Maynard, 'Abstract of a letter'.
132. Maynard, 'Abstract of a letter'.
133. *The Boston News-Letter*, 23 February to 2 March 1719.
134. See Spotswood, to Council of Trade and Plantations, 431.
135. See Angus Konstam, *Blackbeard: America's Most Notorious Pirate* (Hoboken, New Jersey, 2006), 286–93.
136. 'The Tryal and Condemnation of ten Persons for Piracy Eight of wch. were Executed two repriev'd till his Majestys Pleasure be known Decr 13th 1718', CO 23/1, fo. 79v, PRO.
137. 'Tryal and Condemnation', fo. 79v.
138. 'Tryal and Condemnation', fo. 79v.
139. 'Tryal and Condemnation', fo. 79v.
140. 'Tryal and Condemnation', fo. 80r.
141. 'Tryal and Condemnation', fo. 80r.
142. 'Tryal and Condemnation', fo. 79v.
143. Hosea Tisdell, testimony, trial of Robert Deal, 18 January 1720, *The Tryals of Captain John Rackam, and other Pirates* (Jamaica, 1721), 24.
144. Trial of Charles Vane, *The Tryals of Captain John Rackam*, 40.

145. *General History*, 'Appendix to the First Volume', II [1728], 280. For Vane's 'mutual Civilities' with Blackbeard, see *General History* (first edition, 1724), 107.

146. Woodes Rogers, Proclamation of 5 September, *The Boston Gazette*, 10–17 October 1720.

147. See Rogers, Proclamation.

148. Rogers, Proclamation.

149. See news from 'New Providence, September 4th.', *The Boston Gazette*, 10–17 October 1720.

150. *The Tryals of Captain John Rackam, and other Pirates . . . As Also, the Tryals of Mary Read and Anne Bonny* (Jamaica, 1721), 8.

151. See *The Tryals of Captain John Rackam*, 9, 17.

152. *The Tryals of Captain John Rackam*, 10.

153. See *The Tryals of Captain John Rackam*, 14.

154. See *The Tryals of Captain John Rackam*, 10, 13.

155. See *The Tryals of Captain John Rackam*, 18.

156. *The Tryals of Captain John Rackam*.

157. Dorothy Thomas, testimony, *The Tryals of Captain John Rackam*, 18.

158. Thomas, testimony, *The Tryals of Captain John Rackam*, 18.

159. John Eaton, testimony, *The Tryals of Captain John Rackam*, 33.

160. See testimonies of John Besneck and Eaton, *The Tryals of Captain John Rackam*, 33.

161. James Spatchears, testimony, *The Tryals of Captain John Rackam*, 11, and see Besneck, testimony, *The Tryals of Captain John Rackam*, 33.

162. Spatchears, testimomy, *The Tryals of Captain John Rackam*, 11.

163. See Spatchears, testimomy, *The Tryals of Captain John Rackam*, 11.

164. Spatchears, testimomy, *The Tryals of Captain John Rackam*, 9.

165. Spatchears, testimomy, *The Tryals of Captain John Rackam*, 10.

166. Spatchears, testimomy, *The Tryals of Captain John Rackam*, 10.

167. Spatchears, testimomy, *The Tryals of Captain John Rackam*, 14.

168. Spatchears, testimomy, *The Tryals of Captain John Rackam*, 16.

169. Spatchears, testimomy, *The Tryals of Captain John Rackam*, 16.

170. Spatchears, testimomy, *The Tryals of Captain John Rackam*, 18.

171. Spatchears, testimomy, *The Tryals of Captain John Rackam*, 19.

172. Thomas, testimony, *The Tryals of Captain John Rackam*, 18.

173. Thomas, testimony, *The Tryals of Captain John Rackam*, 18.

174. Thomas, testimony, *The Tryals of Captain John Rackam*, 18.

175. William Falconer, *An Universal Dictionary of the Marine: or, A Copious Explanation of the Technical Terms and Phrases employed in the Construction, Equipment, Furniture, Machinery, Movements, and Military Operations of a Ship* (London, 1769).

176. See N.A.M. Rodger, *The Wooden World: An Anatomy of the Georgian Navy* (London, 1988), 64, and Peter Earle, *Sailors: English Merchant Seamen 1650–1775* (London, 1998), 34.

177. Besneck and Peter Cornelian, testimonies, *The Tryals of Captain John Rackam*, 18.

178. *The Tryals of Captain John Rackam*, 19.

179. *The Tryals of Captain John Rackam*, 19.

180. *The Tryals of Captain John Rackam*, 19.

181. *The Tryals of Captain John Rackam*, 20.

182. See Clinton V. Black, *Pirates of the West Indies* (Cambridge, 1989), 117.

183. Eaton and Besneck, testimonies, *The Tryals of Captain John Rackam*, 33.

184. Verdict and list of those executed, *The Tryals of Captain John Rackam*.

185. See my Chapter VIII, which does not discuss all the novels I have read and counted.

CHAPTER III

1. *A General History of the Robberies and Murders of the most notorious Pyrates* (first edition, London, 1724), 117.

2. *General History*, II [1728], 65, 70.

3. *General History*, II [1728], 75.

4. *General History* (first edition, 1724), 60; the remark about Bonnet's 'married State' was added in the second edition, *General History* (London, 1724), 91.

5. *General History* (first edition, 1724), 62.

6. *General History* (first edition, 1724), 88.

7. Blackbeard's most recent biographer, Angus Konstam, is sceptical of the *General History*'s account of Blackbeard's sexual antics (see Konstam, *Blackbeard*, 199).

8. *General History* (first edition, 1724), 89.

9. *General History* (first edition, 1724), 92.

10. *General History* (first edition, 1724), 94. Cf. *Boston News-Letter*, February 23 to 2 March 1719.

11. *General History* (first edition, 1724), 95.

12. *General History* (first edition, 1724), 96; *General History* (second edition, 1724), 84.

13. See *General History* (first edition, 1724), 92–3, and Spotswood, to Council of Trade and Plantations, 22 December 1718, loc. cit, 431.

14. Maynard, letter.

15. *General History* (first edition, 1724), 99–100. On the Ramillies wig, see Aileen Ribeiro, *Dress in Eighteenth-Century Europe 1715–1789* (New Haven & London, 2002), 28–9.

16. Cf. *General History* (second edition, 1724), 87.

17. See illustrations of 'Blackbeard the Pirate', first edition (1724), facing 86, and second edition (1724), facing 70.

18. *General History* (first edition, 1724), 99.

19. *General History* (first edition, 1724), 99.

20. *General History* (first edition, 1724), 100.
21. *General History* (first edition, 1724), 100.
22. *General History* (first edition, 1724), 117.
23. *General History* (first edition, 1724), 117.
24. *General History* (first edition, 1724), 213.
25. *General History* (first edition, 1724), 119.
26. *General History* (first edition, 1724), 120.
27. *General History* (first edition, 1724), 121.
28. Anne (or Ann) is spelled both ways also in *The Tryals of Captain John Rackam* (1721).
29. *General History* (first edition, 1724), 122.
30. *General History* (first edition, 1724), 122.
31. *General History* (first edition, 1724), 123.
32. *General History* (first edition, 1724), 123.
33. *General History* (first edition, 1724), 123.
34. *General History* (first edition, 1724), 123.
35. *General History* (first edition, 1724), 124.
36. *General History* (first edition, 1724), 126.
37. *General History* (first edition, 1724), 129.
38. *General History* (first edition, 1724), 130.
39. *General History* (first edition, 1724), 130.
40. *General History* (first edition, 1724), 130, 131.
41. *General History* (first edition, 1724), 131.
42. *General History* (first edition, 1724), 131.
43. *General History* (first edition, 1724), 131.
44. 'Appendix', *General History*, II [1728], 285.
45. 'Appendix', *General History*, II [1728], 287.
46. 'Appendix', *General History*, II [1728], 286.
47. *General History* (first edition, 1724), 133.
48. *General History* (first edition, 1724), 133.
49. *General History* (first edition, 1724), 117.
50. *General History* (first edition, 1724), Preface, [v].
51. *General History* (first edition, 1724), 117.
52. The two accounts of the trial of the nine turtlers, for example, are so close in vocabulary, phrasing, even punctuation, as to preclude both accounts being independent verbatim reports of speech and proceedings in the courtroom. *The Tryals of Captain John Rackam* (1721) is the literary source for some parts of the *General History* (first edition, 1724).
53. There is some contradiction between the statement in 'The Life of Mary Read' that the *General History*'s account of the pirate women's lives was 'supported by many thousand Witnesses...at their Tryals' and the statement in the Preface to the *General History* that, if 'we have produced some Particulars which were not so publickly known, the Reason is, we were more inquisitive into the Circumstances of their past Lives, than

other People' (*General History* (first edition, 1724), 117, [v]). On the one hand the evidence at the trial is attested as proof of the *General History's* account and on the other hand any discrepancies are accounted for.

54. See David Cordingly, lives of Mary Read and of Anne Bonny, *The Oxford Dictionary of National Biography* (Oxford, 2004).

55. Thomas Phillips, 'A Journal of a Voyage made in the Hannibal of London, Ann. 1693, 1694', in A. Churchill, ed., *A Collection of Voyages and Travels* (London, 1732), VI, 179.

56. Thomas Philips, 'A Journal', in Churchill, ed., *A Collection*.

57. Thomas Court, 'A Naval Diary', *Transactions of the Cumberland and Westmoreland Antiquarian and Archaeological Society*, N.S. XXXVIII (1938), 241. The naval historian N.A.M. Rodger accepts the word of Thomas Court, but another historian, Suzanne J. Stark, is sceptical of what she calls the 'dubious notion that women went to sea to find their lost lovers' (Suzanne J. Stark, *Female Tars: Women Aboard Ship in the Age of Sail* (London, 1996), 86, and see Rodger, *The Wooden World*, 77).

58. See Neil Rennie, *Far-Fetched Facts: The Literature of Travel and the Idea of the South Seas* (Oxford, 1995), 88; John Dunmore, *Monsieur Baret* (Auckland, 2002).

59. See John Harold Wilson, *All the King's Men: Actresses of the Restoration Stage* (Chicago, 1958), 73.

60. Thomas Heywood, *The Fair Maid of the West*, Part I (London, 1631), IV, i [pp. 47, 52]. For more about piracy in Renaissance England, see Claire Jowitt, *The Culture of Piracy, 1580–1630: English Literature and Seaborne Crime* (Farnham, Surrey, 2010).

61. Daborn, *A Christian turn'd Turke*, stage direction, Scene 2.

62. Francis Beaumont and John Fletcher, *The Double Marriage*, II, i, in *Comedies and Tragedies* (London, 1647). On the conjectured date of first performance, see Cyrus Hoy, Introduction, *The Double Marriage*, in *The Dramatic Works in the Beaumont and Fletcher Canon*, IX (Cambridge, 1994), 97.

63. Beaumont and Fletcher, *The Double Marriage*, II, i (1647).

64. William Wycherley, *The Plain-Dealer* (London, 1677), 'The Persons'.

65. John Gay, *Polly: An Opera. Being the Second Part of The Beggar's Opera* (London, 1729), III, xii (p. 58).

66. Marcus Rediker, *Villains of All Nations: Atlantic Pirates in the Golden Age* (London and New York, 2004), 121.

67. *General History*, II [1728], 1.

68. *General History*, II [1728], 1.

69. *General History*, II [1728], 2.

70. *General History*, II [1728], 3.

71. *General History*, II [1728], 8.

72. *General History*, II [1728], 10, 11.

73. *General History*, II [1728], 12.

74. *General History*, II [1728], 12, and see Manuel Schonhorn, ed., *General History* (London, 1999), 684, n.8.

75. *General History*, II [1728], 12–13.

76. *General History*, II [1728], 13.

77. *General History*, II [1728], 16.

78. *General History*, II [1728], 16.

79. *General History*, II [1728], 22.

80. *General History*, II [1728], 28.

81. *General History*, II [1728], 34.

82. *General History*, II [1728], 34.

83. Henry Watson, Narrative, *CSP, CS, A&WI, 27 October 1697–31 December 1698*, ed. J.W. Fortescue (London, 1905), 108.

84. *General History*, II [1728], 47.

85. See Baldridge, Deposition, in Jameson, ed., *Privateering and Piracy*, 185.

86. *General History*, II [1728], 94.

87. *General History*, II [1728], 97.

88. *General History*, II [1728], 106, 107.

89. *General History*, II [1728], 107.

90. *General History*, II [1728], 109.

91. See Hubert Deschamps, *Les Pirates à Madagascar* ([1949] Paris, 1972), 73–99.

92. See John Robert Moore, *Defoe in the Pillory and Other Studies* (Bloomington, Indiana, 1939), 126–88; Furbank and Owens, *The Canonisation*, 100–9.

93. Maximillian E. Novak, Introduction, Defoe, *Of Captain Misson*, ed. Novak, Augustan Reprint Society, No.87 (Los Angeles, 1961), i. See also John Richetti, *The Life of Daniel Defoe* (London, 2005), 232–3.

94. See Marcus Rediker, 'Libertalia: The Pirate's Utopia', in David Cordingly, ed., *Pirates: An Illustrated History of Privateers, Buccaneers, and Pirates from the Sixteenth Century to the Present* (London, 1996), 124–39, at 126–7.

95. [Defoe?], *Weekly Journal or Saturday's Post*, Saturday, 23 May 1724.

96. [Defoe?], *Weekly Journal*.

97. [Defoe?], *Weekly Journal*.

98. [Thomas Avory,] *The Life of John Buncle* (2 vols; London, 1765), II, 383.

99. [Jonathan Swift], *Travels into Several Remote Nations of the World.... By Lemuel Gulliver* (2 vols; London, 1726), II, iv, 192–3.

100. Rogers, *A Cruising Voyage*, 419.

101. Rogers, *A Cruising Voyage*, 419.

102. Rogers, *A Cruising Voyage*, 419.

103. See, e.g., Culliford, Examination, fo. 255r.

104. Culliford, Examination, fo. 255r, 255v.

105. See Letter from Fort St George, 19 January 1697, *CSP, CS, A&WI, 27 October 1697–31 December 1698*, ed. J.W. Fortescue (London, 1905), 112–13.

106. John Biddulph gives an account of this adventure but without reference to his sources, if any (*The Pirates of Malabar and An Englishwoman in India Two Hundred Years Ago* (London, 1907), 14–15).

107. Bellomont, Boston, 29 November 1699, CO, 5/861, PRO; William Cuthbert, Narrative, *CSP, CS, A&WI, 1699*, ed. Cecil Headlam (London, 1908), 373–4, at 374.

108. Letters, from Bombay, 15 January 1697, and from Calicut, 30 November 1696, *CSP, CS, A&WI, 27 October 1697–31 December 1698*, ed. J.W. Fortescue (London, 1905), 69–70, at 70.

109. Letter, from the President and Council at Surat, 21 April 1697, MS, British Library, E/3/52, fo. 30v. Letter from Bombay, 11 April 1697, *CSP, CS, A&WI, 27 October 1697–31 December 1698*, ed. J.W. Fortescue (London, 1905), 113–14, at 114.

110. William Willock, Narrative, *CSP, CS, A&WI, 27 October 1697–31 December 1698*, ed. J.W. Fortescue (London, 1905), 366–7, at 366.

111. Willock, Narrative, *CSP, CS, A&WI, 27 October 1697–31 December 1698*, 366.

112. Willock, Narrative, *CSP, CS, A&WI, 27 October 1697–31 December 1698*, 366; William Willock, Narrative, MS, British Library, E/3/53, fo. 248r, 248v.

113. William Willock, Narrative (of which there are variant versions), as printed in Charles Grey, *Pirates of the Eastern Seas (1618–1723)* (London, n.d.), 143–4, at 144.

114. William Reynolds, Atchin, 20 August 1697, MS, British Library, E/3/53, fo. 125.

115. Reynolds, Atchin, fo. 125v.

116. Reynolds, Atchin, fo. 125v.

117. Reynolds, Atchin, fo. 125v.

118. Reynolds, Atchin, fo. 125v.

119. Reynolds, Atchin, fo. 125v.

120. Willock, in Grey, *Pirates*, 144.

121. Willock, in Grey, *Pirates*, 144.

122. Reynolds, Atchin, fo. 125v.

123. Reynolds, Atchin, fo. 125v.

124. Reynolds, Atchin, fo. 125v.

125. Reynolds, Atchin, fo. 125v; Willock, in Grey, *Pirates*, 144.

126. Reynolds, Atchin, fo. 126.

127. Reynolds, Atchin, fo. 126.

128. Turner, Deposition.

129. Turner, Deposition; Culliford, at Doctors' Commons, June 1700, in Wilkins, *Captain Kidd*, 77–8, at 77.

130. Joseph Palmer, Examination, 25 April 1701, HCA, 1/15, PRO.

131. Samuel Annesley, 5 December 1698, *Home Miscellaneous Series*, vol. 36, p. 450, quoted in Harihar Das, *The Norris Embassy to Aurangzeb (1699–1702)*

(Calcutta, 1959), 33. On the commerical and political context in India, see Harihar Das, *The Norris Embassy to Aurangzeb (1699–1702)*, 32–3.

132. Annesley, 5 December 1698, in Das, *The Norris Embassy*.

133. Turner, Deposition.

134. Turner, Deposition.

135. See Samuel Burgess, Deposition, 3 May 1698, *CSP, CS, A&WI, 1697–8*, ed. J.W. Fortescue, 227–8, and Robert Ritchie, 'Samuel Burgess, Pirate', in *Authority and Resistance in Early New York*, ed. William Pencak and Conrad Edick Wright (New York, 1988), 118.

136. Frederick Philipse, to Adam Baldridge, New York, 25 February 1695, HCA, 1/98, Pt. 1, fo. 57r., PRO.

137. Philipse, to Baldridge, 25 February 1695, fo. 57r., 57v. (Cf. Baldridge's own record, Deposition, 5 May 1699, in Jameson, ed., *Privateering and Piracy*, 183.)

138. Philipse, to Baldridge, 25 February 1695, fo. 58r.

139. Philipse, New York, 9 June 1698, HCA, 1/98, Pt. 1, fo. 136, PRO.

140. Giles Shelley, to Stephen Delaney, from Cape May, New Jersey, 27 May 1699, in *Manuscripts of the House of Lords* (London, 1908), 330–1.

141. Bellomont, to the Council of Trade and Plantations, 22 July 1699, *CSP, CS, A&WI, 1699*, ed. Cecil Headlam (London, 1908), 360–1, at 361.

142. Bellomont, to the Council of Trade and Plantations, 22 July 1699.

143. Shelley, to Delaney, 27 May 1699, 331.

144. Governor Basse, to William Popple, 9 June 1699, *CSP, CS, A&WI, 1699*, ed. Cecil Headlam (London, 1908), 280–1, at 280.

145. Basse, to Popple, 9 June 1699, 280.

146. James Kelly, *A full and true Discovery of all the Robberies, Pyracies, and other Notorious Actions, of the Famous English Pyrate, Capt. James Kelly, who was Executed on Friday the 12th. of July 1700* (London, 1700); Bellomont, to the Board of Trade, 29 November 1699, in Jameson, ed., *Privateering and Piracy*, 238.

147. Bellomont, to the Board of Trade, 29 November 1699, in Jameson, ed., *Privateering and Piracy*, 239, 240.

148. Kelly, *A full and true Discovery*.

149. Shelley, to Delaney, 27 May 1699, 331.

150. See Baldridge, Deposition, in Jameson, ed., *Privateering and Piracy*, 186–7, and mention of his arrival at New York in HCA, 1/98, Pt. 1, fo. 48, PRO. In 1700 he fraudulently married another pirate's wife with a doctored licence (see Jameson, ed., *Privateering and Piracy*, 197, n.1). Burgess, HCA, 1/98, Pt.1, fo. 50, PRO; Culliford, Examination, fo. 256r.

151. Turner, Deposition.

152. On Chivers, see Hill, *Notes on Piracy*, 126.

153. Matthew Lowth, 'Journal of Loyall Merchant', MS, British Library, L/MAR/A/CXXXII.

154. I refer generally to HCA, 1/98, Pts. 1–2, PRO, and particularly to Lowth, HCA, 1/98, Pt. 2, fo. 257r., PRO.

155. Lowth, 'Journal'.
156. Lowth, 'Journal'.
157. Lowth, 'Journal'.
158. Council of Trade and Plantations, to Mr Secretary Vernon, 13 January 1698, *CSP, CS, A&WI, 27 October 1697–31 December 1698*, ed. J.W. Fortescue (London, 1905), 88.
159. Council of Trade and Plantations, to Vernon, 13 January 1698, 88.
160. Council of Trade and Plantations, to Vernon, 26 February 1698, 121.
161. Narcissus Luttrell, *A Brief Relation of State Affairs from September 1678 to April 1714* (6 vols; Oxford, 1857), IV, 428 and see 429.
162. Thomas Warren, 23 December 1700, HCA, 1/15, PRO.
163. Robert Culliford, 'Peticion of Robt. Cullover', HCA, 1/15, PRO.
164. Lowth, 'Journal'. On Chivers's death in Bombay, see Richard Zacks, *The Pirate Hunter: The True Story of Captain Kidd* (London, 2003), 300.
165. On the problematic pardon, see Jan Rogozinski, *Honor Among Thieves: Captain Kidd, Henry Every, and the Pirate Democracy in the Indian Ocean* (Mechanicsburg, Pennsylvania, 2000), 148.
166. ADM, 1/3666, fo. 250r., PRO.
167. 'Examination of Captain Robert Collover Prisoner in Newgate', 2 October 1701, ADM, 1/3666, fos. 255v, 256r, PRO.
168. Sir Charles Hedges, to my Lord High Admiral, 2 April 1702, British Libraray, Add. MSS. 24107, fo. 207.
169. For further legal details, see Jacob Judd, 'Frederick Philipse and the Madagascar Trade', *New York Historical Society Quarterly*, LV (1971), 354–74, and Ritchie, 'Samuel Burgess, Pirate', 114–37.
170. See Henry Brooke, to Col. Quary, Port Lewis, 12 November 1703, in *CSP, CS, A&WI, 1702–3*, ed. Cecil Headlam (London, 1913), 741–4.
171. See entry for 28 February 1704, 'A Journal of our voyage... in her Majesties ship Scarborrow', British Library, Sloane MS, 3674.
172. Robert Drury, *Madagascar; or Robert Drury's Journal, During Fifteen Years Captivity on that Island* (London, 1729), 291.
173. For Deaan Toakoffu's nickname, see Mervyn Brown, *Madagascar Rediscovered: A History from Early Times to Independence* (Hamden, Connecticut, 1979), 71.
174. Drury, *Madagascar*, 432.
175. Drury, *Madagascar*, 432.
176. Drury, *Madagascar*, 433, 435.
177. Drury, *Madagascar*, 434.
178. Drury, *Madagascar*, 435.
179. Drury, *Madagascar*, 436.
180. Drury, *Madagascar*, 436. For Thomas Collins's possible background with Every, see Manuel Schonhorn, ed., *A General History of the Pyrates*, note, 688.
181. There are some further details about Burgess (at second hand) in Drury, *Madagascar*, 323–4.

182. Drury, *Madagascar*, 438.

183. Drury, *Madagascar*, 439–40. On the authorship debate, see Moore, *Defoe*, 104–25; A.W. Secord, *'Robert Drury's Journal' and Other Studies* (Urbana, Illinois, 1961), 1–71; Furbank and Owens, *The Canonisation* (New Haven and London, 1988), 109–13; Rennie, *Far-Fetched Facts*, 55–8.

184. See *General History*, II [1728], 270–1.

185. See Drury, *Madagascar*, 439; *General History*, II [1728], 271.

186. *General History*, II [1728], 272.

187. One historian's opinion that the poisoning story 'undoubtedly was inserted into the *General History* as a comic interlude' seems overly dogmatic (Rogozinski, *Honor Among Thieves*, 268, n.74). The most reliable researcher of Burgess makes an uncharacteristic error in attributing the poisoning story to Drury (Ritchie, 'Samuel Burgess, Pirate', 130).

188. William Snelgrave, *A New Account of some Parts of Guinea, and the Slave-Trade* (London, 1734), 198.

189. *The Weekly Journal or British Gazetteer*, 10 October 1719.

190. Snelgrave, *A New Account*, 211–12.

191. Snelgrave, *A New Account*, 234.

192. Snelgrave, *A New Account*, 234.

193. Snelgrave, *A New Account*, 211.

194. Snelgrave, *A New Account*, 277.

195. Snelgrave, *A New Account*, 235–6.

196. Snelgrave, *A New Account*, 236.

197. Snelgrave, *A New Account*, 236–7.

198. Snelgrave, *A New Account*, 237.

199. Snelgrave, *A New Account*, 237–8.

200. Snelgrave, *A New Account*, 238.

201. Snelgrave, *A New Account*, 284, 272.

202. See Snelgrave, *A New Account*, 281, 284.

203. See Captain Macrae, letter, Bombay, 16 November 1720, in *The Post Boy*, 22–5 April 1721.

204. Macrae, letter, 16 November 1720.

205. Macrae, letter, 16 November 1720.

206. Macrae, letter, 16 November 1720.

207. See J.H. Parry, *Trade and Dominion: English Overseas Empires in the Eighteenth Century* ([1971] London, 1974), 94.

208. Richard Lasinby, 'Narrative of the Proceedings of the Pyrates', MS, British Library, Miscellaneous Letters Received, 1722, E/1/13, fos. 165–171v, at 166v.

209. Lasinby, 'Narrative', fo. 167.

210. Lasinby, 'Narrative', fo. 168.

211. Voltaire, *Le Mondain*, in *Mélanges*, ed. Jacques van den Heuvel (Pléiade edition, 1961), 203.

212. Macrae, letter, 16 November 1720, fos. 168v–169.

213. Second MS of Lasinby's account, in third person, British Library, Miscellaneous Letters Received, 1722, E/1/13, fos. 175–77v, at 176.

214. Lasinby, 'Narrative', fo. 170.

215. Lasinby, 'Narrative', fo. 170v. I am assuming (to anticipate) that Edward England took part in the capture of the *Nostra Senhora*. Duval names the captain of the *Fancy* (aka *Cassandra*) as 'Siger' (and names Taylor as 'Quarter-master') and Lasinby speaks of 'one Seeger' as 'Commander in Chief' of the pirate alliance ([Duval,] *Lettres curieuses* (1725), reprinted in Albert Lougnon, *Sous le signe* (Paris, 1958), 168, 170, 169; Lasinby, Second MS of 'Narrative', fo. 175). Taylor's unreliable account to (perhaps inadequately reliable) Bucquoy places Taylor himself heroically at the centre of the action and La Buse somewhat incidentally, without mention of Edward England (Jacob de Bucquoy, *Zestien Jaarige reize naa de Indien* [1744], transl. into French and published in part in Alfred and Guillaume Grandidier, *Collection des ouvrages anciens concernant Madagascar* (Paris, 1907), V, 109–12).

216. Lasinby, 'Narrative', fo. 170v.

217. See [François Duval,] *Lettres curieuses sur divers sujets* (1725), reprinted in part in Albert Lougnon, *Sous le signe de la tortue: Voyages anciens à l'Ile Bourbon (1611–1725)* (Paris, 1958), 167ff.

218. Lasinby, 'Narrative', fo. 170v.

219. Lasinby, 'Narrative', fo. 171. Bucquoy (at second hand) gave the takings from the capture of the *Nostra Senhora* as 30 million 'gulden' (Bucquoy, *Zestien Jaarige*, 110).

220. Jacques-Henri Bernardin de Saint-Pierre, *Voyage à l'Isle de France, à l'Isle de Bourbon* (2 vols; Amsterdam, 1773), II, 18.

221. Bernardin de Saint-Pierre, *Voyage*, II, 18.

222. Bernardin de Saint-Pierre, *Voyage*, II, 18, transl. mine.

223. See Lasinby, 'Narrative', fo. 171, and [Duval,] *Lettres curieuses*, 170.

224. John Freeman, Second Mate of the *Ostend Galley*, 'An Account of the Pyrates', MS, British Library, Miscellaneous Letters Received, 1723, E/1/14, fo. 205. Cf.—perhaps—the report of Robert, who was not a witness, who attributes 'la perte de plus de 80 de leurs meilleurs hommes' to jealousies and feuding (Robert, 'Description en générale et en détail de l'ile de Madagascar', MS, published in part in Alfred and Guillaume Grandidier, *Collection des ouvrages anciens concernant Madagascar* (Paris, 1907), V, 64).

225. See Robert, 'Description', 64–5. I give the date supplied by M.I. Guet, *Les Origines de l'Ile Bourbon et de la colonisation française à Madagascar* (Paris, 1888), 219, but Lougnon, *L'Ile Bourbon pendant la Régence* (Paris, 1956), gives 30 December 1721 (179, n. 53).

226. See Freeman, 'An Account', fo. 205, and Guet, *Les Origines*, 219.

227. Bucquoy, *Zestien Jaarige*, 107, English transl. mine. For disputes between Taylor and La Buse, see Robert, 'Description', 67.; for the capture of the Dutch fort, see also Freeman, 'An Account', fo. 205.

228. Letter from Jamaica, 12 May 1723, MS, British Library, Miscellaneous Letters Received, 1723, E/1/14, fo. 161v.
229. Captain David Greenhill, reported in letter from Captain Jeremy Pearce, Letter from Jamaica, 19 June 1723, MS, British Library, Miscellaneous Letters Received, 1723, E/1/14, fo. 163.
230. Bucquoy, *Zestien Jaarige*, 114, transl. mine.
231. Clement Downing, *A Compendious History of the Indian Wars . . . Also the Transactions of Men of War under Commodore Matthews, sent to the East-Indies to suppress the Pyrates . . . With an Account of the Life and Actions of John Plantain, a notorious Pyrate at Madagascar* (London, 1737), 135.
232. Desforges Boucher, Governor of Réunion, *c.* September 1724, quoted in Moreau, *Une Histoire*, 232, transl. mine; and see also unidentified source quoted at 233. For the capture of La Buse, see De Valgny, MS, quoted in Grandidier, *Collection*, V, 66, n.1, and for the hanging of La Buse, see Dumas, Governor of Réunion, 20 December 1730, *Archives Coloniales, Correspondence générale de Bourbon*, V, 1727–1731, in Grandidier, *Collection*, V, 65, n.1.
233. Christopher Hill's 'Radical Pirates?' are the imaginary Misson and Caraccioli and also the imaginary pirates of the 'Republic' of Avery. Marcus Rediker knows that Misson is imaginary but argues that his fictitious Libertalia 'had objective bases in historical fact'. (See Christopher Hill, 'Radical Pirates?', in *The Collected Essays*, III, *People and Ideas in 17th Century England* (Brighton, 1986), 161–87, and Rediker, 'Libertalia', 127.)
234. The pioneering historian of pirate homosexuality was B.R. Burg, *Sodomy and the Pirate Tradition* (New York and London, 1984), but, as Hans Turley has subsequently pointed out, 'the evidence for piratical sodomy is so sparse as to be almost nonexistent'. Turley has solved this problem, however: 'Because of the deviant homosocial world of the pirate, piracy and implicit homoerotic desire go hand in hand'. Turley's case is that in a 'homosocial' world—without women—homosexuality is implicit and can be read between the lines, despite—or perhaps because of—the absence of evidence (Hans Turley, *Rum, Sodomy and the Lash: Piracy, Sexuality, and Masculine Identity* (New York and London, 1999), 2, 9).
235. Downing, *A Compendious History* (London, 1737), 62–3.
236. Downing, *A Compendious History*, 63. For identification of 'Ranter-Bay', see Mervyn Brown, *Madagascar Rediscovered: A History from Early Times to Independence* (Hamden, Connecticut, 1979), 291, n.3.
237. Downing, *A Compendious History*, 64.
238. Downing, *A Compendious History*, 115–16.
239. Downing, *A Compendious History*, 64.
240. Downing, *A Compendious History*, 64.
241. Downing, *A Compendious History*, 64.
242. Sir John Fielding, *A Brief Description of the Cities of London and Westminster* (London, 1776), xv.

243. Samuel Nobber, signed statement, HCA, 1/18, 10, PRO.

244. Magnus Dessen, signed statement, HCA, 1/18, 11, PRO.

245. Dessen, signed statement.

246. See Downing, *A Compendious History*, 116ff.

247. Hubert Deschamps opines that Downing 'a bâti une histoire de Plantain, dont le point du départ seul paraît vraisemblable' (*Les Pirates à Madagascar*, 174), and Downing's twentieth-century editor admits conservatively that his author's writings contain 'inaccuracies, both wilful and involuntary' (William Foster, Introduction, Clement Downing, *A History of the Indian Wars*, ed. William Foster (Oxford, 1924), xxxi).

CHAPTER IV

1. John Gow, Examination of John Smith [alias Gow], 2 April 1725, HCA, 1/55, fo. 105v, PRO.

2. Gow, Examination, fo. 105v.

3. James Belbin, Examination, 2 April 1725, HCA, 1/55, fo. 107v, PRO; Peter Rollson, Examination, 2 April 1725, HCA, 1/55, fo. 108r, PRO.

4. Rollson, Examination, fo. 108r.

5. William Melvin, Examination, 3 April 1725, HCA, 1/55, fo. 116v, PRO; and see Belbin, Examination, fo. 106v.

6. Melvin, Examination, fo. 106v.

7. Melvin, Examination, fo. 107r. The stabbing by Winter and shooting by Gow/Smith are confirmed by Melvin, Examination, fo. 116v.

8. Rollson, Examination, fo. 108r.

9. Melvin, Examination, fo. 116v.

10. Melvin, Examination, fo. 117r.

11. Rollson, Examination, fo. 108v. Rollson declared that he refused to join in the mutinous 'Agreement' (see fo. 108r) but Melvin—himself not innocent—involves Rollson in the violence (see Melvin, Examination, fo. 116v.).

12. Rollson, Examination. Michael Moor confirms Williams's words and murder (see Michael Moor, Examination, HCA, 1/55, fo. 120r).

13. Belbin, Examination, fo. 107r.

14. Smith, Examination fo. 105v.

15. Smith, Examination, fo. 106r.

16. Rollson, Examination, fo. 108v.

17. Smith, Examination, fo. 106r.

18. See Robert Porrenger, Examination, 10 April 1725, HCA, 1/55, fo. 136v, PRO.

19. See Porrenger, Examination, fo. 136v.

20. See J. Gaynam, 'A full and true Account of the Behaviour and Dying Words of Alexander Rob, the Pyrate', *Parker's Penny Post*, Monday, 5 July 1725, 2–3.

21. Gaynam, 'A full and true Account', 2.

22. Gaynam, 'Account', 2.

23. Porrenger, Examination, fo. 136v. See James Fea, to John Gow, 15 February 1725, in Alexander Peterkin, *Notes on Orkney and Zetland* (Edinburgh, 1822), 214.

24. Gaynam, 'A full and true Account', 3.

25. Porrenger, Examination, fo. 136v.

26. Porrenger, Examination, fo. 137r.

27. James Laing, Deposition, Kirkwall, Orkney, 11 March 1725, in *The Literary and Statistical Magazine for Scotland*, vol. 3 (Edinburgh, 1819), 408.

28. James Fea, to John Gow, '10 Mattin of the cloack', 13 February 1725, in Peterkin, *Notes*, 213.

29. Laing, Deposition, 408.

30. Laing, Deposition, 408.

31. Laing, Deposition, 408.

32. Laing, Deposition, 408.

33. Gaynam, 'A full and true Account', 2.

34. James Fea, to John Gow, '10 of the cloack, mattin', 15 February 1725, in Peterkin, *Notes*, 214.

35. John Gow, to James Fea, 15 February 1725, in Peterkin, *Notes*, 214.

36. Gow, to Fea, 15 February 1725, 217.

37. John Gow, to James Fea, 16 February 1725, in Peterkin, *Notes*, 218. For signalling arrangements and 'chince gown', see Laing, Deposition, 409.

38. William Scollay, Deposition, Kirkwall, Orkney, 11 March 1725, in *The Literary and Statistical Magazine for Scotland*, vol. 3 (Edinburgh, 1819), 406.

39. Scollay, Deposition, 407.

40. See *The London Journal*, 12 February 1724–5, 3.

41. *The Daily Post*, 13 March 1725. See also *The London Journal*, 13 March 1724–5, 3.

42. *The Daily Post*, 13 March 1725.

43. See *The London Journal*, 3 April 1724–5, 3.

44. See *The London Journal*, 27 March 1724–5, 3.

45. Gow, Examination, HCA, 1/55, fo. 106r, PRO.

46. See *The London Journal*, 29 May 1725, 2.

47. *The Daily Post*, 27 May 1725.

48. *The Daily Journal*, 27 May 1725.

49. *The London Journal*, 29 May 1725, 2.

50. See *The London Journal*, 5 June 1725, 1.

51. *The London Journal*, 5 June 1725, 1. See also *The Daily Post*, 10 June 1725.

52. James Guthrie, *A True and Genuine Account of the Last Dying Words of John Gow, alias Smith, Captain of the Pirates. As Likewise of the Eight others, who were Executed with him, on June 11th, 1725. At Execution Dock, for Murder and Piracy* (London, n.d. [1725]), 14.

53. Guthrie, *A True and Genuine Account*, 11.

54. Guthrie, *A True and Genuine Account*, 12.

55. *The Daily Journal*, 9 June 1725.

56. *The Daily Journal*, 10 June 1725.

57. *The Daily Post*, 11 June 1725.

58. *The Daily Journal*, 11 June 1725.

59. *The Weekly Journal; or, the British Gazetteer*, 12 June 1725.

60. *The Weekly Journal*, 12 June 1725.

61. *The Daily Post*, 12 June 1725.

62. *Mist's Weekly Journal*, 12 June 1725.

63. Gaynam, 'A full and true Account', 3.

64. Alexander Rob, quoted in Gaynam, 'A full and true Account', 3.

65. *General History of the Pyrates* (third edition, London, 1725), 419.

66. *General History* (third edition, 1725), 421.

67. Rollson, Examination, and Moor, Examination, HCA, 1/55, fos. 108v, 120r.

68. *General History* (third edition, 1725), 425.

69. *General History* (third edition, 1725), 427.

70. *General History* (third edition, 1725), 426–7.

71. Elizabeth Moodie, to James Fea, 22 April 1725, in Peterkin, *Notes*, 223.

72. James Fea, to Elizabeth Moodie, 4 May 1725, in Peterkin, *Notes*, 224.

73. Publication was announced for 'This day about Noon' in *The Daily Post*, 1 July 1725. For the authorship, see Furbank and Owens, *The Canonisation*, 193–4, and *Defoe De-Attributions: A Critique of J.R. Moore's 'Checklist'* (London, 1994), 140.

74. Advertisement, in *The True and Genuine Account of the Life and Actions of the Late Jonathan Wild* (London, 1725).

75. See Furbank and Owens, *Defoe De-Attributions*, 139.

76. *The True and Genuine Account . . . Wild*, 21.

77. *The True and Genuine Account . . . Wild*, 33, 40. For a modern account of Wild, see Gerald Howson, *Thief-Taker General: The Rise and Fall of Jonathan Wild* (London, 1970).

78. See F.W. Chandler, *The Literature of Roguery* (2 vols; London, 1907), I, 111ff.

79. [Richard Savage,] as Iscariot Hackney, *An Author to Lett* (London, 1729), 4.

80. *An Account of the Conduct and Proceedings of the late John Gow alias Smith* (London [1725]), 10.

81. *An Account . . . Gow alias Smith*, 20.

82. *An Account . . . Gow alias Smith*, 45.

83. See *An Account . . . Gow alias Smith*, 41.

84. *An Account . . . Gow alias Smith*, 20.

85. *An Account . . . Gow alias Smith*, iv.

86. *An Account . . . Gow alias Smith*, 23.

87. *An Account . . . Gow alias Smith*, 23.

88. *An Account . . . Gow alias Smith*, 48, 49.

89. *An Account . . . Gow alias Smith*, 51.

90. [Henry Fielding,] as Scriblerus Secundus, *The Author's Farce* (London, 1730), II, iv.

91. Fielding, *The Author's Farce*, II, iv.

92. *An Account . . . Gow alias Smith*, 33, 34, 33; *General History*, I (1726), 429, 430, 429.

93. *An Account . . . Gow alias Smith*, 33; *General History*, I, (1726), 429.

94. *An Account . . . Gow alias Smith*, 39; *General History*, I (1726), 431, 432.

95. *General History*, I (1726), 426.

96. *General History*, I (1726), 427.

97. *General History*, I (1726), 426.

98. *General History*, I (1726), 428.

99. *General History*, I (1726), 429.

100. *General History*, I (1726), 431.

101. *General History*, I (1726), 434.

102. *An Account . . . Gow alias Smith*, 86.

103. Walter Scott, Diary, in J.G. Lockhart, *Memoirs of the Life of Sir Walter Scott* (7 vols; Edinburgh, 1837–8), III, 203–4.

104. Scott, Diary, 17 August 1814, in Lockhart, *Memoirs*, III, 203–4.

105. W.S. Crockett in *The Sir Walter Scott Originals* claims that Gow's betrothed was not a Katherine Gordon but a Katherine Rorieson (*The Sir Walter Scott Originals* (Edinburgh, 1912), 308). Allan Fea in *The Real Captain Cleveland* states that Katherine Rorieson was replaced in Gow's affections by Katherine Gordon (*The Real Captain Cleveland* (London, 1912), 53).

106. Archibald Constable, to Scott, 25 December 1820, *The Letters of Sir Walter Scott*, ed. H.J.C. Grierson (12 vols; London, 1932–7), VII, 12, n.2.

107. For the duration of composition, see Byron to Thomas Moore, 3 March 1814, *Letters and Journals*, ed. Leslie Marchand, IV (London, 1975), 77.

108. Byron, *The Corsair, a Tale* (London, 1814), I, ii.

109. For more on the 'topos', see Neil Rennie, *Pocahontas, Little Wanton: Myth, Life and Afterlife* (London, 2007), 42–3.

110. Byron, *The Corsair, a Tale* (London, 1814), I, xii. Conrad returns by another name in Byron's *Lara*, but that is another story, and not a pirate one.

111. Byron, Note, *The Corsair*, in *The Complete Poetical Works*, ed. Jerome J. McGann, III (Oxford, 1981), 449. On the historical Jean Lafitte and his brother, see William C. Davis, *The Pirates Lafitte: The Treacherous World of the Corsairs of the Gulf* (Orlando, etc., 2005).

112. On the influence of *Die Räuber*, see Peter L. Thorslev, *The Byronic Hero: Types and Prototypes* (Minneapolis, 1962), 75–6. On the development of the Byronic hero, see also Mario Praz, *The Romantic Agony* (Oxford, 1933).

113. Byron, Note, *The Corsair*, in *Complete Poetical Works*, ed. McGann, III, 450. J.J. McGann says that Byron's source 'was probably the Boston *Weekly Intelligencer*' (note, *Complete Poetical Works*, 451).

114. [J.H. Ingraham,] *The Pirate of the Gulf, or Lafitte* (2 vols; London, 1837).
115. Byron, *The Corsair*, I, xvi.
116. Byron, *The Corsair*, I, viii–ix.
117. For the sales of *The Corsair*, see Murray's letter to Byron, quoted in L.A. Marchand, *Byron: A Biography* (3 vols; New York, 1958), I, 433.
118. John Ballantyne, note, in Scott, *Letters*, VI, 427, n.1.
119. Scott, to William Erskine, 27 September 1821, *Letters*, VII, 12.
120. Lockhart, *Memoirs*, V, 126.
121. [Scott,] *The Pirate* (3 vols; Edinburgh, 1822), I, 153; Scott, Diary, 9 August 1814, in *Memoirs*, III, 170.
122. [Scott,] *The Pirate* (1822), I, 5.
123. [Scott,] Note, *The Pirate* (Paris, 1832), 92.
124. [Scott,] Advertisement, *The Pirate*, I, [i].
125. [Scott,] Advertisement, I, ii.
126. [Scott,] Advertisement, I, iii.
127. [Scott,] Advertisement, I, iii.
128. Scott, Diary, in *Memoirs*, III, 204.
129. [Scott,] Advertisement, I, v.
130. [Scott,] Advertisement, I, v–vi.
131. [Scott,] *The Pirate*, II, 217; and Note, *The Pirate* (1832), 279; for Scott's visit, see Diary, 16 August 1814, III.
132. See NLS, MS 3831, fo. 44r, cited in Mark Weinstein and Alison Lumsden, eds., *The Pirate* (Edinburgh, 2001), 495, n.10.
133. See Peterkin, *Notes*, 212–24. Weinstein and Lumsden state in the 'Historical Note' to their edition of *The Pirate* that Scott saw an account of Gow by Peterkin (see *The Pirate* (Edinburgh, 2001), 490).
134. Robert Stevenson, NLS, MS 3831, fos. 44r–45r, cited in Weinstein and Lumsden, eds., *The Pirate*, 490.
135. [Scott,] *The Pirate*, III, 258; Gow, to Fea, 15 February 1725, in Peterkin, *Notes*, 215.
136. See [Cochrane,] *Catalogue of the Library at Abbotsford* (Edinburgh, 1838), 127, 129.
137. See [Scott,] *The Pirate*, III, 90; *General History* (second edition, 1724), 308, 307.
138. *General History* (second edition, 1724), 260; [Scott,] *The Pirate*, III, 207.
139. [Scott,] *The Pirate*, III, 195.
140. [Scott,] *The Pirate*, III, 195.
141. [Scott,] *The Pirate*, III, 165.
142. [Scott,] *The Pirate*, III, 156; *General History* (second edition, 1724), 87, and see revised illustration of 'Blackbeard the Pyrate', facing 70.
143. [Scott,] *The Pirate*, III, 150.
144. [Scott,] footnote, *The Pirate*, 403; *General History* (second edition, 1724), 87.
145. [Scott,] *The Pirate* (1832), III, 157.

146. Byron, *The Corsair*, I, ix, quoted in [Scott,] *The Pirate*, II, 196; [Scott,] *The Pirate*, II, 216.
147. [Scott,] *The Pirate*, I, 170.
148. [Scott,] *The Pirate*, III, 299.
149. [Scott,] *The Pirate*, II, 222.
150. [Scott,] *The Pirate*, III, 91.
151. [Scott,] *The Pirate*, III, 331.
152. See [Scott,] *The Pirate*, III, 344–5.
153. See Thomas Dibdin, *The Reminiscences of Thomas Dibdin* (2 vols; London, 1827), II, 212.
154. Thomas Dibdin, *The Pirate: A Melodramatic Romance, taken from the Novel of that Name* (London, 1822), I, iv, p. 22.
155. Dibdin, *The Pirate*, III, i, 44.
156. Dibdin, *The Pirate*, III, vii, 56.
157. Dibdin, *The Pirate*, III, viii, 63.
158. Dibdin, *The Pirate*, III, viii, 63, 64.
159. Dibdin, *The Pirate*, III, viii, 64.
160. Dibdin, *The Pirate* (London, 1822) BL: 841.E.26.
161. See Henry White, *Sir Walter Scott's Novels on the Stage* ([1927] reprinted Hamden, Connecticut, 1973), 164–5.

CHAPTER V

1. Irving's quotation, which I have followed, substitutes 'youth' in its second line for Marlowe's original 'wealth'.
2. See Washington Irving, 'Abbotsford', written some 17 years later, in *The Crayon Miscellany*, ed. D.K.Terrel (Boston, 1979), 125–68. Irving's letters to his brother Peter give more immediate impressions of Abbotsford (see Irving to Peter Irving, 1, 6, 20 September 1817, *Letters*, I, 1802–23, ed. R.M. Aderman, et al. (Boston, 1978), 500–5).
3. The recollection of Coleridge comes from Charles Robert Leslie, *Autobiographical Recollections*, ed. Tom Taylor (2 vols; London, 1860), I, 34–5. Scott's compliment comes from his letter to Henry Brevoort, who had sent Irving's *History* to Scott, quoted in Pierre M. Irving, *The Life and Letters of Washington Irving* (New York, 1863), I, 240.
4. Pierre M. Irving, 'Abbotsford', 139, 140.
5. For Irving's father's background, see Stanley T. Williams, *The Life of Washington Irving* (2 vols; New York, 1935), I, 3, and Appendix I, at II, 241 ff.
6. On the sources of 'Rip Van Winkle' and 'Sleepy Hollow', see Walter A. Reichart, *Washington Irving and Germany* (Ann Arbor, 1957), 25–30, and also Williams, *Life*, I, 183–4.
7. For the composition of 'Woolfert Webber' and 'Tom Walker', see Washington Irving, *Journals and Notebooks*, III, 1819–27, ed. Walter A. Reichart (Madison, 1970), 262–5, 327–34.

8. [Washington Irving,] as Geoffrey Crayon, Gent., *Tales of a Traveller* (2 vols; London, 1824), II, 237.

9. [Washington Irving,] *Tales*, II, 245–6.

10. Bellomont, to the Board of Trade, 26 July 1699, CO, 5/860, PRO.

11. Bellomont, to Board of Trade, 26 July 1699.

12. Washington Irving, 3 May 1824 (and see 2 June 1824), *Journals*, III, 326 (and 340). See also Pierre M. Irving, to Peter Irving, 31 May 1824, *Letters*, II, 1823–1838, ed. R.M. Aderman, et al. (Boston, 1979), 50.

13. [Washington Irving], *Tales*, II, 250, 251.

14. [Washington Irving,] *Tales*, II, 251.

15. [Washington Irving,] *Tales*, II, 252.

16. [Washington Irving,] *Tales*, II, 258.

17. [Washington Irving,] *Tales*, II, 275, 276.

18. [Washington Irving,] *Tales*, II, 281.

19. [Washington Irving,] *Tales*, II, 282, 283, 282.

20. [Washington Irving,] *Tales*, II, 288.

21. [Washington Irving,] *Tales*, II, 316.

22. [Washington Irving,] *Tales*, II, 301.

23. [Washington Irving,] *Tales*, II, 301, 302.

24. [Washington Irving,] *Tales*, II, 303.

25. [Washington Irving,] *Tales*, II, 316, 315, 313.

26. [Washington Irving,] *Tales*, II, 317, 326, 327.

27. [Washington Irving,] *Tales*, II, 328.

28. [Washington Irving,] *Tales*, II, 336.

29. [Washington Irving,] *Tales*, II, 339.

30. [Washington Irving,] *Tales*, II, 345.

31. [Washington Irving,] *Tales*, II, 363.

32. [Washington Irving,] *Tales*, II, 383–4.

33. [Washington Irving,] *Tales*, II, 387.

34. [Washington Irving,] *Tales*, II, 392.

35. Susan Fenimore Cooper, *The Cooper Gallery; or, Pages and Pictures from the Writings of James Fenimore Cooper, with Notes* (New York, 1865), 72. Cf.: Susan Fenimore Cooper, 'Small Family Memories', in *Correspondence of James Fenimore Cooper*, ed. James Fenimore Cooper (2 vols; New Haven, 1922), I, 52–3; James Fenimore Cooper, to Rufus Wilmot Griswold [10–18 January 1843?], *The Letters and Journals of James Fenimore Cooper*, ed. J.F. Beard, IV (Cambridge, Massachusetts, 1964), 343; James Fenimore Cooper, 1849 Preface to *The Pilot*, ed. Kay Seymour House (Albany, New York, 1986), 5–6. See also Wayne Franklin, *James Fenimore Cooper: The Early Years* (New Haven and London, 2007).

36. James Fenimore Cooper, quoted in Susan Fenimore Cooper, *The Cooper Gallery*, 73.

37. James Fenimore Cooper, Preface, *The Pilot; A Tale of the Sea* (2 vols; New York, 1823), I, vi. The naval historian N.A.M. Rodger also shuns Smollett's

novelistic realism 'as a poor, or rather an over-rich substitute for documentary evidence' (Rodger, *The Wooden World*, I4).

38. Scott, to Maria Edgeworth, 24 February I824, in Lockhart, *Memoirs*,V, 342.

39. On the locations of *The Red Rover*'s composition, see James Fenimore Cooper, *Letters and Journals*, ed. Beard, I, 2I5, 2I2, etc., and see Susan Fenimore Cooper, *The Cooper Gallery*, I78–9.

40. James Fenimore Cooper, *The Red Rover, a Tale* (3 vols; Paris, I827), II, 2I0.

4I. Cooper, *The Red Rover*, II, 209.

42. Cooper, *The Red Rover*, II, 2I0.

43. Cooper, *The Red Rover*, II, 242.

44. Cooper, *The Red Rover*, III, 25. For the cabin decor, see *The Red Rover*, I, I37–9, III, 23.

45. Cooper, *The Red Rover*, III, 20.

46. Byron, *Don Juan*, II, 70, *Complete Poetical Works*, ed. Jerome McGann,V (Oxford, I986).

47. Cooper, *The Red Rover*, III, 92.

48. Cooper, *The Red Rover*, III, I74, I68.

49. Cooper, *The Red Rover*, III, 2I5.

50. Cooper, *The Red Rover*, III, 226.

5I. Cooper, *The Red Rover*, III, 264.

52. Cooper, *The Red Rover*, III, 279, 285, 287.

53. Cooper, *The Red Rover*, III, 287.

54. Cooper, *The Red Rover*, III, 29I.

55. Cooper, *The Red Rover*, III, 292.

56. Cooper, *The Red Rover*, III, 293.

57. Cooper, *The Red Rover*, III, 297.

58. Cooper, *The Red Rover*, III, 308.

59. Cooper, *The Red Rover*, III, 3I2.

60. [John] N[eal], 'Late American Books', *Blackwood's Edinburgh Magazine*, XVIII (September, I825), 3I6–34, at 323.

6I. Cooper, *The Red Rover*, I, 86.

62. See 'Textual Commentary', *The Red Rover*, ed. Thomas and Marianne Philbrick (Albany, New York, I99I), 464–5.

63. Scott, I4 January I828, *The Journal*, ed. W.E.K. Anderson (Oxford, I972), 4I5.

64. Sue's Préface was for *Plik et Plok*, joint edition of *Kernok le Pirate* and *El Gitano* (I83I). On *Kernok*, see Georgette Bosset, *Fenimore Cooper et le Roman d'Aventure en France vers I830* (Paris, I928), II7, I2I–2; on the cultural history of the pirate in France, see Gérard Jaeger, *Pirates, flibustiers et corsaires (Histoire & Légendes d'une société d'exception)* (Avignon, I987).

65. See Scott, 2I October I826, *The Journal*, 2I9.

66. Edward Fitzball, *Thirty-Five Years of a Dramatic Author's Life* (2 vols; London, I859), I, I94. On the American and British productions of *The Red*

Rover, see John D. Gordan, '*The Red Rover* Takes the Boards', *American Literature*, 10 (March, 1938), 66–75. Edward Fitzball's rendering, entitled *The Red Rover; or the Mutiny of the Dolphin: A Nautical Drama*, was performed at the Adelphi, London, in 1828 and again in 1831.

67. In a letter Cooper specifies the year 1711 (see Cooper, to Horatio Greenborough, 30 December 1829, *Letters and Journals*, ed. Beard, I, 399).

68. Cooper, *The Water Witch; or, The Skimmer of the Seas* (3 vols; London, 1830), III, 285, 284.

69. Cooper, *The Water Witch*, III, 290.

70. Charles Maturin, *Bertram; or, The Castle of St. Aldobrand; a Tragedy* (London, 1816).

71. J.C. Cross, *Blackbeard; or, The Captive Princess*, in *The Dramatic Works of J.C. Cross* (2 vols; London, 1812), I, sc. i.

72. Cross, *Blackbeard*, Castlist; sc. ii.

73. Cross, *Blackbeard*, Castlist; sc. ii.

74. Cross, *Blackbeard*, sc. iii.

75. Cross, *Blackbeard*, sc. iv; J.C. Cross, *Blackbeard*, with 'a Description of the Costume' (Dunscombe's Edition, London, n.d.), 5.

76. Cross, *Blackbeard* (n.d.), 5; Cross, *Blackbeard* (1812), sc. iv On 'sailor's petticoat trousers', see: Rodger, *The Wooden World*, 64; Earle, *Sailors*, 34.

77. Cross, *Blackbeard* (1812), sc. v.; Cross, *Blackbeard* (n.d.), 5.

78. Cross, *Blackbeard* (1812), sc. v.

79. Cross, *Blackbeard* (1812), sc. vii.

80. Cross, *Blackbeard* (1812), sc. vii.

81. Cross, *Blackbeard* (1812), sc. x; sc. v.

82. Cross, *Blackbeard* (1812), sc. x.

83. Cross, *Blackbeard* (1812), sc. x.

84. Cross, *Blackbeard* (1812), sc. x.

85. Cross, *Blackbeard* (1812), sc. xii.

86. Cross, *Blackbeard* (1812), sc. xii.

87. Cross, *Blackbeard* (1812), sc. xiii.

88. Cross, *Blackbeard* (1812), sc. xiii.

89. Royal Circus playbill, 1798, illustration in Douglas Botting, *The Pirates* (Amsterdam, 1978), 154.

90. James Fenimore Cooper, Preface (1850), in *The Red Rover*, ed. Warren S. Walker (Lincoln, 1963), 9.

91. J.S. Jones, *Captain Kyd or the Wizard of the Sea. A Drama* (New York, n.d.), I, iii, 14.

92. Jones, *Captain Kyd*, I, iii, 14.

93. Jones, *Captain Kyd*, I, iii, 16.

94. See Cordingly, *Life Among the Pirates*, 155. A case of walking the plank was reported as taking place on 18 July 1822, as cited in Earle, *The Pirate Wars*, 222.

95. Jones, *Captain Kyd*, IV, iii, p. 44.

96. My information about productions is derived from the list provided with the 'Cast of Characters' in Jones, *Captain Kyd*.

97. See J.H. Ingraham, *Captain Kyd: The Wizard of the Sea. A Romance* (London, 1842), in *The Novel Newspaper*, III (London, 1839 [sic]).

98. Captain Marryat, *The Pirate and The Three Cutters* (Paris, 1836), 75.

99. The date and place of Irving's acquisition of Grimm's *Deutsche Sagen* are given in Irving's own hand on his copy, according to Reichart, *Washington Irving*, 146. Irving noted in his journal in Paris on 24 December 1823 that he 'read in German work of Grimms' (*Journals and Notebooks*, III, 1819–1827, ed. Walter A. Reichart (Madison, 1970), 261).

100. Jacob and Wilhelm Grimm, *Deutsche Sagen* (2 vols; Berlin, 1816–18), I, 435–6.

101. Washington Irving, *Wolfert's Roost and Other Tales* (London, 1855), 174.

102. Irving, *Wolfert's Roost*, 176.

103. Irving, *Wolfert's Roost*, 169.

104. Irving, *Wolfert's Roost*, 171, 172.

105. Irving, *Wolfert's Roost*, 172.

106. Irving, *Wolfert's Roost*, 173.

107. Irving, *Wolfert's Roost*, 175.

108. Irving, *Wolfert's Roost*, 176.

109. Irving, *Wolfert's Roost*, 177.

110. Irving, *Wolfert's Roost*, 178, 179.

111. Edgar A. Poe, 'The Gold-Bug', *Tales* (London, 1845), 4.

112. Poe, 'The Gold-Bug', 6.

113. Poe, 'The Gold-Bug', 19.

114. Poe, 'The Gold-Bug', 21, 22, 21.

115. Poe, 'The Gold-Bug', 22.

116. Poe, to Philip P. Cooke, 9 August 1846, *The Letters of Edgar Allan Poe*, ed. J.W. Ostrom (2 vols; Cambridge, Massachusetts, 1948), II, 328.

117. Poe, 'The Gold-Bug', 26.

118. Poe, 'The Gold-Bug', 24, 26.

119. Poe, 'The Gold-Bug', 27.

120. Poe, 'The Gold-Bug', 26.

121. See Poe, 'A Few Words on Secret Writing', *Graham's Magazine*, July 1841, reprinted (with addenda) in Poe, *Complete Works*, ed. James A. Harrison (New York, 1902–3), XIV–XV, 114–49.

122. Poe, 'The Gold-Bug', 36.

123. Poe, 'The Gold-Bug', 36.

124. See A.H. Quinn, *Edgar Allan Poe: A Critical Biography* (New York and London, 1942), 129.

125. Poe, 'The Gold-Bug', 2.

126. Poe, 'The Gold-Bug', 1.

127. Poe, 'The Murders in the Rue Morgue' and 'The Purloined Letter', in *Tales* (London, 1845), 121, 202.

128. [Poe], 'Edgar Allan Poe', *Aristidean*, October 1845, in *Essays and Reviews*, ed. G.R. Thompson (New York, 1984), 869.

129. George Graham published Poe's own accounting of this transaction, 'The Late Edgar Allan Poe', *Graham's Magazine*, XXXVI (March 1850), quoted in Quinn, *Edgar Allan Poe*, 343.

130. See Quinn, *Edgar Allen Poe*, 392.

131. See Henry Nash Smith, *Virgin Land: The American West as Symbol and Myth* (London, 1950), 87.

132. [Maturin M. Ballou,] *Fanny Campbell, the Female Pirate Captain* (Boston, 1845), 15.

133. [Ballou,] *Fanny Campbell*, 43.

134. See Ralph Admiri, 'Ballou, the Father of the Dime Novel', *The American Book Collector*, IV (September–October, 1933), 121.

135. See Jay Monaghan, *The Great Rascal: The Life and Adventures of Ned Buntline* (Boston, 1951), 127.

136. E.Z.C. Judson, review of J.H. Ingraham, *The Midshipman*, quoted by Jay Monaghan, *The Great Rascal*, 88.

137. Ned Buntline, *The Black Avenger of the Spanish Main: or, The Fiend of Blood* (Boston, 1847), Preface and illus., facing 12.

138. Buntline, *The Black Avenger*, 17.

139. Buntline, *The Black Avenger*, 36, 58, 40.

140. Buntline, *The Black Avenger*, 28.

141. Buntline, *The Black Avenger*, 17, 21.

142. Buntline, *The Black Avenger*, Preface.

143. Buntline, *The Black Avenger*, Preface.

144. Buntline, *The Black Avenger*, 64.

145. Patten, 'Dime-Novel Days', *Saturday Evening Post*, CCV, 36 (7 March 1931), 33; quoted by Jay Monaghan, *The Great Rascal*, 250.

146. Cooper, *The Deerslayer: A Tale* (3 vols; London, 1841), I, 15.

147. Cooper, *The Deerslayer*, III, 98.

148. Cooper, *The Sea Lions; or, The Lost Sealers* (3 vols; London, 1849), I, 32, 33.

149. Cooper, *The Sea Lions*, I, 96.

150. For the mention of Kidd, see Cooper, *The Sea Lions*, I, 110. For Cooper's knowledge of Kidd and Gardiner's Island, see Cooper, *The History of the Navy of the United States of America* (2 vols; second edition, Philadelphia, 1840), I, 32–3.

151. For the value, see Cooper, *The Sea Lions*, III, 268.

152. Cooper, *The Sea Lions*, III, 263.

153. Cooper, *The Sea Lions*, III, 273, 299.

154. R.M. Ballantyne, *The Coral Island: A Tale of the Pacific Ocean* (London, 1858), 247.

155. Ballantyne, *The Coral Island*, 248, 247.

156. [Charlotte Brontë], *Jane Eyre: An Autobiography* (3 vols; London, 1847), II, 56.

157. Anthony Trollope, *The Eustace Diamonds* (New York, 1872), 29, 195.

158. Douglas Stewart, *The Pirate Queen: or, Captain Kidd and the Treasure* (London, 1867), 18.
159. Stewart, *The Pirate Queen*, 34, 36, 37.
160. Stewart, *The Pirate Queen*, 38.
161. Stewart, *The Pirate Queen*, 39–40.
162. Stewart, *The Pirate Queen*, 142.
163. Stewart, *The Pirate Queen*, 143–4.
164. Stewart, *The Pirate Queen*, 144.
165. Stewart, *The Pirate Queen*, 146.
166. Stewart, *The Pirate Queen*, 158.
167. Stewart, *The Pirate Queen*, 168.
168. Stewart, *The Pirate Queen*, 174.
169. Stewart, *The Pirate Queen*, 191.
170. Stewart, *The Pirate Queen*, 191.
171. Stewart, *The Pirate Queen*, 235.
172. Stewart, *The Pirate Queen*, 242, 243.
173. Stewart, *The Pirate Queen*, 257.
174. Harriet Beecher Stowe, *Oldtown Fireside Stories* (London, 1871), 148, 151.
175. Stowe, *Oldtown Fireside Stories*, 152–3.
176. Stowe, *Oldtown Fireside Stories*, 153.
177. Stowe, *Oldtown Fireside Stories*, 153.
178. Stowe, *Oldtown Fireside Stories*, 157.
179. Stowe, *Oldtown Fireside Stories*, 168, 169.
180. Stowe, *Oldtown Fireside Stories*, 171.
181. Stowe, *Oldtown Fireside Stories*, 171.
182. Stowe, *Oldtown Fireside Stories*, 171.
183. See: Joan D. Hendrick, *Harriet Beecher Stowe: A Life* (New York, 1994), 392; Justin Kaplan, *Mr Clemens and Mark Twain* (Pelican edition, 1970), 278.
184. Mark Twain, *The Adventures of Tom Sawyer* (London, 1876), 86.
185. Twain, *Tom Sawyer*, 131.
186. Twain, *Tom Sawyer*, 131.
187. Twain, *Tom Sawyer*, 137.
188. Twain, *Tom Sawyer*, 160.
189. Twain, *Tom Sawyer*, 232.
190. Twain, *Tom Sawyer*, 232.
191. Twain, *Tom Sawyer*, 232, 232–3.
192. Twain, *Tom Sawyer*, 233.
193. Twain, *Tom Sawyer*, 233.
194. The date of performance derives from John Gordan, 'The Red Rover Takes the Boards', *American Literature*, 10 (March, 1938), 74.
195. Francis C. Burnand, *An Entirely New and Original Burlesque, Being the very latest edition of a Nautical Tradition told by one of the floating population to the Marines who entitled it The Red Rover; or, I Believe You, My Buoy!* (London, n.d.), 5.

196. Burnand, *The Red Rover*, 8.

197. Mark Twain, *Tom Sawyer* (1876), 137.

198. Francis C. Burnand, *The Red Rover*, 8.

199. Burnand, *The Red Rover*, 21.

200. Burnand, *The Red Rover*, 12, 19.

201. Burnand, *The Red Rover*, Dramatic Personae, and 25.

202. Burnand, *The Red Rover*, 26.

203. Burnand, *The Red Rover*, 39.

204. Burnand, *The Red Rover*, 39.

205. Burnand, *The Red Rover*, 39.

206. Burnand, *The Red Rover*, Dramatis Personae.

207. Burnand, *The Red Rover*, 40.

208. Burnand, *The Red Rover*, 40.

209. Burnand, *The Red Rover*, 40.

210. Burnand, *The Red Rover*, 44.

211. Burnand, *The Red Rover*, 44, 33.

212. Burnand, *The Red Rover*, 45.

213. Burnand, *The Red Rover*, 46.

214. Burnand, *The Red Rover*, Dramatis Personae.

215. Burnand, *The Red Rover*, 46.

216. See Michael Ainger, *Gilbert and Sullivan: A Dual Biography* (Oxford, 2002), 60, 354, 149.

217. Gilbert and Sullivan, *The Pirates of Penzance or The Slave of Duty*, in *The Complete Annotated Gilbert and Sullivan*, ed. Ian Bradley (Oxford, 1996), I, 195.

218. Gilbert and Sullivan, *The Pirates of Penzance*, I, 577, 572.

219. Gilbert and Sullivan, *The Pirates of Penzance*, I, 15.

220. Gilbert and Sullivan, *The Pirates of Penzance*, II, 304–5.

221. Gilbert and Sullivan, *The Pirates of Penzance*, II, 333.

222. Gilbert and Sullivan, *The Pirates of Penzance*, II, 402–4.

223. Gilbert and Sullivan, *The Pirates of Penzance*, II, 426–8.

224. Gilbert and Sullivan, *The Pirates of Penzance*, II, 480.

225. Gilbert and Sullivan, *The Pirates of Penzance*, II, 528.

226. Gilbert and Sullivan, *The Pirates of Penzance*, II, 569.

227. Gilbert and Sullivan, *The Pirates of Penzance*, II, 574, 575.

228. Gilbert and Sullivan, *The Pirates of Penzance*, II, 582–3.

CHAPTER VI

1. Robert Louis Stevenson, 'My First Book—*Treasure Island*', *The Idler*, vol. 6 (August, 1894), 5.

2. Stevenson, 'My First Book', 5.

3. Stevenson, 'My First Book', 5–6.

4. Lloyd Osbourne, 'Note', *Treasure Island*, Tusitala Edition, II (London, 1923), xviii.

5. Stevenson, to W.E. Henley, [24 August 1881], *The Letters of Robert Louis Stevenson*, ed. Bradford A. Booth and Ernest Mehew, III (New Haven and London, 1994), 224. Also Stevenson, to W.E. Henley, [late June, 1881], *Letters*, III, 199.

6. Stevenson, to W.E. Henley, [25 August 1881], *Letters*, III, 225.

7. Stevenson, 'My First Book', 7.

8. Stevenson, 'My First Book', 7.

9. Stevenson, to W.E. Henley, [24–5 August 1881], *Letters*, III, 225. For the generic tradition, see Kevin Carpenter, *Desert Isles and Pirate Islands: The Island Theme in Nineteenth-Century English Juvenile Fiction* (Frankfurt am Main, 1984).

10. Stevenson, to W.E. Henley, [*c*.3 July 1881], *Letters*, III, 206.

11. At 18 Stevenson had accompanied his father on a lighthouse inspection voyage to the Orkney and Shetland islands, and already knew that Scott had preceded him and that *The Pirate* had resulted (see Stevenson, to his Mother, 18–19 June 1869, and 20–22 June 1869, *Letters*, I (New Haven and London, 1994), 177, 186–7). See also Stevenson's introductory 'Note', reprinted in *The Scottish Stories and Essays*, ed. Kenneth Gelder (Edinburgh, 1989), 277–80.

12. Stevenson, 'My First Book', 6.

13. [Defoe,] *The Life and Strange Suprizing Adventures of Robinson Crusoe* (London, 1719), 213 (and see 330, where Crusoe 'carry'd on board…my Parrot').

14. Thomas Stevenson, to Stevenson, 26 February 1882, in Paul Maixner, ed., *Robert Louis Stevenson: The Critical Heritage* (London, 1981), 127.

15. Rogers, *A Cruising Voyage*, 125.

16. Stevenson, *Treasure Island*, *Young Folks*, 'Textual Notes', *Treasure Island*, ed. Wendy R. Katz (Edinburgh, 1998), 253; Stevenson, *Treasure Island* (London, 1883), 120, 126; see also Stevenson, to his Father, [early March, 1882], *Letters*, III, 291.

17. Stevenson, 'My First Book', 9.

18. Stevenson, 'My First Book', 6, 7.

19. Stevenson, chapter heading to Chapter I, *Treasure Island*.

20. Stevenson, *Treasure Island*, [vi].

21. See Eric Quayle, *Ballantyne the Brave: A Victorian Writer and his Family* (London, 1967), 217.

22. Stevenson, *Treasure Island*, 2; Charles Kingsley, *At Last: A Christmas in the West Indies* (2 vols; London and New York, 1871), I, 20.

23. Stevenson, to Henley, [25 August 1881], *Letters*, III, 225.

24. Stevenson, to Henley, [early September, 1881], *Letters*, III, 226.

25. Stevenson, *Treasure Island*, 81.

26. *General History of the Pyrates* (second edition, 1724), 27, and *General History* (first edition, 1724), 103. Kip Wagner and L.B. Taylor, *Pieces of Eight: Recovering the Riches of a Lost Spanish Treasure Fleet* (London, 1967), is a

novelized account of adventurous twentieth-century marine archaeology off the east coast of Florida.

27. See *General History* (first edition, 1724), 140.

28. Stevenson, *Records of a Family of Engineers*, in *The Works of Robert Louis Stevenson*, Edinburgh Edition, XVIII (Edinburgh, 1896), 187–389, at 241.

29. Stevenson, *Treasure Island*, 85.

30. *General History* (first edition, 1724), 213.

31. *General History* (first edition, 1724), 213.

32. *General History* (first edition, 1724), 240, 217. At his trial at Cape Corso, Scudamore denied the charges, but was quoted as declaring that he did not want 'to go to Cabo Corso, and be hang'd like Dog' and had no 'mind to go to Cabo Corso, and be hang'd and sun-dry'd' (*A Full and Exact Account, of the Tryal of all the Pyrates lately taken by Captain Ogle, on Board the 'Swallow' Man of War, on the Coast of Guinea* (London, 1723), 36, 35).

33. *A Full and Exact Account*, 53.

34. Stevenson, 'My First Book', 7; and see *General History* (first edition, 1724), 138.

35. Stevenson, to W.E. Henley, [late May, 1883], *Letters*, IV, 129.

36. *General History* (second edition, 1724), 123.

37. Stevenson, *Treasure Island*, 85.

38. *General History* (first edition, 1724), 195, 196.

39. Stevenson's reuse of Israel Hands was noticed in 1943 by Tom Haber, 'Robert Louis Stevenson and Israel Hands', *The English Journal*, 32, 7 (1943), 399. The fullest account of Stevenson's use of the *General History of the Pyrates* is in Harold F. Watson, *Coasts of Treasure Island* (San Antonio, Texas, 1969), 150–6, but Watson consulted an edition of 1932.

40. *General History* (first edition, 1724), 98.

41. *General History* (first edition, 1724), 98.

42. *General History* (first edition, 1724), 99.

43. Two unequivocal textual debts in *Treasure Island* to Johnson's *History* (the name of Ben Gunn and Silver's 'hanged like a dog, and sun-dried') are not to be found in the abridged and reworded version of Johnson's work that was sold with Stevenson's effects in 1914, appended to another eighteenth-century biographical anthology originally by a different author, the combined works ascribed and entitled as: Captain Charles Johnson, *The History of the Lives and Actions of the most famous Highwaymen, Street-Robbers, &c. &c. &c. To which is added, A Genuine Account of the Voyages and Plunders of the most noted Pirates* (Edinburgh, 1814) (sold as Anderson 1914, II, 261: see Roger Swearingen, *The Prose Writings of Robert Louis Stevenson: A Guide* (London, 1980), 69). We do not know what edition of Johnson's work Stevenson used for *Treasure Island*, but we can be sure it was not the edition of 1814 listed in the catalogue of the sale in 1914.

44. Stevenson, to W.E. Henley, [24 August 1881], *Letters*, III, 224.

45. Wycherley, *The Plain-Dealer*, III, 50; Herman Melville, *Moby-Dick*, ed. Hayford and Parker (New York, 1967), 110. Stevenson knew Melville's fictionalized travel books *Typee* and *Omoo*, and called Melville in praise 'a howling cheese', but there are no signs he knew *Moby-Dick* (Stevenson, to Charles Baxter, 6 September 1888, *Letters*, VI (New Haven and London, 1995), 207).

46. On disabled sea-cooks, see, for example, Rodger, *The Wooden World*, 122.

47. Stevenson, *Treasure Island*, 1.

48. Stevenson, *Treasure Island*, 48, 52.

49. On *Treasure Island* and *King Solomon's Mines*, see: Henry Rider Haggard, *The Days of My Life* (2 vols; London, 1926), I, 220; Lilias Rider Haggard, *The Cloak That I Left: A Biography of the Author Henry Rider Haggard K.B.E.* (London, 1951), 121–2.

50. Stevenson, *Treasure Island*, 259.

51. R.L. Stevenson, *The Master of Ballantrae: A Winter's Tale* (London, Paris, etc., 1889), 51.

52. Stevenson, *Treasure Island*, 276.

53. Stevenson, *Treasure Island*, 181, 222.

54. Stevenson, *Treasure Island*, 178.

55. For 'gentlemen of fortune', see, e.g., *Treasure Island* (1883), 87, and *General History of the Pyrates* (first edition, 1724), 163, 203. For 'rules', see, e.g., *Treasure Island* (1883), 239, and *General History* (first edition, 1724), 169–72.

56. Stevenson, 'A Humble Remonstrance', reprinted from *Longman's Magazine* in *Henry James and Robert Louis Stevenson: A Record of Friendship and Criticism*, ed. Janet Adam Smith (London, 1948), 95.

57. Stevenson, *Treasure Island* (1883), 260.

58. Stevenson, *Treasure Island*, 101, 203.

59. Stevenson, *Treasure Island*, 216–17.

60. At a very early stage, on or about 6 September 1881, Stevenson did mention the possibility of 'a sequel', though uncertain as yet of its 'practicability from the storyteller's point of view' (Stevenson, to Alexander H. Japp, [6 September 1881], *Letters*, III, 228).

61. See Stevenson, *Treasure Island*, 87, 291.

62. See: James Henderson's recollection, reprinted in J.A. Hammerton, ed., *Stevensoniana* (Edinburgh, 1907), 60; James Dow, 'Robert Louis Stevenson and the *Young Folks* Reader', in Rosaline Masson, ed., *I Can Remember Robert Louis Stevenson* (Edinburgh and London, 1922), 209.

63. Stevenson, to his Parents, 5 May [1883], *Letters*, IV, 119.

64. J.M. Barrie, *Margaret Ogilvy* (London, 1896), 12.

65. Barrie, *Margaret Ogilvy*, 12.

66. Barrie, *Margaret Ogilvy*, 19.

67. Barrie, *Margaret Ogilvy*, 46.

68. J.M. Barrie, Preface, R.M. Ballantyne, *The Coral Island* (London, 1913), vi.

69. Barrie, Preface, vii.

70. J.M. Barrie, 'The Freedom of Dumfries', M'Connachie and J.M. Barrie, *Speeches by J.M. Barrie* (London, 1938), 83–4.

71. Barrie, *Peter Pan*, IV, in *The Plays*, ed. A.E. Wilson (London, 1942), 558.

72. Barrie, *Peter Pan*, I, 521.

73. For Sylvia's smile, see Dolly Parry, unpublished diary, 1890–1914, quoted by Andrew Birkin, *J.M. Barrie and The Lost Boys* (London, 1979), 51 (and cf. 69) and see also photographs of Sylvia, e.g. 74.

74. The account of Barrie and Sylvia Llewelyn Davies's meeting and conversation is attributed to 'family accounts' by one biographer (Janet Dunbar) and 'family legend' by another (Lisa Chaney), in particular to 'Sylvia's sister-in-law', Margaret Llewelyn Davies, by the first biographer and to 'Peter Llewelyn Davies's wife, Margaret' (Sylvia's daughter-in-law) by a third (Andrew Birkin). (Janet Dunbar, *J.M. Barrie: The Man Behind the Image* (London, 1970), 115; Lisa Chaney, *Hide and Seek with Angels: A Life of J.M. Barrie* (London, 2005), 150; Birkin, *J.M. Barrie and the Lost Boys*, 305.) For Porthos, see George du Maurier, *Peter Ibbetson* (2 vols; London, 1892), I, 162–3.

75. J.M. Barrie, *The Little White Bird* (London, 1902), 142.

76. Barrie, *The Little White Bird*, 149.

77. Barrie, *The Little White Bird*, 217.

78. On classical Pan and his latter-day incarnations (but not Peter Pan), see John Boardman, *The Great God Pan: The Survival of an Image* (London, 1997).

79. 'The Child's Map of Kensington Gardens', frontispiece, *The Little White Bird*.

80. See Birkin, *J.M. Barrie and the Lost Boys*, 79.

81. See Denis Mackail, *The Story of J.M.B.* (London, 1941), 309.

82. Barrie, *The Little White Bird*, 268.

83. Barrie, *The Little White Bird*, 268–9.

84. I quote what Roger Lancelyn Green calls both 'the first draft' and 'the first complete draft', finished 'on 1 March 1904' (Green, *Fifty Years of 'Peter Pan'* (London, 1954), 58, 65), transcribed in *Fifty Years*, 59–65, at 60.

85. Barrie, 'first draft', transcribed in Green, *Fifty Years*, 61.

86. Barrie, 'first draft', transcribed in Green, *Fifty Years*, 61, 63.

87. For the date of the first drafting of *Peter Pan*, see the photograph of the MS page, dated 'November 23 - 1903', in Birkin, *J.M. Barrie and the Lost Boys*, 100.

88. Arthur Llewelyn Davies did, however, request the other copy of *The Boy Castaways* when in a Nursing Home after an operation for a (subsequently fatal) facial cancer (see Birkin, *J.M. Barrie and the Lost Boys*, 138).

89. The chapter headings of *The Boy Castaways* are conveniently reprinted in Green, *Fifty Years*, 24–5.

90. The caption is quoted by Green, *Fifty Years*, 26, who correctly notes that the word 'dog' is ambiguous.

91. J.M. Barrie, 'To the Five: A Dedication', *Peter Pan or The Boy Who Would Not Grow Up*, in *The Plays*, ed. A.E. Wilson (London, 1942), 497.

92. The photograph (with caption) is reproduced in Birkin, *J.M. Barrie and the Lost Boys*, 91.

93. He lived briefly at Guilford Street and then at Grenville Street (see J.M. Barrie, *The Greenwood Hat: A Memoir of James Anon, 1885–1887* (London, 1937), 18, 19).

94. As Peter Hollindale very properly notes in his edition of *Peter Pan*, the name of Peter Pan's island has taken various forms in Barrie's works, as Never Land in the play as published and Neverland in *Peter and Wendy* (1911). (See Peter Hollindale, ed., *Peter Pan and Other Plays* (Oxford World's Classics, 1995), 311, note.)

95. On the naming of Wendy, not a known name before *Peter Pan*, see Barrie, *The Greenwood Hat*, 195. Poor Margaret Henley died as a child, as Barrie noted, 'when she was about five; one might call it a sudden idea that came to her in the middle of her romping' (*The Greenwood Hat*, 197).

96. Barrie, *Peter Pan*, I, 522.

97. In his 'Scenario for a Proposed Film of *Peter Pan*' Barrie stated that the film's fight between pirates and redskins should be 'more realistic' than in the play. 'There it has to be mere pretence, but here we should see real redskin warfare that will be recognised as such by all readers of Fenimore Cooper, etc.'. What is remarkable is that redskin reality is to be recognized by readers of Fenimore Cooper. The redskin 'pretence' of the play is no different from the 'realism' of Fenimore Cooper. (Barrie, 'Scenario', reprinted in Green, *Fifty Years*, 171–218, at 201.)

98. Stevenson, to J.M. Barrie, [early December 1892], *Letters*, VII, 447.

99. Stevenson, *Sydney Morning Herald*, 14 February 1890, reprinted in R.C. Terry, ed., *Robert Louis Stevenson: Interviews and Recollections* (London, 1996), 153.

100. Barrie, *Peter Pan*, II, 526.

101. Barrie, *Peter Pan*, IV, 554.

102. Barrie, *Peter Pan*, II, 526.

103. Barrie, *Peter Pan*, II, 526.

104. Barrie, *Peter Pan*, III, 541.

105. Marguerite Steen [Jane Nicholson], *William Nicholson* (London, 1943), 98.

106. Steen, *William Nicholson*, 98–9.

107. Daphne du Maurier, *Gerald: A Portrait* (London, 1934), 110.

108. A photograph of Gerald du Maurier as Hook can be seen in Birkin, *J.M. Barrie and the Lost Boys*, 110.

109. I am thinking particularly of the evolutionary story told in Freud's *Three Essays on the Theory of Sexuality* (1905), but also of psychoanalysis and even psychology more generally. By 'Romantic ideology', I refer—particularly, by way of a significant sample—to Wordsworth's *The Prelude, or Growth of a Poet's Mind* (1805), a sexless work, a century earlier.

110. Stevenson, to Henley, [25 August 1881], *Letters*, III, 225.

111. I agree with Jacqueline Rose that '*Peter Pan* is a classic in which the problem of the relationship between adult and child is unmistakably at the heart of the matter' (Rose, *The Case of Peter Pan* (London, 1984), 5). For me, however, Freud's *Three Essays on the Theory of Sexuality* is not a textbook of psychological fact any more than is, for example, Wordsworth's *The Prelude*, though both works are Romantic accounts of the 'growth of the mind'.

112. Barrie, *Peter Pan*, IV, 546.

113. Barrie, *Peter Pan*, IV, 550.

114. Barrie, *Peter Pan*, IV, 550.

115. Barrie, *Peter Pan*, III, 539.

116. Barrie, *Peter Pan*, III, 541, 539.

117. Barrie, *Peter Pan*, V, 568.

118. Barrie, *Peter Pan*, V, 574.

119. J.M. Barrie, *When Wendy Grew Up: An Afterthought* (London, 1957), 15.

120. Barrie, *When Wendy*, 31.

121. Barrie, *When Wendy*, 32.

122. For the two latter suggestions, see Birkin, *J.M. Barrie and the Lost Boys*, 105.

123. J.M. Barrie, *Peter and Wendy* (London, n.d. [1911]), 56.

124. Barrie, *Peter and Wendy*, 68.

125. Barrie, *Peter and Wendy*, 69.

126. Barrie, *Peter and Wendy*, 139, 202.

127. Barrie, *Peter and Wendy*, 172.

128. Barrie, *Peter and Wendy*, 227.

129. Barrie, *Peter and Wendy*, 234. See Stevenson, *Treasure Island*, e.g., 96.

130. Barrie, *Peter and Wendy* (1911), 201. See Stevenson, *Treasure Island*, 64.

131. Barrie, *Peter and Wendy*, 203.

132. Barrie, *Peter and Wendy*, 204.

133. Barrie, *Peter and Wendy*, 206.

134. Barrie, *Peter and Wendy*, 210.

135. Barrie, *Peter and Wendy*, 229.

136. Barrie, *Peter and Wendy*, 230.

137. Barrie, *Peter and Wendy*, 233–4.

138. For the dating of the 'Scenario', see Green, *Fifty Years*, 169. The 'Scenario' was unpublished (as well as unfilmed) but is transcribed in Green, *Fifty Years*, 171–218.

139. J.M. Barrie, 'Scenario', in Green, *Fifty Years*, 183.

140. Barrie, 'Scenario', in Green, *Fifty Years*, 196–7.

141. Barrie, 'Scenario', in Green, *Fifty Years*, 197.

142. See Birkin, *J.M. Barrie and the Lost Boys*, 278.

143. J.M. Barrie, 'Captain Hook at Eton', in M'Connachie and J.M. Barrie, *Speeches by J.M. Barrie* (London, 1938), 115–29, at 115.

144. Barrie, 'Captain Hook at Eton', 115.
145. Barrie, 'Captain Hook at Eton', 116.
146. Barrie, 'Captain Hook at Eton', 116.
147. Barrie, 'Captain Hook at Eton', 118.
148. Barrie, 'Captain Hook at Eton', 117.
149. Barrie, 'Captain Hook at Eton', 122.
150. Barrie, 'Captain Hook at Eton', 123.
151. Barrie, 'Captain Hook at Eton', 125.
152. Barrie, 'Captain Hook at Eton', 126.

CHAPTER VII

1. Leslie Baily, *Gilbert and Sullivan and their World* (London, 1973), 63.
2. J.M. Barrie, to R. Golding Bright, 31 October 1912, *Letters of J.M. Barrie*, ed. Viola Meynell (London, 1942), 60.
3. J.M. Barrie, to R. Golding Bright, 4 December 1918, *Letters*, 61.
4. J.M. Barrie, to Lady Cynthia Asquith, 27 April 1921, *Letters*, 189.
5. Nicholas Llewelyn Davies, interview by Andrew Birkin, 1 January 1976, J.M. Barrie website, <http://www.jmbarrie.co.uk>, accessed 14 January 2013.
6. See Roger Lancelyn Green, *Fifty Years of 'Peter Pan'* (London, 1954), 170.
7. Cynthia Asquith, *Portrait of Barrie* (London, 1954), 160.
8. Asquith, *Portrait*, 160.
9. Asquith, *Portrait*, 160.
10. Asquith, *Portrait*, 160.
11. See: Jack Lodge, 'The Career of Herbert Brenon', *Griffithiana*, 57/58, October 1996, 71; Frederick C. Szebin, '*Peter Pan* Escapes Cinematic Neverland', *American Cinematographer*, October 1995, 97–101.
12. J.M. Barrie, to Cynthia Asquith, 14 November 1924, *Letters*, 201.
13. Barrie, to Asquith, 14 November 1924, *Letters*, 201.
14. Barrie, 'Scenario for a Proposed Film of *Peter Pan*', in Green, *Fifty Years*, 171.
15. See Barrie, 'Scenario', 178, 189.
16. See Barrie, 'Scenario', 181, 186.
17. See Barrie, 'Scenario', 194.
18. Barrie, 'Scenario', 195, 196.
19. Barrie, 'Scenario', 182.
20. Barrie, 'Scenario', 172.
21. Barrie, 'Scenario', 183, and see 201.
22. Barrie, 'Scenario', 183.
23. Quotations from *Peter Pan*, screenplay by Willis Goldbeck [and James Barrie], Paramount Picture, 1924.
24. Goldbeck and Barrie, *Peter Pan*.
25. Goldbeck and Barrie, *Peter Pan*.

26. Goldbeck and Barrie, *Peter Pan*.

27. Goldbeck and Barrie, *Peter Pan*.

28. Goldbeck and Barrie, *Peter Pan*.

29. See *Peter Pan*, V, 2, in J.M. Barrie, *The Plays*, ed. A.E. Wilson (London, 1942), 568.

30. Barrie, 'Scenario', 209.

31. Goldbeck and Barrie, *Peter Pan*, and see *Peter Pan*, V, 2, in *The Plays*, 574.

32. Goldbeck and Barrie, *Peter Pan*, and see *Peter Pan*, V, 2, in Barries, *The Plays*, 575; and 'Scenario', 214.

33. See Lodge, 'The Career', 73.

34. See Lodge, 'The Career', 75.

35. *Variety*, 31 December 1924.

36. *Variety*, 31 December 1924.

37. *Variety*, 31 December 1924.

38. '*Peter Pan* as a Film', *The Times*, 15 January 1925.

39. Barrie, to Asquith, 14 November 1924, *Letters*, 201.

40. Llewelyn Davies, interview.

41. I would like to thank Kevin Brownlow for generously lending me a copy of *The Sea Hawk* from his collection of silent films.

42. Rafael Sabatini, *The Sea-Hawk* (London, 1915), 28.

43. Sabatini, *The Sea-Hawk*, 19.

44. Sabatini, *The Sea-Hawk*, 216.

45. Sabatini, *The Sea-Hawk*, 98.

46. Sabatini, *The Sea-Hawk*, 225.

47. *Variety*, 11 June 1924.

48. *Variety*, 11 June 1924.

49. *Variety*, 11 June 1924.

50. Rafael Sabatini, *Captain Blood: His Odyssey* (London, 1922), 162. Sabatini himself cites Morgan and Esquemeling's *Bucaniers* as historical sources for his *Captain Blood* (see Sabatini, 'Historical Fiction', in *What is a Book?*, ed. Dale Warren (New York, 1935), 23–39, at 39).

51. Sabatini, *Captain Blood*, 183, 165.

52. Sabatini, *Captain Blood*, 192.

53. Sabatini, *Captain Blood*, 201.

54. Sabatini, *Captain Blood*, 211.

55. Sabatini, *Captain Blood*, 284.

56. Sabatini, *Captain Blood*, 286.

57. See Maurice Trace, 'Captain Blood', *Screen* 9.5, No. 104, Winter 2001, 7.

58. See Trace, 'Captain Blood', 6.

59. Steve Smith, Jr, 'Pictorial Side of *Captain Blood*', *American Cinematographer*, September 1924, 20.

60. Smith, 'Pictorial Side', 6.

61. Smith, 'Pictorial Side', 20.

62. Smith, 'Pictorial Side', 20.

63. The *Daily Graphic*, quoted in Jeffrey Richards, *Swordsmen of the Screen: From Douglas Fairbanks to Michael York* (London, Henley, and Boston, Massachusetts, 1977), 251.

64. Richards, *Swordsmen*, 6.

65. *Variety*, 10 September 1924.

66. *Variety*, 10 September 1924.

67. *Variety*, 10 September 1924.

68. Albert Smith, quoted in Trace, 'Captain Blood', 7.

69. *The Black Pirate* (1926), dir. Albert Parker.

70. The names of the classic pirate films do not appear in the Index of Thomas Schatz, *The Hollywood Genre: Formulas, Filmmaking and the Studio System* (New York, 1981); neither does the term 'Swashbuckler'.

71. Flavel, 'To all Masters, Mariners, and Seamen', iii.

72. Le Comte de Lautréamont [Isidore Ducasse], *Les Chants de Maldoror* (Paris and Bruxelles, 1874), 31–2, transl. mine.

73. Fairbanks, quoted in Edwin Schallert, 'Yo, Ho, and a Bottle of Rum', *Picture-Play Magazine*, XXIII, 6 (February, 1926), 16.

74. Fairbanks, in Schallert, 'Yo, Ho', 16.

75. Fairbanks, in Schallert, 'Yo, Ho', 16.

76. Fairbanks, in Schallert, 'Yo, Ho', 17.

77. Fairbanks, in Schallert, 'Yo, Ho', 17.

78. Barbara Little, 'The Pirates Are Coming', *Picture-Play Magazine*, XVIII, 1 (March 1923), 46.

79. Little, 'The Pirates', 46–7.

80. Little, 'The Pirates', 47.

81. Little, 'The Pirates', 47.

82. Little, 'The Pirates', 47.

83. Schallert, 'Yo, Ho', 17.

84. John C. Tibbets and James M. Welsh, *His Majesty the American: The Films of Douglas Fairbanks, Sr.* (South Brunswick, New York and London, 1977), 150.

85. See Jeffrey Vance, *Douglas Fairbanks* (Berkeley, Los Angeles and London, 2008), 204.

86. David Michaelis, *W.C. Wyeth: A Biography* (New York, 1998), 274.

87. R.J.B. Denby, 'Doug Shoots Tomorrow's Perfect Film', *Liberty*, 15 May 1926, quoted in Vance, *Douglas Fairbanks*, 209.

88. See Vance, *Douglas Fairbanks*, 213.

89. Fairbanks, quoted in Schallert, 'Yo, Ho', 108.

90. See David Niven, *Bring On the Empty Horses* (London, 1975), 196. Further, more reliable, details are provided by Douglas Fairbanks, Jr, in interview with Jeffrey Vance, cited in Vance, *Douglas Fairbanks*, 217. For a careful analysis of the stunt, see Rudy Behlmer, '*The Black Pirate* Weighs Anchor', *American Cinematographer* (May, 1992), 34–40, at 34.

91. Allene Talmey, *Doug and Mary and Others* (New York, 1927), 35.

92. A story confirmed by Billie Dove, in 1994 interview with Jeffrey Vance, cited in Vance, *Douglas Fairbanks*, 220.
93. *Variety*, quoted in Behlmer, '*The Black Pirate*', 37.
94. Mordaunt Hall, 'Fairbanks's Pirate Film Whimsical and Beautiful', *New York Times*, 14 March 1926, 5, quoted in James Robert Parish and Don E. Stanke, *The Swashbucklers* (New Rochelle, New York, 1976), 64–5, and in Vance, *Douglas Fairbanks*, 222.
95. *Treasure Island* (1934), dir. Victor Fleming.
96. On Beery, see Niven, *Bring On the Empty Horses*, 329.
97. See: Frank Thompson, ed., *Between Action and Cut: Five American Directors* (Metuchen, New Jersey, and London, 1985), 43.
98. See Thompson, ed., *Between Action and Cut*, 43.
99. *Treasure Island* (1934).
100. Victor Fleming, quoted in Frank Thompson, ed. *Between Action and Cut*, 43.
101. See Thompson, ed., *Between Action and Cut*, 43.
102. See: Stevenson, to Charles Scribner, ?20 October 1887, *Letters*, VI, 40 (and see 49); Swearingen, *The Prose Writings*, 63.
103. *Treasure Island* (1934).
104. *Treasure Island* (1934).
105. *Kinematograph Weekly*, no. 1431 (20 September 1934), 19.
106. *Monthly Film Bulletin*, vol. 1, no. 8 (1 September 1934), 70.
107. See Vance, *Douglas Fairbanks*, 13.
108. F. Scott Fitzgerald, *The Last Tycoon* (London, 1949), 43.
109. Fitzgerald, *The Last Tycoon*, 43
110. *Variety*, 29 January 1935 (or 1936?), quoted in John Davis, 'Captain Blood', *The Velvet Light Trap, Review of Cinema* (1971), 1, 27.
111. Warner to Hearst, 20 February 1935, in *Inside Warner Bros. (1935–1951)*, ed. Rudy Behlmer (New York, 1985), 20.
112. Harry Joe Brown to Hal Wallis, 11 June 1935, in *Inside Warner Bros.*, 21.
113. Hal Wallis to Mervyn LeRoy, 11 June 1935, in *Inside Warner Bros.*, 21.
114. See: Errol Flynn, *My Wicked, Wicked Ways* ([1959] London, 1961), 178; Jack L. Warner with Dean Jennings, *My First Hundred Years in Hollywood* (New York and Toronto, 1964), 235.
115. Warner, *My First Hundred Years*, 234, 235.
116. According to cameraman Hal Mohr, interviewed by John Davis, in Davis, 'Captain Blood', 29.
117. See Davis, 'Captain Blood', 30–1.
118. See: Davis, 'Captain Blood', 28; Jeffrey Richards, *Swordsmen*, 253.
119. Wallis to Curtiz, 28 August 1935, in *Inside Warner Bros.*, 23.
120. Wallis to Curtiz, 28 August 1935, in *Inside Warner Bros.*, 23.
121. Wallis to Curtiz, 30 September 1935, in *Inside Warner Bros.*, 24.
122. Wallis to Curtiz, 9 September 1935, in *Inside Warner Bros.*, 24.
123. Rafael Sabatini, *Captain Blood: His Odyssey* (London, 1922), 39, 166.

124. *Captain Blood* (1935).
125. *Captain Blood* (1935).
126. *Captain Blood* (1935).
127. *Film Daily*, undated, quoted in Davis, 'Captain Blood', 31.
128. *Variety*, 1 January 1936.
129. *Variety*, 1 January 1936.
130. See Rudy Behlmer, Introduction to Howard Koch and Seton I. Miller, *The Sea Hawk* (Screenplay), ed. Rudy Behlmer (Madison, Wisconsin, and London, 1982), 14.
131. Words from a popular song, 'Music, Music, Music', sung by Teresa Brewer, topping the charts in 1950.
132. Wallis to Harry Joe Brown, 14 December 1935, quoted in Behlmer, Introduction, 15.
133. Delmer Daves to Rudy Behlmer, 1968, quoted in Behlmer, Introduction, 16.
134. See Ian Hamilton, *Writers in Hollywood 1915–1951* (London, 1991), 115.
135. See Harry Kelsey, *Sir Francis Drake: The Queen's Pirate* (New Haven and London, 1998), 63.
136. See the list, compiled from Warner files, of books used for research by the Warner screen writers, in Behlmer, Introduction, 43.
137. Seton Miller to Walter MacEwen, 18 March 1940, in Behlmer, ed., *Inside Warner Bros.*, 111.
138. See Behlmer, ed., *The Sea Hawk* (Screenplay), note 5, 209.
139. Henry Blanke to Wallis, 6 September 1938, quoted in Rudy Behlmer, Introduction, 19.
140. See Behlmer, Introduction, 20.
141. Seton Miller to Walter MacEwen, 18 March 1940, quoted in Behlmer, ed., *Inside Warner Bros.*, 110.
142. Miller to MacEwen, 18 March 1940, quoted in Behlmer, ed., *Inside Warner Bros.*, 110.
143. Miller to MacEwen, 18 March 1940, quoted in Behlmer, ed., *Inside Warner Bros.*, 111.
144. See Behlmer, Introduction, 26.
145. See Behlmer, Introduction, 37–8 and fig. 2, 44.
146. See Behlmer, Introduction, 29, 37.
147. See Behlmer, Introduction, 36–7.
148. See Behlmer, Introduction, 29, 37.
149. Flynn, *My Wicked, Wicked Ways*, 182.
150. Flynn, *My Wicked, Wicked Ways*, 184.
151. Wallis to Curtiz, quoted in Behlmer, Introduction, 30.
152. Henry Blanke to Wallis, 14 March 1940, in Behlmer, ed., *Inside Warner Bros.*, 109.
153. Wallis to Blanke and Tenny Wright, 3 April 1940, quoted in Behlmer, ed., *Inside Warner Bros*, 36.

154. Frank Mattison to Tenny Wright, *c.* 19 February 1940, quoted in Behlmer, ed., *Inside Warner Bros*, 32.
155. Added scene for British prints of *The Sea Hawk* (1940).
156. *The Sea Hawk* (1940).
157. *The Sea Hawk* (1940).
158. Poster, illustration to documentary, 'The Sea Hawk: Flynn in Action', accompanying *The Sea Hawk* film.
159. See Behlmer, Introduction, 41.

CHAPTER VIII

1. 'Jack (I won't mention his name)', a film producer at Universal, quoted by Richard Brooks, Interview, *Movie*, 12, Spring 1965, 3.
2. Rafael Sabatini, *The Black Swan* (London, 1932), 186.
3. Sabatini, *The Black Swan*, 13, 178.
4. Sabatini, *The Black Swan*, 198.
5. *The Black Swan* (1942).
6. Script of *The Spanish Main*, Reel 2, Section 2B, p. 5, BFI Library, London.
7. Script of *The Spanish Main*, Reel 3, Section 3A, p. 3.
8. Script of *The Spanish Main*, Reel 4, Section 4A, p. 4.
9. Script of *The Spanish Main*, Reel 4, Section 4A, p. 4.
10. Script of *The Spanish Main*, Reel 4, Section 4A, p. 2.
11. Script of *The Spanish Main*, Reel 4, Section 4A, p. 2.
12. *Kinematograph Weekly*, 31 January 1946, 22.
13. *Today's Cinema*, 29 January 1946, 26.
14. *Today's Cinema*, 29 January 1946, 26.
15. *Kinematograph Weekly*, 18 March 1943, 21; E.A. Cunningham, *Motion Picture Herald*, 17 October 1942, 958.
16. Cunningham, *Motion Picture Herald*, 17 October 1942, 958.
17. Maureen O'Hara, with John Nicoletti, *'Tis Herself: An Autobiography* ([1997] London, 2005), 214; and see Flynn, *My Wicked, Wicked Ways*, 214.
18. Douglas Stewart, *The Pirate Queen; or, Captain Kidd and the Treasure* (London, 1867), 38.
19. Stewart, *The Pirate Queen*, 39–40.
20. Bret Harte, *The Queen of the Pirate Isle* (1886), 14.
21. Richard Hughes, *A High Wind in Jamaica* (London, 1929), 145–6.
22. Gustave Alaux, 'La Régate du capitaine Borgnefesse', *Bulletin du Cercle nautique de Chatou*, December 1935, quoted in Gérard Jaeger, *Pirates, flibustiers et corsaires* (Avignon, 1987), 157.
23. Charles de La Roncière, *Le Flibustier mysterieux: Histoire d'un trésor caché* (Paris, 1934), 109.
24. Robert Desnos, 'Lament for the Pirate' (unpublished?), quoted in Jaeger, *Pirates*, 157.

25. Desnos, 'Lament', quoted in Jaeger, *Pirates*, 158, translation mine.
26. Henri Musnik, *Les Femmes pirates: Aventures et légendes de la mer* (Paris, 1934), 19.
27. See Musnik, *Les Femmes pirates*, 23–56.
28. James Bridie and Claude Gurney, *Mary Read* (London, 1935), III, iii, p. 75.
29. Bridie and Gurney, *Mary Read*, III, iii, p. 75.
30. Bridie and Gurney, *Mary Read*, III, iii, p. 75.
31. Bridie and Gurney, *Mary Read*, III, iii, p. 75.
32. Frank Shay, *Mary Read: The Pirate Wench* (London, 1934), 149.
33. For Skinner, see *General History* (first edition, 1724), 135.
34. Shay, *Mary Read*, 152.
35. Shay, *Mary Read*, 162, 189, 236.
36. Shay, *Mary Read*, 285, 286.
37. Philip Rush, *Mary Read, Buccaneer* (London and New York, 1945), Note, 6.
38. Shay, *Mary Read*, 51; Rush, *Mary Read*, 43.
39. Rush, *Mary Read*, 97.
40. Rush, *Mary Read*, 97.
41. Rush, *Mary Read*, 97.
42. Rush, *Mary Read*, 104.
43. Rush, *Mary Read*, 128.
44. Rush, *Mary Read*, 146, 163, 128.
45. Rush, *Mary Read*, 134.
46. Rush, *Mary Read*, 170.
47. Rush, *Mary Read*, 170–1.
48. Rush, *Mary Read*, 171.
49. Rush, *Mary Read*, 172.
50. Rush, *Mary Read*, 172.
51. Rush, *Mary Read*, 176.
52. Rush, *Mary Read*, 192, 198.
53. Hergé, *Le Trésor de Rackham le Rouge* ([1945] 1973), 62.
54. [Gustave Alaux,] *Cahiers de Louis-Adhémar-Timothée Le Golif, dit Borgnefesse* (Paris, 1952), 55.
55. See Jenifer G. Marx, 'Brethren of the Coast', in David Cordingly, ed., *Pirates: An Illustrated History* (London, 1996), 37. Jenifer Marx gives a false (and hoaxing?) attribution for Le Golif to P. Labat, *Memoirs 1693–1705* (1734, reprinted 1971), 35.
56. Manuel Schonhorn, Commentary and Notes, *General History* (London, 1999), 674; John Carlova, *Mistress of the Seas* (New York, 1964), Introduction, 11.
57. Carlova, *Mistress of the Seas*, 11.
58. Carlova, *Mistress of the Seas*, 13.
59. Carlova, *Mistress of the Seas*, 97, 234, 163, 234.

60. Carlova, *Mistress of the Seas*, 82, 80.
61. Carlova, *Mistress of the Seas*, 87.
62. Carlova, *Mistress of the Seas*, 179.
63. Carlova, *Mistress of the Seas*, 179.
64. Carlova, *Mistress of the Seas*, 179.
65. Carlova, *Mistress of the Seas*, 180.
66. Carlova, *Mistress of the Seas*, 178.
67. Carlova, *Mistress of the Seas*, 184–5.
68. Steve Gooch, Prefatorial remarks, *The Women Pirates Ann Bonney and Mary Read* (London, 1978).
69. Gooch, Prefatorial remarks, *The Women Pirates*.
70. Carlova, *Mistress of the Seas*, 47, 57.
71. Gooch, *The Women Pirates*, 57.
72. Gooch, *The Women Pirates*, 39.
73. Gooch, *The Women Pirates*, 45.
74. Gooch, *The Women Pirates*, 64, 72.
75. Gooch, *The Women Pirates*, 73.
76. George MacDonald Fraser, *The Pyrates* (London, Glasgow, etc., 1983), 15, 69, 16, 56.
77. Fraser, *The Pyrates*, 17, 23, 295, 51.
78. Fraser, *The Pyrates*, 192, 82, 95.
79. Robert Desnos, 'Lament', quoted in Jaeger, *Pirates*, 158.
80. Fraser, *The Pyrates*, 142.
81. Fraser, *The Pyrates*, 308–9.
82. Fraser, *The Pyrates*, 308.
83. Fraser, *The Pyrates*, 301.
84. Fraser, *The Pyrates*, 309.
85. Fraser, *The Pyrates*, 309–10.
86. Fraser, *The Pyrates*, 319, 360, 403.
87. Fraser, Afterthought, *The Pyrates*, 406.
88. Fraser, Afterthought, *The Pyrates*, 408.
89. Pamela Jekel, *Sea Star: The Private Life of Anne Bonny, Pirate Queen* (New York, 1983), 62.
90. Jekel, *Sea Star*, 303, 277, 280.
91. Jekel, *Sea Star*, 283.
92. Jekel, *Sea Star*, 283.
93. Jekel, *Sea Star*, 283.
94. Jekel, *Sea Star*, 283.
95. Jekel, *Sea Star*, 331–2.
96. Jekel, Acknowlegements, *Sea Star*, 390.
97. Mace Taxco, Preface, *Anne Bonney and Mary Read: Women Buccaneers* (Albuquerque, New Mexico, 1998), vi.
98. Taxco, Preface, *Anne Bonney and Mary Read*, vi.
99. Taxco, *Anne Bonney and Mary Read*, 260.

100. Taxco, *Anne Bonney and Mary Read*, 261–2.
101. Taxco, *Anne Bonney and Mary Read*, 150.
102. Taxco, *Anne Bonney and Mary Read*, 304.
103. Taxco, *Anne Bonney and Mary Read*, 304.
104. Taxco, *Anne Bonney and Mary Read*, 321.
105. Taxco, *Anne Bonney and Mary Read*, 347. For William Cormac, see: Carlova, *Mistress of the Seas*, 17; Jekel, *Sea Star*, 5.
106. Taxco, *Anne Bonney and Mary Read*, 341.
107. Taxco, *Anne Bonney and Mary Read*, 348, 335, 362.
108. See Taxco, *Anne Bonney and Mary Read*, 30.
109. Jacqueline Church Simonds, *Captain Mary, Buccaneer* (Simsbury, Connecticut, 2000), 26, 178, 43.
110. Simonds, *Captain Mary*, 57, 58.
111. Simonds, *Captain Mary*, 202.
112. Simonds, *Captain Mary*, 280.
113. For a firsthand account of the mundane 'misery and extremities' of ordinary shipboard conditions, see Barlow, *Journal*, I, 60–1. For shipboard circumstances, see also Rodger, *The Wooden World*, 60–8, and Earle, *Sailors*, 85–6.
114. *The Pirates Own Book, or Authentic Narratives of the Lives, Exploits and Executions of the Most Celebrated Sea Robbers* (Philadelphia, 1837), 387.
115. Philip Gosse, *The History of Piracy* (London and New York, 1932), 204, 202, 203.
116. See Carlova, *Mistress of the Seas*, 96.
117. Gosse, *The History of Piracy*, 203, 205. Gosse's apparent misreadings of the *General History* in his *History of Piracy* are baffling as he had previously produced an edition of the *General History*, a reprint of the third edition of 1725, entitled *A General History of the Pirates*, ed. Philip Gosse (Kensington, London, 1925), and *A Bibliography of the Works of Capt. Charles Johnson* (London, 1927).
118. John Robert Moore, *Defoe in the Pillory and Other Studies* (Bloomington, Indiana, 1939), 127.
119. Moore, *Defoe in the Pillory*, 188.
120. See Daniel Defoe, *A General History of the Pyrates*, ed. Manuel Schonhorn (London, 1999) and—on Moore's arguments about the work—see Furbank and Owens, *The Canonisation*, 100–9.
121. See Linda Grant De Pauw, *Seafaring Women* (Boston, 1982), 57–9, 33. Cf. Carlova, *Mistress of the Seas*, 17, 18.
122. De Pauw, *Seafaring Women*, 33.
123. See Moore, *Defoe*, 127 and 235, n. 4.
124. Cordingly, *Life Among the Pirates*, 74.
125. Cordingly, *Life Among the Pirates*, 76, and see 75.
126. See Julie Wheelwright, 'Tars, tarts and swashbucklers', in *Bold in Her Breeches: Women Pirates Across the Ages*, ed. Jo Stanley (London, 1995), 180, 184.

127. Ulrike Klausmann and Marion Meinzerin, *Women Pirates and the Politics of the Jolly Roger*, transl. Austin and Levis (Montreal, etc., 1997), 192.
128. Klausmann and Meinzerin, *Women Pirates*, 192.
129. Klausmann and Meinzerin, *Women Pirates*, 192.
130. See Carlova, *Mistress of the Seas*, 81 and 78.
131. David Cordingly, *Heroines and Harlots:Women at Sea in the Great Age of Sail* (London, 2001), 89.
132. Cordingly, *Heroines and Harlots*, 92.
133. Cordingly, *Heroines and Harlots*, 92–3.
134. Cordingly, *Heroines and Harlots*, 93.
135. Cordingly, *Heroines and Harlots*, 96.
136. Cordingly, *Heroines and Harlots*, 97.
137. Cordingly, *Heroines and Harlots*, note 33, p. 298.
138. See Carlova, *Mistress of the Seas*, 17, and also, for example, Elizabeth Garrett (aka James L. Nelson), *The Sweet Trade* (New York, 2001), in which Anne Bonny's mother and father are William Cormac and Peg Brennan, the names and characters invented by Carlova.
139. See Gilles Lapouge, *Pirates, boucaniers, flibustiers* (Paris, 2002), 160–5.
140. David Cordingly, 'Bonny, Anne', *The Oxford Dictionary of National Biography* (2004).
141. Rediker, *Villains*, 103–4.
142. Rediker, *Villains*, 111–12.
143. Rediker, *Villains*, 107.
144. See Rediker, *Villains*, 115–17.
145. Rediker, *Villains*, 118.
146. Rediker, *Villains*, 121.
147. John Gay, *Polly: An Opera* (London, 1729), I, xiv.
148. J.M. Barrie, *Peter Pan*, IV, 558, in *The Plays*, ed. A.E. Wilson (London, 1942).
149. The sail-splitting stunt is in *Pirates of the Caribbean: Dead Man's Chest* (2006). For the Disney history, see, e.g., Jason Surrell, *Pirates of the Caribbean: From the Magic Kingdom to the Movies* (New York, 2005).

Works Cited in Notes

ABBREVIATIONS
ADM: Admiralty Papers
BFI: British Film Institute
CS: Colonial Papers
CSP, CS, A&WI: Calendar of State Papers, Colonial Series, America and West Indies
HCA: High Court of Admiralty
PRO: Public Record Office (The National Archives)
SP: State Papers

Account of the Conduct and Proceedings of the Late John Gow alias Smith, An (London, [1725]).

Account of the Behaviour, Dying Speeches, and Execution of... William May, John Sparcks, William Bishop, James Lewis, and Adam Foreseith, for Robbery, Piracy and Felony; at the Execution-Dock: On Wednesday the 25th of November, 1696, An (London, 1696).

Admiri, Ralph, 'Ballou, the Father of the Dime Novel', The American Book Collector, IV (September–October, 1933), 121–9.

Ainger, Michael, Gilbert and Sullivan: A Dual Biography (Oxford, 2002).

[Alaux, Gustave,] Cahiers de Louis-Adhémar-Timothée Le Golif, dit Borgnefesse (Paris, 1952).

Alderson, Nicholas, Benjamine Franks, Jonathan Fredway, Depositions, MSS, British Library, E/3/53, fos. 147, 153, 200v.

Arraignment, Tryal, and Condemnation of Captain William Kidd, for Murther and Piracy, upon Six several Indictments, at the Admiralty-Sessions, held... at the Old-Baily, on Thursday the 8th. and Friday the 9th. of May, 1701. Who, upon full Evidence, was found Guilty, receiv'd Sentence, and was accordingly Executed at Execution-Dock, May the 23d., The (London, 1701).

'Asiatic campaigns of Thut-mose III, The', in Ancient Near Eastern Texts, ed. James B. Pritchard (Princeton, 1955).

Asquith, Cynthia, Portrait of Barrie (London, 1954).

Atlas Maritimus (London, 1728).

Augustine, The City of God, transl. Henry Bettenson (Penguin edition, 1972).

[Avory, Thomas,] The Life of John Buncle (2 vols; London, 1765).

Baer, Joel H., '"Captain John Avery" and the Anatomy of a Mutiny', Eighteenth-Century Life, 18 (1994), 1–26.

Baily, Leslie, *Gilbert and Sullivan and their World* (London, 1973).

Baldridge, Adam, Deposition, 1699, in J.F. Jameson, ed., *Privateering and Piracy* (New York, 1923), 180–7.

Ballantyne, John, note, in Scott, *Letters* (1932–37),VI, 427, n.1.

Ballantyne, R.M., *The Coral Island: A Tale of the Pacific Ocean* (London, 1858).

[Ballou, Maturin M.,] *Fanny Campbell, the Female Pirate Captain* (Boston, 1845).

Barlow, Edward, *Journal of his Life at Sea in King's Ships, East and West Indiamen and other Merchantmen from 1659 to 1703*, transcribed by Basil Lubbock (2 vols; London, 1934).

Barrie, J.M., 'Captain Hook at Eton', in M'Connachie and J.M. Barrie, *The Speeches by J.M. Barrie* (London, 1938).

Barrie, J.M., Preface, R.M. Ballantyne, *The Coral Island* (London, 1913).

Barrie, J.M., 'The Freedom of Dumfries', in M'Connachie and J.M. Barrie, *Speeches by J.M. Barrie* (London, 1938).

Barrie, J.M., *The Greenwood Hat: A Memoir of James Anon, 1885–1887* (London, 1937).

Barrie, J.M., *The Letters of J.M. Barrie*, ed. Viola Meynell (London, 1942).

Barrie, J.M., *The Little White Bird* (London, 1902).

Barrie, J.M., *Margaret Ogilvy* (London, 1896).

Barrie, J.M., *Peter and Wendy* (London, n.d. [1911]).

Barrie, J.M., *Peter Pan or The Boy Who Would Not Grow Up*, in *The Plays*, ed. A.E. Wilson (London, 1942).

Barrie, J.M., 'Scenario for a Proposed Film of *Peter Pan*', in Roger Lancelyn Green, *Fifty Years of 'Peter Pan'* (London, 1954), 171–218.

Barrie, J.M., *When Wendy Grew Up: An Afterthought* (London, 1957).

Basse, Jeremiah, to William Popple, 9 June 1699, *CSP, CS, A&WI, 1699*, ed. Cecil Headlam (London, 1908), 280–1.

Beattie, Stuart, '*Pirates of the Caribbean*: The True Story', Channel 5, UK, 29 May 2011.

Beaumont, Francis, and John Fletcher, *The Double Marriage*, in *Comedies and Tragedies* (London, 1647).

Behlmer, Rudy, '*The Black Pirate* Weighs Anchor', *American Cinematographer* (May, 1992), 34–40.

Behlmer, Rudy, ed., *Inside Warner Bros. (1935–1951)* (New York, 1985).

Behlmer, Rudy, Introduction to Howard Koch and Seton I. Miller, *The Sea Hawk* (Screenplay), ed. Rudy Behlmer (Madison, Wisconsin, and London, 1987).

Belbin, James, Examination, 2 April 1725, HCA, 1/55, fo. 107, PRO.

Bellomont, Governor the Earl of, to the Board of Trade, Boston, 8 July 1699, CO 5/860, PRO, and in J.F. Jameson, ed., *Privateering and Piracy* (New York, 1923), 213–18.

Bellomont, Lord, to the Board of Trade, 26 July 1699, CO, 5/860, PRO, and in J.F. Jameson, ed., *Privateering and Piracy* (New York, 1923), 224–32.

Bellomont, Lord, to the Board of Trade, Boston, 29 November 1699, CO, 5/861, PRO, and in J.F. Jameson, ed., *Privateering and Piracy* (New York, 1923), 237–44.

Bellomont, Lord, to the Council of Trade, Boston, 25 May 1700, *CSP, CS, A&WI, 1700*, ed. Cecil Headlam (London, 1910), 269.

Bellomont, Lord, to the Council of Trade and Plantations, 22 July 1699, *CSP, CS, A&WI, 1699*, ed. Cecil Headlam (London, 1908), 360–1.

Bellomont, Lord, to the Council of Trade and Plantations, 24 October 1699, CO 5/860, PRO.

Bellomont, Lord, to the Council of Trade and Plantations, Boston, 24 August 1699, *CSP, CS, A&WI, 1699*, ed. Cecil Headlam (London, 1908).

Bellomont, Lord, to the Council of Trade and Plantations, Boston, 26 July 1699, in *CSP, CS, A&WI, 1699*, ed. Cecil Headlam (London, 1908), 374.

Bernardin de Saint-Pierre, Jacques-Henri, *Voyage à l'Isle de France, à l'Isle de Bourbon* (2 vols; Amsterdam, 1773).

Besneck, John, Peter Cornelian, and John Eaton, testimonies, *The Tryals of Captain John Rackam* (Jamaica, 1721).

Biddulph, John, *The Pirates of Malabar and An Englishwoman in India Two Hundred Years Ago* (London, 1907).

Birkin, Andrew, *J.M. Barrie and the Lost Boys* (London, 1979).

Black, Clinton V., *Pirates of the West Indies* (Cambridge, 1989).

Boardman, John, *The Great God Pan: The Survival of an Image* (London, 1997).

Boccaccio, Giovanni, *Il Decameron*, ed. Aldo Rossi (Bologna, 1977).

Bonner, Willard, *Pirate Laureate: The Life and Legends of Captain Kidd* (New Brunswick, 1947).

Bosset, Georgette, *Fenimore Cooper et le Roman d'Aventure en France vers 1830* (Paris, 1928).

Bostock, Henry, Master of the sloop *Margaret*, Deposition, 19 December 1717, enclosure with Governor Hamilton, to the Council of Trade and Plantations, in *CSP, CS, A&WI, August 1717–December 1718*, ed. Cecil Headlam (London, 1930), 150.

Boston News-Letter, The: 23 February to 2 March 1719; 4 November to 11 November 1719; 18 July to 25 July 1723; 25 July to 1 August 1723.

Boswell, James, *Journal of a Tour to the Hebrides*, ed. F.A. Pottle and C.H. Bennett (New York, 1936).

Botting, Douglas, *The Pirates* (Amsterdam, 1978).

Bradinham, Robert, Examination, 25 April 1701, HCA, 1/15, PRO.

Bradinham, Robert, Examination, *CSP, CS, A&WI, 1700*, ed. Cecil Headlam (London, 1910), 277.

Bradinham, Robert, testimony, *The Arraignment, Tryal, and Condemnation of Captain William Kidd* (London, 1701).

Brathwait, Richard, 'A Sayler', *Whimzies: Or, a New Cast of Characters* [1631], in *A Critical Edition of Richard Brathwait's 'Whimzies'*, ed. Allen H. Lanner (New York and London, 1991), 213–17.

Bridie, James, and Claude Gurney, *Mary Read* (London, 1935).

[Brontë, Charlotte,] *Jane Eyre: An Autobiography* (3 vols; London, 1847).

Brooke, Henry, to Col. Quary, Port Lewis, 12 November 1703, *CSP, CS, A&WI, 1702–3*, ed. Cecil Headlam (London, 1913), 741–4.

Brooks, Richard, Interview, *Movie*, 12, Spring 1965.

Brown, Mervyn, *Madagascar Rediscovered: A History from Early Times to Independence* (Hamden, Connecticut, 1979).

Brownlow, Kevin, *The Parade's Gone By* (London, 1968).

Buckmaster, Edward, Examination, 6 June 1699, in J.F. Jameson, ed., *Privateering and Piracy* (New York, 1923), 197–200.

Bucquoy, Jacob de, *Zestien Jaarige reize naa de Indien* [1744], transl. into French and published in part in Alfred and Guillaume Grandidier, *Collection des ouvrages anciens concernant Madagascar* (Paris, 1907),V, 103–39.

Buntline, Ned, *The Black Avenger of the Spanish Main: or, The Fiend of Blood* (Boston, 1847).

Burg, B.R., *Sodomy and the Pirate Tradition* (New York and London, 1984).

Burgess, Samuel, Deposition, 3 May 1698, *CSP, CS, A&WI, 27 October 1697–31 December 1698*, ed. J.W. Fortescue (London, 1905), 227–8.

Burgess, Samuel, HCA, 1/98, Pt.1, fo. 50, PRO.

Burnand, Francis C., *An Entirely New and Original Burlesque, Being the very latest edition of a Nautical Tradition told by one of the floating population to the Marines who entitled it The Red Rover; or, I Believe You, My Buoy!* (London, n.d.).

Byron, George Gordon, *The Corsair*, in *Complete Poetical Works*, ed. Jerome McGann, III (Oxford, 1981).

Byron, George Gordon, *Don Juan*, in *Complete Poetical Works*, ed. Jerome McGann,V (Oxford, 1986).

Byron, George Gordon, *The Corsair, a Tale* (London, 1814).

Byron, George Gordon, to Thomas Moore, 3 March 1814, *Letters and Journals*, ed. Leslie Marchand, IV (London, 1975).

Byron, William, *Cervantes: A Biography* (London, 1979).

'Captain Kid's Farewel to the Seas', in J.F. Jameson, ed., *Privateering and Piracy* (New York 1923), 253–7.

Carlova, John, *Mistress of the Seas* (New York, 1964).

Carpenter, Kevin, *Desert Isles and Pirate Islands: The Island Theme in Nineteenth-Century Juvenile Fiction* (Frankfurt am Main, 1984).

Casson, Lionel, *Ships and Seafaring in Ancient Times* (London, 1994).

Cervantes Saavedra, Miguel de, *El Ingenioso Hidalgo Don Quixote de la Mancha* (Lisboa, 1695).

Chandler, Frank W., *The Literature of Roguery* (2 vols; London, 1907).

Chaney, Lisa, *Hide and Seek with Angels: A Life of J.M. Barrie* (London, 2005).

Charlevoix, Pierre-Francois-Xavier de, *Histoire de l'Isle Espagnole ou de S. Domingue* (2 vols; Paris, 1730).

Cicero, *De officiis* (Loeb edition, 1913).

Cicero, *De re publica* (Loeb edition, 1988).

Clerke, Jo., 'The Marshalls farther Account of Charges', ADM, 1/3666, fos. 210–11, PRO.

[Cochrane,] *Catalogue of the Library at Abbotsford* (Edinburgh, 1838).

Constable, Archibald, to Scott, 25 December 1820, *The Letters of Walter Scott*, ed. H.J.C. Grierson (12 vols; London, 1932–7),VII, 12, n. 2.

Cooper, James Fenimore, *The Deerslayer: A Tale* (3 vols; London, 1841).

Cooper, James Fenimore, *The History of the Navy of the United States of America* (2 vols; second edition, Philadelphia, 1840).

Cooper, James Fenimore, *The Letters and Journals of James Fenimore Cooper*, ed. J.F. Beard (6 vols; Cambridge, MA, 1960–8).

Cooper, James Fenimore, Preface, *The Pilot; A Tale of the Sea* (2 vols; New York, 1823).

Cooper, James Fenimore, 1849 Preface to *The Pilot*, ed. Kay Seymour House (Albany, New York, 1986).

Cooper, James Fenimore, Preface (1850), in *The Red Rover*, ed. Warren S. Walker (Lincoln, 1963).

Cooper, James Fenimore, *The Red Rover, a Tale* (3 vols; Paris, 1827).

Cooper, James Fenimore, *The Sea Lions; or, The Lost Sealers* (3 vols; London, 1849).

Cooper, James Fenimore, *The Water Witch; or, The Skimmer of the Seas* (3 vols; London, 1830).

Cooper, Susan Fenimore, *The Cooper Gallery; or, Pages and Pictures from the Writings of James Fenimore Cooper, with Notes* (New York, 1865).

Cooper, Susan Fenimore, 'Small Family Memories', in *Correspondence of James Fenimore Cooper*, ed. James Fenimore Cooper (2 vols; New Haven, 1922), I, 52–3.

Cordingly, David, 'Bonny, Anne', *The Oxford Dictionary of National Biography* (Oxford, 2004).

Cordingly, David, *Heroines and Harlots: Women at Sea in the Great Age of Sail* (London, 2001).

Cordingly, David, *Life Among the Pirates: The Romance and the Reality* (London, 1995).

Cordingly, David, 'Read, Mary', *The Oxford Dictionary of National Biography* (Oxford, 2004).

Council of Trade and Plantations, to Mr Secretary Vernon, 13 January 1698, *CSP, CS, A&WI, 27 October 1697–31 December 1698*, ed. J.W. Fortescue (London, 1905), 88.

Council of Trade and Plantations, to Mr Secretary Vernon, 26 February 1698, *CSP, CS, A&WI, 27 October 1697–31 December 1698*, ed. J.W. Fortescue (London, 1905), 121.

Courbin, Alain, *Le Territoire du vide: L'Occident et le désir du rivage 1750–1840* (Paris, 1988).

Court, Thomas, 'A Naval Diary', *Transactions of the Cumberland and Westmoreland Antiquarian and Archaeological Society*, N.S. XXXVIII (1938).

Craton, Michael, *A History of the Bahamas* (London, 1962).

Creagh, David, testimony, *The Tryals of Joseph Dawson, Edward Forseith,* [etc.]. *For several Piracies and Robberies by them committed, in the Company of Every, the Grand Pirate* (London, 1696).

Crockett, W.S., *The Sir Walter Scott Originals* (Edinburgh, 1912).

Cross, J.C., *Blackbeard; or, The Captive Princess,* in *The Dramatic Works of J.C. Cross* (2 vols; London, 1812).

Cross, J.C., *Blackbeard,* with 'a Description of the Costume' (Dunscombe's Edition, London, n.d.).

Culliford, Robert, at Doctors' Commons, June 1700, in Harold T. Wilkins, *Captain Kidd and his Skeleton Island* (London, Toronto, etc., 1935), 77–8.

Culliford, Robert, 'Examination of Captain Robert Collover Prisoner in Newgate', 2 October 1701, ADM, 1/3666, fos. 255–6, PRO.

Culliford, Robert, 'Peticion of Robt. Cullover', HCA, 1/15, PRO.

Cunningham, E.A., *Motion Picture Herald,* 17 October 1942.

Cuthbert, William, Narrative, *CSP, CS, A&WI, 1699,* ed. Cecil Headlam (London, 1908), 373–4.

Daborn, Robert, *A Christian turn'd Turke: or, The Tragicall Lives and Deaths of the two famous Pyrates, Ward and Dansiger* (London, 1612).

Daily Journal, The: 27 May 1725; 9 June 1725; 10 June 1725; 11 June 1725.

Daily Post, The: 13 March 1725; 27 May 1725; 10 June 1725; 11 June 1725; 12 June 1725; 1 July 1725.

Dampier, William, *A New Voyage Round the World* (London, 1697).

Dann, John, testimony, *The Tryals of Joseph Dawson* [etc.] (London, 1696).

Dann, John, Examination, 3 August 1696, in J.F. Jameson, ed., *Privateering and Piracy* (New York, 1923), 165–71.

Das, Harihar, *The Norris Embassy to Aurangzeb (1699–1702)* (Calcutta, 1959).

Davis, John, 'Captain Blood', *The Velvet Light Trap, Review of Cinema* (1971), 1.

Davis, William C., *The Pirates Lafitte: The Treacherous World of the Corsairs of the Gulf* (Orlando, etc., 2005).

De Pauw, Linda Grant, *Seafaring Women* (Boston, 1982).

de Souza, Philip, *Piracy in the Graeco-Roman World* (Cambridge, 1999).

[Defoe, Daniel,] *The Life and Strange Surprizing Adventures of Robinson Crusoe* (London, 1719).

[Defoe, Daniel,] *The Life, Adventures, and Pyracies, of the Famous Captain Singleton* (London, 1720).

[Defoe, Daniel,] *Weekly Journal or Saturday's Post,* Saturday, 23 May 1724.

[Defoe, Daniel,] *A New Voyage Round the World, by a Course never sailed before* (London, 1725).

[Defoe, Daniel,] 'A Review of the State of the British Nation', 18 October 1707, in Defoe's *Review,* ed. A.W. Secord, Facsimile Book 10 (New York, 1938), vol. IV, no. 107.

Dekker, Rudolf, and Lotte Van de Pol, *The Tradition of Transvestism in early Modern Europe,* transl. (London, 1989).

Dennis, John, 'To the Master of the Revels. Writ upon the first acting of a Play call'd *the Successful Pyrate*', *The Critical Works*, ed. E.N. Hooker (2 vols; Baltimore, 1939–43), II.

Deschamps, Hubert, *Les Pirates à Madagascar* ([1949] Paris, 1972).

Dessen, Magnus, Statement, HCA, 1/18, 11, PRO.

Dibdin, Thomas, *The Pirate: A Melodramatic Romance, taken from the Novel of that Name* (London, 1822).

Dibdin, Thomas, *The Reminiscences of Thomas Dibdin* (2 vols; London, 1827).

Doh, Herman, *A Critical Edition of 'Fortune by Land and Sea'* (New York and London, 1980).

Dow, James, 'Robert Louis Stevenson and the *Young Folks* Reader', in Rosaline Masson, ed., *I Can Remember Robert Louis Stevenson* (Edinburgh and London, 1922), 206–9.

Downing, Clement, *A Compendious History of the Indian Wars . . . Also the Transactions of Men of War under Commodore Matthews, sent to the East-Indies to suppress the Pyrates . . . With an Account of the Life and Actions of John Plantain, a notorious Pyrate at Madagascar* (London, 1737).

Drury, Robert, *Madagascar; or Robert Drury's Journal, During Fifteen Years Captivity on that Island* (London, 1729).

du Maurier, Daphne, *Gerald: A Portrait* (London, 1934).

du Maurier, George, *Peter Ibbetson* (2 vols; London, 1892).

Dunbar, Janet, *J.M. Barrie: The Man Behind the Image* (London, 1970).

Dunmore, John, *Monsieur Baret* (Auckland, 2002).

[Duval, François,] *Lettres curieuses sur divers sujets* [1725], reprinted in part in Albert Lougnon, *Sous le signe de la tortue: Voyages anciens à l'Ile Bourbon (1611–1725)* (Paris, 1958), 167ff.

Earle, Peter, *The Sack of Panamá* (London, 1981).

Earle, Peter, *Sailors: English Merchant Seamen 1650–1775* (London, 1998).

Earle, Peter, *The Pirate Wars* (London, 2003).

East India Company, Letter from President and Council, Surat, 21 April 1697, Abstract, MS, British Library, E/3/53, fo. 27.

Eaton, John, and John Besneck, testimonies, *The Tryals of Captain John Rackam* (Jamaica, 1721).

Elston, John, Deposition, 27 May 1698, in *Archives of the State of New Jersey*, First Series, II, 225.

Esquemeling, John, *Bucaniers of America: or, a true Account of the most remarkable Assaults committed of late upon the Coasts of the West Indies, by the Bucaniers of Jamaica and Tortuga, both English and French* (London, 1684).

Evelyn, John, *The Diary*, ed. E.S. de Beer (6 vols; Oxford, 1955).

?Every, Henry, 'A Copy of Verses Composed by Capt. Henry Every now gone to Sea to Seek his Fortune', 388/4, fo. 59, PRO.

Exquemelin, A.O., *The Buccaneers of America*, transl. Alexis Brown (Penguin Books, 1969).

Falconer, William, *An Universal Dictionary of the Marine: or, A Copious Explanation of the Technical Terms and Phrases employed in the Construction, Equipment, Furniture, Machinery, Movements, and Military Operations of a Ship* (London, 1769).

Fea, Allan, *The Real Captain Cleveland* (London, 1912).

Fea, James, to John Gow, '10 Mattin of the cloack', 13 February 1725, in Alexander Peterkin, *Notes on Orkney and Zetland* (Edinburgh, 1822), 213.

Fea, James, to John Gow, '10 of the cloack, mattin', 15 February 1725, in Alexander Peterkin, *Notes on Orkney and Zetland* (Edinburgh, 1822), 214–15.

Fea, James, to John Gow, 15 February 1725, in Alexander Peterkin, *Notes on Orkney and Zetland* (Edinburgh, 1822), 216.

Fea, James, to Elizabeth Moodie, 4 May 1725, in Alexander Peterkin, *Notes on Orkney and Zetland* (Edinburgh, 1822), 224.

[Fielding, Henry,] as Scriblerus Secundus, *The Author's Farce* (London, 1730).

Fielding, Sir John, *A Brief Description of the Cities of London and Westminster* (London, 1776).

Fitzball, Edward, *Thirty-Five Years of a Dramatic Author's Life* (2 vols; London, 1859).

Fitzgerald, F. Scott, *The Last Tycoon* (London, 1949).

Flavel, John, *Navigation Spiritualized, or, A New Compass for Seamen* (eighth edition, London, 1760).

Flynn, Errol, *My Wicked, Wicked Ways* ([1959] London, 1961).

Foster, William, Introduction, Clement Downing, *A History of the Indian Wars*, ed. William Foster (Oxford, 1924).

Franklin, Wayne, *James Fenimore Cooper: The Early Years* (New Haven and London, 2007).

Fraser, George MacDonald, *The Pyrates* (London, Glasgow, etc., 1983).

Full and Exact Account, of the Tryal of all the Pyrates lately taken by Captain Ogle, on Board the 'Swallow' Man of War, on the Coast of Guinea, A (London, 1723).

Freeman, John, Second Mate of the *Ostend Galley*, 'An Account of the Pyrates', MS, British Library, Miscellaneous Letters Received, 1723, E/1/14, fo. 205.

Freud, Sigmund, *Three Essays on the Theory of Sexuality* [1905], transl. James Strachey ([1949] London, 1974).

Furbank, P.N. and W.R. Owens, *The Canonisation of Daniel Defoe* (New Haven and London, 1988).

Furbank, P.N. and W.R. Owens, *Defoe De-Attributions: A Critique of J.R. Moore's 'Checklist'* (London and Rio Grande, 1994).

Gale, to Thomas Pitt, junr., Carolina, 4 November 1718, enclosed with Craggs to Council of Trade and Plantations, *CSP, CS, A&WI, March 1720–December 1721*, ed. Cecil Headlam (London, 1933), 10.

Gardiner, John, 'Narrative', 17 July 1699, CO, 5/860, 64 xxi, PRO, and in J.F. Jameson, ed., *Privateering and Piracy* (New York, 1923), 220–3.

Garrett, Elizabeth, *The Sweet Trade* (New York, 2001).

Gay, John, *Polly: An Opera. Being the Second Part of The Beggar's Opera* (London, 1729).

Gaynam, J., 'A full and true Account of the Behaviour and Dying Words of Alexander Rob, the Pyrate', *Parker's Penny Post*, Monday, 5 July 1725, 2–3.

General History of the Robberies and Murders of the most notorious Pyrates, and also their Policies, Discipline and Government, from their first Rise and Settlement in the Island of Providence, in 1717, to the present Year 1724. With the remarkable Actions and Adventures of the two Female Pyrates, Mary Read and Anne Bonny, A ([first edition] London, 1724).

General History of the Pyrates, from their first Rise and Settlement in the Island of Providence, to the present Time. With the remarkable Actions and Adventures of the two Female Pyrates Mary Read and Anne Bonny, A (the second Edition, with considerable Additions, London, 1724).

General History of the Pyrates, from their first Rise and Settlement in the Island of Providence, to the present Time. With the remarkable Actions and Adventures of the two Female Pyrates Mary Read and Anne Bonny, A (the third Edition, London, 1725).

General History of the Pyrates, . . . A, I (the fourth Edition, London, 1726).

[General] History of the Pyrates, . . . The, II (London, n.d. [1728]).

Gilbert, W.S., and A. Sullivan, *The Pirates of Penzance or The Slave of Duty*, in *The Complete Annotated Gilbert and Sullivan*, ed. Ian Bradley (Oxford, 1996), I.

Godin, Stephen, 13 June 1718, Extracts of several letters from Carolina, *CSP, CS, A&WI, August 1717–December 1718*, ed. Cecil Headlam (London, 1930), 336–7.

Goldbeck, Willis, and J.M. Barrie, Screenplay for *Peter Pan*, Paramount Picture, 1924.

Gooch, Steve, *The Women Pirates Ann Bonney and Mary Read* (London, 1978).

Gordan, John D., '*The Red Rover* Takes the Boards', *American Literature*, 10 (March, 1938), 66–75.

Gosse, Philip, *The History of Piracy* (London and New York, 1932).

Gow, John, Examination of John Smith [alias Gow], 2 April 1725, HCA, 1/55, fo. 105, PRO.

Gow, John, to James Fea, 15 February 1725, in Alexander Peterkin, *Notes on Orkney and Zetland* (Edinburgh, 1822), 215.

Gow, John, to James Fea, 16 February 1725, in Alexander Peterkin, *Notes on Orkney and Zetland* (Edinburgh, 1822), 218–19.

Green, Roger Lancelyn, *Fifty Years of 'Peter Pan'* (London, 1954).

Grey, Charles, *Pirates of the Eastern Seas 1618–1723* (London, n.d.).

Grimm, Jacob and Wilhelm, *Deutsche Sagen* (2 vols; Berlin, 1816–18).

Guet, M.I., *Les Origines de l'Ile Bourbon et de la colonisation française à Madagascar* (Paris, 1888).

Guthrie, James, *A True and Genuine Account of the Last Dying Words of John Gow, alias Smith, Captain of the Pirates. As Likewise of the Eight others, who were Executed with him, on June 11th, 1725. At Execution Dock, for Murder and Piracy* (London, n.d. [1725]).

Haber, Tom, 'Robert Louis Stevenson and Israel Hands', *The English Journal*, 32, 7 (1943), 399.

Haggard, Henry Rider, *The Days of My Life* (2 vols; London, 1926).

Haggard, Lilias Rider, *The Cloak That I Left: A Biography of the Author Henry Rider Haggard K.B.E.* (London, 1951).

Hamilton, Alexander, *A New Account of the East Indies, Being the Observations and Remarks of Capt. Alexander Hamilton, Who spent his Time there from the Year 1688 to 1723* (2 vols; Edinburgh, 1727).

Hamilton, Governor, to Council of Trade and Plantations, received London 6 January 1718, *CSP, CS, A&WI, August 1717–December 1718*, ed. Cecil Headlam (London, 1930), 149.

Hamilton, Ian, *Writers in Hollywood 1915–1951* (London, 1991).

Hammerton, J.A., ed., *Stevensoniana* (Edinburgh, 1907).

Harte, Bret, *The Queen of the Pirate Isle* (1886).

Heywood, Thomas, *The Fair Maid of the West*, Part I (London, 1631).

Heywood, Thomas, and William Rowley, *Fortune by Land and Sea. A Tragi-Comedy* (London, 1655).

Hedges, Sir Charles, undated MS, HCA, 15/1, PRO.

Hedges, Sir Charles, to my Lord High Admiral, 2 April 1702, British Library, Add. MSS. 24107, fo. 207.

Heller-Roazen, Daniel, *The Enemy of All: Piracy and the Law of Nations* (New York, 2009).

Hendrick, Joan D., *Harriet Beecher Stowe: A Life* (New York, 1994).

Hergé, *Le Trésor de Rackham le Rouge* ([1945] 1973).

Herriot, David, in 'The Information of David Herriot and Ignatius Pell', Appendix, *The Tryals of Major Stede Bonnet, and other Pirates* (London, 1719).

Hill, Charles, *Notes on Piracy in Eastern Waters* (Bombay, 1923).

Hill, Christopher, 'Radical Pirates?', in *The Collected Essays*, III, *People and Ideas in 17th Century England* (Brighton, 1986), 161–87.

Holinshed, Raphaell, *The First and second volumes of Chronicles* (London, 1587).

Hollindale, Peter, ed., Barrie, *Peter Pan and Other Plays* (Oxford, 1995).

Homer, *The Odyssey*, transl. A.T. Murray (Loeb edition, 1919).

Houblon, James, 10 August 1694, 388/4, fo. 55, PRO.

Howson, Gerald, *Thief-Taker General: The Rise and Fall of Jonathan Wild* (London, 1970).

Hoy, Cyrus, Introduction, *The Double Marriage*, in *The Dramatic Works in the Beaumont and Fletcher Canon*, IX (Cambridge, 1994).

Hughes, Richard, *A High Wind in Jamaica* (London, 1929).

Ingraham, J.H., *Captain Kyd: The Wizard of the Sea. A Romance* (London, 1842), in *The Novel Newspaper*, III (London, 1839 [sic]).

Ingraham, J.H., *The Pirate of the Gulf, or Lafitte* (2 vols; London, 1837).

Irving, Pierre M., *The Life and Letters of Washington Irving* (4 vols; New York, 1862–64).

Irving, Washington, 'Abbotsford', in *The Crayon Miscellany*, ed. D.K. Terrel (Boston, 1979), 125–68.

Irving, Washington, *Journals and Notebooks* (3 vols), III, 1819–1827, ed. Walter A. Reichart (Madison, 1970), in *The Complete Works of Washington Irving*.

Irving, Washington, *Letters*, I (1802–1823), II (1823–1838), ed. R.M. Aderman, et al. (Boston, 1978, 1979), in *The Complete Works of Washington Irving*.

[Irving, Washington,] as Geoffrey Crayon, Gent., *Tales of a Traveller* (2 vols; London, 1824).

Irving, Washington, *Woolfert's Roost and Other Tales* (London, 1855).

Jaeger, Gérard, *Pirates, flibustiers et corsaires (Histoire & Légendes d'une société d'exception)* (Avignon, 1987).

Jameson, J.F., ed., *Privateering and Piracy in the Colonial Period: Historical Documents* (New York, 1923).

Jekel, Pamela, *Sea Star: The Private Life of Anne Bonny, Pirate Queen* (New York, 1983).

Johnson, Charles, *The Successful Pyrate* (London, 1713).

Johnson, Samuel, *A Dictionary of the English Language* (2 vols; London, 1755).

Jones, J.S., *Captain Kyd or the Wizard of the Sea. A Drama* (New York, n.d.).

'Journal of our voyage . . . in her Majesties ship Scarborrow, A', British Library, Sloane MS, 3674.

Jowitt, Claire, *The Culture of Piracy, 1580–1630: English Literature and Seaborne Crime* (Farnham, Surrey, 2010).

Judd, Jacob, 'Frederick Philipse and the Madagascar Trade', *New York Historical Society Quarterly*, LV (1971), 354–74.

Kaplan, Justin, *Mr Clemens and Mark Twain* (Pelican edition, 1970).

Katz, Wendy R., ed., *Treasure Island* (Edinburgh, 1998).

Kelly, James, *A full and true Discovery of all the Robberies, Pyracies, and other Notorious Actions, of the Famous English Pyrate, Capt. James Kelly, who was Executed on Friday the 12th. of July 1700* (London, 1700).

Kelsey, Harry, *Sir Francis Drake: The Queen's Pirate* (New Haven and London, 1998).

Khán, Kháfi, 'Muntakhabu-l Lubáb', in *The History of India, as Told by its Own Historians*, ed. H.M. Elliot and John Dowson (8 vols; London, 1867–77), VII.

Kidd, William, Declaration, CO 5/860, 65 xix, PRO.

Kidd, William, letter to the Earl of Orford, 11 April 1700, British Library, Add. MSS, 70036, fo. 104.

Kidd, William, 'Narrative', 7 July 1699, in J.F. Jameson, ed., *Privateering and Piracy* (New York, 1923), 205–13.

Kidd, William, New Gate, 12 May 1701, to Robert Harley, in J.F. Jameson, ed., *Privateering and Piracy* (New York, 1923), 252–3.

Kinematograph Weekly: 20 September 1934; 18 March 1943; 31 January 1946.

King of Pirates: Being an Account of the famous Enterprises of Captain Avery, The Mock King of Madagascar. With his Rambles and Piracies; wherein all the Sham Accounts formerly publish'd of him, are detected. In Two Letters from himself; one during his Stay at Madagascar, and one since his Escape from thence, The (London, 1720).

Kingsley, Charles, *At Last: A Christmas in the West Indies* (2 vols; London and New York, 1871).

Klausmann, Ulrike, and Marion Meinzerin, *Women Pirates and the Politics of the Jolly Roger*, transl. Austin and Levis (Montreal, etc., 1997).

Knox, Robert, *An Historical Relation of the Island Ceylon, in the East Indies: Together, With an Account of the Detaining in Captivity the Author and divers other Englishmen now Living there, and of the Author's Miraculous Escape* (London, 1681).

Knox-Shaw, Peter, *The Explorer in English Fiction* (London, 1987).

Koch, Howard, and Seton I. Miller, *The Sea Hawk* (screenplay), ed. Rudy Behlmer (Madison, Wisconsin, and London, 1982).

Konstam, Angus, *Blackbeard: America's Most Notorious Pirate* (Hoboken, New Jersey, 2006).

La Roncière, Charles de, *Le Flibustier mysterieux: Histoire d'un trésor caché* (Paris, 1934).

Labat, R.P., *Nouveau Voyage aux isles de l'Amerique* (8 vols; Paris, 1742).

Laing, James, Deposition, Kirkwall, Orkney, 11 March 1725, in *The Literary and Statistical Magazine for Scotland*, vol. 3 (Edinburgh, 1819).

Lapouge, Gilles, *Pirates, boucaniers, flibustiers* (Paris, 2002).

Lasinby, Richard, 'Narrative of the Proceedings of the Pyrates', MS, British Library, Miscellaneous Letters Received, 1722, E/1/13, fos. 165–171v.

Lasinby, Richard, Second MS of Lasinby's 'Narrative', in third person, British Library, Miscellaneous Letters Received, 1722, E/1/13, fos. 175–77v.

Lautréamont, le Comte de [Isidore Ducasse], *Les Chants de Maldoror* (Paris and Bruxelles, 1874).

Le Pers, MS, printed in Pierre Margry, *Relations et mémoires inédits pour servir à l'histoire de la France dans les pays d'Outre-mer* (Paris, 1867), 282–9.

Léry, Jean de, *Histoire d'un voyage fait en la terre du Bresil* (La Rochelle, 1578).

Leslie, Charles Robert, *Autobiographical Recollections*, ed. Tom Taylor (2 vols; London, 1860).

Letters, from Bombay, 15 January 1697, and from Calicut, 30 November 1696, *CSP, CS, A&WI, 27 October 1697–31December 1698*, ed. J.W. Fortescue (London, 1905), 69–70.

Letter from Bombay, 11 April 1697, *CSP, CS, A&WI*, ed. J.W. Fortescue (London, 1905), 113–14.

Letter from Fort St. George, 19 January 1697, *CSP, CS, A&WI, 27 October 1697–31 December 1698*, ed. J.W. Fortescue (London, 1905), 112–13.

Letter from the President and Council at Surat, 21 April 1697, MS, British Library, E/3/52, fo. 30v.

Letter from Jamaica, 12 May 1723, MS, British Library, Miscellaneous Letters Received, 1723, E/1/14, fo. 161v.

Lévi-Strauss, Claude, 'Le Champ de l'Anthropologie', in *Anthropologie Structurale Deux* (Paris, 1973), 11–44.

Lewis, Frank R., 'John Morris and the Carthagena Expedition, 1739–1740', *Mariner's Mirror*, XXVI (1940), 257–69.

'Life and Adventures of Capt. John Avery, The', in *The Monthly Miscellany: or, Memoirs for the Curious*, November, 1708, II (London, 1708), 344–53.

Life and Adventures of Capt. John Avery, The (London, 1709).

Lithgow, William, *The Totall Discourse, of the rare Adventures, and painefull Peregrinations of long nineteen Yeares Travayles* (London, 1632).

Little, Barbara, 'The Pirates Are Coming', *Picture-Play Magazine*, XVIII, 1 (March 1923).

Llewelyn Davies, Nicholas, interview by Andrew Birkin, 1 January 1976, J.M. Barrie website, <http://www.jmbarrie.co.uk>, accessed 14 January 2013.

Lockhart, John G., *Memoirs of the Life of Sir Walter Scott* (7 vols; Edinburgh, 1837–38).

Lodge, Jack, 'The Career of Herbert Brenon', *Griffithiana*, 57/58 (October 1996).

Loff, Gabriel, Examination, *CSP, CS, A&WI, 1699*, ed. Cecil Headlam (London, 1908), 372.

London Journal, The: 12 February 1724–5; 13 March 1725; 27 March 1725; 3 April 1725; 29 May 1725; 5 June 1725.

Longus, *Daphne and Chloe*, ed. J.M. Edmonds (Loeb edition, 1916).

Longus, *Daphne and Chloe*, transl. Paul Turner (Penguin edition, 1968).

Lorrain, Paul, *The Ordinary of Newgate his Account of the Behaviour, Confession, and Dying- Words of Captain William Kidd, and other Pirates that were Executed at the Execution-Dock in Wapping, on Friday May 23 1701* (London, 1701).

Lougnon, Albert, *L'Ile Bourbon pendant la Régence* (Paris, 1956).

Lowth, Matthew, HCA, 1/98, Pt. 2, fo. 257, PRO.

Lowth, Matthew, 'Journal of Loyall Merchant', MS, British Library, L/MAR/A/CXXXII.

Luttrell, Narcissus, *A Brief Relation of State Affairs from September 1678 to April 1714* (6 vols; Oxford, 1857).

Lynch, Sir Thomas, to Sec. Lord Arlington, 17 December 1671, *CSP, CS, A&WI, 1669–1674*, ed. Noel Sainsbury (London, 1889).

Mackail, Denis, *The Story of J.M.B.* (London, 1941).

Macrae, Captain, letter, Bombay, 16 November 1720, in *The Post Boy*, 22–5 April 1721.

Marchand, L.A., *Byron: A Biography* (3 vols; New York, 1958).

Marlowe, Christopher, *The Jew of Malta*, in *The Complete Plays*, ed. J.B. Steane (Penguin edition).

Marryat, Captain, *The Pirate and the Three Cutters* (Paris, 1836).

Marx, Jenifer G., 'Brethren of the Coast', in David Cordingly, ed., *Pirates: An Illustrated History* (London, 1996), 36–57.

Maturin, Charles, *Bertram; or, The Castle of St. Aldobrand: a Tragedy* (London, 1816).

Maynard, Lieutenant Robert, 'Abstract of a letter from Mr. Maynard, first Lieutenant of His Majesty's Ship the Pearl, the Station-Ship at Virginia, to Mr. Symonds, Lieutenant of His Majesty's Ship the Phoenix, the Station-Ship at New York', *The Weekly Journal or British Gazetteer*, 25 April 1719.

Melville, Herman, *Moby-Dick*, ed. H. Hayford and Hershel Parker (New York, 1967).

Melvin, William, Examination, 3 April 1725, HCA, 1/55, fo. 116, PRO.

Michaelis, David, *W.C. Wyeth: A Biography* (New York, 1998).

Middleton, Philip, Narrative, 4 August 1696, MS, British Library, 10R/H/36, 199.

Middleton, Philip, testimony, *The Tryals of Joseph Dawson* [etc.] (London, 1696).

Mist's Weekly Journal, 12 June 1725.

Monaghan, Jay, *The Great Rascal: The Life and Adventures of Ned Buntline* (Boston, 1951).

Monthly Film Bulletin, vol. 1, 8 (1 September 1934).

Moodie, Elizabeth, to James Fea, 22 April 1725, in Alexander Peterkin, *Notes on Orkney and Zetland* (Edinburgh, 1822).

Moor, Michael, Examination, HCA, 1/55, fo. 120, PRO.

Moore, John Robert, *Defoe in the Pillory and Other Studies* (Bloomington, Indiana, 1939).

Morgan, Henry, 'A True Accompt and Relation of my last Expedition agst the Spaniards by vertue of a Comission given unto mee by his Excy Sr Tho. Modyford', 31 January 1671, MS, British Library, Add. 11268.

Moreau, Jean-Pierre, *Une Histoire des pirates des Mers du Sud à Hollywood* (Paris, 2007).

Morison, S.E., *The European Discovery of America: The Northern Voyages* (New York, 1971).

Morris, John, letter, Liverpool, 6 November 1739, in J.H. Davies, ed., *The Letters of Lewis, Richard, William and John Morris, 1728–65* (2 vols; Aberystwyth, 1907, 1909).

Musnik, Henri, *Les Femmes pirates: Aventures et légendes de la mer* (Paris, 1934).

Musson, Captain Mathew, to the Council of Trade and Plantations, received London 5 July 1717, *CSP, CS, A&WI, January 1716–July 1717*, ed. Cecil Headlam (London, 1930), 338.

N[eal, John], 'Late American Books', *Blackwood's Edinburgh Magazine*, XVIII (September, 1825), 316–34.

New Dictionary of the Terms Ancient and Modern of the Canting Crew, A (London, 1699).

'New Providence, Sept. 4th', news from, *The Boston Gazette*, 10–17 October 1720.

Niven, David, *Bring On the Empty Horses* (London, 1975).

Nobber, Samuel, Statement, HCA, 1/18, 10, PRO.

Novak, Maximillian E., Introduction, Defoe, *Of Captain Misson*, ed. Novak, Augustan Reprint Society, No.87 (Los Angeles, 1961).

O'Hara, Maureen, with John Nicoletti, *'Tis Herself: An Autobiography* ([1997] London, 2005).

Osbourne, Lloyd, 'Note', *Treasure Island*, Tusitala Edition, II (London, 1923).

Owen, Abel, and Samuel Arris, Deposition, 4 July 1699, CO, 5/860, 64xxiii, PRO.

Palmer, Joseph, Examination, 29 July 1699, CO, 5/15, PRO.

Palmer, Joseph, Examination, 25 April 1701, HCA, 1/15, PRO.

Parish, James Robert, and Don E. Stanke, *The Swashbucklers* (New Rochelle, New York, 1976).

Parry, J.H., *Trade and Dominion: English Overseas Empires in the Eighteenth Century* ([1971] London, 1974).

Paul, 'Titus', *The New English Bible* (New York, 1971).

Pepys Ballads, The, ed. W.G. Day (5 vols; Cambridge, 1987).

Pearce, Captain Jeremy, Letter from Jamaica, 19 June 1723, MS, British Library, Miscellaneous Letters Received, 1723, E/1/14, fo. 163.

Penn, William, to Mr Secretary Vernon, 26 February 1700, *CSP, CS, A&WI, 1700*, ed. Cecil Headlam (London, 1910), 83.

Perkins, Samuel, Deposition, 1698, in J.F. Jameson, ed., *Privateering and Piracy* (New York, 1923), 175–8.

Peterkin, Alexander, *Notes on Orkney and Zetland* (Edinburgh, 1822).

'*Peter Pan* as a Film', *The Times*, 15 January 1925.

Philbrick, Thomas and Marianne, eds, *The Red Rover* (Albany, New York, 1991).

Philipse, Frederick, New York, 9 June 1698, HCA, 1/98, Pt. 1, fo. 136, PRO.

Philipse, Frederick, to Adam Baldridge, New York, 25 February 1695, HCA, 1/98, Pt. 1, fo. 57, PRO.

Phillips, Thomas, 'A Journal of a Voyage made in the Hannibal of London, Ann. 1693, 1694', in A. Churchill, ed., *A Collection of Voyages and Travels* (6 vols; London, 1732), VI.

Phillips, William, account, Dublin, 8 August 1696, SP 63/358, fos. 127v–130r, PRO.

'Plan du Port de l'isle Ste Marie', British Library, Add. MSS, 15319, fo. 34.

Piracy destroy'd: Or, A short Discourse shewing the Rise, Growth and Causes of Piracy of late ... In a letter from an Officer of an East-India Ship lately arriv'd in the River (London, 1701).

Pirates Own Book, or Authentic Narratives of the Lives, Exploits and Executions of the Most Celebrated Sea Robbers, The (Philadelphia, 1837).

[Poe, Edgar Allan,] 'Edgar Allan Poe', *Aristidean*, October 1845, in *Essays and Reviews*, ed. G.R. Thompson (New York, 1984).

Poe, Edgar Allan, 'A Few Words on Secret Writing', reprinted (with addenda) in Poe, *Complete Works*, ed. James A. Harrison (New York, 1902–3).

Poe, Edgar Allan, 'The Gold Bug', *Tales* (London, 1845).

Poe, Edgar Allan, *The Letters of Edgar Allan Poe*, ed. J.W. Ostrom (2 vols; Cambridge, MA, 1948).

Poe, Edgar Allan, 'The Murders in the Rue Morgue', *Tales* (London, 1845), 116–50.

Poe, Edgar Allan, 'The Purloined Letter', *Tales* (London, 1845), 200–18.

Pope, Dudley, *Harry Morgan's Way: The Biography of Sir Henry Morgan 1635–1684* (London, 1977).

Porrenger, Robert, Examination, 10 April 1725, HCA, 1/55, fo. 136, PRO.

Praz, Mario, *The Romantic Agony* (Oxford, 1933).

Quayle, Eric, *Ballantyne the Brave: A Victorian Writer and his Family* (London, 1967).

Quinn, A.H., *Edgar Allan Poe: A Critical Biography* (New York and London, 1942).

Randolph, Edward, 'To the Honourable Commissioners of his Majesty's Custom', 10 November 1696, in *Colonial Records of North Carolina*, ed. William L. Saunders, I (Raleigh, North Carolina, 1886).

Reasons for Reducing the Pyrates at Madagascar: And Proposals humbly offered to the Honourable House of Commons, for effecting the same (London, 1707).

Rediker, Marcus, 'Libertalia: The Pirate's Utopia', in David Cordingly, ed., *Pirates: An Illustrated History of Privateers, Buccaneers, and Pirates from the Sixteenth Century to the Present* (London, 1996), 124–39.

Rediker, Marcus, *Villains of All Nations: Atlantic Pirates in the Golden Age* (London and New York, 2004).

Reichart, Walter A., *Washington Irving and Germany* (Ann Arbor, 1957).

Rennie, Neil, *Far-Fetched Facts: The Literature of Travel and the Idea of the South Seas* (Oxford, 1995).

Rennie, Neil, *Pocahontas, Little Wanton: Myth, Life and Afterlife* (London, 2007).

Reynolds, William, Atchin, 20 August 1697, MS, British Library, E/3/53, fo. 125.

Ribeiro, Aileen, *Dress in Eighteenth-Century Europe 1715–1789* (New Haven and London, 2002).

Richards, Jeffrey, *Swordsmen of the Screen: From Douglas Fairbanks to Michael York* (London, Henley, and Boston, Massachusetts, 1977).

Richetti, John, *Defoe's Narratives: Situations and Structures* (Oxford, 1975).

Richetti, John, *The Life of Daniel Defoe* (London, 2005).

Riley, Sandra, *Bloody Bay* (New York, 1980).

Ringrose, Basil, 'The Dangerous Voyage and Bold Attempts of Captain Bartholemew Sharp, and others', in John Esquemeling, *Bucaniers of America* (2 vols; London, 1684–5), II.

Ritchie, Robert C., *Captain Kidd and the War Against the Pirates* (Cambridge, Massachusetts, and London, 1986).

Ritchie, Robert C., 'Samuel Burgess, Pirate', in *Authority and Resistance in Early New York*, ed. William Pencak and Conrad Edick Wright (New York, 1988), 114–37.

Ritchie, Robert C., 'Stede Bonnet', *The Oxford Dictionary of National Biography* (Oxford, 2004).

Robert, 'Description en générale et en détail de l'ile de Madagascar', MS, published in part in Alfred and Guillaume Grandidier, *Collection des ouvrages anciens concernant Madagascar*, V (Paris, 1907).

Robert: Dictionnaire historique de la langue française, Le (3 vols; Paris, 2000).

Roch, Jeremy, Journals, in *Three Sea Journals of Stuart Times*, ed. Bruce S. Ingram (London, 1936).

Rodger, N.A.M., *The Wooden World: An Anatomy of the Georgian Navy* (London, 1988).

Rogers, Pat, *Grub Street: Studies in a Subculture* (London, 1972).

Rogers, Woodes, *A Cruising Voyage Round the World* (London, 1712).

Rogers, Woodes, Proclamation of 5 September, *The Boston Gazette*, 10–17 October 1720.

Rogers, Woodes, to the Council of Trade and Plantations, *CSP, CS, A&WI, August 1717–December 1718*, ed. Cecil Headlam (London, 1930).

Rogozinski, Jan, *Honor Among Thieves: Captain Kidd, Henry Every, and the Pirate Democracy in the Indian Ocean* (Mechanicsburg, Pennsylvania, 2000).

Rollson, Peter, Examination, HCA, 1/55. fo. 108, PRO.

Rose, Jacqueline, *The Case of Peter Pan or The Impossibility of Children's Fiction* (London, 1984).

Rush, Philip, *Mary Read, Buccaneer* (London and New York, 1945).

Sabatini, Rafael, *The Black Swan* (London, 1932).

Sabatini, Rafael, *Captain Blood: His Odyssey* (London, 1922).

Sabatini, Rafael, 'Historical Fiction', in *What is a Book?* ed. Dale Warren (New York, 1935), 23–39.

Sabatini, Rafael, *The Sea-Hawk* (London, 1915).

[Savage, Richard,] as Iscariot Hackney, *An Author to Lett* (London, 1729).

Schallert, Edwin, 'Yo, Ho, and a Bottle of Rum', *Picture-Play Magazine*, XXIII, 6 (February, 1926), 16–17.

Schatz, Thomas, *The Hollywood Genre: Formulas, Filmmaking and the Studio System* (New York, 1981).

Schonhorn, Manuel, ed., *A General History of the Pyrates* (London, 1999).

Scollay, William, Deposition, Kirkwall, Orkney, 11 March 1725, in *The Literary and Statistical Magazine for Scotland*, vol. 3 (Edinburgh, 1819).

Scott, Walter, Diary, in J.G. Lockhart, *Memoirs of the Life of Sir Walter Scott* (7 vols; Edinburgh, 1837–8), III.

Scott, Walter, *The Journal*, ed. W.E.K. Anderson (Oxford, 1972).

[Scott, Walter,] *The Pirate* (3 vols; Edinburgh, 1822).

Scott, Walter, to William Erskine, 27 September 1821, *Letters*, ed. H.J.C. Grierson (12 vols; 1932–7), VII, 12.

'Seaman's Song of Captain Ward, the Famous Pirate of the World, and an Englishman Born, The', Appendix I, in Daniel J. Victus, ed., *Three Turk Plays from Early Modern England* (New York, 2000), 345–8.

Secord, A.W., *'Robert Drury's Journal' and Other Studies* (Urbana, Illinois, 1961).

Shay, Frank, *Mary Read: The Pirate Wench* (London, 1934).

Shelley, Giles, to Stephen Delaney, from Cape May, New Jersey, 27 May 1699, in *Manuscripts of the House of Lords* (London, 1908), 330–1.

Simonds, Jacqueline Church, *Captain Mary, Buccaneer* (Simsbury, Connecticut, 2000).

Sloane, Hans, *A Voyage to the Islands madera, barbados, Nieves, S. Christophers and Jamaica* (2 vols; London, 1707).

Smith, Steve, Jr, 'Pictorial Side of *Captain Blood*', *American Cinematographer*, September 1924.

Smollett, Tobias, *The Adventures of Roderick Random* (2 vols; London, 1748).

Snelgrave, William, *A New Account of some Parts of Guinea, and the Slave-Trade* (London, 1734).

Spanish Main, The, Script, British Film Institute Library, London.

Spatchears, James, testimony, *The Tryals of Captain John Rackam* (Jamaica, 1721).

Spotswood, Alexander, to the Council of Trade and Plantations, 22 December 1718, *CSP, CS, A&WI, August 1717–December 1718*, ed. Cecil Headlam (London, 1930), 431.

Spotswood, Alexander, to Secretary of State James Craggs, 22 October 1718, in *The Official Letters of Alexander Spotswood*, ed. R.A. Brock (2 vols; Richmond, Virginia, 1882 and 1885), II, 305.

Stark, Suzanne J., *Female Tars: Women Aboard Ship in the Age of Sail* (London, 1996).

Steen, Marguerite [Jane Nicholson], *William Nicholson* (London, 1943).

Stevenson, Robert Louis, 'A Humble Remonstrance', reprinted from *Longman's Magazine* in *Henry James and Robert Louis Stevenson: A Record of Friendship and Criticism*, ed., Janet Adam Smith (London, 1948), 86–100.

Stevenson, Robert Louis, Interview, *Sydney Morning Herald*, 14 February 1890, reprinted in *Robert Louis Stevenson: Interviews and Recollections*, ed. R.C. Terry (London, 1996).

Stevenson, Robert Louis, *The Letters of Robert Louis Stevenson*, ed. Bradford A. Booth and Ernest Mehew (8 vols; New Haven and London, 1994–5).

Stevenson, Robert Louis, *The Master of Ballantrae: A Winter's Tale* (London, Paris, etc., 1889).

Stevenson, Robert Louis, 'My First Book—*Treasure Island*', *The Idler*, vol. 6 (August, 1894).

Stevenson, Robert Louis, 'Note', reprinted in *The Scottish Stories and Essays*, ed. Kenneth Gelder (Edinburgh, 1989), 277–80.

Stevenson, Robert Louis, *Records of a Family of Engineers*, in *The Works of Robert Louis Stevenson*, Edinburgh Edition, XVIII (Edinburgh, 1896), 187–389.

Stevenson, Robert Louis, *Treasure Island* (London, 1883).

Stevenson, Thomas, to Stevenson, 26 February 1882, in Paul Maixner, ed., *Robert Louis Stevenson: The Critical Heritage* (London, 1981).

Stewart, Douglas, *The Pirate Queen; or, Captain Kidd and the Treasure* (London, 1867).

Stow, John, *The Annales of England* (London, 1605).

Stow, John, *A Survay of London* (London, 1598).

Stow, John, *A Survey of London*, corrected [etc.] by John Strype, in 6 books (London, 1720).

Stowe, Harriet Beecher, *Oldtown Fire Stories* (London, 1871).

Sue, Eugène, *Plik et Plok* (1831).

Surrell, Jason, *Pirates of the Caribbean: From the Magic Kingdom to the Movies* (New York, 2005).

Swearingen, Roger, *The Prose Writings of Robert Louis Stevenson: A Guide* (London, 1980).

[Swift, Jonathan,] *Travels into Several Remote Nations of the World . . . By Lemuel Gulliver* (2 vols; London, 1726).

Szebin, Frederick C., '*Peter Pan* Escapes Cinematic Neverland', *American Cinematographer*, October 1995, 97–101.

Talmey, Allene, *Doug and Mary and Others* (New York, 1927).

Taxco, Mace, *Anne Bonney and Mary Read: Women Buccaneers* (Albuquerque, New Mexico, 1998).

Tertre, Jean Baptiste du, *Histoire generale des Antilles* (4 vols; Paris, 1667–71).

Thomas, Dorothy, testimony, *The Tryals of Captain John Rackam* (Jamaica, 1721).

Thompson, Frank, ed., *Between Action and Cut: Five American Directors* (Metuchen, New Jersey, and London, 1985).

Thorslev, Peter L., *The Byronic Hero: Types and Prototypes* (Minneapolis, 1962).

Tibbets, John C., and James L. Welsh, *His Majesty the American: The Films of Douglas Fairbanks, Sr.* (South Brunswick, New York and London, 1977).

Tisdell, Hosea, testimony, *The Tryals of Captain John Rackam* (Jamaica, 1721).

Today's Cinema, 29 January 1946.

Trace, Maurice, 'Captain Blood', *Screen* 9.5, No. 104, Winter 2001, 5–8.

Trollope, Anthony, *The Eustace Diamonds* (New York, 1872).

True Account of the Behaviour, Confession and last Dying Speeches, of Captain William Kidd, and the rest of the Pirates, that were Executed at Execution Dock in Wapping, on Friday the 23d of May 1701, A (London, 1701).

True and Genuine Account of the Life and Actions of the Late Jonathan Wild, The (London, 1725).

True Relation, of the Lives and Deaths of the two most Famous English Pyrats, Purser and Clinton, A (London, 1639).

'Tryal and Condemnation of ten Persons for Piracy Eight of wch. were Executed two repriev'd till his Majestys Pleasure be known Decr 13th 1718, The', CO 23/1 fos. 79v–80r, PRO.

Tryals of Captain John Rackam, and other Pirates . . . As Also, the Tryals of Mary Read and Anne Bonny, The (Jamaica, 1721).

Tryals of Joseph Dawson, Edward Forseith, William Day, William Bishop, James Lewis, and John Sparkes, The. For Several Piracies and Robberies by them committed, in the Company of Every the Grand Pirate (London, 1695).

Tryals of Major Stede Bonnet, and other Pirates, The (London, 1719).

Turley, Hans, *Rum, Sodomy and the Lash: Piracy, Sexuality, and Masculine Identity* (New York and London, 1999).

Turner, Theophilus, Deposition, *CSP, CS, A&WI, 1699*, ed. Cecil Headlam (London, 1908), 289.

Turner, Theophilus, Deposition, British Library, Sloane MS., 2902, fo. 230.

Turner, Theophilus, Deposition, 8 June 1699, CO, 5/714, 70, PRO, and in J.F. Jameson, ed., *Privateering and Piracy* (New York, 1923), 200–1.

Twain, Mark, *The Adventures of Tom Sawyer* (London, 1876).

Vaissiere, Pierre de, *Saint-Domingue: La Société et la vie créoles sous l'ancien régime (1629–1789)* (Paris, 1909).

Vance, Jeffrey, *Douglas Fairbanks* (Berkeley, Los Angeles and London, 2008).

Variety, 11 June 1924; 10 September 1924; 31 December 1924; 1 January 1936.

Vickers, John, Deposition, enclosed in Lt. Governor Spotswood to the Council of Trade and Plantations, *CSP, CS, A&WI, January 1716–July 1717*, ed. Cecil Headlam (London, 1930), 140–1.

Villon, François, *Le Grant Testament* (Paris, 1489).

[Voltaire,] *Candide, ou l'optimisme* (1759).

Voltaire, *Le Mondain*, in *Mélanges*, ed. Jacques van den Heuvel (Pléiade edition, 1961).

Wagner, Kip, and L.B. Taylor, *Pieces of Eight: Recovering the Riches of a Lost Spanish Treasure Fleet* (London, 1967).

Waith, Eugene M., *The Pattern of Tragicomedy in Beaumont and Fletcher* (New Haven, 1952).

Ward and Danseker, Two notorious Pyrates, Ward an Englishman, and Danseker a Dutchman (London, 1609).

Warner, Jack, with Dean Jennings, *My First Hundred Years in Hollywood* (New York and Toronto, 1964).

Warren, Thomas, 23 December 1700, HCA, 1/15, PRO.

Watson, Harold F., *Coasts of Treasure Island* (San Antonio, Texas, 1969).

Watson, Henry, Narrative, *CSP, CS, A&WI, 27 October 1697–31 December 1698*, ed. J.W. Fortescue (London, 1905), 106–8.

Weekly Journal; or British Gazetteer, The, 10 October 1719; 12 June 1725.

Weinstein, Mark, and Alison Lumsden, eds., Scott, *The Pirate* (Edinburgh, 2001).

Wheelwright, Julie, 'Tars, tarts and swashbucklers', in *Bold in Her Breeches: Women Pirates Across the Ages*, ed. Jo Stanley (London, 1995).

White, Henry, *Sir Walter Scott's Novels on the Stage* ([1927] reprinted Hamden, CT, 1973).

Williams, Stanley T., *The Life of Washington Irving* (2 vols; New York, 1935).

Willock, William, Narrative, MS, British Library, E/3/53, 6484.

Willock, William, Narrative, *CSP, CS, A&WI, 27 October 1697–31 December 1698*, ed. J.W. Fortescue (London, 1905), 366–7.

Willock, William, Narrative, in Charles Grey, *Pirates of the Eastern Seas (1618–1723)* (London, n.d.), 143–4.

Wilkins, Harold T., *Captain Kidd and his Skeleton Island* (London, 1935).

Wilson, John Harold, *All the King's Men: Actresses of the Restoration Stage* (Chicago, 1958).

Wordsworth, William, *The Prelude, or Growth of a Poet's Mind* [1805], in *The Prelude: A Parallel Text*, ed. J.C. Maxwell (Penguin edition, 1972).

Wycherley, William, *The Plain-Dealer* (London, 1677).

Zacks, Richard, *The Pirate Hunter: The True Story of Captain Kidd* (London, 2003).

Index